SOUTHERN BIOGRAPHY SERIES
Bertram Wyatt-Brown
Editor

PUBLISHED WITH THE ASSISTANCE OF THE
V. RAY CARDOZIER FUND

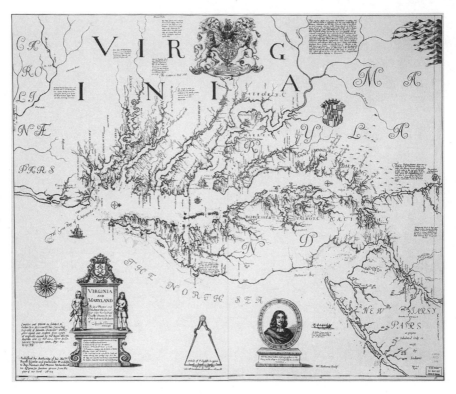

Augustine Herrman's Map of Virginia, 1673

Collections of the Library of Congress

SIR WILLIAM BERKELEY

AND THE FORGING OF

COLONIAL VIRGINIA

WARREN M. BILLINGS

LOUISIANA STATE UNIVERSITY PRESS ⚜ BATON ROUGE

Copyright © 2004 by Louisiana State University Press
All rights reserved
Manufactured in the United States of America
First printing

Designer: Melanie O'Quinn Samaha
Typeface: Minion
Typesetter: Coghill Composition Co., Inc.
Printer and binder: Thomson-Shore, Inc.

Library of Congress Cataloging-in-Publication Data

Billings, Warren M., 1940–
Sir William Berkeley and the forging of colonial Virginia / Warren M. Billings.
    p.   cm. — (Southern biography series)
Includes bibliographical references and index.
ISBN 0-8071-3012-5 (hardcover : alk. paper)
1. Berkeley, William, Sir, 1608–1677.   2. Governors—Virginia—Biography.
3. Virginia—History—Colonial period, ca. 1600–1775.   I. Title.   II. Series.
F229.B53B55   2004
975.5'02'092—dc22
2004011060

For Carol

Contents

PREFACE

Sir William Berkeley and I share an acquaintance of four decades and more. We first met during my undergraduate days at the College of William and Mary, the place where I initially sharpened my taste for early American history. I grew more familiar with him in the time of my apprenticeship as a doctoral student. Later still we were usually in each other's company whenever I rummaged the records in search of a deeper understanding of seventeenth-century Virginians and their world.

His name was synonymous with Bacon's Rebellion—the most serious challenge to British royal authority in North America before the American Revolution—but our repeated encounters divulged another Berkeley. The Berkeley of my acquaintance dominated the Old Dominion as did few of its chief executives, colonial or modern. This Berkeley invented the General Assembly as a bicameral representative legislature, he spurred the rise of Virginia's planter aristocracy, he promoted the development of Carolina, he rebuilt Jamestown, he almost diversified the colony's economy, and he turned himself into a Virginian.

So commanding a presence as his, it seemed to me, resulted from a singular conjunction of personality and place that explained not only Berkeley but the very shape of Virginia itself. The better I knew him, the greater became my appreciation of why no one ever attempted his biography or seldom probed his administration deeply. Berkeley was an enigmatic man. The challenge of writing about his life arose not so much from wrestling with an innately peculiar individual. Because his personal papers and official records were scattered, and most had vanished down the centuries after his death, the test lay in documenting the dimensions of his being. That realization dampened my enthusiasm and fended off the lure of taking him on as a subject for a book. Temptation finally got the better of me in the mid-1980s, about the time I finished editing the papers of one of his successors, Francis Howard, fifth baron Howard of Effingham, and I resolved to write this book.

The book could not proceed, however, until I tracked down and read all of Berkeley's surviving papers. Those artifacts, like so many potsherds from an archaeological site, lay obscurely tucked away in a field of manuscript repositories that ran from the United States to Sweden to the British Isles to the Netherlands and thence to the United States once more. My recovery of many items, I freely admit, resulted as much from luck as from my cleverness at detection. Individual documents, often as not, furnished the best clues to the identity or whereabouts of others. I transcribed each paper I found into a digital database that I initially intended as nothing more than a handy reference aid. This burgeoning trove found life in its own right, blossoming at length as *The Papers of Sir William Berkeley, 1605–1677*, which will appear in the future.

Pieced together, the extant documentary record yielded a surprisingly ample restoration of the vessel that once was the whole Berkeley, but, like a smashed pot dug from the ground, important bits of Berkeley's character and personality were beyond salvage. Most notably, massive destruction of his letters and other writings foiled any deep sounding of the interior man. It was not always possible, for instance, to fathom how he internalized cues that guided his mental processes, let alone how he thought or how his thinking took shape in action. Despite the missing pieces, the following pages depict Berkeley in ways never seen before, just as they illuminate my quest to understand him in the context of the colony he called home.

American scholars have long been guilty of misspeaking Berkeley's name. Customarily, they say *Burke-lee*, as in Berkeley, California. That was a pronunciation unknown to the governor or to his contemporaries, who said *Bark-lee*. Seventeenth-century Britons cast their phonetic interpolation in written form variously as Barclay, Barklee, Barkley, Barkly, Bartlett, Bartley, and, as the governor always preferred, Berkeley.

Direct quotations from original manuscripts are rendered according to the prescripts set forth in the section on selection, rendition, and annotation of documents in *The Papers of Sir William Berkeley* Web site, www.uno.edu/history/berkeley.htm. Obsolete usages are thus regularized only to the extent that modern orthography is imposed upon proper names, whereas archaic abbreviations and symbols are expanded, and sentences begin with capitals and end in appropriate terminal punctuation. Citations to case reports, law dictionaries, statutory abridgments, treatises, and other legal works of the period invariably refer to witnesses that are in my library. Biographical details about Virginians who appear throughout the book arise from an electronic database I compiled for colonial officeholders between 1619 and 1699. Derived from vital statistics, places of origin, kin connections, occupations, offices, and landholdings, the database goes uncited. Dates are rendered in the old style, meaning that they are ten days behind modern reckoning. Then, too, during the seventeenth century the English commenced a new year on 25 March, not 1 January. In the interval writers customarily employed double dates—for example, 1 January 1600/01. That usage is retained here, but 1 January is considered the start of any given year.

I avow my deep gratitude to the following individuals, whose advice, close commentary, and constant encouragement sustained me in immeasurable ways while the book took form. Colleagues at the University of New Orleans were unfailingly supportive. Gerald P. Bodet, Arnold R. Hirsch, and Joe Louis Caldwell, by turns my department chairmen, ensured a convenient writing environment. Marie Erickson, head of reference at the Law Library of Louisiana, proved singularly adept at efficiently filling numerous interlibrary loan requests that put vital, if sometimes recondite, books, journal articles, and other source materials at my fingertips. Barbara M. Tearle, sometime director of the Bodleian Law Library at the University of Oxford, helped in locating pertinent information within the university archives. The Reverend Thomas Buckley, S.J., was instrumental in arranging a contact with the Venerable English College in Rome, where I tracked down a vital clue to Berkeley's whereabouts during the early 1630s.

Leigh Anne Plasse Baltazar, Edward L. Bond, Patricia Brady, Emory G. Evans, Mark F. Fernandez, William M. Kelso, Karen Ordahl Kupperman, John Rushton Pagan, James F. Sefcik, Thad W. Tate, Sandra Gioia Treadway, and Bertram Wyatt-Brown read the manuscript in whole or in part at various stages of its evolution, and their comments helped transform it into a better book. Elizabeth Gratch expertly copyedited the manuscript and thus spared me the embarrassment of obvious errors of grammar and style. Lee C. Sioles and the staff at the LSU Press moved the book expeditiously and saw to its handsome design.

A nod of appreciation goes to the staff of the Colonial National Historical Park at Jamestown for graciously allowing me to examine the field notes, reports, and artifacts that Louis R. Caywood amassed during his excavations at the Green Spring House site in 1955.

Beverly A. Straube, curator at the Association for the Preservation of Virginia Antiquities' Jamestown Rediscovery Project, taught me much about the pottery recoveries at Green Spring. Her knowledge of seventeenth-century technology was equally invaluable.

William M. Kelso, director of archaeology at Jamestown Rediscovery, deepened my understanding about the construction of the 1663 statehouse in light of his team's reassessment of the foundations, which were first excavated and described by Colonel Samuel H. Yonge more than a century ago.

A stint as an Alexander W. Weddell Lecturer at the Virginia Historical Society in 1988 and tenure as the nineteenth Mary S. Carroll Lecturer at Mary Baldwin College four years later provided my earliest public occasions to sketch initial assessments of Berkeley. Those musings underwent additional refinement as a result of suggestions that I received from the participants in an (Omohundro) Institute of Early American History and Culture colloquium at Williamsburg in 1993.

Generous university research stipends underwrote travel and other incidentals of research. A sabbatical leave in 1997 allowed time to begin crafting the manuscript, and my appointment as Visiting Williams Professor of Law at the University of Richmond in the fall of 2002 enabled me to put the finishing touches to it.

Above all, I acknowledge Carol D. Billings. This book is for her.

Abbreviations Used in the Notes

Add.MS	Additional Manuscripts, British Library
ADM	Admiralty Papers, Public Record Office
ADWI	Accomack County Deed, Will, and Inventory Books (*This and all other county court record group abbreviations refer to microfilm copies of original manuscript records deposited at the Library of Virginia in Richmond.*)
AOB	Accomack County Order Books
BL	British Library, London
C	Chancery Papers, Public Record Office
CCDWI	Charles City County Deed, Will, and Inventory Books
CCOB	Charles City Order Books
CO	Colonial Office Papers, Public Record Office
CsmH	Henry E. Huntington Library, San Marino, California
CSPD	Calendar of State Papers, Domestic Series, Public Record Office
DLC	Library of Congress, Washington, D.C.
DNB	*Dictionary of National Biography*
HCA	High Court of Admiralty Papers, Public Record Office
HDWI	Henrico County Deed, Will, and Inventory Books

HLRO	House of Lords Record Office, Westminster
HOB	Henrico County Order Books
IWDWI	Isle of Wight County Deed, Will, and Inventory Books
IWOB	Isle of Wight County Order Books
LC	Lord Chamberlain's Accounts, Public Record Office
LDWI	Lancaster County Deed, Will, and Inventory Books
LNDWI	Lower Norfolk County Deed, Will, and Inventory Books
LNOB	Lower Norfolk County Order Books
LOB	Lancaster County Order Books
MdAA	Maryland Hall of Records, Annapolis, Maryland
MOB	Middlesex County Order Books
N	New York State Library, Albany
NcAr	North Carolina Department of Archives and History, Raleigh
Nhi	New-York Historical Society, New York City
NoDWI	Northampton County Deed, Will, and Inventory Books
NoOB	Northampton County Order Books
NuDWI	Northumberland County Deed, Will, and Inventory Books
NuOB	Northumberland County Order Books
PC	Privy Council Minutes, Public Record Office
PCR	Privy Council Registers, Public Record Office
PRO	Public Record Office, Kew
RDWI	Rappahannock Deed, Will, and Inventory Books
SDWI	Surry County Deed, Will, and Inventory Books
SO	Signet Office Docquet Books, Public Record Office
SOB	Surry County Order Books
SP	State Papers, Public Record Office
T	Treasury Office Papers, Public Record Office
Vi	Library of Virginia, Richmond
ViHi	Virginia Historical Society, Richmond
ViU	Alderman Library, University of Virginia, Charlottesville

ViWC   Research Department, Colonial Williamsburg Foundation,
    Williamsburg

WDWI   Westmoreland County Deed, Will, and Inventory Books

WOB   Westmoreland County Order Books

YDWI   York County Deed, Will, and Inventory Books

YOB   York County Order Books

Sir William Berkeley
and the Forging of
Colonial Virginia

1

EARLY YEARS

lizabeth Berkeley felt pangs that signaled the onset of labor. As her pains sharpened, her servant women hurriedly readied a room in her father's house. They set out the clean bed linens, fresh clothes, and every other necessity their mistress had gathered in anticipation of what lay ahead. When the women had done all they could to make the chamber warm and snug, their mistress took to her bed. A midwife was summoned. She soothed her charge and eased her through the long hours of her travail.[1]

Although delivering a child was always risky for women in the seventeenth century, Elizabeth Berkeley may have feared little beyond travail because all her previous pregnancies had ended safely. This birth would be no different. On a wintry day in early 1605, she bore a son, whom she called William, after her father, Sir William Killigrew.[2]

1. David Cressy, *Birth, Marriage, and Death: Ritual, Religion, and the Life-Cycle in Tudor and Stuart England* (Oxford, 1997), 50–59.

2. The year of Berkeley's birth is established by a pedigree that was prepared in conjunction with a Herald's Visitation of Somerset in 1623 (MS 2C.22264AB, College of Arms, London). This document dispels persistent confusion about the time of Berkeley's birth. Earlier biographical sketches give different years (*Dictionary of National Biography*, 2:368–69; *Dictionary of American Biography*, 2:217–18; *Encyclopedia of Virginia Biography*, 1, under "Berkeley"; R. C. Bald, "Sir William Berkeley's *The Lost Lady*," *Library* 17 [1936–37]: 394–426; and Gerard Eades Bentley, *The Jacobean and Caroline Stage: Plays and Playwrights* [Oxford, 1941–46], 3:20–25). I mistakenly accepted 1606 in "Berkeley and Effingham: Who Cares?" *Virginia Magazine of History and Biography* 97 (1989): 34, which I composed before I came across the pedigree.

The newborn boy entered the favored world of the English gentry, blessed with sound health and hardy kindred. Elizabeth Berkeley was of a consequential lineage. Cecil blood coursed through her veins. Her mother, Margaret Saunders Killigrew, was related to the late William Cecil, first baron Burghley, lord chancellor in the reign of the Virgin Queen. Sir William Killigrew's people were an avidly adventurous, often useful, and occasionally scandalous lot of Cornishmen whose loyalty to the Crown and connections to the Cecils profited them handsomely. Elizabeth's father and uncles won knighthoods and seats in the House of Commons. William, John, and Henry Killigrew also held local office in Cornwall and fought against Spain. John besmirched the family escutcheon by thieving cattle, consorting with pirates, and amassing huge debts that his brothers struggled to clear. The staunchly Protestant Henry fled England during Mary Tudor's reign and picked up the skills of diplomacy, which later led him to be one of Queen Elizabeth's much-traveled emissaries on the Continent.[3] Queen Elizabeth employed William as a groom of her privy chamber and constable of Launceton Castle. Her patronage benefited him not only in these and like offices but in lucrative grants of fees and lands as well. Sir William Killigrew also enjoyed additional preferments in the next reign, even as he continued to sit in Parliament until his death in 1622. He maintained a town house in London and a residence at the manor of Hanworth in Middlesex, and here he sometimes played host to the queen and to her successor, James I.[4]

Here, too, Elizabeth Killigrew bloomed into womanhood. Margaret and William educated their daughter in ways that prepared her to fulfill the main social expectation of highborn English maidens of the time—contracting advantageous marriages and bearing children, preferably boys. Elizabeth satisfied that purpose after she married Sir Maurice Berkeley around the year 1597 and started a household of her own.

Sir Maurice Berkeley (1579?–1617) sprouted from a Somerset sprig of the abundantly branched Berkeley family tree. The Berkeleys were an ancient tribe. Tradition held that they descended from Norse corsairs who scourged the British Isles during the Viking age. Whatever their origins, by the fourteenth century their constant loyalty to the Crown had netted them much in wealth, social stature, and political clout. The Somerset Berkeleys arose less anciently. They traced their roots in and about the town of Bruton to Maurice's grandfather and namesake, who stood stoutly with the Tudors. Henry VIII knighted the elder Maurice and bestowed a dissolved monastery in Bruton upon him, which he refitted into his

---

3. P. W. Hasler, comp., *The House of Commons, 1558–1603* (London, 1981), 2:394–97.
4. Ibid., 397–98.

seat and called Bruton Abbey. Kin, mutual interests, and friendships soon bound Squire Berkeley and his descendants to the Pouletts, the Phelipses, the Hoptons, the Portmans, the Halswells, and numerous other magnates who governed Somerset and took turns serving in the House of Commons. Such, then, were the surroundings that shaped the grandson. As preparation for his undoubted high place in society, the younger Maurice Berkeley attended Queen's College, Oxford, and the Middle Temple, London, as had his father, uncles, and grandsires before him. He married in his teens and entered Parliament soon thereafter, largely, it seems, through the contrivance of his father-in-law. In his mature years he earned his knighthood while soldiering with Robert Devereaux, second earl of Essex, sat as a justice of the peace for Somerset, and remained a member of the House of Commons until his death.[5]

Still, for all the advantages of pedigree and connection, Sir Maurice Berkeley did not reach the heights of his grandfather or his sons. Although he owned or leased various properties in Somerset, Gloucestershire, and London, his holdings would never be reckoned as grand. Bruton Abbey and its considerable acreage passed to him eventually, yet its profits were never wholly his to enjoy because his mother, who had a life interest in the estate, outlasted him. He turned elsewhere in search of income and bought shares in the East India Company, the Virginia Company of London, and the Irish Company. His investments mingled with those of other enterprising gentlemen to underwrite overseas commercial ventures that set the groundwork for England's first colonial empire, but his stocks failed to bring in huge returns. At bottom great wealth never came his way for a plain reason: he took few measures to curb his extravagant appetites. And he died very much in debt.[6]

5. Ibid., 1:430–33; Arthur Collins, *The Peerage of England: Containing a Genealogical and Historical Account of All the Peers of England . . .* (London, 1756), 5:185–90; E. H. Bates, ed., *Quarter Sessions Records for the County of Somerset*, vol. 1 (Taunton, Somerset, 1907); S. W. Bates-Harbin, *Members of Parliament for the County of Somerset* (Taunton, Somerset, 1939), 134–35; Thomas Garden Barnes, *Somerset, 1625–1640: A County's Government during the "Personal Rule"* (Cambridge, Mass., 1961), 18–40; Theodore K. Rabb, *Jacobean Gentleman: Sir Edwin Sandys, 1561–1629* (Princeton, 1998).

6. Theodore K. Rabb, *Enterprise and Empire: Merchant and Gentry Investment in the Expansion of England, 1575–1630* (Cambridge, Mass., 1967), 1–102, 240; Samuel M. Bemiss, comp., *Three Charters of the Virginia Company of London, with Seven Related Documents; 1606–1621*, in Earl Gregg Swem, ed., *Jamestown 350th Anniversary Booklets* (Williamsburg, Va., 1957), 29; Susan Myra Kingsbury, ed., *Records of the Virginia Company of London* (Washington, D.C., 1906–35); Alexander Brown, *The First Republic in America: An Account of the Origin of This Nation . . .* (Boston, 1898); Philip Barbour, ed., *The Complete Works of Captain John Smith (1580–1631) in Three Volumes* (Chapel Hill, N.C., 1981), 1:98 n. 21; 2:273, 274, 301; 3:224, 225 n. 1. Dame Elizabeth Berkeley owned shares in the Virginia Company in her own right as well.

Berkeley fared little better in politics. Faithfully attentive to his magisterial duties on the Somerset bench, he nonetheless failed to distinguish himself sufficiently to attain higher judicial office. Nor did his parliamentary tenure lead to better things. Always a back bencher in the commons, Berkeley earned a reputation as a bit of a hothead, most notably during the Addled Parliament. That fame, plus his religious sensibilities, brought him close to ruination. He inclined toward those Anglicans who wanted to purge the Church of England entirely of its Romish habits and cleanse it completely of what they supposed were its ecclesiastical malpractices. Consequently, he heeded the plaints of a constituent, the Reverend Edward Peacham.

Rector of the parish of Hinton St. George in Somerset, the elderly Parson Peacham was a quarrelsome, puritanical priest continually at odds with his diocesan superiors. He went up to London in spring 1614, just before the dissolution of the Addled Parliament, and conferred with Berkeley regarding a petition against purported clerical abuses that certain Somerset freeholders had sent to the House of Commons. At about that time church authorities finally lost patience with Peacham. They hauled him before the Court of High Commission on a charge of insulting his bishop, and for that offense the court quickly deprived him of his orders before it dispatched him to cool his heels in London's Gatehouse prison. A subsequent search of Peacham's house turned up the draft of a sermon that attacked the church and hurled barbed words at King James I even as it seemed to counsel rebellion. The text raised such fears of conspiracies and treacheries that an alarmed Privy Council ordered Peacham to the Tower pending his further examination and likely trial as a traitor. Investigators soon learned of the conference between the priest and Berkeley. That intelligence led to an urgent summons for Berkeley and two of Peacham's other gentry neighbors to appear before the Privy Council for questioning. Their responses evidently sufficed to ward off their being charged with Peacham, but all three remained under suspicion well after the parson's trial and conviction for treason.[7]

Scanty detail about Maurice and Elizabeth Berkeley casts their lives as hus-

7. Rabb, *Jacobean Gentleman*, 76, 80, 112, 117, 165, 177, 183n, 196, 197; "Edward Peacham," *DNB*, 15:576–78; Stephen R. Gardiner, *History of England from the Accession of James I to the Outbreak of the Civil War, 1603–1642* (London, 1901), 2:272–82; T. B. Howell, comp., *A Complete Collection of State Trials and Proceedings for High Treason and Other Crimes and Misdemeanors from the Earliest Period to the Year 1783* (London, 1816), 2:870–83; order for the appearance of Sir Maurice Berkeley, Sir Nicholas Halswell, and John Poulett, 2 Nov. 1614, Privy Council Register, 2/28, 611, PRO; Calendar of State Papers, 1611–18, 276, PRO; John Chamberlain to Sir Dudley Carleton, 31 Mar. 1614, in Norman Egbert McClure, ed., *The Letters of John Chamberlain* (Philadelphia, 1939), 1:521. Peacham was eventually tried and convicted at Taunton but never faced execution because he died in the town jail.

band and wife or as father and mother in shadow, so there remains little with which to illuminate the extent of their influence on their children beyond remarking the obvious. They gave William and his siblings a cozy life and ties of kin that each might turn to some future benefit. In addition to William, they produced four sons and two daughters. Charles (1600–1665), their firstborn, was followed in turn by Henry (1601–23?), Maurice (1603–27), John (1607–78), Margaret (1611–?), and Jane (1613–?). The five boys went on to knighthoods and public careers as adults, though of them only Charles, William, and John are the ones about whom there is much to know.[8]

Sir Charles Berkeley enjoyed lifelong connections to the Stuarts. Knighted in his twenties, he inherited Bruton Abbey upon his grandmother's death, where he later received both George Abbott, archbishop of Canterbury, and Prince Charles as houseguests. He served Charles I in various ways before he went into exile with Charles II. Steadfastness earned him a seat on the Privy Council and the place of comptroller of the royal household, before he appointed him Lord Berkeley of Rathdown and Viscount Fitzharding. John figured prominently in events leading up to the Civil War in which he played a significant role before he, too, joined the court-in-exile. Charles II subsequently turned him into the Baron Berkeley of Stratton and a privy councillor. The baron was a proprietor of Carolina and the Northern Neck of Virginia as well as lord lieutenant of Ireland, and he built a grand London town house on Berkeley Square, which sat opposite the mansion of his inveterate enemy, Edward Hyde, first earl of Clarendon. As for the girls, no details survive about Margaret. Jane married a wealthy widower named John Davis, and she lived long enough to be named a beneficiary in William's will.[9]

Sir Maurice died when Will, as relatives and friends always called him, was twelve. Father bequeathed son land in Somerset and "moderate annuities to sup-

---

8. Berkeley pedigree. Of the seven siblings only Jane was born at Bruton Abbey (Douglas L. Haywood, ed., *The Registers of Bruton, Co. Somerset* [n.p., n.d.], 1:68).

9. Phyllis Couzens, *Bruton in Somerset: Some Account of Its History* (Sherborne, Dorset, 1972), 47–48; Collins, *Peerage of England*, 5:190; *DNB*, 2, under "Berkeley, William"; William S. Powell, *The Proprietors of Carolina* (Raleigh, 1963), 29–33; "Sketch of the Character of John, Lord Berkeley," Add. MS 36,270, fols. 110–14, BL; Bernard Falk, *The Berkeleys of Berkeley Square & Some of Their Kinfolk* (London, 1944), 34–97; Richard Ligon, *Severall Circumstances to prove that M^{ris} Jane Berkeley and Sr William Killigrew have combined together to defraud me of an estates left unto me by Henry Killigrew Esq.; for payment of his debts, for which I lye now in prison* (London, 1654), 14; William Waller Hening, ed., *The Statutes at Large; Being a Collection of All the Laws of Virginia from the First Session of the Legislature, in the Year 1619*, facsimile ed. (1809–23; rpt., Charlottesville, Va., 1969): 2:258–60. Karen Ordahl Kupperman brought the Ligon pamphlet to my attention, and it identified John Davis by name.

port his pretenses in the world." The portion was about as much as a fourth son might expect, especially when it came from a much indebted estate. Will therefore rose to manhood always knowing the restraints of a pinched purse. Even so, reduced circumstances did not prevent his securing a proper education. If anything, modest means led him to excel whenever opportunities for betterment presented themselves.[10]

Particulars of the boy's upbringing are scarce, though his adult papers portray him as someone of quick wits and broad learning. Will, like any other British youngster, got his first training at his mother's knee and by observing his elders. Those lessons instilled rules that controlled relations between parent and child or servant and master, but they equally taught the mores that governed the larger world of English society and his privileged place in it. Rustic occupations were ever the way of the country gentry too, so Will absorbed the practices of the soil almost from birth. Given his father's involvement in local and national politics, at an early age Will also came to appreciate public life, its responsibilities, and its possibilities. Similarly, he knew about faraway places such as Virginia from his parents, who had financial interests in the colony dating back to the days of its first settlers. A friend to Sir Walter Ralegh, Sir Maurice also was active in the running of the Virginia Company as an ally of Sir Edwin Sandys and the Ferrar brothers, Nicholas and John, who staunchly advocated the production of exotic staples as the means of saving the struggling colony. Members of the extended Berkeley clan who tried their skill at making silk and iron there or who invested in the burgeoning Virginia trade filled Will's head with tales of a strange new world, and their talk of ways to capitalize on the promise of Virginia was commonplace long before the lad passed into his early teens.[11]

At about the age of six or seven Will began his first formal education at a grammar school, which was a place remarkably different from its modern American counterpart. There he learned to read and write in Latin and in English. Gaining those fundamental skills enabled him to tackle the more complex subjects of grammar, logic, and rhetoric, plus smatterings of history and mathematics, which grounded the necessary foundations for further instruction at one of

10. Will of Sir Maurice Berkeley, 1617, Probate Registers, 11/130, PRO; "Sketch of the Character of John, Lord Berkeley"; John Chamberlain to Sir Dudley Carleton, 5 Apr. 1617, McClure, *Letters of John Chamberlain*, 2:70.

11. Michael Strachan, *Sir Thomas Roe, 1581–1644: A Life* (London, 1989), 118–34; Wesley Frank Craven, *The Dissolution of the Virginia Company: The Failure of a Colonial Experiment* (1932; rpt., Gloucester, Mass., 1964), 327; Eric Gethyn-Jones, *George Thorpe and the Berkeley Company: A Gloucestershire Enterprise in Virginia* (Gloucester, 1982); John Chamberlain to Sir Dudley Carleton, 14 Nov. 1616, McClure, *Letters of John Chamberlain*, 2:34.

the universities. And so, just as he turned eighteen, Will followed his forebears to Queen's College, Oxford. He and John both signed the subscription book on 14 February 1622/23, though he quickly transferred to St. Edmund Hall, while John remained enrolled at Queen's.[12]

Institutionally affiliated with Queen's, St. Edmund Hall was a throwback to medieval times, when such hostels were an integral part of the university scene. Their decline came slowly over the length of the sixteenth century, and their diminution marked a gradual transformation of Oxford from a university in England anchored in the authority of the Church Universal to an English university grounded in the norms of Tudor society. The changeover was far from complete when Will matriculated, but by 1623 families such as his regarded university education as essential to a son's preparation for his rightful place in society.[13]

Contemporary records suggest something of the atmosphere and flavor of Will's undergraduate experiences. The Reverend Doctor John Tomlinson, protégé of Archbishop Richard Baxter, had served as principal of St. Edmund since 1610. His faculty consisted of nine masters and readers, including the Reverend Matthew Nicholas, who subsequently became dean of St. Paul's Cathedral Church in London. Generally, accommodations at the hall were adequate. A cook, a butler, a manciple (i.e., provisioner), and a "bible clerke," who doubled as the porter, constituted the house staff. Students swore "to be true to our commons." Their "allowance of bread, drinke and meate [was] reasonably provided," by the manciple, who laid out "readie money," and they had "always single beere." Students and faculty celebrated the daily office of morning prayer between 5 and 6 A.M. on weekdays and at 8 A.M. on Sundays and holy days. Each evening at dinner the bible clerk read a chapter from sacred Scripture, and everyone heard him "with silence." The porter closed the gates for the night at nine o'clock, though students could go into town after hours if Dr. Tomlinson or their tutors granted them leave. "Lectures, disputations, theames, and such like" formed one of the bases of instruction. Additionally, there were "weeklie correc-

12. Subscription Register, SP 39, fol. 84, Oxford University Archives, Bodleian Library; Joseph Foster, comp., *Alumni Oxonienses: The Members of the University of Oxford, 1500–1714* (London, 1892), 1:114; Kenneth Charlton, *Education in Renaissance England* (London, 1965), 89–131; Anthony Fletcher, *Gender, Sex, and Subordination in England, 1500–1800* (New Haven, Conn., 1995), 297–342. Simon Bailey, the Oxford University archivist, provided a photographic copy of the page from Subscription Register that bears the signatures of William and John Berkeley.

13. Mark H. Curtis, *Oxford and Cambridge in Transition, 1558–1642: An Essay on Changing Relations between the English Universities and English Society* (Oxford, 1959), 36–40, 50–53, 260–81; Charlton, *Education in Renaissance England*, 131–69; A. B. Emden, "St. Edmund Hall, Oxford," in H. E. Salter and Mary D. Lobel, eds., *The Victoria History of the Counties of England, Oxfordshire* (London, 1954), 3:319–55; Nicholas Tyacke, ed., *The History of the University of Oxford* (Oxford, 1997), 4:1–135.

tions" of student work, though the "bachelours and schollars [were] negligent in the speakinge of latine." And every undergraduate had his own tutor.[14]

A good tutor was key to gaining well from a university education. Tutors instructed by artful example and potent precept, and, as they did, they inspired subtle, influential relationships with their pupils. Those affinities were quite difficult for someone else to apprehend fully, because tutors and students seldom wrote down their experiences of one another. Existing records do not tell who actually tutored Will. Whoever he was, he had a very profound effect upon the lad because Berkeley retained a disciplined intellect and steady appetite for knowledge all his life.

Modest means combined with quick intelligence to motivate Will, who received his bachelorship within fifteen months of his arrival at St. Edmund Hall. Attaining a B.A. did not necessarily signify that one had completed his degree. Usually, the distinction meant only that an undergraduate had qualified for higher studies that would lead him to a master's diploma in time. Evidently, however, Berkeley's mother and brother Charles bore something else in mind because Will was admitted to the Middle Temple two months before St. Edmund awarded his bachelorship. The plan, it seems, was to equip Will as a barrister or a local magistrate.[15]

He spent two years at the Middle Temple. Like the other inns of court, the Middle Temple existed to ground young men of whatever station in the practice of English common law. Its structure and method of instruction differed not all that much from St. Edmund Hall. Members and students lived, dined, worshiped, and studied together within the walled precincts of the temple. Curricula offerings tended toward the haphazard, and it could take up to seven years to prepare for entry to the bar, though students often had little inclination to pursue a career in the field of law. Instead, the highborn ones regarded whatever time they invested in legal study as an impressive way of rounding off a gentleman's schooling. The temple also afforded an arena for witty students to try their hands at crafting epigrams, poetry, verses, plays, and masques, for there were numerous festal occasions that demanded entertainment or bon mots. Will reveled in the opportunity to hone his gift for words, which contributed later to his reputation for clever conversation and repartee. Outside the temple walls lay the city of London and manifold opportunities for sampling high culture and low

14. Visitationes Aularum, Oxford University Archives, as quoted in Emden, "St. Edmund Hall," 327–28.

15. Curtis, *Oxford and Cambridge in Transition,* 91; Foster, comp., *Alumni Oxonienses,* 1:114; minutes of the parliament of the Middle Temple, 1610–26, entry for 3 May 1624, Middle Temple Library, London.

life. In these circumstances Will learned law as he forged friendships and experiences that stood him well for the remainder of his life. Not least of these bonds
was one he fashioned with his fellow student, Edward Hyde, the future earl of
Clarendon, who would figure prominently in his later career. For all of that he
balked at satisfying his mother's expectations of him. He never answered a call
to the bar, nor did he pursue county office. Instead, he returned to Oxford, entered Merton College, renewed his studies, and in 1629 earned his master of arts
degree. The latter accomplishment led to his election as a college fellow, one of
Merton's senior resident scholars.[16]

Now that Master Berkeley was appropriately prepared, he appeared willing to
settle into the contemplative life of an academic, but after a little while that pro-
fession failed to sate inner yearnings that tugged at him. He petitioned the war-
den and fellows in February 1630 for an extended leave of absence, which his
colleagues promptly granted. Some months later, armed with a passport from
the Privy Council, he and two companions set out "to travill into the partes beyond the Seas for the space of three yeares next insuing, with a promise not to
goe to Rome."[17]

Thomas Coryat (1577?–1617), who toured Europe early in the seventeenth century, popularized the idea that foreign excursions had a wholesome effect upon
Stuart gentlemen such as Will Berkeley. To Coryat's way of thinking, purposeful
travel in strange places widened the outlook as it increased awareness of a greater
world that lay beyond the British Isles. He gave voice to his views in *Coryat's
Crudities, hastily gobled up in five moneths travells in France Savoy, Italy, Rhetia
commonly called the Grisons country, Helvetia alias Switzerland, some parts of high
Germany and the Netherlands; newly digested in the hungry aire of Odcombe in the
county of Somerset, and now dispersed to the nourishment of the travelling members
of this kingdom* (London, 1611), which was a pioneering travelogue that heightened an English thirsting after foreign sights. Thus, by the 1630s British gentlemen abroad, although not yet legion, were hardly unknown on the Continent. If

16. John Fortescue, *A Learned Commendation of the Politique Lawes of England* (London, 1567),
fols. 113–16; Clive Holmes, *Seventeenth-Century Lincolnshire* (Lincoln, Neb., 1980), 77–78; J. H. Glea-
son, *The Justice of the Peace in England, 1558–1640: A Later Eirenarcha* (Oxford, 1969), 84, 88, 90–91;
Anne Hughes, *Politics, Society and Civil War in Warwickshire, 1620–1660* (Cambridge, 1987), 44; Wil-
fred R. Prest, *The Inns of Court under Elizabeth I and the Early Stuarts, 1590–1640* (London, 1972);
Prest, *The Rise of the Barristers: A Social History of the English Bar, 1590–1640* (Oxford, 1986); Walter
C. Richardson, *A History of the Inns of Court: With Special Reference to the Period of the Renaissance*
(Baton Rouge, 1975); Charlton, *Education in Renaissance England*, 169–99; Richard Lane, comp., "A
Booke of Accounts Ano Dom 1638," Middle Temple Library, London.

17. Registrum Collegii Mertonensis, Merton College Library, Oxford; abstract of passport given
to William Berkeley, Edward Wingfield, and Francis Smith, 3 May 1630, PC 2/39, PRO.

anything, the popularity of the grand tour was on the rise, especially now that England was at peace with France and accommodation with Spain seemed at hand. Little wonder, then, that such an excursion appealed to the restlessly curious Berkeley.[18]

Few details of his trip have come to light, though hints indicate the likely itinerary. Stops in France, the Netherlands, and Italy were considered de rigueur. Will first set off to join his brother John, who was with English troops garrisoned in Holland. Time in the trenches gave him a feel for military life, much as it had done for countless others of his countrymen ever since the 1560s, when the Hollanders broke free of Spanish domination and the English first sent soldiers to ensure Dutch independence. The country held other attractions too. Anglo-Dutch mercantile families abounded in Amsterdam, Rotterdam, Leiden, and elsewhere, so there were ample occasions to gain more than a nodding acquaintance of Dutch ways. Will observed evidence of how Netherlands merchants and seafarers were massively extending Holland commerce worldwide, trading with Dutch colonies and anywhere else there was need for a ship's hold to freight goods to market or the chance to earn a guilder. Warehouses in port cities groaned under the weight of cloth from England, tobacco from Virginia, spices from the East Indies, furs from New Netherlands, and sugar from the Caribbean. Their abundant stock spoke powerfully to a rising rivalry between England and Holland that, unbeknownst to Will at the moment, would intervene in how he governed Virginia.[19]

Next, he toured France. That portion of his travels might well have taken him along a route similar to one prescribed by Richard Peacham. Author of the widely appreciated *The Compleat Gentleman: Fashioning him absolute in the most necessary & commendable Qualities concerning Minde or Bodie that may be required in a Noble Gentleman* (London, 1622), Peacham advised visiting Normandy, Paris, the Loire Valley, Picardie, and Orléans. If one were intent upon acquiring a command of French, it was particularly important to go to Orléans, where, as Peacham wrote, "the language is spoken with more elegancie and puritie."[20]

18. Peacham, *Compleat Gentleman*, 200–201; Kevin Sharpe, *The Personal Rule of Charles I* (New Haven, Conn., 1992), 43–46, 65–86. On the development of touring generally and its impact on young Englishmen such as Berkeley, see Janet P. Trevelyan, "Wandering Englishmen in Italy," *Proceedings of the British Academy* 16 (1930): 66–78; Dorothy Carrington, *The Traveller's Eye* (New York, 1947); John Walter Stoye, *English Travellers Abroad, 1604–1667: Their Influence in English Society and Politics* (London, 1952); E. P. de G. Chaney, *The Grand Tour and the Great Rebellion: Richard Lassles and the "Voyage to Italy" in the Seventeenth Century* (Geneva, 1985).

19. "Sketch of the Character of John, Lord Berkeley."

20. Peacham, *Compleat Gentleman*, 205–8, 203.

Once Will passed through France into Italy, he perhaps did as other English travelers and spent a while at Padua, even attending lectures at the university. Then he ignored the restrictions of his passport and went to Rome, because, like everyone else, he would have regarded a visit to the Eternal City as an essential element in his peregrinations and education. He lodged for a time at the Venerable English College, a Jesuit institution that welcomed British visitors of all religious complexions.[21]

Will returned to England in 1632. That he was gone a shorter time than his passport allowed suggests that a lack of money cut short his travels. Dwindling resources certainly entailed him to find a settled existence and a reliable living. One possibility was to return to Oxford and resume his fellowship at Merton College. Another was to find a county office. A third was to finish off his legal studies and answer a call to the bar. Yet none of these choices appealed to him. Instead, he took the course of many other younger, impoverished gentry sons. He sought preferment at court. Family credentials afforded him more than a bit of an edge. He could rely upon his elder brother Charles. His first cousin Henry Jermyn was a favorite of Queen Henrietta Maria. A cousin-in-law, George Kirke, was a groom of the royal bedchamber and a gentleman of the robes, whereas a Merton colleague, the Reverend John Earle, was chaplain to Philip Herbert, fourth earl of Pembroke, the lord chamberlain. Pembroke controlled appointments to the royal household and was lord lieutenant of Somerset; Sir Charles Berkeley was one of his deputies.[22] The combined weight of these relations sufficed to win Will an appointment as a gentleman of the king's privy chamber extraordinary before the year was out.[23]

The position gave Berkeley proximity to Charles I and opportunities with which to fashion a career that was as profitable as it was honorable. How well he used his chance would determine how far he might rise and how quickly.

21. Chaney, *Grand Tour and the Great Rebellion,* 19–91. An entry in the college's Pilgrim Book, 1580–1656, records "Dmo. Barclay" as arriving at the college on All Souls' Day (2 Nov.) 1631.

22. On Jermyn (d. 1684), afterward first earl of St. Albans, and his relationship to Henrietta Maria, see Quentin Bone, *Henrietta Maria: Queen of the Cavaliers* (Urbana, Ill., 1972), esp. 84, 85. George Kirke married Berkeley's first cousin Anne Killigrew.

23. The actual warrant for Berkeley's appointment has disappeared, though Pembroke's account book records its existence, LC 5/132, PRO. On the value of appointments such as Berkeley's, see Kevin Sharpe, "The Image of Virtue: The Court and Household of Charles I, 1625–1642," in David Starkey et al., eds., *The English Court: From the Wars of the Roses to the Civil War* (London, 1987), 226–61, esp. 233–34, 246, 249–51.

2

AT THE KING'S COURT

reeding fitted Will Berkeley for royal service, but nothing about his upbringing quite readied him for what now lay before him. Becoming a courtier put him near the seat of majesty and introduced him to inspirations and personalities unlike any he had known before. His encounters rounded his character and whetted his intellectual propensities. They were lessons in the skills and mannerisms of an accomplished courtier equally. He honed his courtly abilities to an ever finer edge as he quietly observed how daily happenings at court revolved around the person of the king. Charles I chose who might bask in the warmth of his largess or who got his blind eye. His regard determined not only those of his subjects he favored; it dictated the rhythms of his household, the way of politics, and the government of his kingdoms too.

In his seventh year as king Charles stood at the zenith of his reign. He was quite the opposite of his father, whom he had succeeded in 1625. Witty and informal, slovenly and ribald, lazy and difficult, the often irreverent James Stuart was an agile politician. Debate and dealing came easily to him, and he just as pragmatically countenanced a latitudinarian Church of England. Charles was none of those things. Straitlaced and haughty, Charles was regular in habit and understated, though stylish, in dress. A deliberate manner of speaking helped him control a stammer, but it also rendered a natural disposition toward weightiness graver still. Inquisitive and intelligent, he was as unyielding as his father was nimble. Bottomless devotion to the ethics of honor and order permanently stayed the needle of his moral compass in one place, whereas an affliction of great energy drove him relentlessly to apply those principles to every facet of his rule, even to the tiniest detail. Charles was no politician. A monarch, thought he, was aloof to the hurly-burly of politics. His utterances were not subjects to dispute. They were commands to be heeded.

While still a prince, Charles collaborated with James's particular favorite, George Villiers, first duke of Buckingham, and Parliament in framing his father's later foreign and domestic agendas. Those policies carried into the early days of his own rule, as did war with Spain. Buckingham gained his everlasting affection. The duke remained a political powerhouse until Parliament impeached him and an assassin's knife killed him. A sorrowful Charles, bereft of his dearest friend and closest confidant, took the affairs of state more and more into his own hands, which soon set him at odds with Parliament. Never at ease with these legislatures, nor they with him, Charles dismissed his last for a decade in 1629 in favor of personal rule. An outwardly prosperous, peaceable England bore seeming witness to the wisdom of his decision.[1]

Untroubled by Parliament, Charles more readily indulged his keen appetite for learning and the arts, a taste he shared with his beloved French queen, Henrietta Maria. Hunger for refinement went far beyond the mere personal whim of a ravenous aesthete who happened to be king. It bespoke his very vision of kingship, and it drew scores of architects, gardeners, musicians, painters, poets, playwrights, scholars, and other genteel wits, who swelled the precincts of his court.[2]

Court life centered mainly in London at the palace of Whitehall. Within the walls of that gigantic Tudor-built pile sprawled a warren of staterooms, great halls, private apartments, garrets, kitchens, cabinets, galleries, nooks, and crannies. Some of the more than two thousand rooms lodged Charles and Henrietta Maria, who kept separate quarters, but the greater portion answered the residential needs of many others who lived at the palace to serve their sovereigns. Topsy-turvy spatial arrangements, plus a jostling press of hundreds upon hundreds of royal hangers-on and visitors, daily gave Whitehall a bustling, beehive quality that disturbed the king's sense of tidiness. Not unexpectedly, Charles set about taming this bedlam directly upon succeeding his father. Although lack of money

1. Conrad Russell, *Parliaments and English Politics, 1621–1629* (Oxford, 1979); Kevin Sharpe, *The Personal Rule of Charles I* (New Haven, Conn., 1992); Pauline Gregg, *King Charles I* (Los Angeles, 1981); Kevin Sharpe and Peter Lake, eds., *Culture and Politics in Early Stuart England* (Stanford, 1991).

2. R. Malcom Smuts, *Court Culture and the Origins of a Royalist Tradition* (Philadelphia, 1987); Kevin Sharpe and Stephen Zwicker, eds., *Politics of Discourse: The Literature and History of Seventeenth Century England* (Berkeley, 1987); Sharpe, *Personal Rule,* 222–35; John Peacock, "The Politics of Portraiture," in Sharpe and Lake, *Culture and Politics,* 199–229; J. Newman, "Inigo Jones and the Politics of Architecture," in Sharpe and Lake, *Culture and Politics,* 229–57.

always stymied his vision of a remodeled palace, he never abandoned his schemes, not even toward the end of his life, when he languished as a prisoner of Parliament. He achieved greater success with his reorganization of the administration of the various household departments so that, by the time Berkeley arrived at court, royal prescriptions for the duties and perquisites of a privy chamber man were rigidly enforced.[3]

Charles personally considered every candidate whom the lord chamberlain recommended. Whoever passed the royal scrutiny then received a warrant of office from the earl of Pembroke and swore an oath of fidelity to the king. Charles demanded of each gentleman of the privy chamber behavior as virtuous as his own. Anyone who whored, drank to excess, or indulged in other debaucheries quickly lost favor and just as quickly departed the court. Will Berkeley easily met the king's standard. Free of the taint of "lewd & scandalous vices," he was "generally beloved and always found in the best Company." He rapidly gained a good reputation "in the Town and in the Court" as well.[4]

There were two ranks of privy chamber men, extraordinary and ordinary. Those "sworne Extraordinary [were] obliged to noe duty." They could come and go "at their pleasure," whereas the ordinary gentlemen had to perform specific tasks that attached to service in the privy chamber. Once Berkeley achieved ordinary status in 1635, he assumed chamber responsibilities, attended all public occasions, and sometimes acted as Charles's personal envoy. In the latter capacity he automatically enjoyed the "high Distinction of bearing the King's Commands on the faith and credentials of [his] appointment, *without a written or sealed commission.*" Although he collected no salary, he benefited from privileges that normally went with his position. He received lodging in the palace and provender for his horses, plus freedom from arrest or appearance in the law courts and attendance at militia musters.[5]

At one time privy chamber men were among a monarch's most intimate personal attendants. James I diminished their importance after he elevated his body servants of the royal bedchamber to a more august place in the household hierarchy. Charles retained that innovation, and, by the time Berkeley became a privy

3. Kevin Sharpe, "The Image of Virtue: The Court and Household of Charles I, 1625–1642," in David Starkey et al., eds., *The English Court from the Wars of the Roses to the Civil War* (London, 1987), 229–48.

4. Anon., "Sketch of the Character of John, Lord Berkeley," Add. MS 36,270, fols. 104–10, BL.

5. Chap. 1 n. 23; petition of the privy chamber men to Charles I, Jan. 1637/38, SP16/380, fol. 112, PRO; warrant from Philip Herbert, fourth earl of Pembroke, the lord chamberlain, 1635, LC/132, PRO; Nicholas Carlisle, *An Inquiry into the Place and Quality of the Gentlemen of His Majesty's Most Honorable Privy Chamber* (London, 1829), 109–16, 255–58, 288–89.

chamber man, his post lacked the stature it had once commanded, though the advantage of regular access to the king remained. The obligations of office were none too onerous either, which was another of its attractions.[6]

Whether attending Charles or standing at ease, Berkeley could freely partake of frequent opportunities for refining his mastery of courtly craft. Contemplating the many paintings, which hung throughout the palace, increased his appreciation of artistic representation and sharpened his aesthetic sensibilities. Sir Anthony Van Dyck's portraits of Charles and the royal family made particularly lasting visual impressions on Berkeley because they testified powerfully to how personal rectitude and domestic tranquillity empowered a ruler to wield dominion over his subjects. Acquaintance with the works of Inigo Jones brought familiarity with fashionable architectural styles, especially the Italianate idiom that the celebrated Jones introduced to set designs for court masques and for buildings such as the Banqueting House at Whitehall. And those very masques, in which Berkeley participated, embodied themes of chasteness, devotion, honor, valor—the selfsame virtues that Charles cultivated so sedulously in himself and demanded so relentlessly of others.[7]

At another intellectual level John Tradescant, father and son, extended Berkeley's innate curiosity about botany, landscaping, horticulture, silk making, and agricultural experimentation. The Tradescants were much sought after as designers of pleasure gardens, though their reputations stood on much besides their formidable skills at cultivating bushes and tending flowers. John Sr. (1570?–1638) knew more about plants than anybody in the British Isles. His unsurpassed grasp of botany not only raised him to a figure of international proportions, it accounted for his successful introduction of hundreds of foreign plants into English cultivation. Tradescant, who avidly collected exotica too, maintained Britain's first museum of natural history. Known as "John Tradeskins Ark," his museum sat next to his house in Southwark, south of the River Thames, hard by Lambeth Palace. It boasted the finest sampling of American floral and faunal specimens anywhere in Britain. Visiting the ark was therefore well nigh obligatory for droves of courtiers who, like Will Berkeley, came to marvel at its many curiosities. Such was the eminence of Tradescant Sr. that Charles I named him gardener royal in 1630 and gave him charge of all palace gardens.[8]

6. Neil Cuddy, "The Revival of the Entourage: The Bedchamber of James I, 1602–1625," in Starkey et al., *English Court from the Wars of the Roses to the Civil War*, 173–225.

7. Sharpe, *Personal Rule of Charles I*, 223–27; Roy Orgel and Stephen Jones, *Inigo Jones: The Theater of the Stuart Court* (Berkeley, 1973); Kevin Sharpe, *Criticism and Compliment: The Politics of Literature in the England of Charles I* (Cambridge, 1987), 179–265.

8. David Sturdy, "The Tradescants of Lambeth," *Journal of Garden History* 2 (1982): 1–16; Arthur MacGregor, "The Tradescants: Gardeners and Botanists," in Arthur MacGregor, ed., *Tradescant's*

Tradescant died in the spring of 1638, whereupon Charles put his son in his stead. John Jr. (1606–62) was a formidable botanist in his own right. Bred to horticulture as a youth, he trained with his father, who in later years depended upon him to gather specimens from abroad. Indeed, he had just returned from a collecting excursion to Virginia about the time of his father's death. His tenure as king's gardener proved short owing to the onset of the Civil War. Came the conflict, and he left the country in 1642 in the company of Bertram Obert for a stay in Virginia that coincided with Berkeley's first years as governor.[9]

Besides gardening for Charles and Henrietta Maria, the Tradescants maintained the royal silk works. Housed at Oatlands in a building of Inigo Jones's design, the silk works dated to 1616, when a Huguenot sericulturalist, John Bonoeil, became silk master to King James. Bonoeil tried introducing the English to the economic possibilities of his craft. The idea of silk production never caught hold with English men of commerce, but neither did it die a swift death. Instead, Bonoeil and the Tradescants' labors reinforced a belief among colonial promoters that silk making could flourish in Virginia, which was why settlers there were urged with varying degrees of intensity to cultivate silk throughout the seventeenth century. Berkeley knew of such promotions long before he ever set foot at Oatlands. His kin had responded to them back in the days of the Virginia Company. Their participation kindled his own lifelong interest in silk, and now he was drawn to the Tradescants to learn what he could from them. Observing them at work and probing their knowledge of plants and horticultural techniques afforded him much practical information that he would apply to his own later agricultural experiments and garden planning in Virginia.[10]

Standing near the principal ministers of the realm furthered his education in the ways of statecraft. Perhaps as never before, he grasped how government at the center depended upon the goodwill of county families such as his own. He observed court factions vying for position, their grouping and regrouping to ad-

Rarities: Essays on the Foundation of the Ashmolean Museum, 1683, with a Catalogue of the Surviving Early Collections (Oxford, 1983), 3–17; April London, "*Musaeum Tradescantianum* and the Benefactors to the Tradescants' Museum," in MacGregor, *Tradescant's Rarities*, 24–40; Mea Allan, *The Tradescants: Their Plants, Gardens and Museum, 1570–1662* (London, 1964); Prudence Leith-Ross, *The John Tradescants: Gardener to the Rose and Lily Queen* (London, 1984), 13–99, 99–111, 163–80, 181–97; B. Fletcher, *Royal Homes Near London* (London, 1930), 141–45.

9. Leith-Ross, *John Tradescants*, 163–80. Tradescant's name appears in a head right Obert, or Hobert, sued out on 10 Oct. 1642 (Virginia Land Patent Book No. 1, pt. 2, 1637–43: 827, Vi). Likely Obert and Tradescant were friends because the latter allowed the former to claim him as a head right. Obert, whose name indicates he was French and Huguenot, remained in Virginia, where he amassed considerable holdings in Gloucester and Lancaster counties.

10. See chaps. 9 and 11.

vantage, and the king navigating between them. And he witnessed the malign results of ill-considered policies, consequences too often made worse by a ruler whose constant need of revenue strained the allegiances of the gentry throughout his three kingdoms. Nearness opened him to a wider appreciation of Virginia affairs too. He made the acquaintance of Virginia's former governor, Sir Francis Wyatt, and its one-time treasurer and acting secretary, George Sandys, just as he watched the continuing policy debates over the future of that faraway settlement. From the moment Virginia became a royal dominion in 1625, Crown deliberations about its future centered on its management and the methods of making it prosper for the greater good of the nation. The king inclined toward governing through a reconstituted company, but he temporized until the year before Berkeley arrived at court. In 1631 Charles finally charged a commission headed by Henrietta Maria's lord chamberlain, Henry Sackville, fourth earl of Dorset, to propose a solution. Besides Sandys and Wyatt, the Dorset Commission included some two dozen colonial experts, whom Berkeley knew to one degree or another through his parents' participation in the defunct Virginia Company. The Dorset Commission reported a scheme that accorded with Charles's proclivity, but an irresolute monarch and hostile colonials effectively scuttled its recommendations. Charles subsequently turned to the Privy Council for other ideas. Its endeavors halted precipitately when the Crown placated the Virginians after they overthrew Governor Sir John Harvey in 1635. Harvey's ouster led finally to the reappointment of the man Berkeley would one day replace as governor of the colony, and, when Sir Francis Wyatt left England for America in 1639, Charles faced the more pressing problem of quieting his rebellious Scottish subjects, which diverted attention from Virginia.[11]

An equally important element in Berkeley's political education may be traced to his inclusion among two loosely strung sets of courtiers. One, which the poet Sir John Suckling named "The Wits," included Thomas Carew, Lucius Cary, second viscount Falkland, the Reverend William Chillingworth, Sir William Davenant, John Denham, Sir Kenelm Digby, the Reverend John Donne, Sidney Godolphin, Thomas Killigrew, the Reverend Richard Lovelace, Toby Mathews,

---

11. Sharpe, *Personal Rule*, 173–79; Wesley Frank Craven, *Dissolution of the Virginia Company: The Failure of a Colonial Experiment* (1932; rpt., Gloucester, Mass, 1964), 292–337; Theodore Rabb, *Jacobean Gentleman: Sir Edwin Sandys, 1561–1629* (Princeton, 1998), 353–89; Michael Strachan, *Sir Thomas Roe, 1581–1644: A Life* (Salisbury, Wilts., 1991), 220–21; Richard Beale Davis, *George Sandys, Poet-Adventurer: A Study in Anglo-American Culture in the Seventeenth Century* (New York, 1955), 257–60; petition to the Privy Council, 6 Mar. 1631/32, Virginia papers, Sackville MS 712/2, Centre for Kentish Studies, Maidstone, Kent; Jon Kukla, *Political Institutions in Virginia, 1619–1660* (New York, 1989), 81–95; commission to Sir Francis Wyatt, Jan. 1638/39, CO 5/1354, 212–13, PRO.

Walter Montagu, Endymion Porter, George Sandys, Aurelian Townshend, and Suckling himself. They all hovered around that "most gracious and needy sanctuary of those who have no other support," Henrietta Maria, whose infectious fondness for entertainment drew from them a profusion of plays, poems, and masques. The affinity between the Wits and Berkeley was natural enough. Godolphin, Killigrew, and Lovelace were his relations, the rest were his friends, or fellow gentlemen of the privy chamber, and he had a talent for writing.[12]

Sadly, however, all but one of his literary offerings disappeared long ago. The lone exception is a play, which he titled *The Lost Lady, A Tragi-Comedy*.[13] He began writing *The Lost Lady* in the summer of 1637. Months passed as plot, characters, and dialogue took form. After circulating his working draft to his friends for their comments, he polished the piece to a point where at year's end he felt comfortable enough to mount it for an audience. So he arranged with a group of London players known as the King's Men to act the play for Charles and Henrietta Maria during the Christmas season. That initial performance met a favorable reception, which led to stagings at Blackfriars and the Cockpit in early 1638. After *The Lost Lady* closed down, Berkeley contracted with the London printers John Okes and John Coleby for two editions of the text, which he likely distributed as souvenirs. (A third edition appeared in 1640.) He also employed a scribe, who prepared a fancy manuscript copy as a present for the queen.[14]

Set in ancient Greece, *The Lost Lady* has an improbable story line that turns on the actions of numerous characters who become enmeshed in a convoluted play of love and deception. Such intricacies of plot appealed to Stuart audiences. So did Berkeley's use of ghosts, portents, heroes, villains, wordplays, classical allusions, romantic scheming, pratfalls, and political chicanery. Even the play's chattiness and slow-moving pace were standard ingredients of Caroline theatricals. But here was more than mere slavish adherence to the predictable. For Berkeley these very dramatic conventions were devices expressive of something else. Framing *The Lost Lady* against a background of war and intrigue reflected

---

12. Suckling identified the group in a poem known variously as "A Session of Poets" or "The Wits," a text of which appears in Thomas Clayton, ed., *The Works of Sir John Suckling: The Non-Dramatic Works* (Oxford, 1971), 73; Sir Thomas Roe to George Goring, Lord Goring, 8 Apr. 1634, CSPD, 1633–34, 543. On Henrietta Maria's impact upon Caroline theater, see Erica Veevers, *Images of Love and Religion: Queen Henrietta Maria and Court Entertainments* (Cambridge, 1989).

13. R. C. Bald, "Sir William Berkeley's *The Lost Lady*," *Library*, 4th ser., 17 (1936–37): 395–426.

14. George Gerrard to Thomas Wentworth, first earl of Strafford, 7 Feb. 1637/38, Thomas Wentworth, *The Earl of Strafford's Letters and Despatches*, ed. William Knowler (London, 1739), 2:250; Gerard Eades Bentley, *The Jacobean and Caroline Stage* (Oxford, 1941–68), 3:20–25; Josiah Quincy Adams, ed., *Henry Herbert, Master of the Revels, 1623–1673* (New Haven, Conn., 1917), 77.

his inner dismay at the erosion of England's reputation abroad and the decay of the "Halcyon Reign" at home. Strictures against rulers, especially the duplicitous duke of Argos and the unyielding Lord Pindarus, hint at his private misgivings about his own royal master. And the intricate stratagems he had his main characters employ for the sake of their love manifested a growing distaste for the machinations of court politics and a rising frustration with his own lack of advancement.[15]

Berkeley held sour remembrances of the period when England fought France and Spain. During the war years 1625 to 1629 Charles, at the behest of the duke of Buckingham, launched ill-considered attacks on the Spanish at Cádiz and the French at the Isle of Rhé, which sat at the approaches to the port of La Rochelle. Collecting men and supplies strained the Crown's relations with the squirearchy all over the country and cost Charles capital he did not have. Worse still, the campaigns proved miserable fiascoes that sent good English soldiers—Berkeley's brother Maurice among them—to ignominious deaths and left the Crown powerless to shape events on the Continent. Disaster sent ripples of dismay churning across a realm already roiling with discontent. Personal rule quieted but never silenced the outrage. Cádiz and Rhé remained grotesque memories of England's shame, especially for anyone who, like Will Berkeley, had lost relatives to those hideous enterprises.[16]

Closeness to the king yielded Berkeley a steady diet of the disparity between image and reality. In intimate moments, when Charles tossed aside the cloak of majesty, he showed himself to Berkeley as something other than the figure he projected publicly or in the Van Dyck portraits. The private Charles was no regal,

15. D. B. Rowan, ed., *The Lost Lady by Sir William Berkeley* (Oxford, 1987). A manuscript text, which bears Berkeley's handwritten corrections, is in the Folger Shakespeare Library in Washington, D.C. Witnesses to the printed texts are also in the Folger and other libraries (Rowan, *Lost Lady*, xi–xvii). Whereas older critics such as R. C. Bald once dismissed Caroline dramatists as lacking the style, grace, and skill of their Elizabethan or Restoration counterparts, a newer generation of literary scholars and historians now look at the same playwrights in an altogether different light. Their studies examine Caroline plays for clues to the attitudes of the authors toward the era, its politics, and its culture in general. Martin Butler, *Theater of Crisis, 1632–1642* (Cambridge, 1984); Smuts, *Court Culture and the Origins of a Royalist Tradition;* Veevers, *Images of Love and Religion;* Sharpe, *Criticism and Complement;* and Albert H. Tricomi, *Anticourt Drama in England, 1603–1642* (Charlottesville, 1989) provide helpful orientation to this body of work and its arguments, whereas Timothy Raylor's *Cavaliers, Clubs, and Literary Culture: Sir John Mennes, James Smith, and the Order of the Fancy* (Newark, Del., 1994), 295–318, includes a useful bibliography of relevant titles as well.

16. Russell, *Parliaments and English Politics*, 322–91; Berkeley pedigree, 1666, College of Arms, as noted in Thomas Woodcock to WMB, 13 July 1990, Sir William Berkeley Papers Project Archive; Sharpe, *Personal Rule of Charles I*, 8–32, 398; Thomas Garden Barnes, *Somerset, 1625–1640: A County's Government during the "Personal Rule"* (Cambridge, Mass., 1961), 203–58.

godlike creature, ever virtuous and profoundly wise. He was just a man, albeit one whose rank put him at a distance from others. Flesh and blood, he had the same capabilities for good or ill as his privy chamber man or anyone else. Berkeley discerned more to scorn than to cherish, and the longer he attended Charles, the more he came secretly to view the king with the disdain he voiced indirectly in *The Lost Lady*. Hence, in the play scheming sullied virtue, deception besmirched honor, and stubbornness threatened order.

If proximity colored Berkeley's opinions of Charles, then so did his affiliations with Lucius Cary, second viscount Falkland, Sir Edward Hyde, and Sir Thomas Roe. Of the many public men Berkeley encountered throughout the 1630s, those three stand above the rest as perhaps his foremost political mentors. The pensive yet openly charming Falkland (1610–43) hosted the second set of thinkers who embraced Berkeley from time to time. That group—which included Wits, Berkeley's cousin the Reverend Henry Killigrew, Thomas Hobbes, Hyde, and Falkland's brother-in-law Henry Moryson—gathered down in Oxfordshire at Great Tew, the viscount's country seat. (There Berkeley also became friendly with Falkland's wife, Lettice, and her siblings, Francis and Richard Moryson, who would later hold offices under him in Virginia.) Rationalists all, the men of Great Tew championed intellectual tolerance in the firm hope that logical inquiry would one day reunite a broken Church Universal. Skeptics too, their doubts fed their faith in free will and the possibility of redemption for all souls. Predictably, their beliefs inspired their deep disaffection with Archbishop William Laud and King Charles, neither of whom swerved from an unyielding bent for thorough uniformity in church discipline and doctrine. The men of Great Tew found no comfort either in the rigid certainties of Puritans.[17]

As for Hyde (1609–74), he was Falkland's closest friend after Henry Moryson. His acquaintance with Berkeley went back to days when both studied at the Middle Temple. Apparently, however, they did not associate much again until Berkeley joined the Wits and the earl of Pembroke found a place at court for Hyde.[18]

The peripatetic Sir Thomas Roe (1581–1644) gave spacious definition to the word *adventurer*. In his younger years he owned shares in the Virginia Company

17. Edward Hyde, earl of Clarendon, *The History of the Rebellion and Civil Wars in England*, ed. W. Dunn McCray (Oxford, 1888), 178–90; Kenneth Murdock, *The Sun at Noon: Three Biographical Sketches* (New York, 1939), 98–139; Kurt Weber, *Lucius Cary, Second Viscount Falkland* (New York, 1940), 66–82, 82; Hugh Trevor-Roper, "The Great Tew Circle," in Trevor-Roper, *Catholics, Anglicans and Puritans: Seventeenth-Century Essays* (London, 1987), 166–231; G. E. Aylmer, "Presidential Address: Collective Mentalities in mid-Seventeenth-England: IV, Cross Currents: Neutrals, Trimmers and Others," Royal Historical Society *Transactions*, 5th ser., 39 (1988): 1–23.

18. Russell, *Parliaments and English Politics*, 13 and n. 1.

of London, sat in the Addled Parliament of 1614, visited Turkey, journeyed to India, and explored the South American coast. Occasionally, he used his influence with the Crown to boost members of the Berkeley clan. He was also someone who argued for allying Protestant England and Holland against the Catholic Hapsburg Antichrist, a view that found no favor with Charles. That difference of opinion mattered little because toward the end of 1636 Charles named Roe chancellor of the Order of the Garter. The appointment not only gave Sir Thomas an opportunity to serve his master directly; it also threw him into regular contact with Berkeley before and during those occasions when all the privy chamber men waited on the king at Garter ceremonies.[19]

Roe, Hyde, and Falkland were dubious of Charles's policies toward the church, Parliament, Scotland, Ireland, and Europe. Each of them chafed at a sovereign whom they considered weak and untrustworthy, but none was a radical. Quite the contrary, each stoutly believed in political continuity and in monarchy as the bedrock of British society. Men of peace, they regarded violent change, especially wars, as self-destructive. Therefore, they saw no choice but to use their prodigious talents to mediate between Charles and his censors. Berkeley imbibed from them an immutable devotion to the Crown and an equally abiding wariness of Stuart kings. Their distaste for Laud's churchmanship likewise reinforced in him a realization that people of faith were seldom driven in directions they devoutly refused to walk. Those were lessons he rarely forgot.

Five years at court taught yet another lesson: keen courtly abilities alone could not ensure aggrandizement. Being a privy chamber man brought Berkeley neither riches nor power. His brothers caught more of the regal ear than he, as did friends and acquaintances, all of whom seemed always to enjoy greater favor with the king. He was merely a run-of-the mill courtier, who at the age of thirty-two approached his middle years. Money, or more aptly his short supply of it, concerned him too. Income from his inheritance and other sources barely offset the cost of keeping up a gentleman's appearance.

Prospects appeared to brighten about the time he began work on *The Lost Lady*. Charles granted him a monopoly on the manufacture and sale of "snow & ice within in this our Kingdom of England & Dominion of Wales" for "the term of 14 years."[20] To satisfy the requirements of the Monopolies Act of 1624, Berkeley

---

19. Roe to John Drury, 24–28 Jan. 1636/37, SP 16/345, fol. 55, PRO; Strachan, *Sir Thomas Roe.*

20. Texts of Charles's letters patent no longer exist, but the grant of the monopoly can be documented by other evidence. Sir John Suckling's poem "The Wits" provided one clue to it. "To *Will Berkeley*," Suckling noted, "all the wits meant well, / But first they would see how his snow would sell" (Clayton, *Non-Dramatic Works of Sir John Suckling*, 73). Suckling wrote the verse in the summer of 1637, and so it seems likely that Berkeley received the monopoly that year also (ibid., 266–67). Then there is the draft of a warrant from Charles II that ordered the renewal of the letters patent.

claimed that privilege, asserting that he had invented a new method of marketing ice for which he was entitled to an exclusive right to the profits of his "invention."[21] The nature of his invention is unknown. It may have been nothing beyond a contrivance to circumvent the statute and to stifle competitors, who also dreamed of finding fortunes in ice. On the other hand, Berkeley may have actually designed some type of icehouse. Whatever the case, the monopoly augured an improvement in his finances.[22]

Another possibility involved his own plan for tallying the "number & qualitie of such forraigners as either reside or resorte into . . . England." He launched that scheme when he petitioned Charles on 31 January 1637/38 "to erect an office of Registering the names of all straingers except your Majesties servants, Embassadors with their servants & Marchants." Enrolling such persons in this manner would "prevent Deceipt in them who have their secret ends." It could not succeed, he averred, unless "your Majestie would be pleased to prohibit all persons to lodge or vent howses to the said straingers without a Ticket" from the registry office. Those tickets would cost one shilling per person, and they would be renewed annually. Berkeley proposed that he be appointed registrar. As compensation for his "paines & charges," he should receive "one third part of the profit that thence shall arise reserving & being accomptable to your Majestie for the remainder in such sort as shall be thought convenient."[23]

Charles "gratiously inclined to favor his servant in this his humble suite." Before "shewing" his "Royall pleasure," he looked to his solicitor-general, Edward Littleton, for an opinion "touching the legallitie" of Berkeley's proposition. Littleton sought the counsel of customs officials. They concluded that "the granting of [the petition] can be noe wayes prejudiciall to his Majesties customes as haveinge noe relation thereunto." Charles then turned to the Privy Council, which rejected the idea. So the scheme came to nothing, and Berkeley missed a shot at still greater financial security.[24]

Dated 22 Dec. 1665, the document explicitly states that Charles revived the monopoly because "it has formerly pleased Our late dear father of Blessed Memory to give & grant unto Sir William Berkeley Knight present Governor of Virginia full power licence & authority to gather make & take snow & Ice" (SP44/22, PRO).

21. See 21 and 22 Jac. I, c. 3, sec. vi, Cay, *Abridgment,* 2: under "monopolies."

22. The latter supposition receives some credence because Berkeley introduced icehouses at Jamestown. It is further reinforced by the use of icehouses in England after the Restoration and the revival of the patent in 1665. See J. Paul Hudson, *A Pictorial Booklet on Early Jamestown Commodities and Industries* (Williamsburg, 1957), 76; and Mark Girouard, *Life in the English Country House: A Social and Architectural History* (New Haven, Conn., 1978), 262.

23. Petition to Charles I, 31 Jan. 1637/38, SP16/380, PRO.

24. SP 16/38; PC2/49, PRO.

If the Privy Council dashed Berkeley's expectations in January 1638, Charles sent them soaring later that year. In September he dispatched Berkeley to the Netherlands on the highly delicate mission of seeking out Henrietta Maria's mother, Marie de Medici, and persuading her to stay put. Months earlier Marie had noisily made known her desire to visit her daughter, a prospect that did not please her son-in-law by any means. The expense of entertaining her would drain the royal coffers of money Charles could ill afford to squander on the dowager queen and her entourage. Then there were the political ramifications of such a visit. Her son, Louis XIII, had exiled Marie from France, meaning that her appearance at the English court would offend the French. Charles had no wish for that. An even more gnawing apprehension was the likely effect of her visit upon Charles's political fortunes. Just being in England at all, the queen mother and her Catholic servants would fuel perennial fears of papist conspiracies. These worries seemed all the more upsetting because Charles's growing difficulties with the Scots added generously to rising disaffection with the king. All things considered, then, Marie's presence would serve no purpose other than to accelerate the decline in Charles's popularity. Hence, the king's wish to keep Marie off British soil.[25]

To hold her at bay, both Charles and Secretary of State Sir John Coke looked first to the Crown's ambassador to the Netherlands, Sir William Boswell. Anticipating that Boswell might fail at dissuading Marie, the king pulled out another stop. Charles undoubtedly hoped that, by dispatching one of his very own privy chamber men to her, Marie would recognize the depth of his desire and remain on the Continent.

Speed was of the essence. Charles personally ordered a pay warrant for two hundred pounds that enabled Berkeley to travel in a manner befitting a royal emissary. Henrietta Maria and Charles hastily wrote private letters that expressed their affection even as they counseled how it would be better if Marie remained where she was. Coke promptly drew up detailed instructions too. He told Berkeley that, once the royal missives were delivered, he should leave Marie and report to him. That done, Berkeley should go next to The Hague and confer privately with Stadtholder William, prince of Orange. Finally, he should convey certain dispatches to Boswell and return to London.[26]

September passed into October before all was ready and Berkeley got his final orders. Then he rode down from London to the Kentish port of Margate, where

25. Victor-L. Tapié, *France in the Age of Louis XIII and Richelieu*, trans. D. McN. Lockie (Cambridge, 1974), 240–41, 389; Boswell to Coke, 20/30 Sept. 1638, SP34/154, PRO.

26. Abstract of warrant for travel expenses, Sept. 1638, SO 3/11, PRO.

on 4 October he boarded an awaiting vessel. Casting off immediately, her crew shook her sails loose from their lashings, and she picked up seaway. She had just cleared the harbor when one of her lookouts spied an inward-bound Dutch merchantman. Her skipper hailed the Hollander, seeking news of Marie de Medici. Back came the reply that Marie was lodged at Vlissingen, where she waited for her passage to Britain. Plotting their course accordingly, the English stood southward toward their destination. They berthed at Vlissingen a day later, but the queen mother was nowhere to be found. She had left town some while earlier. Questioning a house servant who remained behind, Berkeley determined that "her Majesty lay at Hernvliet a smal Dorpe [i.e., village] neere the Bril where she had ten dayes expected a wind to carry her to England so thither I made and arriv'd the Saterday night following [6 October], and presented their Majesties letters." He succeeded no better than had Boswell. As he informed Coke, he dickered with Marie for four days straight, but neither his "best art" nor the written entreaties of Charles and Henrietta Maria "perswaded her." Only "contrary winds could checke her stay an hower."[27]

Thoroughly frustrated, Berkeley took his leave of the queen mother on 10 October and traveled on to The Hague. The next day he called at Boswell's residence and gave Coke's letter to the ambassador. Either Boswell lodged him or he fended for himself while he sought his audience with the Prince William. He remained until 7 December, when he sailed to London, bearing a batch of letters from Boswell. Marie was already in England.[28]

Back at court, Berkeley was rewarded for his failed efforts. Charles granted him a yearly pension of three hundred pounds and more besides. On 11 December he signed letters patent that conferred on Will and his brother John lifetime rights to "The office of Clarke of the Treasury of the Court of common Pleas at Westminster under the Chief Justice of that Court for the time being . . . after the Death or other determination of the estate or interest of George Duncomb gentleman the present Officer, With all fees, rights, & profitts belonging to the said place, as amply as the now Clerke or any other have held the same."[29]

27. Berkeley to Coke, 10 Oct. 1638, SP 84/154, PRO.

28. Ibid.; Boswell to Coke, 11/21 Oct. 1638, SP 84/154, fols. 287–88, PRO; Jean Paget, sieur de la Serre, *Histoire de Lentree del Reyne Mere du Roy Tres Chretien, dans la Grande Bretagne* (London, 1639).

29. Pension from Charles I, 11 Dec. 1638, and letters patent from Charles I, 11 Dec. 1638, both in SO 3/12, PRO. Various authorities have claimed that Berkeley received a seat on the Canada Council too. So did I, when I wrote "Berkeley and Effingham: Who Cares?" *Virginia Magazine of History and Biography* 97 (1989): 34, but the future governor and the Berkeley who sat on that council were different individuals. The latter was a Scot with ties to the Scottish merchants Sir William Alexander and

Were these benefactions and the mission to Marie de Medici signs that the king now considered Berkeley worthy of greater things? Will could only hope they were. Whatever Charles intended as a future reward, it meant little when set beside the political woes that undermined his personal rule in every quarter.

The king's most immediate concern as 1638 ran into the new year was to pacificy the Scots. His northern kingdom bubbled in turmoil. Hard economic times and fury with bishops, a new prayer book, or anything else that smacked of "English" and "popish" liturgical adornments sparked off riots in Edinburgh in July 1637. The trouble was that Charles had little appreciation of the sources of the disturbances or the depth of feeling that inspired them. Rioting played to a disposition in him always to see popular dissent in any form as an assault upon royal authority. His Scottish and English advisors disagreed about the means of preventing the tumult from growing into something more serious, which was unfortunate because their divisions mainly buttressed the king's natural inclination to ignore advice and to formulate ill-conceived policies on his own. Consequently, Charles quickly alienated nonconformist and moderate Scots alike just as he handily distanced himself from those of his Scottish subjects who should have been his natural allies. Equally ominous was the militancy of the Covenanters. In the Scots who signed the National Covenant in February 1638 lay not merely the kernel of religious opposition but also the flower of warlike resistance. The commitment of the Covenanters to fight for their church preferences matched the king's conclusion that, were he to take the field personally against them, he would bring the Covenanters to their senses. And, so, in June 1638 a call went out to the county lords lieutenant to raise troops for an army to join Charles at York the following spring. The order set the stage for the First Bishops' War.[30]

In March 1639 the Privy Council directed that Berkeley and the other "Gents of the privie Chamber both ordinary and extraordinary with their Retinue and Attendants (which is as it is conceaved will amount to 600 or 800 horse) shall, with their Officers, being under the imediate Command of the Lord Chamber-

Robert Charlton. Francis L. Berkeley alerted me to the conflation of the two: Francis Berkeley to WMB, 16 Sept. 1989, Berkeley Papers Archive. To complicate matters a bit further, two of the governor's contemporaries were named William Berkeley as well. One was a London merchant of Puritan leanings, while the second was the governor's nephew, an admiral in the royal navy who died in combat during the Second Anglo-Dutch War.

30. Conrad Russell, *The Fall of the British Monarchies, 1637–1642* (Oxford, 1991), 1–71; Peter Donald, *An Uncounselled King: Charles I and the Scottish Troubles, 1637–1641* (Cambridge, 1990); Mark Charles Fissell, *The Bishops' Wars: Charles I's Campaigns against Scotland, 1638–1640* (Cambridge, 1994), 1–18.

laine, bee appointed to attend as a Guard for his Majesties person." Expecting a quick victory over the Scots and its attendant rewards, Berkeley got none of the one and little of the other. In truth not much about the First Bishops' War went as expected. Supplies and equipment were slow in arriving, and so were the troops. Even when soldiers appeared, they were poorly armed and poorly trained. Disagreements between Charles and his commanders fed dissension in the ranks and poisoned morale. Determined as always, Charles forbore until his army was as ready as it ever would be, and in May 1639 he sallied forth to meet the Scots. Alexander Leslie, an officer hardened by soldiering on the Continent, commanded the Covenanters, who waited above the border to meet the English. He anticipated that a strong show of force would convince the king to refrain from imposing his view of liturgy and ecclesiastical polity upon the Scots. Armageddon never came. A skirmish near the Scottish town of Kelso sent both sides scurrying for the bargaining table, and in mid-June they agreed to the Treaty of Berwick, which put off further conflict. A few weeks later Charles tapped Berkeley for knighthood, and in August the newly minted Sir William Berkeley returned to London with the rest of the royal staff.[31]

Negotiating his way out of war may have caused Charles to seem greathearted rather than weak because peace was the thing that everyone said they wanted. Berkeley's distant kinsman, John Poulett, Lord Poulett, voiced that hope. "If you saw our men," he wrote a friend, "with their feathers and buff cotes and bigg lookes you would say the Scotts are like to have but a bad bargeyn in meddling with us. For my part that am not yet come to my buff cote and feathers I pray for peace and that the shock of our arms may not be tried." But at what price had peace, or at least the postponement of conflict, come? Charles returned to Whitehall still wedded to his religious policies and to his methods of dealing with the Scots. Now he faced reckoning with a campaign that had been both expensive and abortive. The drain on the Exchequer compelled him all along to borrow against anticipated revenues, and he had to sell or hock much of his jewelry just to keep the army afield. In mid-August rumors flew around London that the king must soon call a Parliament to find more money, but no writs were forthcoming. As the fall of 1639 neared, it was clear that the Scots were not pacified, and it was equally certain that the treaty proclaimed at Berwick would not hold for much longer. Everyone who advised the king now agreed that the Crown must return Scotland to obedience, though everyone disagreed about means. It

31. Order-in-council regarding privy chamber men, 19 Mar. 1638/39, SP 16/396, 123–34, PRO; David Matthew, *Scotland under Charles I* (London, 1955), 293; Fissell, *Bishops' Wars*, 18–39; Donald, *Uncounselled King*, 118–79; list of knighthoods conferred, 1558–1752, Add. MS 32,102, BL; Pauline Gregg, *King Charles I* (Los Angeles, 1981), 283–95.

was Lord Deputy Thomas Wentworth, first earl of Strafford, lately called out of Ireland to become principal minister, who finally persuaded his master to seek help from Parliament. The writs went out on 12 February 1639/40, summoning lords and commons to Westminster on 13 April.[32]

Berkeley was too insignificant to do more than to fall back into the customary routines of his duties as a privy chamber man and to observe the play of these events from the sidelines. His relative obscurity contrasted noticeably with his brother John, whose star was in the ascendant. A veteran of the Scots campaign too, John had been knighted at Berwick on the same day as Will, and he won a seat in the new House of Commons. Considering the outcome of the session, perhaps Will had reason not to be overly envious of his brother's good fortune.[33]

Sir John Berkeley and his fellow members went up to Westminster to address the grievances of the localities they represented and to listen to Charles's brief for money. Charles went up to the Parliament house expecting only to receive money. The refusal of both to find common ground quickly guaranteed a fleet session. Charles opened the Short Parliament on 13 April. Three weeks later he dissolved it. Empty-handed, he remained committed to crushing the Covenanters, and so began the Second Bishops' War.[34]

Once again, Berkeley and others in the royal household burnished their cuirasses, honed their sabers, oiled their pistols, blacked their boots, and saddled their horses for a northward march. Offsetting the expenses of his preparation were some added funds he received after the king gave him a substantial sum of money from fines levied in the Court of Star Chamber. Sir Francis Windebank assisted in procuring the grant, which indicates the hand the secretary of state played in assigning Berkeley his role as a staff officer in the upcoming campaign.[35]

Taking the fight to the Scots, Charles faced similar difficulties as those he had confronted the year before and more. The Covenanters played a better game at building support for their cause across England, especially after a pro-Scottish party judiciously worked only those issues that garnered a broad following for its cause. That gambit polarized English politics as it bred widespread mutiny and desertion in Charles's army of a sort not seen in living memory. The spectacle of troops murdering officers or anyone else they thought to be papists demoralized already dispirited soldiers, who were worse equipped than in 1639. This time, too, Alexander Leslie decided to invade England rather than wait for Charles to cross into Scotland, so the general aggressively pushed his considerable force south

---

32. Poulett to Smyth, 19 Apr. 1639, Ashton Court MS, Bristol Record Office, as quoted in Fissell, *Bishops' Wars*, 38; Sharpe, *Personal Rule*, 822–23.

33. William S. Powell, *The Proprietors of Carolina* (Raleigh, N.C., 1968), 30.

34. Sharpe, *Personal Rule*, 849–77.

35. Abstract for letters patent from Charles I, June 1640, SO 3/12, PRO.

looking for a fight. The battle came below Newcastle-upon-Tyne at Newburn on 28 August 1640.[36]

Alexander Leslie and the Covenanters roundly defeated their enemy.

Leslie's victory left the English army in an untenable place and compelled Charles to run for safer ground. He retreated all the way back to York in the first days of September, there to contemplate his next move. The Scots were at his heels. His army was weaker following its clash with Leslie, but there were still nearly twenty thousand men under his command. He could fight another day, and he was wont to do just that. Two strategic considerations—the political fall-out from Newburn and money—pressed another course upon him. News of the debacle sent shivers of alarm throughout London and gave added voice to cries for peace. Charles, as he always did, chose not to heed such noises, and, had they been the only impulse toward negotiating with the Scots, he would have ignored the peace table. What he could not gainsay was that, without money to maintain his army, he could not fight for the time being. And thus began the negotiations that ended the following May with the Treaty of London.[37]

Berkeley emerged to the fore in the weeks just after Newburn. He acted as a go-between who dickered for exchanges of prisoners. Also a courier, he ferried messages between the lines or brought dispatches back and forth from the army, Secretary Windebank, and the king. He showed a flair for spying too, although his talent for using the information lacked finesse. At one point, for example, he discovered that three dozen English lords had invited the Scots to invade and were colluding with the Covenanters. He passed the intelligence along to Windebank, who in turn informed Charles. Then, according to Windebank, "His Majesty was no sooner in his chair than the Lords by mouth of the Earl of Bristol demanded justice on Sir Wm. Berkley for having said that the rebels had the hands of 37 of the nobility that invited them to come into England." If, noted the secretary, "he be not able to make it good, they are sharp upon him, but I hope he will be able to clear himself." Berkeley claimed that his intelligence came directly from the mouth of Alexander Leslie, but he had neither written evidence nor Leslie to corroborate his claims. Unproven, the accusations gained Berkeley a harsh rebuke. No longer useful, he retreated to the background, having been soured by his experiences.[38]

36. Russell, *Fall of the British Monarchies*, 145–46; Fissell, *Bishops' Wars*, 39–62, 264–86.

37. Russell, *Fall of the British Monarchies*, 146–205.

38. Sir Francis Windebank to Sir Edward Hyde, 29 Sept. 1640, Clarendon Papers, 19:33–34; Windebank to Charles I, 29 Sept. 1640, Clarendon Papers, 19:142; Sir Henry Vane to Windebank, 6 Sept. 1640, SP 16/476, 66, PRO; Vane to Windebank, 7 Sept. 1640, SP 16/476, 76, PRO; Vane to Windebank, 9 Sept. 1640, SP 16/477, 5, PRO; William Hamilton, first earl of Lanark, to Alexander Leslie, 11 Sept. 1640, SP 16/477, 16, PRO; Vane to Windebank, 24 Sept. 1640, SP 16/477, 23, PRO.

3

A Time to Leave, a Time to Begin Anew

erkeley remained at York until late October 1640, when the king decamped for London to open a new parliament. He rode into town still smarting from his recent embarrassment. The sting lessened once he fell back into the customary routines of a privy chamber man, though the memory of his embarrassment lingered amid other frustrations that fretted him. Quietly, he took stock of his situation and tried to calculate his best interest. Soldiering had dealt him a hard knock. Instead of catching a warrior's glory and greater preferment, he had netted the humiliation of failed campaigns and the compounding shame of severe reprimands. The Bishops' Wars sharpened his already low regard for his master and fueled his long-standing annoyance at his lack of advancement. Like everyone else, he also had good cause to wonder how the consequences of Charles's failure to subdue the Scots would touch him directly.

That was a concern that caught more and more of his attention once Parliament assembled at Westminster. Opening day, 3 November 1640, was full of pomp and circumstance, but pageantry barely hid the fissures that separated king from legislature. Charles's speech from the throne did little to disguise the rifts either. Those fractures widened in the ensuing months as haggling with the Scots; Parliament's impeachments of Thomas Wentworth, first earl of Strafford, Archbishop William Laud, and Lord Keeper Sir John Finch; the Root and Branch Petition; the Affair of the Five Members; the Triennial Act; the Army Plot; and the abolition of Star Chamber and the High Commission all wedged Charles's kingdoms ever nearer the brink of civil war.[1]

As Berkeley anxiously watched the drift of these events, he saw in them less and less that encouraged him generally and more and more that threatened him personally. His pocketbook particularly depended upon his share from the treasury of the Court of Common Pleas. Such gifts were among the special privileges that Parliament was now determined to abolish, and in February 1641 the House of Lords sought to recall his patent. The lords' proceedings against him resulted in costly litigation that ultimately failed to sustain his claim. Charles had also given him a portion of the fines levied in Star Chamber. When Parliament dismantled that much-hated court, he lost even more income. Gone, too, was his monopoly on the sale of ice.[2]

The Army Plot to spring the impeached earl of Strafford from the Tower of London threatened something beyond deflation of his purse. Sir John Berkeley, Henry Jermyn, Sir John Suckling, and other of his intimates were numbered among the conspirators. Perhaps Berkeley knew of their plans, or he may even have been involved with them, but nothing directly linked him to the plotters. Even so, the glimmer of suspicion fell on him for a time, though he escaped incrimination. The plot speeded Parliament's adoption of a bill of attainder that doomed the hapless Strafford to a traitor's death on Tower Hill.[3]

Diminished income, brushes with the Army Plot, and Strafford's beheading brought home to Berkeley the precariousness of his own place at court vis-à-vis a highly changeable political situation. He did not cleave unflinchingly to the king. Nor did he waste great sympathy on Charles's most vocal opponents. A squeezed wallet and political moderation put him on ground that grew increasingly difficult to hold. With ever more of his perch disappearing almost daily, he realized that he must soon take sides or else find a way of avoiding such a choice altogether. By the time Strafford perished, on 12 May 1641, Berkeley had already concluded that he would leave the court and go abroad in search of a new beginning. That determination involved two others: how to exit gracefully and what to do next. He looked to his kin for suggestions and help, which brought the omnipresent Sir Thomas Roe into the picture.

1. Conrad Russell, *The Fall of the British Monarchies, 1637–1642* (Oxford, 1991), 206–74.

2. Petition to the House of Lords, 4 Feb. 1640/41, Main Papers, HLRO; 17 Car. I, c. 10, sec. 3, John Cay, comp., *An Abridgment of The Publick Statutes in Force and Use of The Publick Statutes in Force and Use From Magna Carta, in the ninth year of King Henry III. To the eleventh year of his resent Majesty King George II. Inclusive* (London, 1739), under "Liberties and rights."

3. Conrad Russell, "The First Army Plot of 1641," Royal Historical Society *Transactions*, 5th ser. 38 (1988), 85ff.; Russell, *Fall of the British Monarchies*, 274–303.

Returning in June 1640 from an embassy to Hamburg, Roe got a chair at the Privy Council and won a seat in the commons. For a brief instant that fall he was even under consideration to succeed Sir John Coke as secretary of state, but the moment flit away as quickly as it had come. Roe's friendship with Laud tainted him. Once Parliament struck at the archbishop, Roe ceased regular attendance in the House or at the council, and in April 1641 he informed Speaker William Lenthall that Charles had named him envoy to the Imperial Diet at Ratisbon and asked leave to depart. Amid his own travel preparations Roe hurriedly considered Berkeley's plea for assistance. He recommended Constantinople, where he had lived during the days when he was ambassador to the Turks. There was a vacancy, he knew, because of the recent retirement of his successor, Sir Peter Wyche, and he urged Berkeley to go after it. Having done what he could for Berkeley on short notice, Roe crossed the Channel for Ratisbon on 10 May 1641. Among those who shared cabin space with him aboard the *Leghorn Merchant* were Sir John Berkeley, Sir William Davenant, Jermyn, Suckling, and several other Army Plotters who escaped to the Continent.[4]

Berkeley seized on Sir Thomas's advice and began lobbying for Constantinople shortly after Roe's departure, but for reasons that are no longer clear, he suddenly reversed himself in favor of another opportunity. Sir Richard Cave, Roe's nephew, explained the outcome of that reversal after the fact. Berkeley, he wrote to Roe on 20 August 1641, "goes Governor for Verginia, he hath quitted his designe and interest for Constantinople, and hath incouraged me to fall upon it." That Cave wrote to inform his uncle of the change in plan indicates that Roe went to Ratisbon believing Berkeley was bound for the Middle East, just as Cave's intelligence reinforces an impression of a precipitous alteration in Berkeley's intentions.[5]

4. Michael Strachan, *Sir Thomas Roe, 1581–1644: A Life* (Salisbury, Wilts., 1989), 241–52, 253–55. On seventeenth-century Englishmen in Turkey generally, see Daniel Goffman, *Britons in the Ottoman Empire, 1642–1660* (Seattle, 1998).

5. Cave to Roe, 20 Aug. 1641, SP 16/483, 74, PRO. Largely for want of information, scholars in the past glossed over the circumstances that led to Berkeley's becoming governor. See Thomas Jefferson Wertenbaker, *Virginia under the Stuarts, 1607–1688* (Princeton, 1914), 84; Wesley Frank Craven, *The Southern Colonies in the Seventeenth Century, 1607–1689*, in Wendell Holmes Stephenson and E. Merton Coulter, eds., *A History of the South* (Baton Rouge, 1949), 164; Richard L. Morton, *Colonial Virginia* (Chapel Hill, N.C., 1960), 1:146; Jon Kukla, *Political Institutions in Virginia, 1619–1660* (New York, 1989), 105; Warren M. Billings, John E. Selby, and Thad W. Tate, *Colonial Virginia: A History* (White Plains, N.Y., 1986), 48; David Hackett Fischer, *Albion's Seed: Four British Folkways in America* (New York, 1989), 209. R. C. Bald, "Sir William Berkeley's *The Lost Lady*," *Library*, 4th ser., 17 (1936–37): 397, was closer to the truth than he realized when he suggested that disaffection with being a courtier impelled Berkeley to leave England.

If Berkeley ever recorded the reasons for his about-face, that document has not surfaced. Nevertheless, the considerations that drove him seem plain enough. The Ottoman Empire was an alien place to him, whereas Virginia was not. His familiarity with the colony reached back to his boyhood and to times when his relations had chased fortunes there. He met men at Whitehall who had once lived in Virginia, and he was acquainted with the policy debates over its future. Besides, governing Virginia was potentially more prestigious and lucrative than being at Constantinople. Ultimately, if subsequent actions reveal prior thinking, a primary motive for his decision was akin to that of tens of thousands of his fellow Britons who were pulling up stakes and migrating to the Western Hemisphere. He saw in Virginia a place to satisfy ambitions that he could not sate in England.

Yet a barrier in the person of Governor Sir Francis Wyatt stood in the way. To surmount that hurdle, Berkeley entreated the king to appoint him in Wyatt's stead and pressed his brother Charles and his friends Lucius Cary, second viscount Falkland, and Sir Edward Hyde to level the path for him. Each was well suited to help. Falkland was now secretary of state, having replaced Sir John Coke. Sir Charles Berkeley was personally close to the king, and Hyde had recently come over to King Charles's side. The three worked promptly. Indeed, they brushed Wyatt aside with startling speed. On 31 July 1641, a mere ten weeks from the time Will Berkeley resolved to leave the court, Charles named him governor and captain-general of Virginia. The new governor's commission and instructions passed the seals in a matter of days too, and the sealing enabled Berkeley to swear his oath of office in the Privy Council chamber on 10 August.[6]

Nothing in that sequence of events or cast of characters reveals the pivotal consideration in the appointment: Why did Charles so readily substitute Berkeley for Wyatt? Berkeley was a novice. The first governor without direct links to the defunct Virginia Company, either by way of his investment, membership on its committees, or tenure in the colony, he lacked personal connections with powerful interests who saw in a revived company the means of managing the settlement. His knowledge of Virginia itself was entirely vicarious, and he lightly grasped the dynamics of colonial politics. On balance he had little that commended him as a successor to Wyatt, apart from being the king's privy chamber man and from a prominent family. Wyatt, by contrast, was an able administrator

6. Russell, *Fall of the British Monarchies*, 289; abstract of warrant for commission to Sir William Berkeley, 31 July 1641, indexes 4214, fol. 25, PRO; commission from Charles I, 10 Aug. 1641, C.66/2895, PRO; instructions from Charles I, 10 Aug. 1641, CO 5/1354, 224–41, PRO; Pauline Gregg, *King Charles I* (Los Angeles, 1981), 335–37.

with a long record of service in Virginia. He was the company's last governor and the Crown's first, and he had won great respect for his skill at steering Virginia through the troubled 1620s. His admirable reputation accounted for his reappointment in 1639, when Charles sent him back to quiet the settlers after they overthrew Sir John Harvey. An evenhanded, tactful man, Wyatt was widely popular with Virginians, especially those who ranked at the head of the colony's nascent political establishment. He managed his duties well and enjoyed the confidence of his superiors, and no one in Virginia clamored for his removal.

Charles's weighing of the merits of each man is unrecorded. Berkeley's arguments in favor of his appointment are gone too, and there are no clues to be gleaned from collateral documentation. Lacking direct testimony, circumstantial evidence suggests the reason Charles chose as he did. Virginia rarely figured high in his thinking. It mattered even less in August 1641 because he was greatly preoccupied with issues far weightier than who governed that faraway plantation for him. His relations with Parliament had degenerated steeply after Strafford's execution, and he was about to head north to Scotland. Notably, on the very day that Berkeley received his commission, the king left London. And so it seems that a vexed Charles hurriedly chose to gratify his privy chamber man without regard to how his decision affected Wyatt or Virginia.[7]

And what of Wyatt? What method, if any, did he employ to keep his job? Apparently, once he fathomed what he was up against, he bowed to powers he could not overcome and scrambled to cut the best deal he could. To that purpose, he relied on George Sandys to negotiate with Berkeley. Their dickering stretched into early September before both sides came to an understanding, and on 4 September they initialed an agreement that rewarded Wyatt handsomely. Berkeley pledged to protect Wyatt from any diminution of his expected salary. He warranted that he would not take up his duties "untill the fourteenth day of January [1641/42] next ensueing" and to compensate Wyatt if he entered "upon that government before the time here prefixed." Next Berkeley pledged to pay Wyatt three hundred pounds, in three annual installments, as "some satisfaction of the great losses hee shall susteine by his removeall." Then he agreed to buy "Sir Francis his dwelling house in James Citty att the rate hee paide . . . for it, with further allowance of what hee hath expended thereuppon." Wyatt retained a seat on the Virginia Council of State, which was an unprecedented concession

7. *DNB*, 63:1092–93; J. Frederick Fausz and Jon Kukla, eds., "A Letter of Advice to the Governor of Virginia, 1624," *William and Mary Quarterly*, 3d ser., 34 (1977): 105–30; Susan Myra Kingsbury, ed., *Records of the Virginia Company* (Washington, D.C., 1906–35), 1:418, 443, 444, 472, 490, 507; 2:523, 530; commission from James I, 24 Aug. 1624, Kingsbury, ed., *Records of the Virginia Company*, 2:501–4; commission from Charles I, 1639, accession 27,402, Vi; Kukla, *Political Institutions in Virginia*, 81–105.

to a retiring governor that was never repeated again. Berkeley promised not to be "swayd" by any of Wyatt's adversaries, and he also guaranteed to restore several councillors "that are left out of my Commission, and [to] ranke them in their [former] places." Lastly, he agreed to permit "noe recrimminations reheareings or reversals of Judgments which have or shall bee given or determined by Sir Francis and the Councell there without express order of the King or the Lords of his Majesties privie Councell."[8]

The role of four other signatories to the agreement is revealing. Falkland, Sir Charles Berkeley, and Hyde acted as guarantors of Berkeley's performance, which marks them as the potent allies who lobbied on his behalf. William Claiborne signed the document too. He was one of the Virginia councillors left out of the commission, and he was friendly with Wyatt. More significantly, his signature identifies him as another of Wyatt's intermediaries. It also indicates Berkeley's early association with one of the most powerful of his new constituents.[9]

Claiborne (1600–1677), long a resident of Virginia, first shipped over with Wyatt in 1621 to become the colony's first surveyor-general. He subsequently used his surveying skills to accumulate ample landholdings while he built business networks that ran from the Chesapeake watershed to the London mercantile community and back. One of those networks linked him closely with another colonial magnate, Councillor Samuel Mathews. Claiborne's commerce set him against the interests of the Lords Baltimore and the Maryland settlers, who ruined his trading ventures at Kent Island and caused a passionate, lifelong enmity toward Marylanders. Growing fortune put him in the midst of Virginia's emerging political elite, and in 1624 he joined the Council of State, where with Mathews he led the dominant faction. Charles I appointed him secretary of the colony, an office that ranked second only to the governor-general in its political weight, and he held it for a decade. Siding with those of his council colleagues who demanded a greater say in governing, he helped expel Governor Harvey from office when Sir John refused to defer to their wishes. He emerged from the Harvey feud much stronger for having taken this stance, which made him someone whom Berkeley approached cautiously.[10]

8. Articles of agreement with Sir Francis Wyatt, 4 Sept. 1641, Main Papers, HLRO.

9. Ibid.

10. Nathaniel G. Hale, *Virginia Venturer: A Historical Biography of William Claiborne, 1600–1677* (Richmond, 1951); Annie Lash Jester and Martha Woodroof Hiden, comp., *Adventurers of Purse and Person, Virginia 1607–1625*, 2d ed. (Princeton, 1964), 131–33; Sarah S. Hughes, *Surveyors and Statesmen: Land Measuring in Colonial Virginia* (Richmond, 1979), 9–12, 38–44; J. Mills Thornton III, "The Thrusting Out of Governor Harvey: A Seventeenth-Century Rebellion," *Virginia Magazine of History and Biography* 76 (1968): 11–26.

About the time Berkeley met Claiborne, he also encountered another important Virginian, Richard Kemp, who was in London minding his affairs. Kemp (1600?–1649) displaced Claiborne as secretary in 1634, so the two men were often at odds. A provocative fellow by nature, he clashed with the anti-Harveyites on the Virginia council, he disagreed with Wyatt, and he kindled a singularly nasty feud with a York County clergyman, the Reverend Anthony Panton. Kemp and Sir Francis clashed in 1640, after Claiborne disclosed that he had won the Crown's consent to his proposal for a colonial signet officer, who would certify all public records. The king permitted the governor and council to implement the recommendation, if they chose. Kemp opposed the suggestion because the existence of a signet officer would diminish his power and perquisites. Wyatt, on the other hand, approved of the scheme. The council adopted it, and Claiborne became keeper of the seal. When that happened, Kemp huffily stole away to London in hopes of reversing the council's action. There was another reason for Kemp's being in the metropolis in the summer of 1641. He aimed at settling scores with the Reverend Mr. Panton. Kemp and the equally impulsive Panton deeply detested each other. At one point in the 1630s Kemp persuaded the council to banish Panton to England, which set off messy litigation that bounced back and forth from Whitehall to Jamestown for the better part of a decade. Whether Kemp and Berkeley were acquainted before they took their respective oaths of office together is impossible to say, but the secretary was obviously someone Berkeley needed to know.[11]

Panton and Kemp's legal tussles unexpectedly snared Berkeley and threatened to scuttle his new job. On hearing of Berkeley's appointment, Panton immediately discovered Kemp's evil hand in the nomination, and, after calculating how best to confound his enemy, he fired off an objection to Parliament. Berkeley, who had no inkling of any of this, busily readied himself for his adventure. He recruited some three dozen servants. Five were women, whom he probably intended to use as household servants, whereas the men were destined to become field hands and other sorts of helpers. Clothing for them, a proper wardrobe for him, books, furnishings, tools, foodstuffs, and "neccessaryes" cost a thousand pounds to procure and pack. He scouted for a willing sea captain who knew the way to Virginia. Finding one was no simple matter. To begin with, Berkeley intended to cross the Atlantic during its stormiest seasons, when all but the hardiest of masters flinched at wrestling their ships through mountainous swells in a

11. H. R. McIlwaine, ed., *Minutes of the Council and General Court of Colonial Virginia, 1622–1632, 1670–1676*, 2d ed. (Richmond, 1979), 473–74, 494–97, 482, 483; CO 1/10, fols. 25–26, 88, 168–73; PC 2/51, 191–99, PRO.

tempest-whipped ocean. Even if he contracted with an agreeable captain, he still faced the prospect of endless holdups. Skippers kept to no set schedules, and none of them would sail until his supercargo had found a complete payload. Luck favored Berkeley. In October he located a master who agreed to pick him up, and around 25 October he and his servants left London for their port of embarkation. They had not gone far, however, before the House of Lords ordered him to answer Panton's protest.[12]

Berkeley rushed back to town and hastily drew up a petition that he hoped would satisfy the lords. In it he reminded them that, after they had deprived him of "his whole substance" back in February, "hee had recourse to his Majestie for the Government of Virginia." Charles gave Berkeley the office "under the great Seale of England." Berkeley then "proceeded with all due regard" to Wyatt's interests and yielded "to all faire motions on [the former governor's] behalfe that his neerest freind" Claiborne propounded to him. The deal done, and seeing no further impediment to his appointment, he properly went ahead with his own preparations for the voyage to Virginia, and he stood to lose the money he had advanced "upon his owne charge" if he were "deteyned" much longer. Then he came to the heart of his plea. He emphatically denied any collusion with Secretary Kemp. With equal force he stated that Panton was "altogether unknowne unto [me] and his complainte without ground neither charging [me] with any cryme." If future allegations "shalbee proved against [me] your petitioner shall humbly submitt to the weight of youre Lordshipps censure." He concluded on a hopeful note, praying that the House "would be honorably pleased to comiserate his cause, and to suffer your humble petitioner to depart."[13]

His words wrought the desired result, and the lords pursued him no further. Free to go, he rejoined his party, hoping perhaps that there would be no future Pantons to threaten him or his relationships with the Virginians and his superiors. His departure date is uncertain, but it can be approximated. The lords concluded their inquiry on 5 November, so Berkeley likely sailed within a few days of his leaving London.

As winter was nearing, the captain of his ship bypassed the shorter North Atlantic route in favor of a safer but lengthier passage. He dropped down from England toward the Portuguese coast, where he caught breezes that blew him south to the Canaries and beyond. Below the 20th parallel, the winds prevailed

12. Henry Robinson to Sir Henry Mildmay, 5 Nov. 1641, SP 16/485, 61, PRO; petition of Anthony Panton to the House of Lords, 3 Oct. 1641, Main Papers, fols. 102–4, HLRO; petition of Richard Kemp to the House of Lords, 3 Nov. 1641, fols. 104–5, HLRO.

13. Berkeley to the House of Lords, 3 Nov. 1641, Main Papers, fols. 103–4, HLRO; orders of the House of Lords, 4 and 5 Nov. 1641, Journals of the House of Lords, 4:421, 424, HLRO.

from the northeast. Picking them up, the ship rode to the West Indies. At last she beat northward to the headlands of the Chesapeake Bay. Berkeley formally took up his duties on 8 March 1641/42, and it was therefore likely that the ship made landfall sometime during the first days of February at the latest. Tacking into the bay, she worked her way cautiously past the dangerous Middle Shoal and made for the mouth of the James River. If her captain knew the way, she continued to Jamestown; if not, he hove to and fetched a pilot who guided him upriver.[14]

The reach to the capital gave Berkeley his first glimpses of Virginia. His feelings, whatever they were, must be imagined because his reckoning of them is gone now. Surely, thankfulness was one. He could rejoice at having survived the trip.

Little in his previous experience ever challenged his endurance quite like his first crossing of the Atlantic. Whenever he went on deck, he saw only the vastness of endless sea and sky. Leaving his cabin became an indulgence after a while. Travelers, royal governors-general included, got in the sailors' way, and so he rarely went topside. Blue-water vessels like his were tiny things that rarely exceeded a waterline length of a hundred feet. They were short on comfort too. Round bottomed and bluff ended, they bobbed corklike in rolling sea swells and groaned ceaselessly under the unrelenting strain of wave against hull as driving winds hissed noisily through spar and line. Passengers of his quality billeted astern near the captain's cabin. His tight quarters proved only marginally better than those in the 'tween decks, where ordinary wayfarers hung their hammocks. Decent meals, especially hot food, were luxuries seldom substituted for the steady fare of wormy biscuits, stale cheese, and flat ale. And nothing quelled the stench of rotting excrement and putrefying garbage that forever wafted up vilely from the bilges and permeated everything.

At the first opportunity Berkeley scanned both sides of the James River. His eyes strained for indications of a countryside that matched that of his imagination, and, like other newcomers, he sought things that made the new surroundings familiar. Winter was not the most welcoming of times in Tidewater Virginia. Heavy, damp cold hung in the air. Its bite reminded him of English weather, but little else about the scenery along the James resembled the west of England or the outskirts of London. He beheld only scattered plantation houses and outbuildings, which sat along the water's edge. Nothing about them compared in aspect or splendor with any of the great houses that he had known since child-

14. Arthur Pierce Middleton, *Tobacco Coast: A Maritime History of Chesapeake Bay in the Colonial Era* (Newport News, Va., 1953), 1–30.

hood. Farther back from the shoreline, he could make out barren fields that awaited spring cultivation and stands of timber. Hardwoods spiked sharply upward, their leaf-bare limbs marking a stark contrast with interspersing evergreens. Both projected bleakness against a backdrop of leaden skies. As he searched to find something familiar, perhaps that unvoiced doubt and anticipation that rush suddenly in on anyone about to abide the consequences of life-turning choices, whisked through his mind. Had he made the right decision? Was he up to the task before him? Would leading Virginians accept him? How should he approach them? Who would be his friends? Who were his enemies? What opportunities for financial gain awaited him?

Whatever his inner thoughts, they yielded to another sensation once the ship berthed along Jamestown wharf and he touched dry land again—the unalloyed delight of feeling terra firma beneath him. The ground seemed to roll underfoot like the sea, especially if he bent down for any reason. That sensation went away in a matter of days as his body accustomed itself to being ashore once more, and he spent his first weeks on dry land settling into the house he had purchased from Wyatt. Wyatt was there too, although presumably he had moved to other quarters.

The General Assembly was also in town, working on Wyatt's proposed reforms of local government. Out of regard for his replacement, Sir Francis prorogued the assembly until 18 April, and on 8 March 1641/42 he handed the government over to Berkeley. With his administration legally in place, Berkeley could continue acquainting himself with Virginia and its people.[15]

---

15. Warren M. Billings, *A Little Parliament: The Virginia General Assembly in the Seventeenth Century* (Richmond, 2004), 5–25; Conway Robinson, comp., "Notes and Excerpts from the Records of Colonial Virginia," Conway Robinson Papers, ViHi, 235.

4

SETTLING DOWN

ettling down meant more to newcomers than unpacking and starting afresh. It also meant reconciling to separation from Britain and coming to terms with Virginia. Experienced colonists pungently named those collective adjustments the "seasoning." Seldom easy, seasoning could be swift or so gradual as to be almost unnoticeable. Sometimes seasoning came not at all, and for unnumbered immigrants their inability to endure inexorably resulted in hurtful or deadly consequences, but, for those who eventually fit themselves to different lives, settling down was one of many experiences that turned them into Virginians. So it was for Berkeley.

A place to live and something to do were among the first adjustments that faced any new free immigrant. For Berkeley the house he had purchased from Sir Francis Wyatt afforded him comfortable, if less than spacious, shelter. A perquisite of office, a three thousand–acre plot of ground known as the "Governor's Land" provided rental income and also enabled him to take up farming almost at once. In these things he enjoyed advantages that few other settlers could command immediately upon their arrival in Virginia, but the greater part of his seasoning turned on how he adjusted to his role as the colony's leading citizen and chief executive.

In the first place he had to overcome fallout from the suddenness of his appointment. He arrived in the colony friendless and all but unannounced. Virginians who counted politically were not overly eager to have such a stranger to come among them. They respected Wyatt for his capabilities, his record of service to the colony, and his deference to them. By contrast, they knew little of their new governor beyond the obvious. He was a king's man with clout sufficient to shunt Sir Francis aside. And so they eyed him warily as they probed for signs of weakness or signals of his readiness to befriend them. For his part Berkeley needed to move with resolute swiftness to establish a suitable relationship with them, one that isolated potential enemies as it cemented a loyal following. Circumstances of the moment complicated how he might go about that.

He took up his government amid the apprehensions of a motherland in turmoil and a colony in flux. His charge presented an exquisite trial of skills in that it compelled him to hold Virginia constant and to steer between competing factions of leading settlers while he carried out King Charles's orders and kept the goodwill of the king's enemies in Parliament. Ruling in the interests of sovereign and settler required a willingness to take liberties with his instructions, which had changed little in wording or content since the Crown first indited them back in the 1620s. Consequently, the royal mandates entailed upon him certain expectations that no longer matched colonial political realities, and he had to develop a nimbleness of purpose that allowed him to hew to the spirit of those commandments while he adjusted to unforeseen contingencies.

Practical concerns, not sentiment, bound Virginians' allegiances to Charles I. The king guaranteed colonial land titles and political arrangements. Royal indecision kept at bay those courtiers and London merchants who saw in a revived Virginia Company the means of managing the colony in a profitable manner. Civil war in the British Isles would put colonial loyalties to the test. Gathering strife compelled the settlers to take sides, which threatened commercial relationships that were vital to colonial prosperity. Closer to home, a mere seven years had passed since the Council of State overthrew Governor Sir John Harvey following a dispute over his power to act independently of the councillors' wishes. Most of the very men who ran off Harvey still sat around the council table, and how well Berkeley got on with them would quickly dictate the fate of his administration.

If he had not fully grasped the task he faced beforehand, then he surely recognized its enormity from the moment he first regarded Virginia and its sole metropolis. Jamestown can scarcely have inspired him. Here was no great city, no enormous palaces, no royal court, no signs of a capital, nor any other trapping to reinforce his dignity as the king's vice-regent. Instead, here was a village, tinier than many a little English country hamlet of his acquaintance. Houses of differing scale and fabrication sheltered the residents. Thatch-roofed cottages of wattle and daub quartered recent immigrants or poorer town dwellers. Several brick homes dotted the scene too, though frame structures were the more prevalent

SETTLING DOWN / 41

type of permanent living quarters. Whatever the construction, every building looked small when set against the houses and palaces he knew in England. Overall Jamestown added up to an indifferent vista.[1]

Even so, the place had come far since 1607. "James Cittie" sat some sixty miles inland from the seacoast on a pear-shaped peninsula whose stem of an isthmus fastened it to the north bank of the James River. This almost-island had seemed an ideal place to the original adventurers who threw up the fort out of which the metropolis grew. Settling there guarded against invasion from the sea or attack by the Indians. Geography added another advantage too. The river channel ran close to shore, which permitted deep-draft vessels to anchor near the water's edge and to off-load supplies with relative ease. Military considerations aside, the locale was anything but suitable. Nature, far from making the island a fit town site, rendered it quite undesirable for urban living. Its distance from the ocean worked against Jamestown becoming a consequential port. Wetlands accounted for much of the terrain. Dry ground, such as it was, rimmed the perimeter or ridged fingerlike into watery muck. No springs or creeks fed the residents' need for potable water. Wells, when dug, were often so shallow as to invite contamination or so deep as to tap the brackish aquifer that supplied marsh and river alike. The murky wetness of the marsh spawned unimaginable multitudes of pestiferous insects that spread misery and disease as they dined hungrily on settlers and livestock with equal ferocity. Sultry summers and dreary winters added their own dashes of unpleasantness to what was a decidedly disagreeable spot.[2]

Colonists stubbornly clung to Jamestown in spite of its drawbacks. Fort and town were practically the same throughout the two decades the Virginia Company ran the colony. Both brushed ruination in 1610, when the fort was nearly abandoned, and again in 1616, when the rage to grow tobacco drew all but fifty

---

1. The Governor's Land was situated on the mainland just above and to the west of Jamestown Island. Marked off in the 1620s as a perquisite for the chief executive, it afforded an incumbent income from tenants as well as from farming. Some of the tract underwent archaeological investigation in the 1970s; see Alain Charles Outlaw, *Governor's Land: Archaeology of Early Seventeenth-Century Virginia Settlements* (Charlottesville, Va., 1990). But those digs revealed little about Berkeley's uses of it. See also Plat of Governor's Land, 1683, William Salt Papers, Staffordshire Record Office, Stafford, England.

2. John Smith, *A True Relation of Such Occurrences and Accidents as Hath Hapned in Virginia . . .* (1608), in Philip L. Barbour, ed., *The Complete Works of Captain John Smith (1580–1631) in Three Volumes* (Chapel Hill, N.C., 1986), 1:29; John L. Cotter, *Archaeological Excavations at Jamestown, Virginia* (Washington, D.C., 1958), 152–53. Once thought to have eroded into the James River, most of the original fort was rediscovered during archaeological investigations that began in the mid-1990s. The results of those digs are annually reported in William M. Kelso, et al., *Jamestown Rediscovery* (Richmond, 1995–); and on the Jamestown Rediscovery Web site at www.apva.org.

inhabitants to other settlements that offered more arable land on which to plant. Deputy Governor Samuel Argall stopped the decline after he embarked on a vigorous rebuilding effort that resulted most notably in repairs to the company storehouse and the raising of a new frame church. His persistence so vexed residents that they complained boisterously to the company in London. Those protests provided one in a series of justifications that prodded company leaders to revamp their operation, and the changes, enacted in 1618, moved Virginia from a quasi-military outpost toward a more traditional agriculturally bound society. As a result, the settlers got new forms of land tenure, rules akin to English local law, a better resident administration, and a more representative management entity, the General Assembly.[3]

The company left the decision of where to convene the assembly to the settlers. Governor Sir George Yeardley picked Jamestown and for an obvious reason. Within town precincts lay a building, Argall's church, roomy enough to seat large gatherings. There was also a company-owned governor's house where the chief executive and his council could meet. And so Yeardley turned Jamestown into Virginia's first capital. The transformation came at a propitious moment because of the company's simultaneous effort to polish the town into a more attractive place. Surveyor-general William Claiborne projected the earliest major expansion of Jamestown. Called "New Towne," the development rose downriver of the existing village. Claiborne marked off two parallel streets that ran on a rough east-west axis. One, known as the River Road, followed the James until it linked up with another that passed the fort on its way over the isthmus to the mainland. Cross-streets joined the second thoroughfare, or "Backe Street," as the residents soon named it.

Discontinuities bred by the Anglo-Indian War of 1622–32, the downfall of the Virginia Company, and the transfer of the colony to the Crown all impeded growth for much of a decade, though New Town attracted its share of developers. Future governor Harvey, for one, took up a large parcel between Back Street and the River Road in the eastern extremity of the suburb. There he cultivated an orchard and gardens and raised various buildings, including his residence. Councillor of State George Menifie lived nearby. Other neighbors were John Chew, a substantial merchant, Secretary Ralph Hamor, and the always tart councillor

---

3. Wesley Frank Craven, *The Dissolution of the Virginia Company: The Failure of a Colonial Experiment* (New York, 1932), 47–81; Sigmund Diamond, "From Organization to Society: Virginia in the Seventeenth Century," *American Journal of Sociology* 63 (1958): 457–75; Virginia Land Patent Book 1, pt. 1, 1624–37, Vi; Sarah Shaver Hughes, *Surveyors and Statesmen: Land Measuring in Colonial Virginia* (Richmond, 1979), 8–10; Warren M. Billings, "Vignettes of Jamestown," *Virginia Cavalcade* 45 (1996): 169–71.

Richard Stephens, who often quarreled with Harvey. Sometime acting governor Dr. John Pott, the infamous poisoner of native chieftains, and Sir Francis Wyatt constructed houses a bit farther west. Edward Blaney, William Peirce, and Roger Smith, each of whom sat in the General Assembly around the time of Berkeley's arrival, also built in the area. Hamor, Pott, and Stephens were dead by 1642, though the day would come when Berkeley named Stephens's son governor of Albemarle and wed the son's widow.

As the danger from the Indians receded, the fort fell into disuse. The distinction between New Town and the old quarter diminished too, so that by the close of the 1620s Jamestown consisted of assorted residences, a church, and a storehouse. As yet no taverns lodged colonists who came to town to press suits at court or to transact other affairs, nor was there a purpose-built statehouse from which to conduct the colony's business.[4] Instead, the church still doubled as the meeting hall for the General Assembly, the governor's front parlor provided the venue for sessions of the Council of State and the Quarter Court, and the secretary of the colony used his residence as a public record office.

The character and look of Jamestown had altered substantially during the administration of Sir John Harvey. Charles I named Sir John governor and captain-general in 1628 and commanded him to develop the capital. Harvey's incentive ran deeper than the king's instructions. His house was a "rendezvous for all sorts of strangers" and "a general harbour for all comers," and for those reasons, as much as any, he convinced the General Assembly to enact legislation that refurbished Jamestown significantly. A law of February 1631/32, for instance, declared the town to be Virginia's sole port of entry. Another statute compelled craftsmen to "worke" their trades and to refrain from planting tobacco, whereas a 1633 act gave the town storekeeper oversight of the colony's official weights and measures. Yet one more law promised to anyone who built "on James Island . . . A graunt of a convenient proportion of ground for howsing & a garden plot."[5]

Reporting to the Privy Council in January 1638/39, Harvey told of the progress of his endeavors. Town dwellers had recently constructed a dozen new stores, houses, and other sturdy buildings, including a "faire" brick residence, which belonged to Secretary Richard Kemp. "Wee have," he continued, "contributed to

4. For a discussion of statehouses at Jamestown, see Warren M. Billings, *A Little Parliament: The Virginia General Assembly in the Seventeenth Century* (Richmond, 2003), 141–49.

5. Sir John Harvey to the Privy Council, 18 Jan. 1638/39, CO 1/10, fols. 8–13; William Waller Hening, ed., *The Statutes at Large; Being a Collection of All the Laws of Virginia from the First Session of the Legislature, in the Year 1619*, facsimile ed. (1809–23; rpt., Charlottesville, Va., 1969), 1:163, 208, 221; Nell Marion Nugent, comp., *Cavaliers and Pioneers: Abstracts of Virginia Land Patents and Grants* (Richmond, 1934–79), 1:123.

the building of a brick church," while the General Assembly had lately enacted "A Levye . . . for the building of a State howse." And he noted somewhat proudly, every "foote of ground for half a mile together by the Rivers syde" was being utilized for housing or commercial purposes.[6]

As the report showed, Harvey's prompting added significantly to the building stock, which enlarged the inhabited area and resulted in greater consolidation between New Town and the old quarter. Specific references to Secretary Kemp's dwelling suggest it was the first of its kind at Jamestown, whereas the remark about the brick church noted an improvement of the town's sacred space. Sir John's hope for a purpose-built statehouse never materialized. Instead, the General Assembly later used the proceeds from the levy to buy Harvey's house and tenement as an alternative.[7]

Wyatt followed up on Harvey's schemes, albeit in a less ambitious fashion. He pushed a bill through the General Assembly of January 1639/40 that specifically designated Jamestown as the colony's "chief town." An unusual statute, it was the first to compel the governor and his successors to reside at Jamestown. Wyatt complied with it by buying the Kemp house after the secretary decided to put up a new one for himself near Middle Plantation (later Williamsburg). Another of Wyatt's legislative proposals led to the regulation of retail liquor sales, which indicated the existence of publicans and public houses in the capital. Then, too, the assembly reenacted its earlier commitment to the "makeing of a Town" as part of a statute that required "auncient proprietors" to seat their town lots or lose them. The same law authorized the governor and council to project a "platt forme" to the east of the original fort. Whether Wyatt actually oversaw the construction is unclear. Perhaps not, seeing as the act passed shortly before he sold out to Berkeley. Whoever supervised the job, the rectangular earthen bastion stood guard until the 1660s, when the General Assembly replaced it with a larger fortification on an upriver site.[8]

To Berkeley, Jamestonians appeared as nondescript as the town he beheld. He encountered residents who were mostly young English males, though he saw an occasional African Virginian too. Renters rubbed elbows with propertyless freemen who scratched out paltry livings as day laborers or petty miscreants. Small planters farmed the land beyond the town limits. Substantial citizens, such as

6. Harvey to the Privy Council, Jan. 1638/39.

7. Billings, *Little Parliament*, 141–49.

8. Hening, *Statutes at Large*, 1:226, 229; Jon Kukla, ed., "Nine Acts of the Grand Assembly of Virginia, 1641," 7, MS, Vi. (I am indebted to Jon Kukla for the copy in my possession.) The site of the earthen bastion is now located on National Park Service (NPS) property. It was recently confirmed by excavations conducted by Colonial Williamsburg archaeologists for the NPS.

Chew and Menifie, mingled commerce with trade and agriculture in their scramble for money and place. A smattering of brewers and coopers, bricklayers and masons, lime burners and potters, carpenters and nailers, sawyers and turners, smiths and shipwrights, managed to flourish in their customary occupations, but Berkeley met no one who rose to his intellectual propensities or who came close to his background and social stature. Initially, that loss of affinity affected him keenly. He confessed as much to David Pieterez de Vries, a Dutch merchant mariner who called on him in the fall of 1642. They talked long of commerce and seafaring, but all the while Berkeley pressed de Vries to winter over at Jamestown. He desperately wanted the company of the Hollander, who had "seen the world, and had sailed as a Commander over all of it," because he "was fond of, and in need of society."[9]

Political considerations tempered his "need of society" and colored how Governor-General Berkeley approached his constituents. Foremost among King Charles's instructions were orders to build towns across Virginia. Accordingly, he must encourage new towns by demanding that every planter who owned more than five hundred acres of land build "within convenient time" a "house of Brick of 24. foot long and 16. foot broad with a Cellar to it" at Jamestown or in some other location. Because "the Buildings at James Town [were] for the most part decayed, and the place found to be unhealthy," Charles authorized Berkeley "to choose such other Seate for the Cheife Town" as he deemed fit, and it would retain "the Ancient name of James Town."[10]

Those commandments proceeded out of a decades-old belief in compact settlements as the key to controlling Virginia and mining its riches. The conviction originated with the owners of the Virginia Company. They modeled the first settlement in the manner of fortified garrison towns in Ulster that had proven effective in the conquest of Northern Ireland. Such an outpost would not only protect the colonists, but it would be equally useful in the quest for trade with the natives and the development of diverse products that investors expected to market in England. Virginia proved a more difficult land to exploit than anyone connected with the place ever imagined, but faith in the value of towns persisted, and it drove some of the reforms to local administration that company officials embodied in the Great Charter of 1618. John Rolfe's successful experiments with a highly desirable West Indian strain of tobacco set loose changes that turned Virginia in

9. "Voyages of David Pieterez de Vries," New-York Historical Society *Collections*, 2d ser., 2 (1857): 129.

10. Instructions to Sir William Berkeley, Aug. 1641, Warren M. Billings, ed., *The Old Dominion in the Seventeenth Century: A Documentary History of Virginia, 1606–1689* (Chapel Hill, N.C., 1975), 54.

a different direction. Scattered plantations and tobacco, not towns and economic diversity, pointed to prosperity, or so it seemed to those who imitated Rolfe.

Thus, the primary features of a colony grounded in land, bound labor, and tobacco were all in place well before Berkeley became governor. The population grew too, increasing tenfold after 1618 as Virginia-bound vessels swelled a flood of immigrants that did not ebb for a half-century. A tiny fraction were Africans, French Huguenots, Scots, Irish, and other Europeans. The rest were English. Situated somewhere between penury and magnificence, English settlers fit into that social grade that Stuart Britons had labeled the "middling sort." They quit villages and countryside all across England, though most left the southeast and the counties that reached from the Thames Valley to the West Country. The manner of their removal to Virginia controlled what befell them next. Those with no more to offer than strong backs and mighty arms bargained themselves into indentured servitude for the price of a ticket to Virginia. Young, single, and mostly male, such immigrants totaled upward of three-quarters of the colony's settlers.

Money and personal associations favored another, smaller complement of young men who bought their passage as well as those of their families and bondservants. Their cohort represented virtually every occupational calling, though its greater part marched from mercantile families. Ties to proven settlers or to the Virginia Company gave certain individuals advantages that started them on the way toward fixing their collective grip upon colonial politics. They constituted an emerging ruling class whose only claim to power was their ability to succeed. Leaders unused to leading, they lacked habits and carriage of a rank apart. Insecurity sharpened their resentments of intrusions on their prerogatives, real or imagined, yet they were determined to share largely in setting the course of Virginia's future. Fractious though they were, they managed to chart the basic outlines for self-government, a legal order, and a structured society that were clearly visible by Berkeley's landing.[11]

11. Edmund S. Morgan, *American Slavery, American Freedom: The Ordeal of Colonial Virginia* (New York, 1975), 412; "A List of the Number of men women and children Inhabitinge in the severall Counties within the Colony of Virginia. Anno Domini *1634*," CO 1/8, 155, PRO; Bernard Bailyn, "Politics and Social Structure in Virginia," in James Morton Smith, ed., *Seventeenth Century America: Essays in Colonial History* (Chapel Hill, N.C., 1959), 90–115; Wesley Frank Craven, *White, Red, and Black: The Seventeenth-Century Virginia* (Charlottesville, Va., 1971), 1–39; James Horn, "Servant Immigration to the Chesapeake in the Seventeenth Century," in Thad W. Tate and David Ammerman, eds., *The Chesapeake in the Seventeenth Century: Essays on Anglo-American Society* (Chapel Hill, N.C., 1979), 51–96; Russell R. Menard, "British Migration to the Chesapeake Colonies in the Seventeenth Century," in Lois Green Carr, Philip D. Morgan, and Jean Russo, eds., *Colonial Chesapeake Society* (Chapel Hill, N.C., 1988), 99–133; James Horn, *Adapting to a New World: English Society in the Seventeenth Century Chesapeake* (Chapel Hill, N.C., 1994), 19–78; Alison Games, *Migration and the Origins of the English Atlantic World* (Cambridge, Mass., 1999), 1–72.

In turn, hordes of new Virginians altered the Tidewater landscape from what it had been when natives alone ranged over it. Trees and game disappeared as settlements radiated outward from Jamestown. Plantations spread on both sides of the James River from the fall line (at modern-day Richmond) to the Chesapeake Bay and also covered much of the Peninsula, the land between the James and the York rivers. Others dotted the Eastern Shore, while some were just beginning in 1642 to inch northward across the York in the direction of territory drained by the watersheds of the Rappahannock and Potomac rivers.

These settlement patterns impinged on Berkeley in several ways. Just like any other colonist who brought servants to Virginia at his own cost, he could claim a head right of fifty acres per laborer, and over time that device allowed him to amass vast properties. He also held a measure of control over who received real estate across the colony. His signature on land patents validated them. Signing them became an onerous, routine chore, but from the landowner's point of view it was among his singular gubernatorial duties. That responsibility fell within his more general instruction to "assign such proportion of land to all Adventurers and Planters as have been usefull heretofore in the like cases either for Adventures of money, Transportation of people thither according to the Orders of the late Company, and since allowed by his Majesty."[12]

Establishing title to land had vexed planters ever since the Virginia Company went bankrupt. Charles I threw once and future claims into limbo after he declared Virginia a Crown province because his proclamation made no specific mention of any land grants the company had issued after its institution of the head right system in 1617. The first royal governors followed the company policies with tacit royal sanction, but a decade passed before Charles explicitly endorsed the practice and confirmed existing holdings. That guarantee was not as good as it seemed on its face, because reviving the Virginia Company still remained an option when Berkeley became governor. Years earlier, the Dorset Commission had favored revival, but its recommendation was stillborn, yet King Charles clung to the idea when he appointed Berkeley. Virginians, on the other hand, were of divided counsel. Some adamantly opposed a revived company in

12. W. Stitt Robinson Jr., *Mother Earth: Land Grants in Virginia, 1607–1699* (Williamsburg, 1957), 10–26; "Instructions to Berkeley," Billings, *Old Dominion*, 54–55. Because it was unlawful for a chief executive to sign his own patents, there were special patenting procedures that dated to the 1620s that applied to Berkeley. Instead of initiating his claims in a county court, as was the practice with ordinary planters, he brought them to the Council of State. The councillors validated them with special orders-in-council, and those signed orders took the place of the more conventional patents. Recording clerks tallied the orders with the other council records, most of which were consumed by fire in 1865, and the loss prevents an accurate reckoning of the lands Berkeley acquired by patent.

any form and had done so ever since the company's dissolution. Just as stoutly, other colonists supported its revival. The more vocal of the Virginia revivalists petitioned the House of Commons in 1641 to recharter the company. Their entreaty reached Westminster while Berkeley was still in England, and he left knowing that he must confront a most sensitive issue whose implications reached quite beyond his mere power to distribute land.[13]

Control over land distribution was one of the responsibilities that involved him with the natives politically. Clearing ground for tobacco took its toll on the Indians, especially the Powhatans, who bore the brunt of contact with the English. A loosely aligned group of Algonkian-speaking peoples, who originally inhabited much of what is now eastern Virginia, they took their name from the paramount leader who had forged their alliance before 1607. Their relations with the English were edgy from the earliest days of contact, and the pressure of a never-ending stream of settlers eventually led Powhatan's successor, Opechancanough, to attack the aliens in the hope of forever driving them away. Opechancanough's warriors struck massively in March 1622, hitting English settlements all along the James and even assailing trading vessels where possible. Their assault, which started the Anglo-Indian War of 1622–32,[14] almost succeeded. A third of the colonists died on the day of the attack. Fighting, famine, and disease felled many more within the ensuing twelve months. In the face of such losses Governor Wyatt painstakingly mobilized able-bodied survivors and harassed the Powhatans. He landed a major blow in 1624, when he engaged the Indians in a pitched battle at Pamunkey, one of the enemy strongholds in what is now New Kent County. Despite the victory, the fight degenerated into a war of attrition that dragged on another eight years. Both sides suffered frightful losses in a lethal game of stroke-counterstroke that settled nothing and only hardened animosities that remained long after peace was declared.[15]

13. Thomas Cary Johnson, ed., *A Proclamation for setling the Plantation of Virginia, 1625* (Charlottesville, Va., 1946); Robinson, *Mother Earth*, 35; Billings, *Little Parliament*, 11–13; Richard Beale Davis, *George Sandys, Poet-Adventurer* (London, 1955), 257–64.

14. Ethnohistorians J. Frederick Fausz and Helen C. Rountree have made a convincing brief for the argument that between 1607 and 1677 the English and the Powhatans fought four wars for possession of eastern Virginia. See Fausz, "Patterns of Anglo-Indian Aggression and Accommodation along the Mid-Atlantic Coast," in William W. Fitzhugh, ed., *Native Cultural Institutions in Eastern North America* (Washington, D.C., 1985), 225–68; Fausz, "An Abundance of Blood Shed on Both Sides: England's First Indian War, 1609–1614," *Virginia Magazine of History and Biography* 98 (1990): 3–56; Rountree, *Pocahontas's People: The Powhatan Indians through Four Centuries* (Norman, Okla., 1990), chap. 2.

15. Sir Francis Wyatt and the Council of State to Henry Wriothesley, third earl of Southampton, and the Virginia Company, 2 Dec. 1624, Susan Myra Kingsbury, ed., *Records of the Virginia Company* (Washington, D.C., 1906–35), 4: 507–8; William L. Shea, *The Virginia Militia in the Seventeenth Cen-*

For their part the Powhatans regrouped and clung to as much of their traditional territory as they could without provoking the colonists unduly. At the same time, the Indians eagerly sought trade goods from the English. The conundrum was how to take the best the aliens had to offer, keep the strangers at a distance, and retain cultural identity. That was not an easy riddle to crack, given the rapidity with which Virginia expanded after 1632. Almost daily, the natives faced competition for the richest farmland, the loss of game animals, marauding swine and cattle who constantly fed on crops, and the tension of living in proximity to strangers who hated them. Insults invited retaliation, which caused raids and punishing skirmishes that occurred sporadically after peace returned.[16]

Intermittent armed strife helped Opechancanough repair the damage to his power as paramount chief. The flare-ups stoked his own implacable hostility to the English, but, more important, they served as burning reminders to his people that his goal of destroying the colonists remained a worthy national aspiration. He and they had come close to succeeding in 1622, and they might again, providing they followed him. Therefore, Opechancanough worked quietly and patiently to rebuild his reputation and his forces against the day when he could loose the full fury of his might on the English once more. Just as he had done in the past, he contrived to lull his enemy into false feelings of security by feigning a tranquil pose. On one occasion he even had certain of his subordinate chiefs intervene on behalf of a colonist who was convicted before the Council of State "for his contempt in killing of an indian." Although the Englishman stood to suffer no more than a fine of twenty pounds sterling, "the great men interceded to the board," certifying "they [were] satisfied concerning the same," and the settler got off scot-free.[17]

Such gestures, while welcomed, scarcely persuaded the English of Opechancanough's peaceful intent. Pacific overtures could not hide the fact that the natives, though diminished, still threatened Virginia militarily. Ten years of war left too many horrific reminders for the English to drop their guard. If those souvenirs were insufficient, then the General Assembly made certain that no settler forgot that the colony remained a dangerous place. It created 22 March a holy day of remembrance. As prescribed in law, colonists all across Virginia gathered annually in their churches to commemorate "our deliverance from the Indians at that bloudie massacre which happened upon the 22d of March 1621[/22]." Public

tury (Baton Rouge, 1983), 25–58; Helen C. Rountree, "The Powhatans and the English: A Case Study of Multiple Conflicting Agendas," in Rountree, ed., *Powhatan Foreign Relations, 1500–1722* (Charlottesville, Va., 1993), 173–206; "Instructions to Berkeley," Billings, *Old Dominion,* 54.

16. Shea, *Virginia Militia in the Seventeenth Century,* 56.

17. Robinson, "Notes," 32.

acts of memory reinforced a shift in the way the English thought about Indians after 1622. No longer were settlers disposed to maintain friendly relations, for there was now vast disinterest in educating, converting, or intermingling with the natives. Instead, Indians were to be avoided as much as possible, used when necessary, and exterminated when they got in the way. Natives were just one more obstacle to English possession of Virginia, and many a colonist looked to that hoped-for day when the barbarians, like weeds of a field, might be cut down forever. Inspired thus, settlers remained wary, arrogant, and generally hostile to anything Indian.[18]

That change of heart carried important policy implications for how the provincial government dealt with the natives in peacetime. Guarding against the distinct likelihood of future clashes required three things of the governor-general and the General Assembly: a competent military establishment, a ready stockpile of weaponry, and a strategy to manage Anglo-Indian relations. Harvey worked a considerable improvement in colonial defenses before he retired. Taking a page from Wyatt's wartime scheme, he insisted that outlying colonists fortify their plantations, and he encouraged the completion of a palisade across the width of the Peninsula. Then he reorganized the militia, which he decentralized by putting local commanders in charge of individual units. To address the matter of arms and ammunition, he got the General Assembly to require every free adult white male to own and maintain a musket at his own expense. Thereby he spared provincial and local authorities the necessity of stockpiling small arms at public cost. The General Assembly also levied duties on ships arriving from abroad as a means of financing the purchase of gunpowder and heavy ordnance.[19]

Seamlessly melding those measures into an integrated Indian policy proved illusory after a measure of peace was restored in 1632. Defense planning could do nothing to divert the press of increased English immigration upon the natives, nor was it an anodyne for periodic skirmishing that grew commonplace during the 1630s. Then there were the inherent complexities of the Indian trade. Trafficking with the natives was hugely profitable, and, well before Berkeley's arrival, William Claiborne and Samuel Mathews had emerged as the colony's premier Indian traders. Jealously guarding their interests, they soon clashed with Sir John Harvey over Indian policy. They objected robustly when Sir John negotiated an end to war in 1632, before they had exacted a measure of revenge for the governor's disruption of their trading networks and toppled Harvey.[20]

18. Hening, *Statutes at Large,* 1:123, 202.

19. Shea, *Virginia Militia in the Seventeenth Century,* 39–54.

20. J. Frederick Fausz, "Merging and Emerging Worlds: Anglo-Indian Interest Groups and the Development of the Seventeenth-Century Chesapeake," in Lois Green Carr, Philip D. Morgan, and Jean B. Russo, eds., *Colonial Chesapeake Society* (Chapel Hill, N.C., 1988), 54–73; Michael Leroy

Berkeley's instructions mirrored Harvey's. They strictly enjoined Berkeley to "forbid all persons whatsoever to receive into their houses the person of any Indian or to converse or trade with them" without his special license. That mandate necessarily compelled him to balance the commercial interests of a privileged few against the defensive needs of an entire colony. Sir John Harvey's experience was a cautionary example of the pitfall that threatened if Berkeley strayed too far in one direction or the other. A way around that trap lay in his dexterity at neutralizing the influence of potential adversaries such as Mathews and Claiborne. Doing that depended upon his mastery of the Council of State, the General Assembly, local government, and his own office.[21]

In one guise or another the Council of State had existed since Virginia's earliest days, so its place as a primary mechanism of governance was firmly fixed in 1642. By that date anywhere from ten to eighteen men normally sat around the council table, assuming that everyone attended sessions. They included the governor-general, who presided, the secretary of the colony, and the treasurer. A full complement rarely showed up. Absences seldom, if ever, impeded work because a long-standing rule created the governor and any five members as a quorum, and those six could always act for the entire membership.

Company officials originally envisioned the council as a board of sound military men who advised the governor-general and acted as something of a counterbalance to executive authority. That purpose broadened considerably after the company revised its management scheme in 1618, and by Berkeley's day councillors owned wide powers that touched Virginia politically as well as militarily. When there was no chief executive, the senior councillor became governor pro tempore. The secretary of the colony and the treasurer supervised a range of colony-wide administrative activities. Other members held the high command of the militia or control of lesser provincial offices. Councillors, sitting together as the Quarter Court, adjudicated all felonies and decided appeals from local jurisdictions. They also joined the governor-general and burgesses in the General Assembly to enact laws for the colony.

In keeping with a habit that began with the company and lasted until 1776, councillors derived their authority from a section of the governor's commission of office that named them to their places. Ranked in order of seniority, they served for life. A governor-general could dismiss any of them for cause, and he could fill vacancies. His powers of appointment nominally allowed leeway in

Oberg, *Dominion and Civility: English Imperialism and Native America, 1585–1685* (Ithaca, N.Y., 1999), 176–79.

21. "Instructions to Berkeley," Billings, *Old Dominion,* 54.

crafting a pliant council, but none of Berkeley's predecessors had much luck on that account because few vacancies occurred during their terms in office.

At first the company picked members from the upper stations of English society, but highborn Britons rather quickly shied away from accepting appointments, and, as early as the late 1610s, success at settling, experience with Indian relations, nearness to Jamestown, personal or kin connections, and skill in Virginia politics counted preeminently in the calculation for nominees. By the 1640s, therefore, councillors increasingly arose from among those relentlessly grasping settlers who regarded a seat at the council table as the ultimate prize in their quest for stature. Aggressive pursuit of preferment mixed with modest experience of ruling to make such men acutely sensitive to their newfound dignity, which they guarded with a zeal that approached ferocity.[22]

Therein lay the likelihood of trouble because the reach of conciliar authority in relation to the governor-general remained constitutionally and politically unsettled in 1642. At issue was whether the council could act independently of the chief executive, or he of them, whenever irreconcilable policy disputes arose. Berkeley arrived in Virginia quite aware how that very lack of clarity had given rise to the ouster of Sir John Harvey and to contentiousness that afterward confronted Sir Francis Wyatt. He knew, too, that neither his commission nor his instructions resolved the ambiguity. And he appreciated that any attempt to draw a line in ways that favored him invited discord. Tense relationships between Mathews, Claiborne, Secretary Richard Kemp, and the rest of the council allowed him some latitude to set the boundaries. And he might concoct a power base in the General Assembly.[23]

As Berkeley found the General Assembly, it still resembled the original plan of the Virginia Company. It first took life in 1619 as a unicameral body that consisted of the governor-general, his councillors, and burgesses, who were elected from various subdivisions across the colony. More a resident managerial entity than a legislature, it drew limited powers of governance from the Great Charter of 1618 and the corporation's amplifying directives, which it exercised at annual sessions.

In no time at all the General Assembly easily won the affections of leading settlers because it gave them a voice in colonial affairs unlike any they had previously enjoyed. But contentment became apprehension after the Crown dis-

22. Billings, *Little Parliament*, 5–25, 68–73, 149–55; Philip Alexander Bruce, *Institutional History of Virginia in the Seventeenth Century* (New York, 1910), 1:653–90; 2:358–74.
23. Commission to Sir William Berkeley, 10 Aug. 1641, C. 66/2896, PRO; "Instructions to Berkeley," Billings, *Old Dominion,* 52.

solved the company. A heedless Charles I made no provision for the assembly when he proclaimed Virginia a royal colony, which abruptly undercut the body's very constitutional existence. Utility and popularity compelled its continuation, irrespective of its tenuous legal underpinnings, and the colonists pressed Whitehall hard to legitimate it. Persistence finally succeeded when Wyatt returned to Jamestown in 1639 bearing Charles's instructions to summon the General Assembly annually—orders that were repeated to Berkeley too.

Left to its own devices, the fledgling General Assembly turned in an altogether unexpected direction. It, rather than the Crown or Parliament, became the primary lawgiver for Virginia. That change of purpose launched a decades-long passage from a corporate appendage to a little Parliament, and by the end of the Wyatt administration the assembly had already arrogated to itself pertinent attributes of a popularly based representative legislature. Members assumed the right to decide who might sit as a burgess. They protected themselves from arrest during sessions, curtailed the governor's authority to levy taxes, and mandated specific expenditures of public revenues. The latter claim pointed toward a right of taxation, and that privilege was asserted during the Harvey administration. Then there were takings of powers to erect local subdivisions, regulate the church, and enact defense legislation. As early as 1632, with Governor Harvey's blessing, the assembly also assumed exclusive responsibility for periodic revision of the laws in force, and that rule remains good precedent to this day.

Increasingly, the General Assembly exercised its widening prerogatives in a parliamentary way. Governors-general summoned the assembly by writ, a document that called for the election of burgesses and set the date of the meeting. Members gathered at the Jamestown church to hear its parson, or some other divine, invoke God's blessings on their deliberations. An address by the governor opened the session and set the legislative agenda. Bills got debated, but none passed into law without the concurrence of the governor and a majority of councillors and burgesses. Its work done, the assembly dissolved to await its recall on another day.

For all of that, the General Assembly had a long way to go before it achieved more than a shadow of resemblance to Parliament. Structurally, it was quite primitive, its procedures remained fluid, and its members had still much to learn about the business of lawmaking. It relied on a loosely defined committee system to expedite its work. Here the likeness to Parliament was closer than elsewhere because the use of committees was nearly as novel at Westminster as it was at Jamestown. On the other hand, the newness of the assembly as legislature meant that its rules of order, which dictated the course of bills and the courtesies to be observed during floor debates, were in a state of being and becoming. Secretary

John Pory, the only early assemblyman ever to have sat in the House of Commons, instructed the first General Assembly in the rudiments of procedure. His lessons guided subsequent assemblies, and other regulations emerged through gradual precedental refinements. That said, the assembly's rules of order differed markedly from those in Parliament, and the difference continued for as long as the assembly stayed unicameral. Then, too, whereas Parliament relied upon a covey of clerical assistants, the General Assembly managed with little trained staff. Instead, the clerk of the Council of State did double duty. Besides recording council judgments and Quarter Court decisions, he kept the assembly journals, drafted bills, acted as reading clerk, tallied votes, and engrossed the official texts of the statutes. Parliament also had its speakers in the Houses of Lords and Commons. The General Assembly lacked comparable officers. To be sure, Governor Yeardley designated Secretary Pory "speaker" in 1619, but the designation seems to have been more a recognition of Pory's prior parliamentary service than anything else because Pory discharged few of the duties that normally attached to the office in England. Significantly, no one followed his example in succeeding sessions primarily because the single-house design of the assembly precluded the need for a speaker.[24]

As in England, a place among the burgesses was the only elective office in Virginia. What qualified one colonist above another is now obscure. There were no formal qualifications for elections. Typically, burgesses came of the same class of settlers from which the councillors sprang, and they obviously developed sufficient popular followings to ensure their success at the polls. They represented a hodge-podge of constituencies that ran from private plantations to church parishes to counties. Anywhere from one to four members might be chosen from a single district, for there was yet no limit to the number the voters might elect. The burgesses themselves were still very much novice politicians, endowed with only elementary understandings of English law or the arts, the mysteries, and the creative possibilities of legislating. All during the 1620s common concerns about the fate of the colony and the assembly united them, but the return of peace, their growing sophistication, changing demographic patterns, and different eco-

24. Pory's use of the title of speaker has long been a source of confusion and misunderstanding. It gave rise to a widely held view that the General Assembly began as a two-house legislature, consisting of the Council of State and the House of Burgesses. The assembly did not become bicameral until Berkeley urged the division, which will be discussed in chap. 6. Furthermore, historians, journalists, political scientists, politicians, teachers, and others consistently and mistakenly conflate the House of Burgesses with the General Assembly. From its earliest days the assembly always contained three elements: governor, councillors, and burgesses; after 1643, however, two of them, the councillors and the burgesses, organized into separate houses.

nomic conditions polarized them into nascent factions. One took its lead from Mathews and Claiborne, another looked to Secretary Kemp, and a third was largely leaderless. Berkeley deduced something of these divisions before he left London, and he came primed to use them to his advantage.[25]

If he had gleaned nothing else from his experiences as a courtier, he surely absorbed the lesson that effective government at the center must depend upon willing government in the localities. Springing from that web of kith and kin whose strands stretched across the realm to Parliament and Whitehall, he had witnessed firsthand how Charles I's alienation of local magnates and rural parsons rendered Britons ungovernable to the point of undermining the monarchy irreparably. That was a mistake he intended not to repeat in Virginia.

Once in the colony, he quickly discerned that local government was the most plastic of all its political entities, given that its form was barely a decade old. Finding an effective means of local government had been a source of bedevilment ever since settlements radiated outward from Jamestown. Company officials tried to fix the problem in 1618 by dividing Virginia into four corporations, each with a court to handle routine administrative and judicial matters. At the same time, the company also promoted the growth of large-scale private settlements whose undertakers received legal authority over their plantations. To these creations the General Assembly of March 1623/24 added a series of monthly courts, which it invested with limited civil and criminal jurisdiction. The patchwork sufficed until the 1630s, when the assembly acted on advice from a royal commission, headed by Archbishop William Laud, and replaced it with a uniform system patterned after English county courts. Staffing the new courts were "commissioners of the peace," a sheriff, and a clerk, all of whom were nominally gubernatorial appointees. Commissioners, who quickly came to be called "justices," adjudicated small civil causes and petty misdeeds and attended to various administrative routines. Sheriffs held police power, while clerks maintained a record of all public and private transactions that came before their respective courts.

The change of structure was Governor Harvey's most durable accomplishment. By pushing the Laud Commission recommendations into law, Sir John determined a permanent design for local institutions, and it was one that delineated a basic division of political power between county and province. On the other hand, Sir Francis Wyatt deserved major credit for encouraging the General Assembly to assign ever greater responsibilities to the courts, and he also did much to regularize county government before he retired. Indeed, he and the assembly were amid comprehensive refinements to the scope and nature of the

25. Billings, *Little Parliament,* chaps. 1, 4, 5, 6, and 10.

courts' jurisdiction when Berkeley landed at Jamestown. But Wyatt put the final disposition of those adjustments on hold out of deference to his successor.

Establishing the county courts had one other long-term effect, a consequence that would abet Berkeley's aim of forging ties between himself and local magnates. Institutionally, the county courts allowed a few colonists to set themselves up as a ruling class. A yearning for stature and wealth was the prickly urge that drove ambitious colonists to Virginia. Seats on local benches offered fulfillment. Uniting power with position, they opened access to land, laborers, social networks, and strategic marriages. Holding the office of justice symbolized one's arrival at the head of Virginia society, and the race to the top was at full tilt when Berkeley took over.[26]

As he settled down, he may not have appreciated all of the implications of Virginia's institutional arrangements or the dimensions of its emerging society, but he was hardly ill equipped to make requisite adjustments in timely fashion. As the king's vice-regent, he was the single most important public figure in the colony. Whereas his commission and instructions granted to him enormously broad powers of political rule and military authority, the imprecision of their warrant gave him abundant latitude to decide how best to use his prerogatives. Beyond that, he enjoyed advantages his predecessors never had.

Despite potential bad effects of the troubles in Britain and simmering discontents among leading colonists, Virginia was quieter than it had been in decades. Relative peace meant that Berkeley could concentrate on improving upon the county courts, the General Assembly, or the economy instead of warring on the Indians. Being the first governor without prior association with the Virginia Company or the colony was a bit of a blessing too. Free of that past, he might act the part of honest broker and equitably compose issues that divided colonial politicians and in such fashion as to build a loyal following among the antagonists.

Whether he knew it or not, his greatest assets were his personal attributes. In a world where family mattered, he came of a background unequaled by any previous governor. He was no made-up gentleman in the manner of Sir George Yeardley or Sir John Harvey, who were knighted to "grace [them] the more" with

26. Ibid., chap. 10; Warren M. Billings, "The Growth of Political Institutions in Virginia, 1634 to 1676," *William and Mary Quarterly*, 3d ser., 31 (1974): 225–42; Billings, "Justices, Books, Laws and Courts in Seventeenth-Century Virginia," *Law Library Journal* 85 (1993): 277–97; Emily J. Salmon and Edward D. C. Campbell Jr., *The Hornbook of Virginia History: A Ready-Reference Guide to the Old Dominion's People, Places, and Past*, 4th ed. (Richmond, 1994), 159–71.

a gentility that was not theirs by birth. Berkeley was born genteel.[27] His people stood many rungs higher on society's ladder than the estimable Sir Francis Wyatt. The Berkeleys took care of their own and found him a place at court, and, when the time came, they helped in making him governor. Will Berkeley had daily seen Charles I in person, had conversed with him, and acted as the king's personal emissary. No Virginian ever approached that degree of proximity, so he projected an aura of might that exalted him more highly than anyone among them. His time at court imparted lessons in the intrigues and arts of politics. He recognized in stagecraft an essential ingredient of statecraft. Observing how Charles mixed the two, he learned when and where to draw the line between them.

Aloof but accessible, Berkeley was an urbane, witty man. Elegant etiquette complemented a keen ear for smartly coined sentences. Sharp-eyed intelligence joined an innate curiosity that made him an agile visionary, alert to new ideas and temperamentally at ease with the accumulation of knowledge through first-hand experience. Above all else, however, he claimed kinship with his fellow colonists in one important respect. For him, as for them, Virginia promised something better than he had left behind in England. Chasing his dream, he set out to become Virginia's chief planter as well as its chief executive.

27. The paraphrase derives from John Chamberlain's remark to Sir Dudley Carleton about the time James I knighted Yeardley, Chamberlain to Dudley, 28 Nov. 1618, in Norman E. McClure, ed., *The Letters of John Chamberlain* (Philadelphia, 1939), 2:188.

5

THE HOUSE AT GREEN SPRING

uty pressed in upon Berkeley soon after he took his oaths. He recommissioned local officials, and where necessary he filled the empty seats on the county benches. Sessions of the Quarter Court eased him into his role as Virginia's chief judge. Meetings with the General Assembly acquainted him personally with the colony's leaders. Death suddenly vacated the place of treasurer and gave him the opportunity to name a replacement. Despite the crush of mastering administrative routines, charting a political agenda, and handling the unexpected, he made ample time to ease himself into the planter elite.

Moving to Virginia and compensating Sir Francis Wyatt drained his finances, though he had enough capital on hand to carry through until his wages came from Whitehall. As it turned out, his "severall pension[s] and allowance[s] from his majestie" were not forthcoming because "the vnkind differences now in England" forced the Crown to suspend payment. Strapped, Berkeley looked to the General Assembly for help. It responded generously in March 1643 with a levy of two shillings per head on every ratepayer in the colony. The tax was rendered in comestibles or livestock that he might sell or consume as he saw fit.[1]

These gifts tided him over while he searched for other income. Months earlier,

1. William Waller Hening, ed., *The Statutes at Large; Being a Collection of All the Laws of Virginia from the First Session of the Legislature, in the Year 1619,* facsimile ed. (1809–23; rpt., Charlottesville, Va., 1969), 1:280–82.

in fact, he had leased a hundred acres of the Governor's Land to a local politician named Robert Hutchinson for an "Annual rent of fower barrells of Merchantable Indian Corne sheld at my howse at James Citty." First of many ensuing rental agreements down the years, the Hutchinson lease identifies rents as a significant source of Berkeley's accumulating wealth. Leasing property under his control produced something of equal, if not greater, value. His deals initiated durable relationships with established planters. Some renters were as prominent as Hutchinson. Others were decidedly less so, but all depended upon him, and, after a fashion, most became his loyalists.[2]

Property bought from Sir Francis Wyatt launched Berkeley as a Virginia land-owner. He quickly added other Jamestown real estate. Two tenements, plus an orchard, were gifts from the General Assembly.[3] He procured another lot, where he started a spacious official residence to replace the house Wyatt had sold to him. Then in June 1643 he cashed head rights on the servants he had brought from England, using them to patent a sizable plot some three miles from James-town. This tract was the finest feather in his cap, for on it he founded the grand villa and vast working farm that turned him into Virginia's foremost planter.[4]

Just shy of a thousand acres, the allotment appealed to him because its fea-tures could be handily fitted into his schemes for its future. Powhatan Creek and the Governor's Land bounded the plot to the north and to the east. Other planta-tions bordered its southern limits. Mostly unclaimed land lay beyond the western property line, which left such room for expansion as need and purse admitted. (He eventually increased the area of his holding to over seven thousand contigu-ous acres.) The parcel was distant enough from Jamestown to bring respite from the affairs of state yet near enough to reach the metropolis speedily in times of

2. Lease to Robert Hutchinson, 20 May 1642, Virginia Land Patent Book 1, pt. 2, 1637–43, 772, Vi. John Soane identified some of Berkeley's tenants by name in a survey of the Governor's Land that he executed in 1683, which is now in the William Salt Library at the Staffordshire Record Office, Stafford. A complete list of all who rented from the governor cannot be compiled because the relevant docu-ments are no longer extant.

3. Hening, *Statutes at Large*, 1:267. The destruction of the James City County court records and other pertinent documents prevents pinpointing either tenement. Archaeological investigations to date have also failed to identify these properties at this writing.

4. Patent to Green Spring, 1 June 1643, Thomas Jefferson Papers, DLC. Claiming a defect in the original survey, Berkeley refiled his patent in 1646, which the council allowed, and the tract was then calculated to contain a total of 1,090 acres (patent to Green Spring and other lands, 6 June 1646, Thomas Jefferson Papers, DLC). Thereafter, his neighbor Robert Wetherall sold him an adjoining 1,000 acres (renewal of title to Green Spring, 17 Mar. 1661/62, Thomas Jefferson Papers, DLC). In 1659 he sued out a claim for another 5,062 acres (grant from Samuel Mathews Jr., 5 Mar. 1658/59, Lee Family Papers, ViHi), and that addition raised the total above 7,000 acres.

necessity. Roads linked it with the capital and neighboring plantations along the James and the Chickahominy and beyond. Better still, Powhatan Creek gave water access to Jamestown. Another small stream on the property, which fell to the James, held the possibility of supporting traffic directly to the river. The land itself once belonged to the native Paspaheghs, so portions of arable ground were already cleared for cultivation. Abundant stands of timber offered ready supplies of wood for fuel and lumber. Topographically, the terrain rose gently upward to a point where it flattened onto a roughly leveled plain. High ground afforded agreeable sites for habitation and suitable soil for brick or pottery making. An icy freshet poured forth good water nearby. It gave the property its English name, Green Spring.[5]

Berkeley picked a spot a short distance from the spring, and there he raised his dwelling, which he called Green Spring House. In the end he created what was arguably the largest stately mansion of its day in English North America. Such was its size that Green Spring House approached a scale that would have favorably impressed his former courtier colleagues.

The place is gone. Ludwells and Lees lived there after Berkeley's death. Their indifferent care accelerated its decline, though a section of the main house lasted to the end of the eighteenth century. It had fallen into such disrepair that the owner, William Ludwell Lee, pulled down the remnant in 1798. Gone, too, are construction records and Berkeley's plantation account books. Now archaeological recoveries and documentary scraps supply the only physical evidence of the Green Spring House. Those bits are too few to do more than conjure evanescent images of the mansion, grounds, and fields that Berkeley cherished deeply.[6]

Like builders of seventeenth-century great country estates in Britain, Berkeley developed Green Spring piecemeal. First to rise was a modest dwelling that formed the core of the much greater mansion that was to follow. Work began shortly after he got his patent, but it slowed owing to the outbreak of the Anglo-

5. "A Letter from Mr. John Clayton Rector of Crofton at Wakefield in Yorkshire, to the Royal Society, May 12. 1688," in Edmund Berkeley and Dorothy Smith Berkeley, eds., *The Reverend John Clayton, a Parson with a Scientific Mind: His Scientific Writings and Other Related Papers* (Charlottesville, Va., 1965), 56.

6. Jane Carson, "Green Spring Plantation in the 17th Century: House Report," MS, 6–8, ViWC. Archaeologists twice dug the house site, first in the 1920s and again in the 1950s. Those were times when historical archaeology was still an infant discipline, and scholarship on Berkeley was only marginally better. The house site belongs to the National Park Service and awaits intensive reexamination (Warren M. Billings, "Imagining Green Spring House," *Virginia Cavalcade* 44 [1994]: 84–95; Virginia Barrett Price, "The Making, Remaking, and Unmaking of Green Spring between 1643 and 1803" [master's thesis, University of Virginia, 2000]). I am indebted to Mrs. Price for providing me with a copy of her fine study.

Indian War of 1644–46 and his unexpected trip to England. Building picked up after the conflict ended, and the house more than doubled in size by the time of Virginia's surrender to Parliament in 1652. Forced retirement and money troubles kept Berkeley from attempting additional enlargements, but a return to stable finances in the later 1650s allowed him to launch the renovation that brought the building to completion during the next decade.[7]

Berkeley initially conceived Green Spring House as a compact two-and-a-half-story structure. He situated its ground floor rooms end to end, more or less on a north-south axis. Two turrets, equidistant from each other, rose on the western facade, suggesting that side was the original location of the main entry. He added a subsequent parallel rank of larger rooms across the south front. To these he later joined two perpendicular bays. As a result, the plan now resembled an inverted letter *U*. He also put up an antechamber between the two arms, which may have sufficed as a new formal entryway. The ultimate renovation changed both the profile and the orientation of the house. It contributed an L-formed extension, only a room wide, that stretched the length of the northern arm to nearly a hundred feet. In this configuration a cross-shaped stairway rose in the center of the extension and faced toward Jamestown. Most striking of all, a Mediterranean-style arcade stretched one floor high across the front. Atop it sat a low railed terrace, and from the terrace visitors gained access to the front door or an overlook of the gardens.

Availability, more than taste, ordained Berkeley's choice of fabric. His contemporaries in England relied upon materials found nowhere in Tidewater Virginia. The region lacked veins of portland stone or slate to quarry into blocks and shingles or galena to mine into lead roofing foil. Importing these basic construction ingredients was so costly as to exceed practicality. Of necessity, he turned to what was at hand. Marl and oyster shells were everywhere abundant.[8] Pulverized then mixed with water and sand, the two combined into an adequate mortar. Bricks substituted for stones as the stuff of foundations, exterior walls, basement flooring, walks, outdoor stairways, and drains. Ceramic tiles took the place of slate or lead roofing. Berkeley's brick makers dug clay pits for tiles and bricks, firing both in the thousands on site. Sawyers cut huge quantities of timber—black walnut, cherry, chestnut, cypress, maple, pine, oak—that carvers and turners embellished into beautifully pleasing alternatives to marble adornments of interior spaces. Berkeley still had to rely upon England or Holland for tools,

7. Billings, "Imagining Green Spring House," 92–94.
8. A naturally occurring composite of clay, carbonates of calcium and magnesium, and bits of primordial shells.

door hinges, nails, screws, bolts, paint, window hardware, glass panes, decorative tile, and hosts of other finishing supplies. All of his skilled craftsmen came from abroad too.

Apart from the normal uncertainties of freighting cargoes over the Atlantic, troubles with the natives and discord in Britain were disruptions that slowed progress on the mansion. Periodic shortages of cash and the job of governing also worked their delays. Then, too, completing the project required more time and expenditure than Berkeley had first imagined. As the years rolled on, Green Spring House became more hobby than chore. Perfecting it allowed him the enjoyment of expressing himself in ways that gratified his penchant for adjusting his architectural tastes to the climate and terrain of Virginia.

Berkeley picked up at court his understanding of the latest trends in Caroline architectural styles and tastes. He knew about Andrea Palladio and his effect upon house builders. Palladio's drawings, published in *I quattro libri dell' architettura* (Venice, 1570), inspired designs that royalty and gentry across Europe found quite appealing. Berkeley routinely saw vivid expressions of those plans in the stage sets, the Banqueting House at Whitehall, and other projects of Inigo Jones, who introduced the English to Palladian precepts. His travels on the Continent reinforced these exposures. In particular Dutch examples such as the Mauritshuis, the stadtsholder's residence in The Hague, alerted him to possibilities of smaller-scale applications of Palladio's ideas.[9]

Another probable influence on Berkeley was Sir Henry Wotton's *Elements of Architecture* (London, 1624). The first book on the subject by an English author, it espoused a different approach to house building than Palladio's. Being philosophical rather than technical, *Elements of Architecture* contained no measured drawings or practical advice. Instead, it stressed ideals that should guide *any* gentleman who set out to have a country estate of his own. Among others Wotton counseled that, in conceiving the layout of rooms, the builder should be at pains that "the *Place* of every part is to be determined by the *Vse*." He meant that "Chambers of *Delight,* All Studies and Libraries," should face east; kitchens, bakeries, and breweries should look "Meridionall"; and butteries, cellars, and pantries should front north. Wotton also connected design to ornament, and therefore Sir Henry recommended sculptures and paintings—especially those from Italy—as the most delectable decorations for the interior. Aviaries and animal

9. Mark Girouard, *Life in the English Country House: A Social and Architectural History* (New Haven, 1979), 119–63, provides a useful, brief discussion of the impact of Palladianism in Caroline England.

parks, fountains and fishponds, gardens and groves, mounts and mazes, were the appropriate outside adornments.[10]

House and grounds said something particular about their creators. The paragon, as Wotton voiced it, was a "proper *Mansion* House and *Home.* Such an achievement then became "the Theater of [the owner's] *Hospitality,* the *Seate* of *Self-fruition,* the *Comfortablist part* of his owne *Life,* . . . A kinde of private *Princedome;* Nay, to the *Possessor* thereof, an *Epitome* of the Whole *World.*" Green Spring House spoke all those things about its creator.[11]

In its final form the design of Green Spring House presented an unusual look. A glimpse of the floor plans reveals a conspicuous similarity to that of Bruton Abbey, the Berkeley family seat. Both were U-shaped, both were asymmetrical, and both contained a succession of rooms that proceeded outward from an original core. The appearance therefore implies that Berkeley borrowed more from the architectural conventions of his youth than from those he imbibed during his court years. Accordingly, Green Spring House may have come closer in overall aspect to a Jacobean than to an Italianate villa. And yet a closer study of its plan shows an orderliness not seen in the abbey scheme. This regularity suggests that Berkeley took inspiration from Palladio and Wotton. Another indication of their influence was the addition of the arcade and terrace. These features made Green Spring House quite unlike any other known period house in Britain or English America, and they demonstrated Berkeley's striving to mark the completed mansion as his own unique creation.[12]

So did his method of landscaping the plantation. The scheme reflected his cognizance of contemporary gardening thought and practice. Fascination with "hortulan affairs" ran long and deep in the English imagination, as it does to this day. More pointedly, pleasure gardening was a particular rage while Berkeley

10. Wotton, *Elements of Architecture,* 7–9, 82–108, 108–23. Wotton was long ambassador to Venice. He collected Italian paintings, sculptures, and glassware for himself and his patrons, and he is often credited with introducing Italian art to the English court. Among his patrons were Robert Cecil, Burghley's son and first earl of Salisbury, and George Villiers, first duke of Buckingham. Wotton, in turn, was a major benefactor of John Tradescant the Elder, and he taught Tradescant how to dress fennel (Prudence Leith-Ross, *The John Tradescants: Gardeners to the Rose and Lilly Queen* [London, 1984], 169; John Parkinson, *Paradisi in Sole Paradisius Terrestris* [London, 1629], 494).

11. Wotton, *Elements of Architecture,* 82.

12. Phyllis Couzens, *Bruton in Selwood: Some Account of Its History* (Sherborne, Dorset, 1972), 101, 102. My vision of the finished house differs from that of Louis R. Caywood, the National Park Service archaeologist who excavated the foundations in 1955. For the contrasting views, see Caywood, *Green Spring Plantation: Archaeological Report* (Yorktown, 1955), 8–12; and Billings, "Imagining Green Spring House," 90–94.

lived, and Stuart Britons ascribed special meaning to their gardens. The transformation of the rural landscape reflected cultural assumptions of seventeenth-century gentlemen about their relationships to nature. Rational, creative beings, such persons had both the ability and the desire to render the world around them ever more beautiful than they found it in its primeval condition. Contemplation of design and its execution drew one nearer to God because a well-ordered garden concentrated one's mind on the Divine ideal.

Executing these views imposed a hierarchical series of interventions in nature. At the borders of a gentleman's estate lay untouched land, not yet subject to his mediation. Next came pastures, which bore the fewest marks of human intrusion. Then followed cultivated fields, orchards, vineyards, and dependencies. The main house and its garden constituted the pinnacle of the hierarchy, so they represented the highest alterations of the rustic environment. Thus, the pleasure garden depended upon combining lovely plantings with man-made accessories to achieve a systematic, artful transformation of nature's handiwork.[13]

Wotton's *Elements of Architecture* spoke to such views, as did most available books about plants and aspects of gardening and landscape design. Among the ones that instructed Berkeley and his contemporaries were those of John Bate, John Gerard, Samuel Hartlib, and John Parkinson. Gerard, a London barber-surgeon and gardener to William Cecil, first baron Burghley, compiled an illustrated encyclopedia of useful plants.[14] First published in 1597, it was reprinted by the botanist Thomas Johnson in a corrected edition of 1633 that incorporated hundreds of new species and illustrations.[15] Parkinson, an apothecary, was herbalist to both James I and Charles I and friend to the Tradescants.[16] His tome became a standard reference after he brought it out in 1640. More accurate and

13. The phrase comes from John Beale, who corresponded with Samuel Hartlib, Hartlib Papers, 67/22/1A, University of Sheffield, Sheffield. My thinking on these matters has been guided by proponents of gardening history. Gardening history is a relatively young discipline. Its emphasis is upon formal English pleasure gardens as they related to country houses and the creators of both, rather than upon the horticultural aspects of gardening (Roy Strong, *The Renaissance Garden in England* [London, 1979], 7). Besides Strong, among the principal studies are John Dixon Hunt and Peter Willis, eds., *The Genius of Place: The English Landscape Garden, 1620–1820* (London, 1975); John Dixon Hunt, *Garden and Grove: The Italian Renaissance Garden in the English Imagination, 1600–1750* (Princeton, 1986); and John Dixon Hunt, *Greater Perfection: The Practice of Garden Theory* (Philadelphia, 2000).

14. John Gerard, comp., *The Herball or Generall Historie of Plantes* (London, 1597).

15. Johnson (1600?–42) reissued his edition of the *Herball* in 1637. He was also an acquaintance of the Tradescants.

16. John Parkinson, *Theatrum Botanicum. The Theater of Plantes, or An Universall and Compleat Herball* (London, 1640).

comprehensive than Gerard's encyclopedia, even with Johnson's improvements, Parkinson's directory of plants described over thirty-eight hundred species, of which about two-thirds were illustrated. Parkinson produced a second book, *Paradisi in Sole Paradisus Terrestris* (London, 1629), which depicted in words and finely wrought woodcuts upward of a thousand flowering plants that were admirably adaptable to gardening. The Bate volume discussed fluid mechanics, and it contained design drawings and material specifications for pumps, fountains, clocks, and other water-powered devices that were helpful in creating or enhancing any pleasure garden. In addition to a section on fireworks displays, it also gave elementary lessons in drawing and painting.[17] Hartlib's book differed from the rest in that it was arguably the earliest wherein an English author tried to express the practice of landscaping as a set of ordered principles that expressed a philosophy of gardening. It even furnished fairly detailed line drawings showing how these precepts might be adapted to real situations.[18]

Inspirations such as these enlivened in Berkeley a well-tuned appreciation for the prevailing conversation about landscaping. Extant traces of how he developed Green Spring hint that much. His layout of pastures, fields, orchards, vineyards, gardens, dependencies, and even a deer park was wholly consistent with the philosophical underpinnings and practical applications that recurred in the writings of Wotton and the others.[19]

He filled his gardens and orchards with plant stock that he obtained abroad or locally. Plants crossed the ocean without too much difficulty. Seeds, properly wrapped and kept dry, made the journey readily enough. Bulbs and rhizomes could be freighted in much the same fashion. Shipping cuttings, saplings, vines, and shrubbery was riskier and rather more demanding of care. Dirt-filled barrels

17. John Bate, *Mechanician. The mysteries of Nature and Art in foure severall Treatises* (London, 1634). Bate's publisher was Ralph Mabb. Coincidentally, Mabb printed Berkeley's plays *Four True tragicomicall Histories of Late Tymes by the names of the Lady Cornelia. The farce of blood. The two Damsells. and the Spanish Lady Don Diego Puedesser* in 1638, but no witness to that volume has ever come to light.

18. Samuel Hartlib, *A Discourse for Division or Setting Out of Land, as to the Best Form* (London, 1655); Hunt, *Greater Perfections*, 179–89, esp. 186–87. Although they were not acquainted personally, Hartlib and Berkeley definitely knew of each other by reputation and through others. A Hartlib associate, Benjamin Worsley, drafted the plan by which Parliament removed Berkeley in 1652. Hartlib was a promoter of sericulture in Virginia, and he was acquainted with Berkeley's silk operations through Berkeley's friend and fellow planter Edward Digges. John Ferrar, sometime deputy treasurer of the Virginia Company, also linked the two.

19. [John Ferrar], *A Perfect Description of Virginia: Being A full and true Relation of the present State of the Plantation . . .* (London, 1649), 14; Berkeley and Berkeley, eds. *The Reverend John Clayton*, 106; Caywood, *Green Spring Plantation*, 15–16.

answered the need for soil. Rainwater quenched thirsty flora. Plants traveled easiest when dormant, but with care and adequate sunlight they could survive a crossing even in their active state. Every flower, bush, shrub, or tree Berkeley planted need not have come from overseas. Prominent planters who preceded him were avid gardeners too. Their seeds and rootstocks supplied him locally, as did species of native vegetation. In time he developed nurseries and at least one large greenhouse, where he bred both ornamentals and fruit trees.[20]

The first grove of fruit trees went in about the time construction started on the house, and it reflected traditional English tastes for apples, apricots, peaches, quinces, and pears. A bit later he set out "a new Orchard" that contained fifteen hundred trees. The two together gave him ingredients for cider, perry, and dried fruits that he could sell. Then, too, if he followed the usual practice, he employed some fruit trees for ornament, plaiting their branches into leafy garden alleys or splaying them against walls for elegant effect.

He also cultivated oranges and lemons. To compensate for the extremes of Virginia's weather, he relied upon a proven method that had long ensured the survival of citrus trees in the British Isles. Sprouting seeds in the nursery, he transplanted their rising saplings into large clay or wooden jardinieres. Lugs attached to the containers allowed workmen to insert poles and move them about. Tended in that fashion, fully grown trees could then be carried in or out of an orangery as the weather allowed.[21]

There were vineyards from which Berkeley got grapes for both raisins and wine. His interest in viticulture responded to his own tastes and an English belief that Virginia soils were capable of fine wine production. Attempts at founding a colonial wine industry reached back to the 1620s, when the Virginia Company recruited a few French vintners to teach the settlers their arts. The Frenchmen passed their learning along to several consequential planters who had flourishing vineyards before Berkeley landed in the colony. He himself became a stalwart advocate of Virginia's promise for wine making, but how well he actually suc-

20. Virginia Ferrar to [?] Dame Berkeley, ca. 9 May 1650, Ferrar Family Papers, Magdalene College Library, Cambridge.

21. [Ferrar], *Perfect Description of Virginia*, 14; Leith-Ross, *Tradescants*, 17. Citrus trees were native to China, India, and Southeast Asia. Having been cultivated in those regions for thousands of years, they made their gradual transit westward to Europe. Two sorts of oranges, sweet and bitter, were probably introduced to the Iberian Peninsula during the Moorish occupation, and growing them in orangeries was commonplace by the seventeenth century. Lemons and limes moved westward more slowly, though they were known to the Spaniards, who cultivated them in the West Indies (Kenneth F. Kiple and Kriemhild Coneè Ornelas, eds., *The Cambridge World History of Food* [Cambridge, 2000], 2:1826, 1800).

ceeded is uncertain. His one known reference to his own vintage came in a letter he wrote to Edward Hyde, first earl of Clarendon, in 1663. There he promised to send his "Lordshipp a Hogshead of Virginia wine for the last year I drank as good of my own planting as ever came out of Italy." On the other hand, that pledge may have spoken more to expectation than to reality, given a later comment of the historian Robert Beverley. Writing in 1705, Beverley remarked that Berkeley had emulated earlier attempts at starting vineyards, but he was quick to note that Berkeley's "Project had a . . . bad Circumstance: For, to save Labour, he planted Trees for the Vines to run upon," implying that the endeavor amounted to little.[22]

Details of how Berkeley equipped the plantation with farm animals and fowl are spotty. More likely than not, he spared himself both the trouble and the added expense of transporting brood stock across the Atlantic. He looked, instead, to his neighbors, which led him to an unexpected windfall. By terms of a provision tax the General Assembly furnished at no cost to him all the cattle, swine, goats, turkeys, hens, and geese that he needed to found his flocks. Whether he followed the traditional methods of British animal husbandry or adopted the colonial habit of letting his livestock range freely is unknown, but in time sales of salt pork and beef gave him yet one more source of income.[23]

Forest products—furniture woods, barrel staves, pitch, tar, and turpentine— were another, but field crops were the mainstays of his agricultural wealth. Berkeley cultivated corn, wheat, barley, rye, rape, and tobacco. Apart from his own need, he sold the cereals for feed or ground them to meal and flour that he marketed to his neighbors or abroad. The rape plant was useful as animal fodder. Oil of rapeseed was desirable both as an edible and a lubricant, so it, too, had market potential. He planted tobacco like everyone else, and he sold his first crop to some Bristol merchants. Although the weed always figured in the mix of his harvests, it was never a favorite of his. Given his beliefs, he quite despised tobacco and devoted much of his life to developing alternatives to it.

22. Edmund Berkeley and Dorothy S. Berkeley, eds., "Another 'Account of Virginia' by the Reverend John Clayton," *Virginia Magazine of History and Biography* (VMHB) 76 (1968): 427; Warren M. Billings, "Durand of Dauphiné: An Itinerant Huguenot in Colonial Virginia" (paper read at the annual meeting of the Huguenot Society of the Founders of Manakin in the Colony of Virginia, Baton Rouge, June 1988), 4–5; [Ferrar], *Perfect Description of Virginia*, 14; Berkeley, *Discourse and View of Virginia* (London, 1662), 7; Berkeley to Clarendon, 18 Apr. 1663, Egerton MS 2395, BL; Robert Beverley, *The History and Present State of Virginia*, ed. Louis B. Wright (Chapel Hill, 1947), 135.

23. A list of the livestock ratepayers could give Berkeley in lieu of cash is in Hening, *Statutes at Large*, 280–82. See also Virginia Dejohn Anderson, "Animals into the Wilderness: The Development of Livestock Husbandry in the Seventeenth-Century Chesapeake," *WMQ*, 3d ser., 59 (2001): 377–409.

He went to Virginia firmly committed to bettering its economy through agricultural diversity. His awareness of the literature and the debates on the merits of diversification was as profound as that of anyone in his generation. That knowledge had been shaped in his youth and during his years as a courtier. His commitment to diversification neatly meshed with certain of his instructions from Charles I. The king commanded him to promote the cultivation of hemp, flax, rapeseed, dyestuffs, pitch, tar, vineyards, orchards, mulberry trees, silkworms, and pig iron as substitutes for tobacco. These orders differed not at all from like mandates directed to each of his predecessors, but he was the first chief executive who fully grasped the possibilities, who had faith in the underlying rationale, and who remained in Virginia long enough to give diversification a chance to prove itself. Becoming governor-general also allowed him the opportunity to test ideas that before his appointment were merely his dreams.[24]

Only through trial and error could Berkeley determine which products had any practicality for his personal enrichment or application colony-wide. He turned the fields of Green Spring into a vast laboratory of agricultural experiments. His first trials centered on rice, sugar, and silk. They taught him an important lesson. Although exotic commodities could be produced in Virginia, the trouble of growing some of them, such as rice and sugar, often far exceeded whatever profits they might give in return.

The allure of rice was plain enough. English herbalists ascribed medicinal properties to rice. John Gerard, for instance, claimed it "doth binde the belly, and also nourish." Cooks had long served it up in stews, tarts, or puddings as well. Rice was not native to Britain, nor would it thrive there. It was, as Gerard remarked, "brought unto us" via Spain, all "purged and prepared, as we see in the maner of French barly." Predictably, rice became one of the exotic staples that early promoters believed could grow in Virginia and free the nation from its dependence on the Spaniards.[25]

High expectations and persistent prodding realized minimal results long be-

24. Affidavit of Richard Payton and Thomas Coscoll, Bristol Deposition Book, 1643–47, 69–70, Bristol Archives Office, Council House, Bristol; Billings, "Sir William Berkeley and the Diversification of the Virginia Economy," *VMHB* 104 (1996): 433–37.

25. Madge Lorwin, *Dining with William Shakespeare* (New York, 1976), 266–67; Karen Hess, ed., *Martha Washington's Booke of Cookery and Booke of Sweetmeats* . . . (New York, 1984), 104–5, 125–26; Gerard, comp., *The Herball, or Generall Historie of Plantes*, 72–73; Kiple and Ornelas, eds., *Cambridge World History of Food*, 1:149–52; William Strachey, *The Historie of Travell into Virginia Britania (1612)*, ed. Louis B. Wright and Virginia Freund (London, 1953), 37–38; H. J., *Nova Britannia: Offering Most Excellent fruites by Planting in Virginia* (London, 1609), 22; Wesley Frank Craven, *The Dissolution of the Virginia Company: The Failure of a Colonial Experiment* (1932; rpt., Gloucester, Mass., 1964), 101, 179, 187–88.

fore Berkeley mounted his attempt. Colonists tried rice culture in the 1610s but soon gave it up as too difficult, especially after John Rolfe's tobacco experiments pointed to an easier, seemingly more profitable alternative. And so the vision of rice fields in Virginia flickered away with the demise of the Virginia Company. If Berkeley knew that, as he surely did, then why his experiment? Probably because his reading the promotional literature had piqued his curiosity and appealed to his sense of adventure. Those writings offered little that was practical, and there were no English horticultural treatises on the plant and its peculiarities. Nor could he have read much about how to finish the grain to suit English tastes. Thus, he sailed from England still not knowing much about how rice was actually grown or prepared, though he was determined to try his hand at it. Once in Virginia, he stumbled upon part of the necessary information. Several West African servants, whether his own or another's is unclear, taught him their way of raising rice.[26]

Supremely confident of his chances, Berkeley procured some seed for a trial. He sowed, reaped, and brought in fifteen bushels of grain on the first try. Then he planted his entire harvest and sold its subsequent yield. He proudly communicated these initial results to one of his correspondents in England, that ceaseless voice of diversification, John Ferrar. Evidently, too, he claimed that he verged on establishing the long-desired rice industry. At least that was how Ferrar presented Berkeley's report in his pamphlet *A Perfect Description of Virginia* (London, 1649). Ferrar praised Berkeley's experiments and doubted "not in short time to have Rice so plentiful as to afford it at 2ᵈ a pound if not cheaper, for we perceive the ground and Climate is very proper for it."[27]

Ferrar was too sanguine, and Berkeley was too self-assured. Rice at Green Spring went nowhere fast. Berkeley never enlisted enough competent laborers to husk and prepare the grain the way the English preferred it. An undesirable product had no market, and, thus, the project was scaled back after only a few years' trial.[28]

26. Kiple and Ornelas, *Cambridge World History of Food*, 1:134.

27. [Ferrar], *Perfect Description of Virginia*, 14. David L. Ransome, editor of the microform edition of the Ferrar Family Papers housed at Magdalene College, Cambridge, has established beyond question Ferrar's authorship of this little treatise. See Ransome, "An Old Man's Dream: John Ferrar and the Promotion of Virginia" (paper delivered at the Samuel Hartlib Papers Conference on Peace, Unification, and the Advancement of Learning in the Seventeenth Century, University of Sheffield, July 1992); and Ransome to Warren M. Billings, 18 May 1991, Sir William Berkeley Papers Project Archive. See also Ferrar's unpublished MS "Virginia Truly and Richly Valued," fol. 5, Ferrar Family Papers, Magdalene College Library, Cambridge and Ransome to Billings, 29 Mar. 1992, Berkeley Papers Archive.

28. Beverley, *History and Present State of Virginia*, 316–17.

Sugar, as Berkeley knew well, was among the most profitable of colonial staple crops, which says why he wanted to take his shot at it too. The odds against his success were formidable. Machinery for grinding sugarcane and the pots for boiling the juice represented a sizable capital outlay. Tending cane was highly labor intensive, and recruiting an adequate work force of field hands, coopers, carpenters, smiths, and potters added considerably to the investment. Boiling the juice was a brutal, demanding skill that called for a deft touch in knowing when the mixture was done. Packing raw sugar, or refining it, and disposing byproducts were also time-consuming. All that aside, the chief obstacle to raising sugarcane in the Tidewater was sugarcane itself. Biologically, sugarcane is a perennial grass that waxes in moist, humid climates and cannot withstand hard winter weather.[29]

So, Berkeley looked for alternatives. He toyed with refining quantities of brown sugar that he imported, first for his own use and then for sale to others in the colony, but that was not an especially lucrative undertaking. Maize seemed a possible alternative to sugarcane. He got the idea from Virginia planters who knew how to make small stores of sugar from cornstalks for their own use. Maize was easily grown, it was plentiful, and its stalks contained a sweet juice. Making sugar from it demanded as much of an outlay for equipment and labor as for sugarcane, however, and in the end this attempt at commercial exploitation was more short-lived than his rice experiment.[30]

Next, he tried silk. Silk was one of the most highly touted of the exotic staples that Englishmen wanted to produce for themselves. Experimental silk manufacture was introduced into Britain in the 1500s. It caught the fancy of James I, who

29. Richard S. Dunn, *Sugar and Slaves: The Rise of the Planter Class in the English West Indies, 1624–1713* (Chapel Hill, 1972), 189–223; Kiple and Ornelas, *Cambridge World History of Food*, 1:438.

30. E.W., *Virginia: More especially the South part thereof, Richly and truly valued* . . . (London, 1650). Although the Indians made sugar from sugar maple trees, that was not a source the colonists took to readily until late in the seventeenth century, and even then they never saw maple sugar as a commercial alternative to the West Indian variety (Beverley, *History and Present State of Virginia*, 136–37). Around the time of his sugar endeavor, Berkeley employed a potter who made sugar cone molds, examples of which Louis Caywood recovered in 1955 (Caywood, *Green Spring Plantation*, pl. 14). Caywood did not recognize them as such, and they drew little attention until the mid-1990s, when Beverly A. Straube, curator of artifacts at the APVA Jamestown Rediscovery Center, identified them for what they were. Straube also connected them to one specific potter who flourished during the first decade of Berkeley's occupancy at Green Spring. Their presence among the Green Spring House artifacts raised several possibilities about their intended purpose on the plantation. The unlikeliest was that Berkeley imported cane or juice that he turned into sugar because in transit the juice would have fermented and the canes would have gone to rot. Berkeley may have exported molds, but that was unlikely too, given that West Indian sugar planters hired their own potters. The existence of the cones, the fact Virginians knew how to turn corn into sugar, and Berkeley's known penchant for experimentation argue that he attempted to make sugar from cornstalks.

expected to wean his kingdoms from their French and Italian suppliers. Soon after he succeeded Elizabeth I, in 1603, he licensed William Stallinge to breed silkworms and the mulberry trees whose leaves fed the worms. A bit later James authorized Stallinge to enclose a plot of ground at Westminster on which to set mulberry trees, and by 1610 Stallinge presented his royal benefactor with nine pounds of woven silk. Stallinge was soon overshadowed by John Bonoeil. A refugee from Languedoc, Bonoeil sprang from a Huguenot community of sericulturalists who dominated the silk industry in France. James appointed Bonoeil to oversee an elaborate silk works he projected at the palace of Oatlands. Charles I maintained the Oatlands operation and went so far as to name the senior John Tradescant his silk master. Such royal championing appealed to gentlemen dabblers, but it failed to prod a critical mass of commercial men, and there would be no seventeenth-century raw silk industry in the British Isles. The vision of national self-sufficiency in silk did not perish. It drifted into efforts to make Virginia prosper.[31]

John Smith, himself a devoted proponent of sericulture, reported on the first venture at founding the industry in Virginia. That try amounted to naught, but the settlers remained under constant orders to farm mulberry trees and silkworms throughout the company period. Company treasurer Sir Edwin Sandys added his own urgent boost. Reacting to a sharp reproof from James I, he enlisted the services of Huguenot vignerons, whom he sent to Virginia to teach the colonists worm raising. Sandys also included a shipment of Bonoeil's *Observations to be Followed, for the Making of fit roomes to keep Silke-wormes in: Also For the Best Manner of planting Mulbery trees to feed them* (London, 1622), which the royal silk master wrote specifically for the colonists' edification. Many of the vignerons died in the Anglo-Indian War of 1622–32, but those who escaped taught their skills to willing English planters. In turn the colonists passed the learning on to others, and by the 1640s there existed a nucleus of planters who routinely manufactured small but marketable amounts of silk.[32]

Berkeley grew up knowing about silk, and he was intrigued by it, though he may not have seen his first actual silk operation until he joined Charles's court and spent time at Oatlands. Probably by then he had already digested Bonoeil's *Observations*. Although Bonoeil deliberately intended his book for Virginia, it became a standard text that circulated in England in both handwritten and

31. Charles E. Hatch Jr., "Mulberry Trees and Silkworms: Sericulture in Early Virginia," *VMHB* 65 (1957): 3–4; Leith-Ross, *John Tradescants*, 93–94.

32. Philip L. Barbour, ed., *The Complete Works of Captain John Smith (1580–1631) in Three Volumes* (Chapel Hill, 1986), 1:151, 159; Hatch, "Mulberry Trees and Silkworms," 4–24; Billings, "Berkeley and Diversification," 443.

printed copies. Quite practical, it was, and remains, an accessible, sensible, even humorous guide to the mysteries of sericulture, and its straightforward instructions were easily followed.[33]

Silk thread came from an insect Bonoeil called a butterfly. Actually, it was a moth. Any moth would do. Customarily, however, Bonoeil and his fellow silk farmers relied on *Bombyx mori,* an unassuming whitish critter with an inch-and-a-half wing span. *Bombyx mori* lived an eight-week life cycle that went from egg (seed), to larva (caterpillar), to pupa (chrysalis), to moth. After hatching, the larva fed voraciously on leaves until it spun its cocoon. It stayed in its chrysalis for nearly two weeks, whereupon it emerged as an adult moth. Females mated, and each one laid some five hundred eggs before she died. Sericulture revolved around that cycle.[34]

Left to themselves, silkworms devoured any succulent green leaves within their reach, and, just as sericulturalists favored the *Bombyx mori,* so they regarded the mulberry tree as the ideal source of worm food. Belonging to the family *Moraceae,* the mulberry was a tree of medium size that shot forth lobed, heart-shaped leaves and bore a delectable, many-seeded fruit. This preference for the mulberry tree was one of the major spurs goading the colonists to take up silk. A species grew natively in Virginia, and it would suffice under systematic cultivation.

Mulberry orchards took between three and five years to mature to the point where they yielded leaves enough to sustain silkworms without permanent injury to the trees. To start an orchard, field hands first extracted seeds from the berries of wild trees, which they dried for planting in nursery beds at springtime. The spouts remained in their beds for a year before they were transplanted for further growth. Periodically cut back to force them to branch out, the saplings reached a height of about seventy-two inches during their second year's development. Now pruned severely, they were dug up in cool weather, balled, and set out in a well-tilled field at intervals that ran anywhere from fifteen to thirty feet. As soon as they leafed out the following spring, the trees were ready to feed the worms.[35]

A single adult tree, by contemporary estimates, supplied just under a hundred pounds of leaves per season. Two dozen trees gave a half-ton. This amount was deemed adequate to feed an ounce of worm eggs over the course of the growing cycle. An ounce of eggs equaled ten thousand worms. Those ten thousand worms

33. Bonoeil's *Observations* circulated in manuscript copies as well as printed texts. Samuel Hartlib owned a long-hand version that informed his writings about sericulture, and it is the source of the quotations used here.

34. Belonging to the same class of insects, Lepidoptera, butterflies flourish in the daytime, whereas moths are nocturnal.

35. Hatch, "Mulberry Trees and Silk Worms," 38–41.

spun an average of between five and six pounds of silk. A commercially viable silk works obviously dictated huge mulberry orchards that spread out over many acres.

Purpose-built silk houses were well lit and kept at constant temperature. In addition to a winding room, there were chambers for racks of paper-lined trays that held eggs, feeding worms, and cocoon spinners. Bonoeil recommended locating a site "In good aire by the Mulberie Trees" on which to

> build a howse of the fashion of a Bowling alley Covered broad and high and also covered wel with reeds or other Materials which may defend the heate and the raigne, And the Sydes of the walls very close beeing In Plaistring or boording or other things that one may Ready finde and att all sides Leave many windows made of wood which Locketh and openeth. Moreover there must be made Casements of paper the which may be taken of and be set one againe . . . There must be left a whole In the howse where you will make your fluue and builded like an Oven . . . ; There must be made provision of earthen pots . . . The ars of the said pots In the Oven; And the mouth towards the howse.

A building erected to these specifications measured roughly forty-two by eighteen by twelve feet, and it could accommodate up to 100,000 silkworms.[36]

During the incubation of the eggs, workers watched them and kept them free of vermin and properly warmed. After the seeds hatched, the larvae matured speedily as they ate mulberry leaves, which servants picked on a daily basis. As the worms finished their cocoons, some were allowed to complete the life cycle in order to breed eggs for the next year's crop. The rest were killed. Vats of boiling water dispatched them and loosened the cocoons, also known as "cods," or "bottoms." When the bottoms cooled, workers removed dead bodies and other detritus before they dried the thread and wound it into balls. The yield ran anywhere between eight and twelve hundred yards of thread per cod.[37]

Given these requirements, Berkeley needed neither complicated equipment nor highly skilled laborers to set up shop. He could obtain mulberry seeds from the wild trees in his woods, and he could get worm eggs locally, whereas a modest shed could serve as experimental quarters. The servants he had on hand could do the work as part of their regular routine. He started a stand of mulberry trees, which he planted after his return from England in the spring of 1645. Three years later he was ready to feed his first batch of worms. The subsequent experiment did "Excellently well and to Evidence to all the world booth the fittnes of Clymate

36. Bonoeil, *Observations*, MS, 10–14, Hartlib Papers, University of Sheffield, Sheffield.
37. Ibid., 14–49.

and the goodnes of the Mulbery leafe: [Berkeley] to his greate Renowne Sent home this yeare 1649 May last a good parsell of Silke worme Bottomes[38] to show the goodnes of the Silke and the assured thriving of them." That success convinced him that he had found an alternative to tobacco that was more promising than anything else he had tried to date. Indeed, he would loudly trumpet the virtues of silk and relentlessly perfect his silk works for the remainder of his days.[39]

Whether building or farming, Berkeley needed large gangs of laborers. Certain artisans and craftsmen were his tenants, and he presumably paid them wages or in kind, but bondservants made up the bulk of his workforce. Like other planters, he looked to indentured servitude as the chief means of furnishing a steady store of hands. Details about his servants—sources of supply, numbers, names, ages, ratios of females to males, places of origin, occupations—are virtually nonexistent, owing to the destruction of the James City County Court records and all but three of his land patents. (Of the latter only the one for the original Green Spring acreage enumerates the servants by name.)[40]

Berkeley also kept slaves, but how many and where, when, or from whom he got them is a complete mystery. And it is entirely uncertain that they were only Africans. The one contemporary mention of his slaves comes from a single informant, the Reverend John Clayton. Rector of James City Parish during the 1680s, Parson Clayton noted that Berkeley had once bought three Turkish slaves, whom he "endeavoured to Convert . . . ; and to encourage them, he offered them their Freedom, and to each of them a Plantation, if they would become Christian." Two of the Turks accepted Berkeley's proffer and converted, but the third "lived a *Mahometan* for many Years, till he was fourscore years Old; when it pleas'd God" that Clayton baptized him and the widowed Dame Frances Berkeley stood as his godmother.[41]

When Berkeley was not enlarging the house or tinkering with his farm projects, he busied himself with learning about the territories beyond the Virginia

---

38. *Bottom* referred to balls of finished thread as well as to cocoons.

39. Ferrar, "Virginia Truly and Richly Valued," fol. 5.

40. Berkeley versus Hunter, 29 Nov. 1660, NoOb, 1657–64, fols. 83–84; patent to Green Spring, 1 June 1643; land grant from Samuel Mathews II, 5 Mar. 1658/59, Lee Family Papers, ViHi; renewal of patent rights to land in New Kent County, 5 Apr. 1674, H. R. McIlwaine, ed., *Minutes of the Council and General Court of Colonial Virginia, 1622–1632, 1670–1676*, 2d ed. (Richmond, 1979), 365.

41. John Clayton, *The Defence of a Sermon, Preach'd upon the Receiving into the Communion of the Church of England, the Honourable Terence Mac-Mahon Baronet, and Christopher Dunn Converts from the Church of Rome* (Dublin, 1701), preface. I am indebted to Edward L. Bond, who called this work to my attention and who provided a photocopy of the relevant passage.

frontiers and fostering his own share of the Indian trade. In 1643, for instance, he secured legislative authorization that permitted a group of friendly planters from James City and Charles City counties to probe "a new river or an un-knowne land bearing west southerly from the Appomattake river" in search of trade possibilities. Some years later he sent militiamen to rout unnamed Indians from an area along the Chowan River, and he allowed colonists to settle there too. Commerce with Francis Yeardley, Abraham Wood, John West, Samuel Ma-thews, William Claiborne, Walter Chiles, and Edward Bland, among the identi-fiable planters-traders of his acquaintance, apparently stirred the ever inquisitive Berkeley in 1649 to scout the unexplored territory for himself. By turns these ventures also caused his encouragement of Bland and Wood, who mounted a later expedition into what is now western North Carolina.[42]

Backing the activities of experienced traders enabled Berkeley to partake of a profitable traffic for the venture of a nominal contribution from his purse. They, not he, purchased trade stuff; they, not he, packed merchandise into the forests; they, not he, dealt with the Indians for the deer hides and other furs that consti-tuted the native side of the exchange; they, not he, marketed the skins through their mercantile outlets to Europe; in short, they, not he, assumed all the great risks of a highly chancy business; and they paid Berkeley licensing fees in the bargain. For him a failed expedition merely meant no more than the loss of in-vestment capital. Failure could cost his partners not only money but possibly their lives as well. Despite the inherent dangers of the business, the prospect of rich returns was the lure that caught them all.

Berkeley's associations with such men had other rewards. His partners were not just any traders; they were some of the most important men in the colony. Claiborne and Mathews ran a trading network that stretched from the James River to Chesapeake Bay to London and back again, which surpassed anyone else's for the value of its traffic.[43]

Edward Bland (d. 1652?) concentrated on areas south of the James. He was one of three brothers who successively oversaw the vast colonial interests of their London mercantile kinfolk. An elder brother, John (d. 1680), went out to Vir-ginia in the 1630s, and, when he returned to England, Edward replaced him and remained until his death. Then followed Theoderick (1630–71), who settled soon

42. Hening, *Statutes at Large*, 1:262; Edward Bland, *The Discovery of New Brittaine*, 1650 (London, 1651); Alan Vance Briceland, *Westward from Virginia: The Exploration of the Virginia-Carolina Fron-tier, 1650–1710* (Charlottesville, 1987), 13–68; [Ferrar], *Perfect Description of Virginia*, 13.

43. J. Frederick Fausz, "Merging and Emerging Worlds: Anglo-Indian Interest Groups and the Development of the Seventeenth-Century Chesapeake," in Lois Green Carr, Philip D. Morgan, and Jean B. Russo, eds., *Colonial Chesapeake Society* (Chapel Hill, 1988), 58–59.

after Edward died. He became speaker of the House of Burgesses, a councillor of state, and one of Berkeley's close friends. Officeholding never interested Edward, but his business was of such magnitude and such were his political ties that he hardly needed the visibility of office to make his presence felt.[44]

Walter Chiles (d. 1653) was drawn to Virginia by the scent of opportunity. Of humble mercantile beginnings, he was a smaller operator than Bland, though he was no mere bubble to be blown heedlessly away. He settled his family in Charles City County in 1632 and took up land near the falls of the Appomattox River six years later. Trading with the local Indians prodded him to discover terra incognita. Politics beckoned too. In January 1642 he entered the General Assembly for the first time and remained an intermittent burgess until his death. Proximity to Berkeley allied the two men politically, and in 1650 Chiles purchased the Kemp-Wyatt-Berkeley House.[45]

Having lived in Virginia since 1618, John West (1590–1659) ranked as one of its grand old men, who was venerated for his long service in public life. His eldest brother, Thomas West, third baron De La Warr, was the governor-general who saved Jamestown from abandonment in 1610, while two other brothers were active participants in colonial affairs throughout the company period. Twice acting governor himself, John West was the senior councillor in 1642, and so he remained until he passed away. His trading was on a smaller scale than that of Bland, Chiles, or the Mathews-Claiborne group, confined as it was to an area that embraced the upper reaches of the York River and its main tributaries, the Pamunkey and the Mattaponi.

Abraham Wood (1610–83?) emigrated when he was a boy of ten. Samuel Mathews taught him the intricacies of commerce with the natives, and he grew up to succeed his mentor as one of the greatest colonial experts on all things Indian. Building Fort Henry, at the falls of the Appomattox River, Wood clustered his activities mostly along Virginia's southwestern frontier and tapped an immensely rich custom in furs. He developed market outlets nearer to Fort Henry too, and they attracted settlers such as Walter Chiles to the edges of Charles City and Hen-

---

44. Annie Lash Jester and Martha Woodroof Hiden, comps., *Adventurers of Purse and Person, Virginia 1607–1625*, 2d ed. (Princeton, 1964), 95–100; Neville Williams, "The Tribulations of John Bland, Merchant: London, Seville, Jamestown, Tangier, 1643–1680," *VMHB* 72 (1964): 19–42; affidavit of John Bland, ca. 1676, CO 1/36, 140–41; Briceland, *Westward from Virginia*, 22–23.

45. Jon Kukla, *Speakers and Clerks of the Virginia House of Burgesses, 1643–1776* (Richmond, 1981), 49–52; due bill from Sir William Berkeley to Peter Stuyvesant, 30 Nov. 1649, Miscellaneous Manuscripts, New York City, Nhi; deed of sale from Sir William Berkeley to Walter Chiles, 23 Mar. 1649/50, Ambler Family Papers, DLC.

rico counties. His grasp of Indian matters naturally turned Berkeley to him for advice. A militia officer and Henrico magistrate, Wood also represented that county in several General Assemblies during the 1640s, which further strengthened the blooming of a trusted, deep friendship that lasted until Berkeley's death.

Ties to Francis Yeardley (d. 1655) bound Berkeley to yet another conspicuous web of merchant-planters. Yeardley, himself a son of a former governor-general, lived in Lower Norfolk County, where he held a captaincy in the local militia and a place on the county court. His business extended south below Lower Norfolk into the uncharted region around Albemarle Sound and north over Chesapeake Bay into the Eastern Shore county of Northampton. A brother, Argoll, was one of Berkeley's councillors. This combination revealed connections unlike the others, for it evidenced the powerful presence of Hollanders in Virginia commerce.[46]

Dutch merchant shippers began nosing around Virginia in search of cargoes during the company years. Some remained behind, taking up residence on the Eastern Shore or in the counties watered by the lower stretches of the James River. To the Dutch their burgeoning Virginia trade paled in comparison to enterprises they had in the West Indies, Africa, or the Orient, but the English colonists came to depend upon them for their ship bottoms, which far exceeded the number of English ones. Indeed, such was the level of Dutch maritime dominance in the 1640s that it threatened to drive England's merchant marine from the high seas altogether. That overwhelming presence signified politically as well as economically for Berkeley, but it also alerted him to the importance of the Dutch to his own personal financial well-being.[47]

In his quest for markets Berkeley developed liberal attitudes toward trade— which is to say, he believed the privilege of commerce should not be restricted to a few London or Virginia merchants nor confined by a few market outlets. He used the powers of his office to throw Virginia open to the Dutch and to extend trade contacts between Virginia and other colonies. The sum of his endeavors was promising. Within a half-dozen years of taking up farming at Green Spring, he was shipping his products through an extensive alliance of English, Dutch, West Indian, and New England merchants that joined his plantation to world markets. His views and his market relationships put him at odds with some colo-

---

46. James B. Lynch Jr., *The Custis Chronicles: The Years of Migration* (Camden, Maine, 1993), 129–43.

47. John R. Pagan, "Dutch Maritime and Commercial Activity in Mid-Seventeenth Century Virginia," *VMHB* 90 (1982): 484–88; Jan de Vries and Ad van der Woude, *The First Modern Economy: Success, Failure, Perseverance of the Dutch Economy, 1500–1815* (Cambridge, 1997), 297, 403–4.

nists, particularly those inclined toward London merchants or the parliamentarians.[48]

Now into his mid-forties, wealthy, and secure as never before, Berkeley wished to consolidate his gains in an age-old, traditional way that guaranteed they would remain in his family. He got married. Every detail about his bride—her origins, her name, her age, the exact date of her wedding, the children she bore, the year she died—is entirely mysterious. The sole fact of the marriage is that it happened in the spring of 1650.[49]

Reinventing himself into a great planter deepened Berkeley's affections for Virginia and advanced the job of turning him into a Virginian. As the change worked its way with him, he came to a clearer appreciation about how to translate his successes at Green Spring to the colony as a whole. In his mind prosperity went hand in glove with holding the settlers loyal to the Crown but mainly free of royal direction. That autonomy would enable Virginia to mature into a deferential, closely knit community with a diversified economy that was linked to open markets around the Atlantic rim. Such a Virginia, he thought, would benefit England as it drew skilled immigrants to its shores and produced desirable commodities similar to those he cultivated on his plantation. Those beliefs were of a piece with his approach to the way he governed during his first ten years in office.

48. E.g., articles of agreement between Sir William Berkeley and Leonard Calvert, governor of Maryland, 3 June 1642, summarized in Hening, *Statutes at Large*, 1:276–77; act to encourage the Dutch trade, Mar. 1642/43, in Hening, *Statutes at Large*, 1:258; due bill to Richard Glover of Amsterdam, Mar. 1646, YOB, 1644–49, 95; declaration concerning the Dutch trade, 5 Apr. 1647, Acts of Assembly, 1642–47, Vi; Peter Stuyvesant to Sir William Berkeley, 24 Nov. 1647, summarized in E. B. O'Callaghan, comp., *Calendar of Historical Manuscripts in the Office of the Secretary of State, Albany, N.Y.* (Albany, 1865–66), 1:270.

49. The existence of the marriage is established through letters of two of Berkeley's contemporaries, Virginia Ferrar and Sir John Berkeley. Both had unique ties to the governor. Virginia was a daughter of John Ferrar and an occasional Berkeley correspondent. To judge from available evidence, she never met the governor except through their exchange of letters. Sir John, Berkeley's younger brother, was a leader of royalist exiles after the execution of Charles I. Nothing in the known record connects him personally to Virginia Ferrar. See Virginia Ferrar to [?] Dame Berkeley, ca. 9 May and 10 Aug. 1650, Ferrar Family Papers, Magdalene College Library, Cambridge; Sir John Berkeley to Sir Edward Hyde, ca. 25 Sept. 1650, Clarendon Papers, 40, fol. 218, Bodleian Library, Oxford.

6

Bargains with Great Men

nauguration day for Governor and Captain-General Sir William Berkeley occasioned little by way of pomp or circumstance at Jamestown. No cannon roared out salutes in booming counterpoint to pealing church bells. No finely caparisoned dignitaries paraded with smartly dressed guardsmen through crowd-thronged streets to the statehouse. No fireworks lit up the night sky in dazzling welcome to him. The day of 8 March 1642 passed all but unnoticed across Virginia. It was of no particular significance other than that it was a convenient time to install the new governor. As it happened, the Council of State, whose presence was legally necessary at inaugurations, was in town for one of its sessions as the Quarter Court, so council clerk Richard Lee docketed the swearing-in as the first order of business.[1]

Berkeley walked the short distance from his house to the former Harvey tenement, which accommodated the council chamber. His appearance at the appointed hour set the formalities in motion. A plain ceremony, the short ritual began as quickly as Secretary Richard Kemp, William Bernard, Henry Browne, Humphrey Higginson, Thomas Pettus, John West, and Christopher Wormeley, who made a quorum, gathered around their table and sat down. West, the senior member, called everyone to order. They grew still. West nodded at Lee, who read

1. A statute of 1632 mandated regular terms in March, June, September, and December, which were to start on the first day of the month (William Waller Hening, ed., *The Statutes at Large; Being a Collection of All the Laws of Virginia from the First Session of the Legislature, in the Year 1619*, facsimile ed. (1809–23; rpt., Charlottesville, Va., 1969), 1:174, 187.

the governor's commission aloud. As the concluding words faded to silence, Berkeley stood, placed his hand on a Bible, and repeated three oaths that Lee intoned in succession. One enjoined, "you shall well and truly, according to the best of your skill knowledge and understanding execute and performe the place of Lieut. and Governour General of the colony and plantation of Virginia according to a commission granted you by his Majestie."[2] The remaining vows were statutory promises of allegiance to the king and to the supremacy of the Church of England that an act of parliament enjoined of all Crown officers. Now Berkeley inducted the councillors, each in the order of his seniority. Then he sat in the president's chair, which symbolized his assumption of office constitutionally. He probably said nothing in the way of an inaugural address because such a speech was neither mandatory nor expected.[3]

In the weeks and months that followed, he started to master the intricacies of being governor-general. A workplace was an immediate concern because there was no purpose-built executive residence. His private house therefore doubled as the "governor's mansion." One of its rooms offered public space to receive visitors who sought his favor or aid. He fashioned another into an office. Little, if anything, in these arrangements aroused feelings of grandeur in him. Neither was there much about the cramped quarters that distanced him from supplicants or inspired awe in them. He regarded the situation as tolerable only because he looked upon it as temporary. Indeed, around the time he acquired the Green Spring tract, he began to build a large townhouse for his official home that remained unfinished for nearly a decade.[4]

He made do in other ways. Members of his household staff—very likely no more than a private secretary and a copyist or two—managed his schedule and assisted with his paperwork. He characteristically prepared all of his correspon-

2. Conway Robinson, comp., "Notes and Excerpts from the Records of Colonial Virginia," Conway Robinson Papers, ViHi, 235; Hening, *Statutes at Large,* 2:567. The full text dates from the 1680s, and it is the earliest surviving example of the royal gubernatorial oath.

3. 7 Jac. 1, sec. 6, John Cay, comp., *An Abridgment of The Publick Statutes in Force and Use of The Publick Statutes in Force and Use From Magna Carta, in the ninth year of King Henry III. To the eleventh year of his resent Majesty King George II. Inclusive* (London, 1739). 2: under "oaths."

4. The few details about the look of the townhouse are recorded in Richard Kemp to Berkeley, 27 Feb. 1644/45, Clarendon Papers, 45, fols. 48–50, Bodleian Library, Oxford. Which of the foundations that National Park Service archaeologists excavated in the 1930s and the 1950s supported the townhouse currently is a matter of some debate. See Warren M. Billings, "Imagining Green Spring House," *Virginia Cavalcade* 44 (1994): 92; Warren M. Billings, *A Little Parliament: The Virginia General Assembly in the Seventeenth Century* (Richmond, 2004), chap. 8 n. 6; Carl Lounsbury, "The Statehouses of Jamestown," MS in the author's possession; and Billings to Lounsbury, 29 Feb. 1996, Sir William Berkeley Papers Project Archive.

dence in his own distinctive but clear hand. Scribes employed by the secretary of the colony indited land patents, election writs, and proclamations. Clerks who served the General Assembly engrossed the clear texts of legislative acts, and the clerk of the Council of State drew up council summonses, election writs, attachments, continuances, arrest warrants, and most other records that needed his signature.[5]

More intermittent than persistent, this stream of state papers did not compel Berkeley to develop a rigid routine for their dispatch. Judicial orders, proclamations, council summonses, and election writs usually received his immediate attention because they initiated business that related to the public aspects of his office. Land patents, the largest class of documents requiring his endorsement, touched private affairs that were somewhat less pressing. He often signed them as quickly as they reached his desk, though he sometimes let them pile up. Occasionally, he even allowed scriveners, who were practiced in replicating his handwriting, to initial them in his stead. Paperwork aside, much that went with being governor turned on presiding at the Council of State and dealing with the General Assembly.[6]

Colonial law required that the Council sit four times a year as the Quarter Court. And there was a tradition, in place by 1642, that one of the sessions should coincide with the meeting of the assembly, which spared councillors the inconvenience of added trips to Jamestown. Few proprieties controlled how the Quarter Court dispatched its business. Procedures were flexible and open to ad hoc adaptations. The mechanism for summoning the court amounted to nothing more than a brief note from the governor that announced meeting dates and urged everyone's presence. Sittings themselves were not limited in length, though they usually lasted around twenty-one days, not including Sundays. The council clerk managed the flow of business through his control of the docket. A crier called the court to order. Once he bade suitors to come forward and plead their actions, governor and councillors took their places to hear matters in the sequence of their filing. Civil actions, that bulkiest species of litigation, invariably crowded the calendar to the bursting point. Their number remained high in the 1640s mainly because the Quarter Court still had cognizance of suits valued greater than three hundred pounds of tobacco and because it took appeals from the county courts no matter their worth. As for criminal cases, the Quarter Court

5. Billings, *Little Parliament*, 115–19, 123–27.
6. Virginia Land Patent Book Nos. 1–3, 1637–51, Vi; patent to Robert Taliaferro and Lawrence Smith, 20 Mar. 1666, ViHi; Billings, *Little Parliament*, 31–45, 173–84; H. R. McIlwaine, ed., *Minutes of the Council and General Court of Colonial Virginia, 1622–1632, 1670–1676*, 2d ed. (Richmond, 1979), app. A.

held exclusive power over life or limb. Felony trials claimed only a small place on the docket, and they were ordinarily adjudicated during a single day that was reserved exclusively for their hearing. Besides trials, the court confirmed land grants, ratified appointments, attended to administrative or legislative concerns, and advised on executive matters.[7]

Berkeley got a crash course in the work of the Quarter Court and the temper of his colleagues from the moment he assumed office. Within days of his inauguration Richard Bennett, William Brocas, Nathaniel Littleton, Samuel Mathews, George Menifie, William Peirce, Thomas Willoughby, Sir Francis Wyatt, and Argoll Yeardley showed up to take their oaths and places at the council table. (That left only William Claiborne, who was still in England, and Treasurer Roger Wingate, who was seriously ill.) Their attendance probably gave Berkeley a first acquaintance of Mathews and his henchmen as well as a quick feel for which of the others might lean to him. Wyatt caused him some unease. Their relationship could hardly have been anything less than tense, given the manner of Wyatt's displacement. His mere appearance was a none-too-happy reminder of what had already passed between the two of them. Sir Francis compounded Berkeley's discomfort on 10 March, when he unexpectedly trapped his successor by objecting to the presence of Henry Browne. Reminding his colleagues that he had suspended Browne in "*October* last," he demanded Berkeley's ruling on Browne's right to remain in council. Berkeley favored Browne because King Charles's nomination legally entitled him to his place. To deny him would repudiate the sovereign's express wishes and disavow the solemn oath of allegiance all had so recently sworn. Berkeley was reluctant to force his view. If he did, he risked irretrievably alienating Wyatt and others at a moment when he was still green to his job. Instead, he turned the matter over to his colleagues for their advice and recommendation. Wyatt gathered support in the ensuing discussion, though the record does not reveal who sided with him or how long the talking spun on. In the end "it was the general opinion of the board that the said Capt. *Browne,* should by virtue of his majesty's commission be reconfirmed in the place of a councillor."[8]

Once the Browne contretemps subsided, the lessons centered more directly on what the Quarter Court did routinely. Berkeley ruled on civil suits, sat in judgment of felons, pardoned a doctor wrongfully accused of murder, issued trading licenses, took counsel on Indian affairs, and even granted a request from Thomas Rolfe, the son of Pocahontas and John Rolfe, for permission to visit his

7. Billings, *Little Parliament,* 164–67.
8. Robinson, "Notes," 235.

Indian relations. The necessity of appointing county sheriffs and justices introduced Berkeley to aspects of conciliar and local politics. He held the power of
appointment, which meant in theory that he could select whomever he wished.
As he swiftly discovered, it was accepted custom for local magistrates to recommend three candidates for sheriff, one of whom he would choose, and it was
habitual for the councillors to ratify his choice. Respecting these traditions, he
"prickt" Joseph Johnson, Henry Poole, and a half-dozen other men as sheriffs.
He displayed an equal receptiveness to suggestions for filling county court vacancies as well.[9]

Then, in June 1642, he got a chance to name three new councillors "in consequence of discontinuences of others." Subject only to royal approval, these positions were his alone to fill, and he used the opportunity with care. One of his
nominations went to Thomas Stegge, who, curiously, was both an ally of Bennett
and Mathews and a friend of Secretary Kemp. The other choices were George
Ludlow and Richard Townshend. Long resident in the colony, the two brought
the experience of local politics to their new offices. Both were justices and burgesses for York County at the time of their appointments. Their attractiveness,
from Berkeley's point of view, was plain enough. Neither man had overt ties to
any council faction.[10]

On his own initiative Berkeley modified a routine but highly important state
paper—the county commission of the peace. Constitutionally, the document
empowered local magistrates, and it bore likeness to its English equivalent. Each
designated members of the bench. Each named senior "justices-in-quorum," one
of whom always had to attend sessions. Each recited responsibilities that were
grounded in custom or statutory usages. Each, in a word, authorized the respective benches to perform their duties. Tailoring of the colonial version began in
1624, when the General Assembly established monthly courts in the corporations
of Charles City and Elizabeth City. A commander, plus an unspecified number
of other commissioners, staffed the courts, which held jurisdiction over petty
civil and criminal matters. But these judges could not act without gubernatorial
authorization. Hence the commission. Although the form was similar to the English model, the content was not. There was a recitation of the governor's authority to consign power to the nominees. That was followed by a statement of

9. From the justices of the peace for Charles City County, ca. 8 Mar. 1641/42, CCOB, 1642, ViHi;
Robinson, "Notes," 235–38, 91. *Prickt* signified that Berkeley wrote an X or a + next to one of the
names to indicate his choice for sheriff. In so doing, he followed English practice. Rolfe (fl 1617–46)
was the son of John Rolfe and Powhatan's daughter Pocahontas.

10. Robinson, "Notes," 237; Cynthia Miller Leonard, comp., *The General Assembly of Virginia,*
July 30, 1619–January 11, 1978: A Bicentennial Register of Members (Richmond, 1978), 20.

the commissioners' responsibilities and limitations, which preceded the governor's authenticating signature. By contrast, the recital clauses in an English commission spoke of a direct delegation from the king to the local justices, and the
grant of power encompassed a much wider ambit of responsibility. Then, too,
the colonial document was rendered in the vernacular rather than in Latin, as
was the case in England.[11]

The content of the Virginia commission of the peace did not change after the
General Assembly set up county courts in the 1630s, largely because the jurisdiction of the new benches differed little from those they replaced. Furthermore,
the county courts lacked royal sanction until they were specifically mentioned in
Berkeley's instructions. Charles I not only recognized the courts, but for the first
time he explicitly assigned his power to dispense justice through Berkeley to the
local magistrates.[12]

Berkeley redrew the commission so as to reflect this constitutional alteration
and others as well. The general domain of the justices was spelled out in greater
detail than ever before, councillors of state received seat and vote in the courts,
and the commission remained in force at his pleasure. These alterations were
intended to bring the document and the courts more in line with English practices, to be sure, but they codified current practice while leaving sufficient leeway
to address contingencies that did not exist in Britain.

No one fought Berkeley's changes. His modifications substantially enhanced
the warrant of the courts' authority, which in turn magnified the office of justice
of the peace itself. Those were reasons enough for the council to go along, but
there was another, less overt cause. Berkeley freely shared his instructions with
his colleagues. His gesture was extraordinary because it allowed them to read the
private communications from King Charles to his vice-regent, and that had
rarely been done in the past.[13]

Berkeley revealed a similar circumspection when he aimed at rectifying anom-
alies in the way Virginians dealt with legacies. English inheritance law fell largely
within the purview of the canons of the Church of England. If someone died
intestate, a diocesan bishop issued a letter of administration naming a person
who took control of the estate, cleared outstanding debts, and distributed any

11. Hening, *Statutes at Large*, 1:124; Michael Dalton, comp., *The Countrey Justice: Containing the Practice of Justices of the Peace Out of their Sessions* (London, 1677), 16–19.

12. The earliest surviving witness to Berkeley's commission of the peace is the one issued to the justices of Northampton County on 30 June 1642 , NoOB, 1640–45, fols. 88–89, Vi.

13. "Instructions from Charles I," 10 Aug. 1641, Warren M. Billings, ed., *The Old Dominion in the Seventeenth Century: A Documentary History of Virginia, 1606–1689* (Chapel Hill, N.C., 1975), 52; Bill-ings, *Little Parliament*, chap. 2.

remainder to the rightful heirs, whereupon that individual received a written release. Similarly, jurisdiction over qualifying executors and probate—the written act of authenticating a will—lay in the ecclesiastical courts. Creditors, executors, next of kin, all stated their interest in the will before a judge, who ruled on its validity. The executor settled the estate and, when that was done, petitioned for an instrument called a *quietus*, or *quieta, est*—that is "he or she is quit"—which certified his or her discharge.[14]

Because there were no bishops or church courts in Virginia, these responsibilities gradually devolved upon secular authorities. Executors and administrators first looked to the church courts in England throughout the company years and later. That was a clumsy, expensive way to fix a mounting problem. Eventually, the Council of State assumed the role of a probate court, and, as a result, governors acted the bishop's part, meaning that they validated all probates and letters of administration. Berkeley's predecessors quickly discovered how initialing these documents became nearly as onerous as signing land patents, and the burden disposed them to seek alternatives. The options were by no means settled in 1642, which left room for experimentation. Ultimately, Berkeley prompted the General Assembly to assign most testamentary record keeping over to the county courts, and, although he still continued to sign discharge papers, the handover reduced his paperwork considerably.[15]

As for the General Assembly, it came and went at the governor's behest. Berkeley was anxious to meet with the members soon after he took office. He needed to report on Parliament's attempt at revitalizing the Virginia Company, and certain of his instructions required legislative action. Wyatt's reforms to local administration were unfinished, and Berkeley must indicate where he stood on their future prospects. And, not least, he wanted to establish himself as the assembly's leader as soon as he could. Presumably, he had only to issue writs that would announce an election of burgesses and name a date for the upcoming session, and all would soon be under way.

Things were not that straightforward. There was the sensitive political matter of what to do with the assembly that Wyatt had convened in January. Because Wyatt prorogued it to 18 April in deference to Berkeley, that assembly remained

14. Billings, *Old Dominion*, 53; Henry Swinburne, *A Treatise of Testaments and Last Wills*, 4th ed. (London, 1677), 75, 297–303; and Henry Conset, *The Practice of the Spiritual or Ecclesaiasticall Courts*, 2d ed. (London, 1703), 406–7.

15. McIlwaine, *Minutes of the Council and General Court*, app. A; letter of administration granted to Ellen Lighthart, 4 Oct. 1646, LNOB, 1646–51, fol. 3; probate granted to Isbell Munds, 10 Mar. 1646, LNOB, 1646–51, fol. 1, Vi; Hening, *Statutes at Large*, 1:302–3; Susie M. Ames, ed., *County Court Records of Accomack-Northampton Virginia, 1632–1640* (Washington, D.C., 1954), xlii–xliv.

in existence legally. Confronted with that reality, Berkeley faced two choices. He could recall the assembly, or he could dissolve it. If he dissolved it, all pending legislation would lapse, meaning that the work on Wyatt's reforms would have been for naught. Moreover, elections, as he found out, required at least a month to conduct, and it took a bit longer to get everyone to town after the polling. In the face of what he regarded as "urgent occasions," summoning the existing assembly was the more elegant alternative. Was reconvening it earlier than 18 April constitutionally permissible? A sitting Parliament dissolved at a change of reigns or when it recessed but was recalled sooner than the date to which it had been adjourned. These precedents had no meaning for the General Assembly in 1642 because they contemplated situations that had never before arisen in Virginia. In the absence of settled local custom, Berkeley looked to his instructions. The controlling clause was no help. It merely obliged him to "Summon the Burgesses of all and Singular of the Plantations" annually or "oftner if urgent occasion shall require." There was nothing that equated *summoning* and *electing* or anything that compelled the dissolution of a standing assembly upon his assumption of office. Legally, he could do as he deemed best. He favored recall.[16]

Governor-general and General Assembly greeted each other on 1 April 1642. Berkeley immediately confirmed rumors about the company's possible revival as more than gossip. He reported that, as he left London, the assembly's agent, George Sandys, had lain a petition before the House of Commons wherein the colonists appeared to favor a resurrected company. The news goaded the assembly to a response. Crafting the reply immediately pushed aside all other legislative business and rapidly magnified divisions between councillors and burgesses. In those splits Berkeley discerned an opening that he exploited to the fullest. Siding with the burgesses who adamantly opposed a revived company in any form, he engineered passage of a sternly worded protest.

"The Declaration against the Company" bore the unmistakable mark of Berkeley's singular flair for the written word. Addressed to Charles I, it started with a tart repudiation of Sandys. It caustically disavowed Sandys's entreaty in "the name of the Adventurers and Planters in Virginia to the honourable House of Commons in Parliament in England for the restoring the Letters Patents of Incorporation to the Late Treasurer and Company." And, lest anyone doubt that Sandys had overstepped, that sharp disclaimer was followed by an equally piquant assertion that it was "neither the meaning nor Intent of the . . . Assembly

16. Craven, *Southern Colonies in the Seventeenth Century*, 151–53; Richard L. Morton, *Colonial Virginia* (Chapel Hill, N.C., 1960), 1:147–48; Richard Beale Davis, *George Sandys, Poet-Adventurer* (London, 1955), 257–64; "Instructions from Charles I," 10 Aug. 1641, Billings, *Old Dominion*, 51.

or Inhabitants here for to give way for the Introducing of the said Company or any other."[17]

Next, the manifesto announced that the assembly had "fully debated and Maturely considered the reasons on both sides as well arguing for as against a Company." Then came a clamorous attack on the wrongheadedness of returning Virginia to its former regime. The gist of that argument rose from the proposition that the "old Corporation [could not] with any possibility be again Introduced without absolute Ruin and dissolution to the Colony." Revival portended "Many illegal proceedings and barbarous Torments" of the sort that were documented in "Depositions taken at a Grand Assembly Anno 1632." Land titles granted after 1625 would face legal challenges, which would imperil all colonists who had patented real estate under royal warrant. The company would monopolize commerce, and the right to trade freely, "which is the Life and Blood of a Common Wealth," would be "impeached." These "Intollerable Calamities" contrasted strikingly with the status quo that "doth so much distinguish our happiness from that of the former times." Summing up, the declaration insisted that the assembly,

> having taken into Serious Consideration these and many other dangerous Effects which must be Concomitant in and from a Company or Corporation have thought fit to Declare and hereby do declare from our selves and all the Commonality of this Colony that it was never desired sought after nor Endeavoured to be sought for either directly or Indirectly by the Consent of any Grand Assembly or the Common consent of the people. And we do hereby further declare and Testifie to all the World that we will never admit the restoring of the said Company or any for or in their behalfs saving to our Selves herein a most faithful and loyal Obedience to his Sacred Majesty our dread Sovereign whose Royall Protection and Allowance and Maintenance of this our Just declaration and protestation we doubt not according to his accustomed Clemency an benignity to his Subjects find.

Then, to give the declaration added heft, the General Assembly enacted it into law. Statutory clauses penalized anyone who advocated covertly or openly "the reducing of this Colony to a Company or Corporation" with the loss of his entire estate "upon due Proof or Conviction of any of the Premises." The act took effect in Virginia immediately and within "five days after the Arrival of this our said Declaration Protestation and Act within the realm of England."[18]

17. Declaration against the Company, n.p., Randolph MS, ViHi. Customarily, engrossed texts of legislative documents and statutes bore the date on which an assembly session began rather than the actual date of adoption.

18. Declaration against the Company.

All the burgesses signed the engrossed text. Berkeley did too. Of the council's seven signatories—Bennett, Browne, Mathews, Peirce, Pettus, Wormeley, and Wyatt—Pettus and Wormeley were two whose stances on the company were unclear before the session. Their names on the document indicated their objections to revival. That Browne was a signer came as no surprise. He was obligated to Berkeley, and here was an occasion to repay a debt. Wyatt's endorsement was curious. Sir Francis was an officer and stockholder in the old Virginia Company as well as a member of the Dorset Commission and George Sandys's relation by marriage. Had he changed his mind? Probably not. More likely, he went along out of regard for the burgesses, who always esteemed him for his evenhanded treatment of them. Much more curious was why Bennett, Mathews, and Peirce signed. The three were staunch advocates of returning Virginia to company rule. They could not have endorsed the declaration out of goodness of heart. Neither were they inclined to stiffen Berkeley's hand. Instead, their signing displayed a calculated bit of political trimming. No one in Virginia could anticipate Parliament's, or the king's, response to the declaration. If the document carried the day, then Bennett, Mathews, and Peirce would have bet on the right horse. If not, they would hide in the crowd of assemblymen who had wagered as wrongly as they.[19]

Of the nine councillors who missed the session, Kemp, Littleton, and Yeardley were hostile to the company. Bernard, Brocas, Higginson, and West, held positions that are no longer discernible. As for Menifie and Willoughby, the one was an ally of Mathews; the other was not. Whether their voices could have altered the outcome is purely guesswork. Their absence reflected on them, but it signified nothing legally because the seven signatories constituted a quorum and then some.[20]

The declaration was speeded on its way toward England directly after it was signed. It reached the king in early summer. Writing from York on 5 July 1642, he replied in part: "Your so earnest desire to continue under our immediate Protection is very acceptable to Us; And that as Wee had not before the least intention to consent to the Introduction of any Company over that Our Colony, So wee are by it much confirmed in our former resolutions as thinking it unfitt to change a forme of Government wherein . . . Our Subjects there (having has so long experience of it) receive so much contentment and satisfaction." Encouraging though his words may have been, they were of no practical effect. Parliament

19. Jon Kukla, *Political Institutions in Virginia, 1619–1660* (New York, 1989), 106–7.
20. Declaration against the Company. The declaration is the sole record to survive from the journals and working papers of the April session.

had already abandoned Sandys, and it was about to field an army against Charles. And until royalist or Roundhead prevailed in battle, the controversies that divided them grabbed more of their attentions than did faraway Virginia.[21]

Months passed before any of this was apparent in Virginia. Meanwhile, Berkeley and the General Assembly moved on to other things. "Full debate and mature consideration" of the declaration warmed passions to such a degree that the "many and weighty Business begun . . . yet [did] remain unfinished." An adjournment to salve chafed sensibilities seemed in order. Although the chance of a break was appealing, it raised a constitutional question. Because the declaration had been signed into law, a recess might be construed as tantamount to a dissolution, in which case pending bills would lapse automatically, and no one, least of all Berkeley, wished that outcome. To "prevent all doubts," the assembly on its own authority "adjourned to the Thursday in Whitson week being the Second day of June next coming." At that time "the whole Body of this present Assembly consisting of the Governor Council and Burgesses shall repair to James City then and there to determine and finish all such matters as shall be found necessary to be concluded and Enacted whether in matters already begun or any Business that shall then begin or be proposed that may redound to the glory of God the Honour of his Majesty and the good of the Colony."[22]

The respite had the hoped-for effect. After the assembly returned from its vacation, it passed the remainder of Wyatt's refinements to county government and brought local administration closer "to the Law and Customs of England in proceedings of the Court and trials of Causes." Additionally, members ratified improved procedures for settling "differences and debates concerning Titles of Land or otherwise" and for delimiting the "Meats and bounds" of church parishes. Berkeley backed repeal of a head tax that funded one of his perquisites. (He did not lose much by way of income because in return the assembly gave him an orchard and two rental properties in Jamestown.) "Settling of Peace and friendship with the Indians . . . in Writing" and authorizing trade negotiations with the Maryland government tucked up all the loose ends but one. The statutes in force needed revision. That was an intricate chore, one that was not easily done, nor quickly, and certainly not by fatigued legislators. Seeing that this assembly could give no more, Berkeley put the task off for another day and sent the burgesses home.[23]

21. Charles I to Berkeley, 5 July 1642, CO 5/1354, fol. 237, PRO.

22. Declaration against the Company.

23. Hening, *Statutes at Large*, 1:267. None of the acts survive, but they were summarized in a remonstrance the General Assembly promulgated on 1 July 1642 (Randolph MS, ViHi). There is no text of the repealed poll tax law either.

In retrospect his first months on the job were successful ones. He grew in stature with the councillors, the burgesses, and the county magistrates. He isolated adversaries without breaching the boundary between opponents and enemies. He accepted Virginia's institutional arrangements largely as he had found them, and he demonstrated a willingness to join with the assembly in bettering them. Above all else, he made good his intention to govern with counsel but without being ruled by his councillors.

Cautious but not timorous, intrepid but not truculent, Berkeley revealed a deftness for navigating around conflicting personalities and steering between competing ambitions without foundering. Defusing Wyatt disclosed his knack for judicious husbanding of political capital. Showing his instructions from the king presaged an openness that abided for as long as he governed. Officiating as first among equals came as a refreshing departure from the antics of Sir John Harvey, who acted as though he still walked the quarterdeck of his ship and the councillors were his junior officers. Treating councillors with courtly deference played not only to their yearnings for a large share in Virginia's governance; it also lessened possibilities of future confrontations, and it was a sign of Berkeley's aim to become one with them.

Keenly aware of the prominence leading settlers ascribed to their nascent legislature, he saw in the General Assembly a likely counterweight to the power of the council. He seized the moment and assisted in drafting the declaration against the company. His support for Wyatt's reforms was a proffer for the burgesses' support too, whereas his approval of tax reform bid for popularity with the voters. Championing their issues was an important cue for the burgesses, for it heightened their collective sense of political worth as never before. As in the council, such a stratagem garnered adherents and corralled prospective foes. It did more besides. It was one in a series of bargains with Virginia's great men that gradually enabled Berkeley to win the upper hand.

Events during the remainder of 1642 favored him quite unexpectedly. Wyatt sailed back to England sometime that summer or fall, never to put his hand in Virginia affairs again.[24] With him out of the way, Berkeley had less to fear from the inevitable comparisons between his government and Wyatt's, nor did he need worry any longer about Sir Francis looking over his shoulder. Happily, too, Wyatt's departure created one of the three council vacancies that Berkeley filled with a member who was more favorably disposed toward him. William Claiborne returned from his extended stay in London before year's end. Berkeley had designs on winning him over, once the right opportunity presented itself, so he

24. Wyatt died in 1644.

treated Claiborne with gingerly respect. The fall council meetings were uneventful, though orders were drawn for the planting of settlements along the Piankatank River in what became Gloucester County. More ominously were portents of trouble with some of the natives. Maryland governor Leonard Calvert sent an urgent plea for a hundred militiamen to go "against the Indians," which the council evidently debated but may not have honored because of Claiborne's hostility to Marylanders. There was also some discussion of recent "outrages" closer to home. What to do about them involved secret preparations for retaliatory strikes. At some point, too, Berkeley sought advice about when to hold the next General Assembly. Everyone opted for 2 March 1642/43.[25]

He drew up the writs and dispatched them to the sheriffs, who polled the voters about four weeks before opening day. The elections produced a fresh crop of burgesses, who showed themselves quite friendly to their governor and to his designs for them. Some were apparent first-timers, whereas a few were veterans of earlier sessions. At least one, Robert Hutchinson, was Berkeley's tenant. Walter Aston, Walter Chiles, and Henry Filmer were linked to Berkeley too. Their presence, as well as the high rate of turnover, might be marks of Berkeley's influence upon the electorate. Such a conclusion seems tempting, even self-evident, given what happened at the session, but it is by no means verifiable. Candidates ran unopposed, and freeholders voted orally, and, like all Virginia canvasses in the seventeenth century, the dynamics of this election are cloaked with a darkness that cannot be brightened analytically.[26]

The General Assembly of March 1642/43 stood among the two or three most important legislatures of the Berkeley administration, and it ranks second in significance only to the founding assembly. Soon after Berkeley opened the session, he encouraged the burgesses to sit separate and apart from the Council of State as a House of Burgesses. The burgesses greeted his proposition enthusiastically, and the General Assembly became bicameral.[27]

Dividing the assembly was an elemental step in its transition from corporate appendage to representative legislature to little Parliament. Indeed, from 1643 onward members of both houses more deliberately turned to Parliament for inspiration, and they consciously modeled their procedures on the habits of the Westminster legislature. There were immediate, practical consequences as well. The new House of Burgesses needed its own chamber and officers. Existing re-

25. Robinson, "Notes," 237.
26. Compare the membership rosters for the sessions of 1642 and 1643 in Leonard, *General Assembly of Virginia*, 20, 21.
27. Kukla, *Political Institutions in Virginia*, 108–19.

cords are unrevealing of how the burgesses dealt with their new space requirements, though they hint broadly at who became the principal officers of the House.[28]

As in the House of Commons, there was now a speaker and a clerk. Both played hands that ensured the orderly dispatch of the General Assembly's legislative business. Mr. Speaker was the mouth of the House, meaning that he presided over debates, made committee assignments, and represented the burgesses in discussions with the governor and council. The clerk, on the other hand, did all of the bill drafting, acted as reader, and managed the house calendar. From the beginning there was one notable difference between the two bodies. Burgesses had free choice of their officers. The commons did not.[29]

By allowing the House of Burgesses this extraordinary privilege, Berkeley gave up a tool comparable to one the Crown used to steer Parliament. Yet there was an underlying political logic to what he did, especially in the context of his own situation in the spring of 1643. He still lacked more than a nucleus of support. His concession was in keeping with his already assiduous courting of the burgesses in search of allies. Besides, it did not cost him all that much. He could charm the House, or he could bring it around with other means at his disposal. More important, his chief concern remained mastering the council, which, to his way of thinking, still posed the greatest hazard to the success of his administration. Inviting the burgesses to found a house of their own lessened that risk on two accounts. Physically separating the councillors from the burgesses curtailed conciliar sway over them. Institutionally, the House itself counterbalanced the council, which would enable him to play the two against each other.[30]

The burgesses' picks for clerk and speaker smack of deals being struck before the actual division of the assembly took place. John Meade (1612–45?) became the first clerk of the House. A trained scribe, he was a protégé of Secretary Kemp, who had brought him out of England to work as Richard Lee's deputy. Meade's training made him a natural to clerk for the burgesses, and he served the budding House in good stead until he died, but his qualifications were of secondary importance. Once the assembly divided, Kemp stood to lose the gift of a place. His animus toward the Mathews-Claiborne group inclined him to favor Berkeley's idea because of its potential for confounding his antagonists. And he was not

28. Billings, *Little Parliament,* 250 n. 22, 259 n. 6.

29. Ibid., 115.

30. William Hakewill, comp., *Modus tenendi Parliamentum: Or, The Old Manner of Holding Parliaments in England* (London, 1641), 15–16, 36–38.

without friends among the burgesses. Therefore, he may well have capitalized on those connections to ensure Meade's election.[31]

Thomas Stegge got the nod for speaker. On its face the choice seems slightly odd because to become speaker Stegge resigned from the council and ran as a representative for Charles City County. Furthermore, he appears not to have been a burgess in any of the previous assemblies, and he never sat in the House of Burgesses after 1643.

Berkeley could have prevented Stegge's election, just as he could have opposed his candidacy for the speakership. He did not, which implies he bargained with the Mathews-Claiborne faction. In return for their support for dividing the assembly, Mathews and Claiborne got a shot at putting one of their own in the speaker's chair. Berkeley readily accepted Stegge, who was beholden to him for his appointment to the council. Kemp liked him as well. And there appears to have been a tacit understanding among all concerned that, after the session concluded, Stegge would return to the council. In the end everyone got something in return for backing the partition of the assembly.[32]

Once it reorganized, the assembly took up the business of a thorough tune-up of the laws in force. A decade had passed since the previous overhaul. In that time accretions of "many and sundry acts and laws" contributed to a disarray that was "very prejudicall to the Collony," especially in light of the institutional changes that were made in 1642. Turning to the task at hand, the newly bicameral General Assembly resorted to a process that originated in the 1630s and remained standard practice throughout the seventeenth century. First, it repealed existing "acts and lawes." Then it surveyed the nullified statutes with a view toward reframing and retaining all those that it deemed as still useful to public purposes. Next, it added legislation to address current imperatives before it debated the draft and passed it. The resulting restatement mingled the old and the new into a code that ordered some seventy acts roughly by the types of activities they regulated.[33]

Years later Berkeley singled out two statutes that were "put into acts by my solicitation." The revised code itself quite clearly documents many more that bore the sign of his hand. Laws that generally tidied up ecclesiastical administra-

---

31. Jon Kukla, *Speakers and Clerks of the Virginia House of Burgesses, 1643–1776* (Richmond, 1981), 137. Stegge returned to the council in June 1643 and attended with regularity thereafter (Robinson, "Notes," 238; LNDWI, 1637–46, 238; LNOB, 1646–50, fols. 70, 112).

32. Edward Hill, an ally of Berkeley's, succeeded Stegge as speaker in the General Assemblies of 1644 and 1645 (Kukla, *Speakers and Clerks*, 37).

33. Hening, *Statutes at Large*, 1:239, 240, 238–82.

tion or commanded conformity to church canons and the "littergie" of the Book of Common Prayer were his doing. So, too, an act that debarred Catholics from office and their priests from settling in the colony. Those particular statutes flowed directly from a royal instruction, which required him to hold spiritual practice true to the established religion. Another of his acts codified an instruction to exempt councillors from "all publick charges and taxes, church duties onely accepted." More generally, he advocated reenactment of all the recent changes in local government. He thereby fostered an increase in the jurisdiction of the county courts in ways that magnified the compass and the eminence of the justices of the peace. In turn, augmenting the courts advanced the division of authority between county and province, it invested emerging county elites with the potential to monopolize local affairs, and it ensured him greater latitude in determining the course of public policy.[34]

The experience of becoming bicameral and revising the laws in force moved the General Assembly way down the road toward becoming a little parliament. It also led to a deeper understanding of how the governor and the burgesses related to one another as politicians. Both had much to learn about the intricacies of legislatures. The interplay between them in succeeding assemblies educated them as both cautiously discovered which responsibilities dwelt exclusively with Berkeley, which belonged mainly to the burgesses, and which were shared prerogatives. His persistent grooming allowed ample leeway for the burgesses to perfect the workings of their House with minimal gubernatorial intrusion. In return, the House usually followed his lead.

Having put the burgesses more or less into his pocket, Berkeley renewed his currying favor with whomever seemed receptive to his blandishments. The death of treasurer Roger Wingate presented him with an opportunity that he cleverly used to diminish Samuel Mathews and William Claiborne. Wingate's passing not only vacated one of the more profitable provincial offices; it also left emptied a seat at the council. The chair went to Richard Moryson. The brother of Lettice, Viscountess Falkland, wife of Berkeley's mentor during his days at court, Moryson was a friendly face. Claiborne accepted the tender of the treasurer's post. By taking the offer, he was now beholden to Berkeley, which lessened his clout and distanced him from Mathews.[35]

34. Petition to the Committee for Foreign Plantations, [21 July 1666], CO 1/16, fols. 183–84, PRO; Hening, *Statutes at Large*, 1:248–49, 260, 241, 277, 268, 279; "Instructions from Charles I," 10 Aug. 1641, Billings, *Old Dominion*, 51; Warren M. Billings, "The Growth of Political Institutions in Virginia, 1634 to 1676," *WMQ*, 3d ser., 31 (1974): 230–45; Billings, "The Transfer of English Law to Virginia, 1606–1650," in K. R. Andrews, N. P. Canny, and P. E. H. Hair, eds., *The Westward Enterprise: English Activities in Ireland, the Atlantic, and America, 1480–1650* (Liverpool, 1978), 226–42.

35. Robinson, "Notes," 33, 238.

It was a different story with Richard Lee. He and Berkeley worked closely to-gether while he clerked for the council and the General Assembly. Proximity led to lifelong friendship that Berkeley nurtured at every opportunity after 1643. The division of the assembly diminished Lee's rewards from the clerkship because the remuneration that accrued from bill drafting and other legislative charges passed from him to the new clerk of the House. Berkeley offset Lee's losses in a novel fashion. He turned to a warrant in his instructions that empowered him to "nominate and appoint all other publique Officers under the degree of the Coun-cill," and he created the post of attorney general for Lee. Berkeley could justify his creation as an advance in the way pleas of the Crown were argued before the Quarter Court. The office had English precedents, because it was the attorney general who prosecuted for the Crown in the royal courts of justice. More practi-cally, a permanent officeholder relieved Berkeley of designating an attorney gen-eral ad hoc at every session of the Quarter Court. From Lee's standpoint the place graced him as a favorite of the governor and rewarded him with fees. Berkeley also named him to the bench of York County, and he sat in the House of Burgesses before he wound up on the Council of State in 1651.[36]

Argoll Yeardley also became an important ally economically as well as politi-cally. The eldest son of a former governor-general, Yeardley eased into politics at an early age, and he entered the council in 1639, while still in his twenties. An active merchant-planter, he found much of his livelihood in commerce with the Dutch. His second wife, Ann Custis, tightened his bonds to the Netherlands even more. She belonged to an Anglo-Dutch family from Rotterdam. Blood ties and common business interests reinforced Yeardley's loose alliance with like-minded merchant-planters who joined the Eastern Shore and the lower James River basin to the Holland trade. Besides Yeardley, the group included Nathaniel Littleton, Thomas Willoughby, Secretary Kemp, Richard Lee, Edmund Scarburgh, Year-dley's brother Francis, and Adam Thoroughgood, a Lower Norfolk County jus-tice, whose daughter Sarah had married a Dutch trader, Simon Overzee. (Overzee later wed Willoughby's daughter Elizabeth.) The network connected to Amsterdam via Berkeley through Richard Glover. Another of the Anglo-Dutch merchants with Virginia interests, Glover trucked mainly around Jamestown and along the York River. The Berkeley-Glover link drew into the mix councillors

36. Ludwell Lee Montague, "Richard Lee 1613?–64, the Immigrant," *Virginia Magazine of History and Biography (VMHB)* 74 (1966): 3–22; "Instructions from Charles I," 10 Aug. 1641, Billings, *Old Dominion*, 52; Robinson, "Notes," 238; Leonard, *General Assembly of Virginia*, xx, 26; John R. Pagan, "Dutch Maritime and Commercial Activity in Mid-Seventeenth-Century Virginia," *VMHB* 90 (1982): 488–90.

George Ludlow, Bridges Freemen, and Ralph Wormeley; burgesses Robert Holt and Stephen Gill; and numerous well-heeled independent merchant-planters.[37]

Yeardley was also instrumental in bringing his brother-in-law John Custis to the governor's attention. Custis had settled in Northampton County about the time of his sister's marriage. His fluency in the Dutch tongue proved the asset that attracted Berkeley, who used him as a translator on more than one occasion. Their association sparked a lifelong intimacy between the two men and profited Custis handsomely. He gained lands, preferments, and the heights of Virginia politics.[38]

Shared visions of the promise of sericulture attracted another group to Berkeley. Much smaller than the Yeardley coalition, it numbered magistrates in Nansemond and Charles City counties, plus others, who experimented with silk before Berkeley appeared on the scene and gravitated toward them. In time the group grew to include Thomas Pettus, Edward Digges, and Sir Henry Chicheley, whom Berkeley enticed to follow his example. They, too, became close friends, especially after he gave them seats on the Council of State and provincial offices.[39]

Berkeley's wooing of the great men got a sudden boost from an unexpected quarter. The Indian leader Opechancanough believed that the arrival of a new governor and turmoil in Britain so preoccupied the colonists that they might drop their guard just long enough for him to deliver a lethal blow. He calculated correctly. Even though Berkeley and the more knowledgeable Indian experts had picked up hints, no one seemed to have detected Opechancanough's massing of forces. Indeed, neither the governor nor the council had done much to beef up armaments or forces in the event of trouble.

Opechancanough attacked on the morning of 18 April 1644. He chose the date deliberately because of its religious significance for the settlers. That year 18 April was Maundy Thursday, one of the holy days in the week between Palm Sunday and Easter Day. Opechancanough knew the English preoccupation with things of the spirit rather than their regard for things of the world would lull his enemies even deeper into carelessness. Their inattention safeguarded the priceless element of surprise on which he banked for victory. The strategy worked to perfection, at least in its initial phases. Over five hundred colonists died in the opening assault. More lost their lives or were taken captive as the fighting spread in

37. James B. Lynch Jr., *The Custis Chronicles: The Years of Migration* (Camden, Maine, 1993), 135–39; YDWI, 1645–49, 95.

38. Nicholas Luccketti, Edward A. Chappell, and Beverly A. Straube, *Archaeology: Excavations at the Ancestral Custis Plantation, Northampton County, Virginia* (Jamestown, Va., 1999), 7–9; Lynch, *Custis Chronicles*, 157–71.

39. Samuel Hartlib, *The Reformed Virginia Silk-Worm . . .* (London, 1655), 31–35.

the days that followed. Stunning though the fatalities were, they scarcely over-whelmed the colony, though it was abundantly clear that Opechancanough meant to drive the English from Virginia. Whether he succeeded depended upon his ability to best the colonists on the field of battle.[40]

Perhaps because Berkeley was mindful of the mistake of Charles I in warring on the Scots without public support, he decided to look immediately to the General Assembly for its blessing and financial backing. A hastily called assembly met on 1 June 1644 to map out a battle plan. The most critical need was military hardware. In the discussion about addressing the shortage, everyone agreed that Berkeley should promptly "repaire for England and Implore his Majesty's gracious assistance for our Releife." The assembly gave him letters of credit and underwrote his travel expenses. Sending him abroad raised political questions about who would be in charge of the government and who would take the fight to Opechancanough. Reluctant to trust that much power to one individual, Berkeley divided the responsibility between Kemp, who became deputy governor, and Claiborne, who became general of the forces. Just as soon as he signed the necessary commissions and drafted other instructions, Berkeley boarded an awaiting vessel, and by 22 June he was headed for London.[41]

There he soon saw the folly of his mission. Civil war turned the British Isles into an armed camp to the discomfort of friend and foe alike. Destruction was everywhere, with more, much more, likely to follow. Queen Henrietta Maria was on the Continent in search of money and support for her husband's cause. The Wits had long since scattered to the winds. Suckling and viscount Falkland were dead, and so were others from the old court circles. Sir John Berkeley led the king's forces in Devonshire and Cornwall. Sir Edward Hyde and Sir Charles Berkeley were in the inner ring of Crown advisors. The war was not going well for the royalists, and Virginia could expect no help from King Charles because he was too absorbed in his fight with the parliamentarians to come to the aid of his remote colony.

Berkeley got caught up in the campaigning in the West Country. Had he chosen, he could have solicited an officer's commission. He did not, possibly because he recalled the unhappy results of last time he fought beside Charles. Officers

40. Robert Beverley, *The History and Present State of Virginia,* ed. Louis B. Wright (Chapel Hill, N.C., 1947), 60–61; William L. Shea, *The Virginia Militia in the Seventeenth Century* (Baton Rouge, 1983), 57–72.

41. Act authorizing Berkeley's return to England, 1 June 1644, Acts of Assembly, Clerk's Office, Chesapeake, Va.; commission to William Claiborne, 1 June 1644, "Acts, Orders and Resolutions of the General Assembly of Virginia: At Sessions of March 1643–1646," *VMHB* 22 (1915): 229–34; Robinson, "Notes," 239.

who had shamed him during the Second Bishops' War now stood beneath the royal standard, and the recollection of his humiliation at their hands had not yet lost all of its bite. Memories aside, something else surely tugged at him: the realization that having a command would mean abandoning the colony for a long while and maybe for good. That was not a prospect he relished because of his deepening attachments for Virginia. And so, he took his leave of the king, bought what arms he could, and went home as quickly as he could find a westbound vessel.[42]

Landing at Jamestown in June 1645, he discovered that the war had gone badly in his absence. Claiborne proved an indifferent general who was bent more on using the militia to settle a personal vendetta with the Marylanders than in defeating the Indians. Berkeley put him aside and took the field himself. He sprang a trap on the natives which resulted in capture or death for a number of subchieftains, though Opechancanough eluded him. Then he pillaged the Indians' cornfields and torched their villages until the coming of cold weather quieted the campaign. The following spring he met with the General Assembly, and together they perfected a plan that ended the war. They recruited a special force of militia for the express purpose of taking Opechancanough. The troops hounded their quarry and cornered him at length. A messenger brought the news to Berkeley, who "with a Party of Horse . . . made a speedy march and surprized him in his Quarters." Jubilantly, he brought his captive to Jamestown, intending to ship him to England, but a militiaman bayoneted the old man as he lay in chains in the town jail. Necotowance, who replaced the dead leader, sued for peace. A jubilant Berkeley presided at the negotiations that produced a draft treaty, which he presented to the General Assembly for its approval.[43]

The compact, ratified in October 1646, was the first Anglo-Indian agreement ever vouchsafed by legislative fiat. That Berkeley submitted it to the assembly's consideration was another of his gestures toward winning favor, but he had an additional purpose in mind as well. Ratification by the General Assembly codified his control of Indian affairs and put the attendant policy matters beyond the reach of the councillors alone. Future changes would require statutory enactment, meaning that the entire assembly must consent to them.

Defeat cost the beaten natives enormously. By terms of their capitulation they acknowledged that they were now tributaries, and, in recognition of that inferior

---

42. *Court Mercurie*, 11 Sept. 1644; Berkeley to Francis Moryson, 11 Feb. 1676/77, Coventry Papers, 77, fol. 426; William S. Powell, *The Proprietors of Carolina* (Raleigh, N.C., 1968), 30–31, 13.

43. William L. Shea, "Virginia at War, 1644–1646," *Military Affairs* 41 (1977): 142–77; Hening, *Statutes at Large*, 1:317–19, 323–26; Beverley, *History and Present State of Virginia*, 61–62; Wesley Frank Craven, "Indian Policy in Early Virginia," *William and Mary Quarterly*, 3d ser., 1 (1944): 65–82.

status, they agreed to pay the governor a yearly gift of twenty beaver skins. They gave up most of their homelands to the colonists. In return they got a reservation north of the York River. Indians were forbidden to consort with settlers without special permission, and they were compelled to wear identifying coats and badges whenever they passed through English settlements. Henceforth, they admitted colonial law, not tribal custom, as the basis for settling all civil or criminal disputes between themselves and the English. The treaty also called for a string of forts along the frontier that would act as a defensive perimeter and an early warning system.

In short, here was a blueprint for the moment and for the future that was predicated on a plain calculus. Lasting peace required subjugation of all Indians who lived in proximity to the settlers. The two peoples should be separated as far as practicable, and the governor should regulate all contact between them.

The Treaty of 1646 formed the core of Anglo-Indian relations for nearly thirty years. However much Berkeley may have wished to honor it, he never succeeded in enforcing it to the letter. Heightened immigration flooded thousands of new settlers into Virginia throughout the 1640s and beyond. Berkeley could not prevent these immigrants from inundating the reservation, and within a decade of the treaty signing there were three new counties carved from it. On a daily basis the stolen hog, the damaged crop, the underhanded deal, the personal insult, the occasional assault, were constant sources of tension that he could do little to relieve. Conversely, Berkeley's predilection for leaving local problems to local magistrates invited treaty violations that caught his notice only when they threatened to get out of hand. Nor was he inclined to rein in the leading traders. *Regulation* did not mean shutting out the bigwigs. Far from it. Those with controlling interests retained their monopolies, but, although their need of his indulgence kept them on his tether, he allowed them free rein. And, like virtually every other Briton, he assumed the worst about the natives even as he accepted the desirability of incorporating them into his designs for Virginia. That duality, no less than desultory injuries and usurpations, kept the relationship between settler and Indian bubbling, but, as long as things stewed just below the flash point, the colony remained at peace.

Winning the war and gaining the peace made Berkeley more popular than ever before, which obviously raised the value of his political stock. He invested some of his dividends in improving Jamestown and reaching out to the Dutch as he held the London merchants at arm's length. Once he comprehended the colonists' attachments for Jamestown, he made no effort to move the capital elsewhere or to advocate the founding of new cities across Virginia, despite his instructions. He elected, instead, to build up Jamestown. Before the war diverted him, he telegraphed his intention to retain Jamestown as the colony's seat of government and principal metropolis. He got the General Assembly to renew legislation making the "James Cittie" Virginia's sole port of entry, and he secured other laws that were designed to lure artisans and leading planters. Those steps attracted assorted artisans and others who followed their traditional occupations. He also attempted to lead by example, which was a reason for starting his townhouse and introducing Virginians to the virtues of ice pits.[44]

Berkeley picked up where he had left off once the hostilities ceased. In 1649 he signed legislation that promoted Jamestown in a major way commercially. He patterned his law on English statutes that had regulated traffic in market towns for centuries. The act set up a "weekly markett" place where colonists from near and far could come and bargain for anything vendible. To that purpose, it specified a town lot "bounded . . . from the Sandy Gutt, comonly called and knowne by the name of Peter Knight's store westward and soe to the gutt next beyond the house of Lancelott Elay eastward, and bounded on the north side with the back river." Markets, which were "holden upon every Wednesday and Saturday," opened for business between eight in the morning and six in the evening. Supervising them was a clerk of the market, who collected fees for his services. A gubernatorial appointee, the clerk assigned vendor space and generally supervised exchanges. He maintained the official weights and measures, registered all sales, and resolved all quarrels over pricing and other terms of exchange.[45]

With this law and other inducements, Berkeley achieved results by midcentury that gave Jamestown a look and feel of a stable community that it had lacked heretofore. It was still a tiny place, despite the cascade of new immigrants who generally regarded plantation society as more congenial to their hopes than urban living. The turf fort, begun around the time of Berkeley's arrival, guarded the river approach to the town. Ships lined refurbished wharves, their holds crammed with cargoes from afar or gorged with tobacco bound for overseas ports. One or more warehouses stood nearby. Residents worked at their crafts or farmed the fields beyond the town limits. Taverns and alehouses afforded momentary relaxation. The brick church, a now familiar landmark, gave spiritual

44. Hening, *Statutes at Large*, 1:245–46, 252, 300, 330, 331; [John Ferrar], *A Perfect Description of Virginia* (London, 1649), 3; J. Paul Hudson, *A Pictorial Booklet on Early Jamestown Commodities and Industries* (Williamsburg, 1957), 76; John L. Cotter, *Archaeological Excavations at Jamestown, Virginia* (Washington, D.C., 1958), 147–50; Mark Girouard, *Life in the English Country House: A Social and Architectural History* (New Haven, Conn., 1978), 262.

45. Hening, *Statutes at Large*, 362; Edmund Wingate, comp., *An Exact Abridgment of all Statutes in Force and Use. From the Beginning of Magna Charta, Untill 1641* (London, 1670), 79–80; Cay, *Abridgment*, 1, under "Clerk of the market."

refuge and a space where parishioners swapped gossip before or after worship. Suitors plied their suits in the James City County court or at the Quarter Court. Out-of-towners crowded the secretary's office or sought audience with their governor. Sessions of the General Assembly spoke to the town's political significance, but further improvements came to an abrupt stop after Berkeley was driven from office.[46]

Before and after the Anglo-Indian War of 1644–46 Berkeley also got two major pieces of legislation through the General Assembly, both of which widened commercial access to Holland and furthered his policy of free trade. The first statute was part of the revised code of March 1642/43. By it the assembly expressly declared that "any merchant, factors or others of the Dutch nation [could] import wares and merchandizes and [could] trade or traffique for the commoditys of the collony in any shipps of their owne or belonging to the Netherlands." The act was a setback for the Claiborne-Mathews faction. It signaled the ascendancy of Yeardley and his cohorts, and, for the first time, Virginia gave statutory recognition of the Dutch as trading partners.[47]

The law did not go unchallenged. Claiborne and Mathews pulled their ties to the London mercantile establishment to alert Parliament, but, because of the Civil War, a response was several years in coming. In February 1646/47 Parliament enacted a bill to encourage what it called English "Adventurers to the several Plantations . . . of America" and to discourage the colonists from trucking with the Dutch. That measure provoked the second piece of Berkeley's legislation.[48]

A text of the parliamentary act reached Jamestown while the General Assembly of April 1647 was in session. Berkeley's response took the form of a statutory declaration openly questioning Parliament's power to bind the colonists because of a "right & priviledge" that "by ancient Charter" permitted "the planters to entertaine trade with any nation or people in amitye with his Majestie." Not only that, but the act intruded upon the "libertye of the Collony & a right of deare esteeme to free borne persons (vidzt) that noe lawe should bee established within the kingdome of England concerninge us, without the consent of a grand Assemblye here." Quite possibly, the declaration continued, Parliament had been misled by the "wylie & spetious pretences" of Londoners and other English traders.

46. Warren M. Billings, "Vignettes of Jamestown," *Virginia Cavalcade* 45 (1996): 172–73; William M. Kelso, Nicholas M. Luccketti, and Beverly A. Straube, *Jamestown Rediscovery V* (Richmond, 1999), 15–20.

47. Hening, *Statutes at Large*, 1:258–59.

48. An Ordinance for encouragement of Adventurers to the several Plantations of Virginia, Bermudas, Barbados, and other places of America, 23 Jan. 1646/47, C. F. Firth and R. S. Rait, eds., *Acts and Ordinances of the Interregnum, 1642–1660* (London, 1911), 1:912.

If so, that was no excuse for "the most honorable houses" to trample upon "the rights, immunities & priviledges of our Charter by as due a Clayme belongeinge to us, . . . [that] were the Conditionall reward & [recompense] propounded for our Undertakings in those rugged paths of Plantation." The declaration closed on a defiant note. Saying "wee doe againe invite the Dutch Nation, & againe publish & declare all Freedome & libertie to them to trade within the Collony," it promised "ourselves & the whole Collony to defend them with our uttermost power & abilitye."[49]

For the next few years Berkeley's commercial policy went unmet by anything coming out of Westminster. Meanwhile, the Dutch in New Amsterdam got wind of the declaration because in November 1647 their governor-general Peter Stuyvesant (1592–1672) wrote seeking to establish a formal trade agreement between the two colonies. As a sweetener, Stuyvesant made Berkeley the gift of a finely bred Spanish horse. Stuyvesant, whom the Dutch West India Company had recently translated from Curaçao to New Amsterdam, was clearly interested in strengthening the company's ties to the Chesapeake, but Berkeley held back from formalizing a relationship between the two colonies. For certain Stuyvesant's letter was hardly Berkeley's first contact with New Netherlands. He dealt there through Sir Henry Moody, who lived on eastern Long Island, and Paulus Leendertsen van der Grist, a New Amsterdamer, well before Stuyvesant appeared on the scene. Subsequently, he used Moody as his go-between on official matters, whereas Leendertsen initiated a series of transactions between himself and the two governors that continued into the 1660s.[50]

Berkeley nearly wrecked his commercial and political successes on the shoals of an ill-considered religious agenda. The source of that misguided policy originated in two of the king's instructions. Charles I was as determined to impose his view of church polity in Virginia as he was bent on enforcing it in Britain. He commanded "That . . . you be carefull Almighty God may be duly and daily served according to the forme of Religion Established in the Church of England

49. Declaration concerning the Dutch trade, 5 Apr. 1647, Acts of Assembly, 1647, Clerk's Office, Chesapeake, Va.

50. Pagan, "Dutch Maritime and Commercial Activity in Mid-Seventeenth-Century Virginia," 472–85; Stuyvesant to Berkeley, 24 Nov. 1647, New York Colonial Documents, 12, New York State Archives, Albany; and E. B. O'Callahagan, comp., *Calendar of Historical Manuscripts in the Office of the Secretary of State, Albany, N.Y.* (Albany, 1865), 270; Henk den Heijer, *De geshiedenis van WIC* (Zutphen, 1994), 85–88; due bill to Stuyvesant, 30 Nov. 1649, Miscellaneous MS, New-York Historical Society, New York City; discharge to Leendertsen, 14 Dec. 1650, Miscellaneous MS, New-York Historical Society. Berkeley was initially acquainted with Moody through his cousin Francis Lovelace (Daniel Lovelace, "Governor, Diplomat, Soldier, Spy: The Colorful Career of Colonel Francis Lovelace [1622–1675]," MS, 10).

both by Your selfe and the people under your charge." His second admonition required administering the oath of allegiance to all colonists as a means of smoking out dissenters. At court Berkeley had witnessed firsthand his master's unforgiving pursuit of orthodoxy and had privately rejected Charles's quest as wrongheaded. Now his personal feelings were quite beside the point. His office obliged him to impose the royal pleasure on the colonists as best he could, but, in attempting to do exactly as the king had bidden him, he invited the great risk of replicating the strife in Britain that set Anglican against Puritan.[51]

From the colony's earliest days distance and neglect spared the settlers the din of the theological disputations that embroiled their kindred in the British Isles. A strange new world, few priests, and scanty institutional buttresses begot a colonial church nearer to the model of James I than that of his son. Virginians read their Bibles, prayed daily and earnestly to a just God, and turned to the Book of Common Prayer for direction in their private or corporate devotions. Their belief that the fundamental tenets of Christianity counted for more than theological correctness promoted an ecumenical view of Anglicanism and an acceptance of heterodox opinions regarding the ambiguities of faith and practice. Attitudes such as these allowed for a polity that bent toward the Church of England without insistence upon unswerving conformity to a single, rigid interpretation of Anglican teachings. In their quiet, accidental way the colonists thus created an environment in which staunch Anglicans and stiff Puritans, and those in between, lived in peace and in harmony as they went about their daily lives and work or when they met in church. Even the odd Catholic found a measure of tolerance and acceptance.[52]

Such churchmanship was not all that different from Berkeley's own notion of what it meant to be Anglican. The similarity eluded him before he left London because he had learned precious little about the state of religion in Virginia during his Whitehall years. Impatient to prove himself diligent in a matter he knew Charles held very close to his heart, he was not about to act the sloth. He would make the colonists conform. And, without carefully considering the consequences, he pushed the General Assembly of March 1642/43 to adopt the king's instructions as statutes.[53]

In and of itself cobbling the king's orders about the "forme of Religion" into law aroused no apparent ill feelings in the assembly. Members could construe

51. "Instructions from Charles I," 10 Aug. 1641, Billings, *Old Dominion*, 51.

52. Edward L. Bond, *Damned Souls in a Tobacco Colony: Religion in Seventeenth-Century Virginia* (Macon, Ga., 2001), 93–144.

53. Hening, *Statutes at Large*, 241–43, 277.

the relevant acts as refined expressions of legislation that had been on the books in one version or another ever since 1624, especially because such improvements were part and parcel of the assembly's restatement of the statutes in force. Such a construction found no favor with dissenters, least of all three Puritan divines from Massachusetts Bay who showed up in January 1643 bearing letters of introduction to Berkeley from Governor John Winthrop.[54]

The three had come at the invitation of colonists who lived in Isle of Wight, Nansemond, and an adjoining part of Lower Norfolk County, where Puritan-leaning settlers were more numerous than just about anywhere in Virginia. That the region also suffered from a shortage of clergy explains why locals of all persuasions looked northward to Boston. It was the nearest place where they might find godly ministers who were willing to attend to their spiritual needs. Their choices only hardened Berkeley's resolve to enforce the new conformity laws.[55]

He expelled the Massachusetts clergymen and ordered all colonists to swear the oath of allegiance or face the consequences. As a result, Anglican and Puritan Virginians skated perilously close to open warfare. Opechancanough's attack and Berkeley's trip to England turned attentions elsewhere. For as long as the fighting continued, the colonists paid more attention to defeating their enemy than to how they prayed or who preached over them. By war's end Berkeley had experienced something of an epiphany too.[56]

The trip to England was a lesson in the horrors of religious strife, and it rekindled something in William Berkeley that he had learned from the Bishops' Wars. No amount of compulsion could force people of faith down paths they refused to tread. They would either kill or die for what they believed. In turn he recognized that, if he wanted to unite the colonists behind him, he must distance himself from an ecclesiastical policy that identified him too closely with the king's religious views. At length he saw in the religious polity he had nearly upset spiritual arrangements that comforted him. Being the king's servant, he still felt driven to devise a means of honoring his duty to Charles while contenting his constituents. His solution, which emerged in a statute from the General Assembly of November 1647, displayed the ingenuity of a nimble mind. The act, with-

54. Ibid., 1:124–25, 180; Edward Johnson to John Ferrar, 25 Mar. 1650, Ferrar Papers, fol. 1160, Magdalene College, Cambridge.

55. LNOB, 1637–46, fols. 1–5, 28, 27, 50, 55, 59; John Bennett Boddie, *Seventeenth Century Isle of Wight County: A history of the County of Isle of Wight, Virginia, during the Seventeenth Century, including abstracts of the county records* (Chicago, 1938), 6–31, 54–61; Jon Butler, ed., "Two 1642 Letters from Virginia Puritans," Massachusetts Historical Society *Proceedings* 84 (1972): 105–9; George Carrington Mason, *Colonial Churches of Tidewater Virginia* (Richmond, 1945), 187–88.

56. Bond, *Damned Souls in a Tobacco Colony*, 150–52.

out saying so directly, repealed the oath of allegiance as a test of conformity and the banishment of dissenting clergy. It reaffirmed the long-standing requirement that "all ministers in their severall cures throughout the colony doe duly upon every Sabboth day read such prayers as are appointed and prescribed unto them" by acts of parliament, the canons of the church, the Book of Common Prayer, and colonial legislation. Additionally, the law authorized vestries in those parishes in which the ministers refused to use the prayer book to withhold the tithes that supported clergy stipends. Such a situation was not likely to arise because vestries had the legal right to engage whom they chose, and conforming or nonconforming vestries would presumably seek out like-minded men of the cloth.[57]

For all of his resourcefulness Berkeley did not put the religious issue completely behind him. Or, more properly, others would not let him. Foremost among those who would not was the Reverend Thomas Harrison.[58] Harrison took up the cure of Elizabeth River Parish, Lower Norfolk County, and became for Berkeley what Anthony Panton had been to him: a fractious clergyman who threatened his hold on power. Difficulties between Harrison, his vestry, and his flock ensued because of his refusal to use the prayer book, and, when the county court could not settle the broils, it fell to Berkeley and the Council of State to compose them. A writ went out ordering Harrison's appearance at Jamestown, but what he said to the council is not known. The best guess is that Harrison promised to be obedient, but his nonconforming ways soon led an aggravated governor to banish him. The peripatetic parson went to Boston, married a cousin of Governor Winthrop, and eventually wound up in Ireland as chaplain to Henry Cromwell, Oliver's brother. His troubles with Berkeley caught the notice of Parliament, and they were among things that led to Berkeley's removal.[59]

The more Charles's power declined, the greater the likelihood that Berkeley would lose his place. Indeed, about the time the Anglo-Indian War of 1644–46 broke out, some in Parliament anticipated Berkeley's overthrow. Chief among them was Robert Rich, second earl of Warwick (1587–1658), who for more than

57. Hening, *Statutes at Large,* 1:341–42.

58. Harrison (1619–82) was from Kingston-upon-Hull, Yorkshire. A tradition, which modern scholars have repeated, holds that he was Berkeley's private chaplain (Philip Alexander Bruce, *Institutional History of Virginia in the Seventeenth Century* [New York, 1910], 1:253–58; John H. Latané, *The Early Relations between Maryland and Virginia,* in Herbert B. Adams, ed., *Johns Hopkins University Studies in Historical and Political Science,* 13th ser., 13 [1895]: 41–44; Bond, *Damned Souls in a Tobacco Colony,* 153). I found nothing in Berkeley's papers or other contemporary evidence to corroborate the story, and it got no credence in Francis Burton Harrison, "The Reverend Thomas Harrison, Berkeley's 'Chaplain,'" *VMHB* 53 (1945): 302–11.

59. Bond, *Damned Souls in a Tobacco Colony,* 153–54.

forty years had had a hand in Virginia and all manner of other colonial enterprises. In November 1643 Parliament named Warwick governor-in-chief and lord
high admiral of all the colonies as well as chairman of a commission it charged
with ruling the overseas plantations.[60]

Civil war prevented Warwick's commission from intruding upon Virginia,
though it did not deter the earl from considering what might be done to establish
Parliament's writ there. His first inclination was to let the Virginians rule themselves, and he was not necessarily averse to leaving Berkeley in place, just so long
as everyone accepted the commission's oversight. He made known those intentions in a letter for public consumption that he sent westward early in 1644. But
he was also quick to reach out to Samuel Mathews, who he knew was friendly to
the parliamentary cause and who was in England at the moment. Much of what
he wrote to Mathews repeated his earlier letter, though he implied that, if Mathews maneuvered Berkeley from office and was elected instead, such a change
would not be unwelcome. Warwick's attitude toward Berkeley hardened after he
learned of the governor's religious policies, but even then he seemed more disappointed than hostile. In the end Mathews stayed in England, the Warwick commission was preoccupied by the turn of events in Britain, and for the time being
Berkeley continued where he was.[61]

Berkeley's ultimate challenge followed the trial and beheading of Charles I. In
July 1649 the parliamentary Council of State officially informed Sir William of
the king's execution and the abolition of the monarchy. The council also enjoined his obedience to the new government, and it ordered him to await further
instructions. Without saying so directly, the dispatches hinted at the council's
willingness to keep him on in return for his changing allegiances.[62]

When Berkeley got the news, he wasted no sorrow on the hapless Charles,
though he was not about to be tempted by the Puritan Parliament. His disdain
for his late master in no way subtracted from his profound conviction that a
people with no king was an unnatural thing. He scorned Britain's new rulers as
odious murderers who were beneath his contempt and in no way worthy of his
fealty. Instead of accepting the new regime, he was determined to hold Virginia
loyal to the Stuarts.

To that end he shot off a stinging remonstrance to London that condemned

---

60. *DNB*, s.v. "Robert Rich"; J. H. Hexter, *The Reign of King Pym* (Cambridge, Mass., 1941), 85;
Charles M. Andrews, *The Colonial Period of American History* (New Haven, Conn., 1934–38), 1:167;
Firth and Rait, *Acts and Ordinances of the Interregnum*, 1:331.

61. Warwick to [?], ca. Mar. 1644; Warwick to Samuel Mathews, same date; Warwick to [?] after
Apr. 1644, Stowe MS 184, 24–26, BL; Kukla, *Political Institutions in Virginia*, 132–37.

62. Order-in-council, 26 July 1644, SP 25/62, PRO.

Parliament, even as he proclaimed Charles II as rightful ruler of the colony. With a touching gesture of loyalty, he returned his commission, which he entrusted to Richard Lee, who delivered it to the would-be king in Brussels. Using a variety of contacts, he also established direct channels of communication with his brothers, Sir Edward Hyde, and other key royalist exiles. Through them he encouraged cavaliers with military backgrounds to come to Virginia and turn it into a base from which to combat the usurpers. To undercut the parliamentary cause in the colony, he dispatched a letter to Charles II asking the putative monarch to displace William Claiborne as treasurer because "an officer of trust should [not] appeare against his Majesties interest." And, to keep the Virginians firm in their proper loyalties, he summoned the General Assembly in October 1649, which passed legislation declaring treasonable utterances that defended regicide or questioned the succession of Charles II.[63]

Even as Berkeley took these steps, the fugitive king was reaching out to him. Charles wrote a series of letters that outlined measures to guard against a probable attack on Virginia and ways to finance the necessary defenses. He gave his letters to Henry Norwood and Francis Moryson. Both men were royalist officers, but, more important, they were close to Berkeley. Norwood was a cousin. Moryson was another brother of Lettice, viscountess Falkland. In the vanguard of royalist émigrés who flooded into the colony after Charles I perished on the block, they were soon men to whom Berkeley turned for counsel and support. Berkeley recommended Norwood to replace Claiborne in the treasurer's post. He also used Norwood as a courier to the exiled king. With Berkeley's encouragement, Moryson entered into Virginia's public life and embarked on a course that eventually made him one of Sir William's most trusted intimates.[64]

For their part the parliamentarians reacted purposefully, if cautiously, to the realization that Berkeley would neither change sides nor willingly yield to them. The Council of State took his inflammatory remonstrance in stride and merely ordered that it "bee referred to the Consideration of the Committee of the Admiralty, who are thereupon to take into their consideration how the Government

63. John Gibbon, *Introductio ad Latinam Blasoniam* (London, 1682), 156; Francis Moryson to Henry Thynne, 2 Apr. 1678, Henry Coventry Papers, 78:220; Hening, *Statutes at Large*, 1:359–61.

64. Charles II to Berkeley, ca. Aug. 1649, reference in *A Voyage to Virginia. By Colonel Norwood*, in Peter Force, ed., *Tracts and Other Papers, Relating Principally to the Origin, Settlement, and Progress of the Colonies in North America, from the Discovery of the Country to the Year 1776* (Washington, D.C., 1836–44), 3, no. 10, 49–50; abstract of a letter from Charles II to Berkeley, ca. 23 Sept. 1649, Pepys MS 2504, Pepysian Library, Magdalene College, Cambridge; Fairfax Harrison, "Henry Norwood (1615–1689)," *VMHB* 33 (1925): 4–7; commission from Charles II, 3 June 1650, CO 5/1354, 238–47, PRO; Kukla, *Speakers and Clerks*, 54–57.

of that Plantation may bee altered." Out of that determination came an August 1650 order-in-council interdicting English trade with Virginia. Two months later Parliament enacted a navigation law that forbade foreign vessels from trafficking in the colony without special licenses.[65]

When Berkeley got texts of these measures, he instantly saw their threat to Virginia and to him. Bent on thwarting their ill effects, he summoned the General Assembly for a day-long meeting on 17 March 1650/51. He opened the session with a speech that excoriated "the men of *Westminster*." At one point he shouted, "Surely Gentlemen, we are more slaves by nature, then their power can make us if we suffer our selves to be shaken by these paper bulletts." Should defiance meet with force, "do but follow me," he beguiled, and "I will either lead you to victory, or loose a life which I cannot more gloriously sacrifice then for my loyalty, and your security." His words resounded in receptive ears. After he finished, "the pretended Act of Parliament was publiquely read in the Assembly where upon" the members of both houses unanimously condemned it with a joint declaration of their own. The two documents subsequently became soldiers in the propaganda war between Cavaliers and Roundheads because Berkeley sent texts of both to friends at The Hague, who printed them for distribution throughout the Netherlands and England.[66]

For Parliament combating Charles II's campaigns to recover his throne took higher priority than reining in Berkeley. Cromwell dispelled the threat from Charles when he utterly routed Charles's army at the battle of Worcester on 3 September 1650. A short while later the parliamentarians sought to end their Virginia difficulties, and they had at least two sources of advice on how to go about doing that. William Claiborne, Richard Bennett, and Thomas Stegge were in London, they favored excluding the Dutch from the Virginia trade, and they knew the situation back home better than anyone at Whitehall. Equally as important, they were willing to accept political realities they could not change, which made them receptive to accommodating to the new regime as Berkeley would not. Their stance fit neatly within recommendations that the commons received from Benjamin Worsley.

Worsley, who enjoyed the confidence of the parliamentary leaders, first outlined his thoughts about the time Charles I went to his death. He pointed out

65. Order-in-council, 14 Dec. 1649, SP 25/3, PRO; order-in-council, 10 Aug. 1650, SP 25/8, PRO; An Act for prohibiting Trade with the Barbadoes, Virginia, Bermuda and Antego, 3 Oct. 1650, Firth and Rait, *Acts and Ordinances of the Interregnum,* 2:425–29.

66. Berkeley, *The Speech of the Honourable Sr. William Berkeley Governour and Capt. Generall of Virginea, to the Burgesses in the Grand Assembly at James Towne on the 17. of March 1650/1* . . . (The Hague, 1651).

that Parliament could never master the colony so long as Berkeley remained in place, nor could Virginia be of any use to England unless the Dutch were eliminated as the colonists' trading partners. A bit later on he drew up a more detailed scheme for conquering the colony. A contingent of redcoats and warships should be dispatched to America under the command of a special commission. The commissioners, he argued, should be colonials faithful to Parliament, and they should turn to force only if Berkeley refused to capitulate. His concluding recommendation was a statute to ban the Dutch from Virginia waters.[67]

Parliament followed Worsley's advice down to the last jot and tittle. During the summer of 1651 troops were rounded up and readied for their mission. Orders went out to the commissioners of the navy to provision the frigates *Frescoe* and *Guinea* for the voyage to the New World. *Frescoe*, it turned out, had a sprung mainmast, so she was abandoned in favor of another frigate, the *John*. Then, on 26 September 1651, the Council of State picked *Guinea*'s captain Edmund Curtis, Robert Dennis—*John*'s skipper—Richard Bennett, William Claiborne, and Thomas Stegge as commissioners and gave them orders for "the reduceing of Virginia to the obedience of this Common-wealth." Two weeks later Parliament adopted the Navigation Act of 1651, which banned colonial trade with the Netherlands. Last-minute preparations kept the flotilla dockside several weeks more before it raised sail and headed westward in the company of merchantmen laden with cargoes of trade goods and some six hundred Scots prisoners of war.[68]

The convoy made its first landfall at Barbados, where the soldiers easily subdued that colony to parliamentary rule. That task done, the fleet scudded northward for Virginia, only to be beset by a storm that scattered it and blew *John* to the bottom of the sea with the loss of all hands, including Dennis and Stegge. The surviving ships reached the capes of the Chesapeake in January 1652 and anchored in the lower James River, near the present-day city of Newport News. Bennett and Claiborne dispatched messengers to Berkeley seeking his surrender. He refused them an answer. A tense standoff followed. Bennett and Claiborne

67. Worsley, "A Memorandum of the Virginia Plantation," ca. Feb. 1649, piece 5; Worsley, "Further Animadversions about Virginia," n.d., piece 6; Worsley to William Strickland, n.d., piece 7; Strickland to Sir Henry Vane, 2 Sept. [1651?], piece 7—all in Samuel Hartlib Papers, bundle 61, piece 5, University of Sheffield, Sheffield.

68. Robert Blake to the commissioners of the navy, 9 Aug. 1651, SP 18/17, fol. 66, PRO; request for permission to provision the *John*, 3 Sept. 1651, SP 18/17, fol. 74, PRO; commission and instructions to Robert Dennis et al., 26 Sept. 1651, SP 25/22, fols. 82–88, PRO; Andrews, *Colonial Period of American History*, 4:34–46; An Act for the increase of Shipping, and Encouragement of the Navigation of this Nation, 9 Oct. 1651, Firth and Rait, *Acts and Ordinances of the Interregnum*, 2:559–62; Robert Deane to the commissioners of the navy, 6 Oct. 1651, SP 18/17, PRO; William H. Gaines Jr., "The Treaty of Jamestown, 1652," *Virginia Cavalcade* 1 (Spring 1952): 20–21.

quietly wooed leading colonists, while Berkeley, ever the dramatist, prepared a spirited show for the invaders. He called out a thousand militiamen and placed them strategically about the little capital and its approaches as if he would contest the enemy. At length Bennett and Claiborne forced the issue. They sailed upriver for Jamestown, and for a few days in early March it looked as though blood might actually run. At the last moment Berkeley gave in.[69]

Threatening bloodshed won three concessions that Berkeley sought once he accepted the folly of protracted resistance. First and foremost, he safeguarded Virginia's political establishment and spared colonists the intrusions of prying outlanders. Next, he preserved the loyalty of his Virginia allies and his standing with Charles Stuart. And he protected the sensibilities and property of Virginians who opposed Parliament.

His ruse easily achieved those strategic results and for a reason that he anticipated all along. He rightly suspected that no one in England wanted a lengthy military struggle in Virginia. Even though he and Bennett and Claiborne stood opposite, they were rivals, not enemies. Bennett and Claiborne cared as much for Virginia as he. Their gravitation to the parliamentarians was born of practicality. They and Berkeley disagreed on economic policy. He favored the Dutch, whereas their business interests tied them tightly to London. They saw in an ascendant Parliament both the means to eliminate the Hollanders as competitors and the way for London merchants to monopolize colonial trade. Berkeley's ability at keeping Virginians faithful to the Stuarts not only threatened Bennett and Claiborne financially, but his noisy condemnation of parliamentary rule put Virginia in a bad place. Sir William had to go, especially after Parliament forbade English traffic to the colony. With the governor out of the way, Bennett and Claiborne were more than willing to ensure the security of Virginia's present political order.

Both sides agreed to a truce once each realized the other's intent. There are no minutes from the negotiations, but the bargaining progressed cordially enough. Berkeley called the General Assembly to town, and its members played some part in the haggling that led to two treaties of surrender that Bennett, Claiborne, and Curtis signed on 12 March.

One preserved Virginia's political integrity. In return for an acknowledgment by the General Assembly that the change of regimes was a "Voluntary Act not forced nor constrained (by a Conquest) upon the Country," Parliament confirmed the settlers' right to "have and Enjoy such freedom and Priviledges as

69. Richard L. Morton, *Colonial Virginia* (Chapel Hill, N.C., 1960), 1:168–73; Kukla, *Political Institutions in Virginia,* 148–57.

belong to the free-born people of England." There would be "a full and Total Remission and Indemnity of all Acts Words or Writings done or spoken against the Parliament of England." Everyone had a year to decide whether to swear loyalty to the new masters or to leave Virginia. Use of the Book of Common Prayer was authorized for "one Year ensuing," providing that "the Major part of the Parishes" consented. Clergymen could stay in their cures if they did not "misdemean" themselves. Colonists could keep their private stores of arms and munitions. The General Assembly could legislate on all matters, just so long as it enacted nothing "contrary to the Government of the Commonwealth of England and the Laws there Established." It alone could lay all "Taxes Customs and Impositions whatsoever," and only it could raise or garrison troops. Virginia's "Ancient bounds and Limits granted by the Charter of the former Kings" would be respected, existing land patents would "remain in full force and strength," and the head right system would continue. Significantly, there was an implied pledge of a "new Charter from the Parliament" that would codify these provisions, which seemed to put a period to resuscitating the Virginia Company.[70]

The second treaty applied expressly to Berkeley and the council. By it Berkeley refrained from taking "any oath, [or] engagement to the Commonwealth of England," and he was permitted to "[pray] for or [speak] well of the king for one whole yeare" in the privacy of his home. His "Lands, howses, and whatsoever else belongeth" to him were his to keep, though he could sell out and "transport" himself wherever he "pleased." If he wanted to go to the Netherlands or England, he could haul his possessions "without any lett in any of the [Dutch] ports, or any molestation by any of the states ships att England whatsoever." In the event he wished to "goe for London or other place in England," he was promised freedom from "any trouble or hinderance or arrest or such like in England, that [he might] follow [his] occasions for the space of six months after [his] arrivall." Debts due by act of assembly would be honored. And he could send someone of his choosing "to give an accompt to his Majestie of the Surrender of his Countrie," providing he bore the messenger's expenses.[71]

So far as is known, there were no formalities of surrender once all the terms were agreed to and reduced to writing. Bennett became governor, and Claiborne resumed his old place as secretary of the colony. The General Assembly got down to the business of altering the laws in force to suit the new political situation. Berkeley was on parole and at liberty to go his own way.[72]

70. Articles of surrender of the General Assembly, 12 Mar. 1651/52, Randolph MS, ViHi.

71. Articles of surrender of the governor and council, 12 Mar. 1651/52, CO 1/11, fols. 129–30, PRO.

72. Warren M. Billings, ed., "Some Acts Not in Hening's *Statutes:* The Acts of Assembly, April 1652, November 1652, and July 1653," *VMHB* 83 (1975): 22–72.

He left Jamestown to begin life as a private citizen, knowing that for the second time in his life his experience of arms had resulted in his humiliation. The stakes were higher than they had been during the Second Bishops' War. Then he was chastised merely for embarrassing his military superiors. Now he defaulted on his sacred duty to the king and lost his master's possession too. These were bitter defeats, and the memory of them inspired a hatred of rebels that never left him.

7

AN ENFORCED RETIREMENT

erkeley rode to Green Spring House knowing he must account to Charles II for his surrender. Weeks went by before he could bring himself to put pen to paper. March became April, and April slipped into May, and, when he dared delay no longer, he wrote an explanation. Entrusting his letter to Colonel Richard Lovelace, he dispatched his former aide-de-camp abroad on 11 May.[1]

The letter Lovelace bore was more remarkable for what it left untold than for what it said. Barely two pages in length, it supplied no hint of how Jamestown had actually fallen to the parliamentary forces. It said nothing about the terms of the capitulation. Instead, it was an apologia crafted in the muted, elegantly deferential language of a courtier who had failed in his duty to keep Virginia out of Parliament's clutches but nevertheless sought his master's forgiveness. Berkeley figuratively threw himself at Charles's feet, "imploring your majesties pardon for delivering up your majesties Colony into the hands of your Ennimies. True it was," he continued, "I could have distroyed the country with those forces I had, but preserve it I could not." Pressed on all sides by colonists who "fearfully and furiously [cried] out for any accomodation" and a Council of State who begged "me to consent to Articles of Surrender," he sued for peace and spared

1. Pass for Francis Lovelace, CO 1/11, 137, PRO. In addition to being Berkeley's aide-de-camp, Lovelace was his cousin and a brother of, the Reverend Richard Lovelace, one of the Wits. His career is detailed in Daniel Lovelace, "Governor, Diplomat, Soldier, Spy: The Colorful Career of Colonel Francis Lovelace of Kent (1632–1675)," MS.

Virginia from destruction. He concluded with a prayer to "god to preserve your Sacred Majestie to give you Victory over your Ennimies to restore you to your Kingdoms and give you more in recompense of those your majestie hath been so long kept from by your Ennimies."[2]

Berkeley calculated his words to cushion the impact of the news they conveyed and to lessen the damage to his reputation. There was another, more personal reason for casting his account as he did. What he could not say, indeed dared not confess, was how his affections for Virginia had compelled him to place its welfare above all else. At no time before his surrender had he ever thought of setting his fellow planters in harm's way merely to contest a lost cause or to prove his own valor. His resort to arms was designed for one quite specific purpose: to extract from the parliamentary commissioners concessions that protected Virginia. Charles would not have understood such loyalty.

With Colonel Lovelace gone for Holland, Berkeley next faced the question of accommodating to private life. His most immediate concern was honoring the articles of surrender that directly affected him. If constrained by the exact letter of the terms, he stood to lose Green Spring House, and he would have a year to sell off his properties before quitting Virginia. Neither Governor Bennett nor Secretary Claiborne intended to hold him to those promises, providing he remained on his good behavior. They signaled as much in October 1652, when they reconfirmed his title to the Green Spring tract and its adjoining acreage. A bit later on the General Assembly of July 1653 used the excuse of the "present warr with the United Provinces" to extend his stay for an additional eight months. That extension came and went. No one noticed, and the subject of his departure never arose again. Paroled, he stayed at Green Spring House, where he lived "resigningly submissive" to Parliament for the remainder of the interregnum.[3]

Those eight years are the least documented of any in his adult life, though there are sufficient clues to trace an outline of his movements. Loss of office led to a swift, hard squeeze to his pocketbook. Gone were his salaries, his rents from the Governor's Land, and the numerous other perquisites that went with being chief executive. His adjustments to those losses came amid international conflict that pinched him too.

In December 1651 envoys from the Netherlands arrived in London seeking repeal of the Navigation Act. Those negotiations failed about the time of Berke-

2. To Charles II, 4 May 1652, Clarendon Papers, 43, fols. 111–12, Bodleian Library, Oxford.

3. Renewal of title to Green Spring, 9 Oct. 1652, Jefferson Papers, DLC; speech to the House of Burgesses, 13 Mar. 1659/60, Jefferson Papers, DLC; William Waller Hening, ed., *The Statutes at Large; Being a Collection of All the Laws of Virginia from the First Session of the Legislature, in the Year 1619,* facsimile ed. (1809–23; rpt., Charlottesville, Va., 1969), 1:384.

ley's surrender, and their breakdown led to the First Anglo-Dutch War (1652–54). But for Oliver Cromwell's becoming lord protector, the fighting might have dragged on longer than it did. Cromwell never thought of the Dutch as enemies. Instead, he regarded them as natural allies because of shared religious convictions, and, though he backed the Navigation Act, he believed the world offered enough commerce for both nations. He brought the fighting to an end with the Treaty of Westminster in 1654, despite the war's popularity with English merchants.[4]

Although the fight never spread to Virginia, it cut Berkeley off from the Dutch merchant fleet and from his markets in Holland just when he was trying to adjust to the fallout of his enforced retirement. The economic depression that followed the peace seems to have soured his financial position even more, and there are indications that he had to scramble to make ends meet. His contacts with New Amsterdam increased, and he tried to extend his traffic with his fellow Virginians. Being a creditor himself, he pressed the General Assembly for back payments and other arrears, and, when necessary, he sued his debtors to recover all that he could from them. None of these remedies yielded quick results, so he was forced to dispose of real estate. One, and possibly more, of his lots at Jamestown went on the block. He sold Secretary Claiborne a parcel from the Chippokes plantation in Surry County for an undisclosed price. A unit in the Jamestown row house netted 27,500 pounds of tobacco from Governor Bennett, who needed a place to live whenever he went up to the capital from his plantation in Isle of Wight County on public business.[5]

For all of his effort Berkeley probably did not regain financial equilibrium much before the latter years of the decade, but impaired income did not stop him from making improvements at Green Spring. He added to the mansion, refined the gardens, continued his agricultural experiments, and worked at bettering his silk-making skills. Silk seemed the most promising alternative to tobacco as a cash crop, especially now that sericulture was again in vogue on both

4. Charles Wilson, *Profit and Power: A Study of England and the Dutch Wars* (London, 1957); Simon Hart, "The Dutch and North America, 1600–1650," *De Halve Maen* 66 (1971): no. 1: 5–6, 15; no. 2: 7–8, 10; no. 3: 7–8; no. 4: 11–12, 16; C. R. Boxer, *The Anglo-Dutch Wars of the 17th Century* (London, 1972), 4–20; J. R. Powell, *Robert Blake, General-at-Sea* (London, 1972).

5. Allowances from the General Assembly, 1 Dec. 1656, Jefferson Papers, DLC; payment of arrears, 13 Mar. 1657/58, MS laws of the General Assembly, ViHi; conveyance to William Claiborne, 17 Sept. 1657, Land Patent Book No. 4, 1655–62, 120, Vi; conveyance to John Phips, 23 Feb. 1656/57, Patent Book No. 4, 1655–62, 69, Vi; receipt from Francis Yeardley, 6 Oct. 1653, LNOB, 1646–51, fol. 64, Vi; Berkeley to Peter Stuyvesant, 11 May 1657, Miscellaneous MS, New York City, Nhi; Berkeley to Thomas Stegge II, 20 Oct. 1657, CCOB, 1655–65, fol. 144, Vi; deed of sale to Richard Bennett, 1 Mar. 1655/56, Hening, *Statutes at Large*, 1:407.

sides of the Atlantic. Governor Edward Digges did his part and prodded the planters to follow Berkeley's example. Claiming "silke will be the most profitable commoditie for the countrey," he persuaded the General Assembly of December 1656 to adopt a law that required every freeholder to raise ten mulberry trees for each hundred acres of land he owned or face a fine for noncompliance. In England members of the influential Samuel Hartlib circle warmed to the prospect of achieving large-scale production in Virginia. Hartlib himself trumpeted the idea in *The Reformed Virginia Silk-Worm* (London, 1655). There he repeated the gist of John Bonoeil's *Observations* and added recent testimonials to successes in Virginia, but he took no notice of Berkeley's feats. Hartlib's overlooking Berkeley was by design rather than by accident. Edward Digges and John Ferrar were his informants on the situation in the colony, and neither was a stranger to Sir William. Given that one of the Hartlib circle, Benjamin Worsley, had counseled Parliament about removing Berkeley, Hartlib's snub was scarcely surprising. Other English Puritans who distrusted Berkeley's politics but knew of his ongoing work with silkworms and diversification conceded the former governor a grudging measure of praise. As one admitted, Berkeley was "a person of most eminent Ingenuitie . . . that hath made very many Tryalls and Experiments."[6]

"Many Tryalls and Experiments" brought Berkeley to ponder the consequences of his effort at modifying the Virginia economy. On the one hand, his endeavor demonstrated his own aptitude for successfully applying diversification schemes to a real-life plantation. On the other hand, few of his fellow planters followed his example. That realization persuaded him to reexamine his approach to the problem, but without power his solutions remained figments of his restless imagination, and he turned to other things.

Proximity to Jamestown allowed him to finger the pulse of the colony without attracting undue notice. He distanced himself from his successors, but it was abundantly plain to him that they were constrained in ways that he was not. They spoke for a regime that never won the loyalty of most planters. The constitutional adjustments that settled commonwealth rule on Virginia weakened their office. Governors became creatures of elective office. Answering to the General Assembly, or more precisely the House of Burgesses, they served two years at a time, or "untill the next meeting of the Assembly." Governing under such conditions demanded qualities of agility that did not abundantly grace Richard Bennett, Edward Digges, or Samuel Mathews Jr.[7]

6. Hening, *Statutes at Large,* 1:420; Thomas Povey to Edward Digges, 1661, Povey letter book, Add. MS 11411, British Library.

7. Warren M. Billings, "Some Acts Not in Hening's *Statutes:* The Acts of Assembly, April 1652, November 1653, and July 1653," *Virginia Magazine of History and Biography (VMHB)* 83 (1975): 27–28.

A kindly, good man, and deeply pious, Bennett had the misfortune to govern amid an unpopular war. He lacked finesse too. His want of savvy tripped him up in 1653, when he tried unsuccessfully to prevent Walter Chiles from becoming speaker of the House of Burgesses. Although Bennett continued in office another two years, he never recovered from his defeat. Digges was no parliamentarian. Neither was he loudly royalist, and his moderation promoted him as an acceptable successor to Bennett. He averted any squabbles with the burgesses because, after an eighteen-month tenure, he resigned to go to London on colony business. Mathews was not so lucky. Scarcely into his twenties, this first Virginia-born governor had almost no political experience. His youthfulness commended him to some of his burgess colleagues, but for others being his father's son tarnished him. In any event he entangled himself in disagreements about revising the statutes in force that nearly led to his expulsion from office.[8]

Avoidable or not, these scrapes bore vivid witness to a spirited, independent House of Burgesses of a sort that Berkeley had never seen in the time of his incumbency. That self-sufficiency was redolent of rising institutional maturity, but it also revealed political alignments among the burgesses. On the whole more royalists than parliamentarians sat in the House during the interregnum. Some were unwavering adherents of the Stuarts, but others, perhaps the majority, merely looked upon monarchy as the only sure foundation for society. While they all quietly hoped and prayed for the restoration of the king, they stooped to expediency and elected governors who were acceptable to their rulers in London. As for control of the House, that was another story. Puritans Edward Major and Thomas Dew presided, respectively, at the General Assemblies of April and November 1652. Subsequently, Speakers Theodorick Bland, Walter Chiles, Edward Hill, Francis Moryson, John Smith, and William Whitby were all of the royalist faction. So were house clerks John Corker, Charles Norwood, and Henry Randolph. Because the burgesses also elected councillors, the royalists put their kind on the Council of State too.[9]

Chiles and the rest shared another affiliation in common. All were cordial to Berkeley, and Norwood was his cousin. Their presence testifies to a number of his allies who sat in both houses of the General Assembly throughout the years of his retirement. In the House were John Carter, Sir Henry Chicheley, Edward

---

8. Jon Kukla, *Political Institutions in Virginia, 1619–1660* (New York, 1989), 169–82, 192–204; Warren M. Billings, *A Little Parliament: The Virginia General Assembly in the Seventeenth Century* (Richmond, 2004), 34–35.

9. Billings, *Little Parliament*, chaps. 2 and 6; Jon Kukla, *Speakers and Clerks of the Virginia House of Burgesses, 1643–1776* (Richmond, 1981), 46–48.

Hill, Warham Horsemanden, Henry Lee, Lemuel Mason, Edmund Scarburgh, Henry Soane, Robert Wetherall, William Whittaker, Abraham Wood, and Francis Yeardley, whereas Argoll Yeardley, Nathaniel Littleton, and George Ludlow were of his following in the council. No one at Jamestown saw anything amiss when any of these former colleagues stopped at Green Spring House. Some were business partners, some lived on adjoining plantations, and some passed that way on their journeys to and from assembly sessions or meetings of the Quarter Court.

Their discreet conversation kept Berkeley fully abreast of the latest political happenings in the capital, but, in receiving their information, he took great care not to give the government the slightest excuse to revoke his parole or to force him to sell Green Spring. That is not to say he shied off conspiring, but the signs of his intrigues are quite meager. Save for one scheme, he covered his tracks beyond recognition. Even in this one instance his footprints were so light that they escaped notice in his day, and they are now nearly undetectable.

The plot was as convoluted as any he contrived in his play-writing days. Its cast of characters included himself, Henry Norwood, Richard Glover, and Argoll Yeardley's brother-in-law Edmund Custis, who was a London-based retailer with Holland connections. The play aimed at funneling money to Charles II and fomenting armed resistance to the commonwealth in the West Indies. Apparently, Berkeley and Norwood hatched their conspiracy at Green Spring House in 1650. They recruited Glover, who was about to return to Amsterdam. A year later Norwood went to Holland. Disguised as his cousin's agent, Norwood brought with him bills of exchange that were drawn on a commercial account Berkeley maintained with Glover. Glover cashed several bills for Norwood, who surreptitiously gave part of the money to royalist exiles. (Norwood may also have spent some more for printing and distributing Berkeley's speech to the General Assembly of March 1651.) For appearance sake Glover brought the leftover cash back to Berkeley when he returned on his next trading voyage to Virginia. So far these transactions looked no more sinister than a routine business matter. But, like the plot of *The Lost Lady*, this one had its own unexpected twist. Glover, on Norwood's order, handed over Berkeley's outstanding bills to Edmund Custis, who redeemed them in London and held the funds while he awaited further developments. In the summertime of 1654 Custis and Norwood teamed up to engineer the next phase of the scheme. Using Berkeley's money, they set about purchasing a large store of small arms and chartering a ship to freight the weapons to the West Indies. Not surprisingly, the vessel they procured belonged to Edmund's brother Robert, and its destination was Barbados, where they expected Francis

Willoughby, fifth lord Willoughby of Parham, leader of the island royalists, to buy their muskets.[10]

In the end the plot came to naught. Agents of Cromwell's spymaster John Thurloe uncovered it, and on Christmas Day 1654 they arrested Norwood, Glover, and Edmund Custis. They also seized the arms that the conspirators had already stockpiled in Glover's house. During the interrogations that followed, Glover revealed that he and the others did business together but not much more. Custis acknowledged a one-time acquaintance with Norwood, and he stiffly insisted that the weapons were purchased for protecting Virginia colonists from the Indians. Norwood was no less steadfast. He admitted to nothing beyond knowing Lord Willoughby casually and remembered their contacts as extending no further than vague discussions about raising silk. Seemingly, the three were persuasive enough to spare them indictments for treason, because Norwood and Custis were briefly imprisoned rather than put on trial. Glover just dropped out of sight. Berkeley's name hardly came up, and the eye of suspicion merely winked at him.

Aside from showing a little of Berkeley as conspirator, his involvement with Norwood, Glover, and Custis intimates that he maintained steady communication with a series of surreptitious confidants in Britain and on the Continent. Ship captains who hauled his goods were an obvious resource. They could gather intelligence openly because everyone looked upon them as conduits for all sorts of information. Royalist émigrés could always be counted upon for news. Sometimes they brought secret messages as well. There were clandestine channels to the court-in-exile too. The two that are known ran directly through Sir Edward Hyde and Berkeley's brothers, Charles and John.

Such tidings as Berkeley gathered were often contradictory and slow in coming. His contacts in Britain told a depressing story. The lord protector's grip was firm and showed no indication of relaxing in the immediate future. Royalist informants on the Continent were even less encouraging. They revealed the debaucheries of the court-in-exile and the ineptitude of Charles's supporters, who

10. Henry Norwood, *A Voyage to Virginia. By Colonel Norwood,* in Peter Force, ed., *Tracts and Other Papers, Relating Principally to the Origin, Settlement, and Progress of the Colonies in North America, from the Discovery of the Country to the Year 1776* (Washington, D.C., 1836–44), 3, no. 10, 49–50; Thomas Burch, ed., *A Collection of State Papers of John Thurloe, Esq.* (London, 1742), 3:65, 66, 72–75; Fairfax Harrison, "Henry Norwood (1615–1689): Treasurer of Virginia, 1661–1673," *VMHB* 33 (1925): 4; James B. Lynch Jr., *The Custis Chronicles: The Years of Migration* (Camden, Maine, 1992), 61–66; Richard S. Dunn, *Sugar and Slaves: The Rise of the Planter Class in the English West Indies, 1624–1713* (Chapel Hill, N.C., 1972), 79–80.

seemed unable to work toward a common purpose. Such news probably weakened Berkeley's faith in the likelihood of the king's restoration anytime soon, and he could do no more than yearn for better days to come.

Starting in 1658, he had reasons to hope such times were nigh. Oliver Cromwell died that September, leaving his son Richard to follow him. Berkeley also got wind of an increasingly unstable situation in England. Reports such as these at once encouraged and alarmed him. The snail's crawl at which news crossed the Atlantic quickened his anxieties. Distance only magnified his uncertainty about which side, if any, controlled Whitehall.

Colonial politicians shared his apprehensions too. At the General Assembly of March 1658/59 Governor Mathews divulged the contents of a letter from London in which council president Henry Lawrence officially told of Cromwell's death. Lawrence also ordered Mathews to proclaim Richard Cromwell the new lord protector. That command immediately provoked a furious debate about whether the letter was authentic and if its contents bound the assembly. The burgesses said yes to both questions, but, to preserve their authority, they forced Mathews to concede that the power to elect provincial "officers" resided with them, and they made him join with them in petitioning the lord protector for confirmation of their "present priviledges." Weakened by his troubles with the burgesses, Mathews had no choice but to agree.[11]

The new lord protector enjoyed a momentary popularity, but he was no Oliver, and he abdicated within a year of his accession. Word of "Tumbledown Dick" Cromwell's renunciation and Sir George Booth's aborted royalist uprising found its way to the colony. Then came tales of the expulsion of the Rump Parliament and rumors that Charles Stuart would soon return to his throne. Mathews, his credibility exhausted, could not abate the uncertainties that gripped Virginia. He appeared not to try, so no one knew what to expect next, and, as 1659 wore on, everyone waited for the latest news from abroad. Things got worse before they got better. In January 1659/60 Mathews died without warning.[12]

How quickly did Berkeley learn of Mathews's death? No one knows, but he may have been one of the first among the great planters outside government circles to hear of it. Mathews Manor, where Mathews is thought to have expired,

11. Henry Lawrence to Samuel Mathews and the Council of State, 7 Sept. 1658, H. R. McIlwaine, ed., *Journals of the House of Burgesses of Colonial Virginia, 1619–1658/59; 1659/60–1693* (Richmond, 1914–15), 115, 116.

12. Ronald Hutton, *The Restoration: A Political and Religious History of England and Wales, 1658–1667* (Oxford, 1985), 3–125; Craven, *Southern Colonies,* 264–65; Richard L. Morton, *Colonial Virginia* (Chapel Hill), 1:184–87; John Frederick Dorman, "Governor Samuel Mathews, Jr.," *VMHB* 74 (1966): 439–52.

sat below Jamestown in Elizabeth City County, and it was easily accessible to Berkeley's mansion by water. Whoever carried the news to Green Spring House could easily have rowed up the James River on a rising tide in a matter of hours after Mathews breathed his last. Berkeley's reaction is also unrecorded, though the implications of his successor's passing were surely apparent to him.

In death Mathews not only left the colony leaderless; he brought to light a defect in Virginia's current constitutional structure that blocked the immediate naming of a replacement. There was no lieutenant governor, and neither the speaker of the House of Burgesses nor the secretary of the colony was entitled to succeed, even temporarily. Back in 1652, no one had foreseen the need to specify who should supplant a governor who suddenly became incapacitated or died while in office. Then it had sufficed merely to entrust the election of governors to the burgesses, which was well and good just so long as they were sitting or there was an incumbent to call them into session. The assembly was in recess in January 1660, and without Mathews there was no constitutional way to bring it together for the purpose of conducting an election. Time was of the essence too. Drawing out the process of naming someone only multiplied the feelings of insecurity that already gripped Virginians.[13]

Councillors who settled the matter devised an elegantly pragmatic solution. Falling back on a practice that antedated 1652, they decided that they should pick an interim governor. That person would then agree to recall the General Assembly promptly. Once the burgesses convened, they would either elect him or find someone else. A quorum of councillors gathered at Jamestown and ran down a list of likely candidates. Culling through the prospects, they discerned various liabilities that eliminated them one by one. Former governor Edward Digges, who had a foot in both the parliamentary and royalist camps, was still in England and therefore unavailable. Secretary Claiborne, councillors Richard Bennett, William Bernard, and Francis Moryson were other possibilities. So were senior burgesses such as Theoderick Bland or Edmund Scarburgh. Bennett, given his past history, was clearly unacceptable, and Claiborne was too closely associated with the parliamentarians. The rest, though able men, had insignificant followings in Virginia and even less stature in England. That left a single choice—Will Berkeley. In the schemers' minds no one else would do. The moment demanded a vigorous leader, and Berkeley's capacity to govern was unmatched. Beyond that, no one else equaled his popularity with the planters at large. The former governor could reconcile the disputes that had riven provincial politics in recent years.

13. Warren M. Billings, "The Return of Sir William Berkeley," *Virginia Cavalcade* 47 (1998): 100–110.

He respected colonial institutions, and his belief in monarchy was an asset that could safeguard Virginia interests in the likely event that Charles returned to the throne. Speaker Bland sent a council delegation over to Green Spring House to present the councillors' proposition.[14]

Berkeley hesitated to accept the offer. Approaching his fifty-sixth year, he was an old man by the reckoning of his century. Although not by nature a sickly individual, unnamed illnesses occasionally stalked him, and he was beginning to feel the burden of accumulating years. Publicly he held back out of fear of what the government in England, Puritan or royalist, might do to him. He was too proud to resume office only to be turned out as soon as the situation clarified in England. In the end he put his fears aside out of his sense of duty and became governor pro tempore.[15]

There is no longer any record of the exact day when Berkeley took over, but the fact of the General Assembly's convening in mid-March narrows the probabilities. The need of timely notice recalling the assembly dictated that his summons circulate at least a month before the meeting. Additionally, he received written nominations for sheriffs from justices of the peace in Charles City and Northumberland counties on 20 February. Five days later Berkeley wrote to Peter Stuyvesant acknowledging the arrival of Nicholas Varleth and Brian Newton, who had come from New Amsterdam to negotiate a trade agreement between the two colonies. And there is a minute on file in the records of Lower Norfolk County that shows him presiding at the Council of State on 9 March. So Berkeley became governor pro tempore some time in early to mid-February. But would he go the whole distance and consent to being elected? An answer to that question was far from certain as the burgesses trickled into the capital and considered whom to chose.[16]

14. Ibid.

15. LNOB, 1646–51, fol. 201, Vi; Berkeley to the House of Burgesses, ca. 13 Mar. 1659/60, Virginia Miscellaneous Papers, 1606–92, 146–47, DLC.

16. From the justices of the peace for Charles City County, 20 Feb. 1659/60, CCOB, 1655–65, 228; from the justices of the peace for Northumberland County, 20 Feb. 1659/60, NuOB, 1652–65, fol. 120; to Peter Stuyvesant, 25 Feb. 1659/60, précis in E. B. O'Callaghan, ed., *Calendar of Historical Manuscripts in the Office of the Secretary of State, Albany, N.Y.* (Albany, 1865), 9:217; LNOB, 1656–66, 66.

8

RETURN TO POWER

he General Assembly came to town on 13 March 1659/60. That day the House of Burgesses took up the matter of choosing a governor. Speaker Theoderick Bland named a committee, which met with Berkeley and offered to nominate him. Berkeley, ever respectful of the burgesses and always mindful of parliamentary courtesies, couched his response in a brief reply to Bland. He spoke of his "pressing feares" of possibly offending Charles II and being "outed" again. His reservations notwithstanding, he would take office but only until a government was settled in London. If the burgesses accepted his proviso, then he was "ready, most thankfully and acknowledgingly[,]to serve," if he "alsoe . . . receive[d] the concurrence of the Councill." The House agreed.[1]

Both sides conferred again in order to flesh out the conditions by which Berkeley would govern, but a week of hard bargaining passed before they were of one accord. "There being in england noe resident absolute and generall confessed power of government of this country," the House insisted on retaining "supreame power" until "such a command and commission come out of England as shall be by the Assembly adjudged lawfull." Next, the burgesses demanded that Berkeley "governe according to the auncient lawes of this country," calling the assembly "once in two years . . . or oftner if he [saw] cause" and forbidding

1. Berkeley to the House of Burgesses, ca. 13 Mar. 1659/60, Virginia Miscellaneous Papers, 1606–92, 146–47, DLC.

him from dissolving the assembly "without consent of the major part of the House." They permitted him to name his own council and secretary of the colony, providing he first sought the burgesses' advice and consent. Then, as if to sweeten the offer, they promised immediate payment of his back dues and other outstanding claims against the provincial government. And, to give added authority to these stipulations, they proposed enacting them into law.

Although the terms stated political realities, they hardly pleased Berkeley. He especially sniffed at the staunch affirmation of legislative preeminence and his subordination to the House, but his objections fell on deaf ears. The burgesses' refusal to budge therefore forced him to choose between yielding to their offer or forgoing his election. He relented, and on 19 March he announced his acceptance in an address to the full House.[2]

Vintage Berkeley, the message reached for the moment as only he could. He thanked the burgesses for showering him with "high honors" of a sort that made "a soberer and modester man than I proud." Such esteem, he was certain, was "rather a mercifull aspect of my former endeavors to serve you then a strict intuition and contemplation of my present abilities." Disclaimers aside, he reminded the House how he had once held "the Commission and Commands of my most glorious master King Charles of ever blessed memory," how "his Royall Sonne . . . sent me a Commission to governe here," how Parliament had turned him out, how it appeared that Parliament itself was overthrown, and how it seemed possible that the monarchy would be restored. His reason for this little history lesson was "onely to mouth" an apparent truth: he had been obedient to "all these unstable governments of divers natures and Constitutions." And, although it was clearly "Ones dutie to live obedient to a government," it was a different matter altogether "to Command under it."

Remarking that sudden, extraordinary events now catapulted him toward his former office, he acknowledged that the terms of his restoration troubled him. If, he said, Virginia "were in the Condition of some of our neighbouring Colonyes," then the difficulties and hazards of his returning would not be so great. At worst they were but an "ill choice" that might be "most willingly resigned" once the situation in England clarified. But for him to take office without knowing who controlled Whitehall carried the risk of harming Virginia, the General Assembly, and him. If Parliament retained power, he "would not voluntarily [make] choice of them for my Supremes." Conversely, if Charles II regained the

2. William Waller Hening, ed., *The Statutes at Large; Being a Collection of All the Laws of Virginia from the First Session of the Legislature, in the Year 1619*, facsimile ed. (1809–23; rpt., Charlottesville, Va., 1969), 1:530–31; judgment for payment of arrears.

throne, the king might well be angered by what the burgesses were about to do, in which case they and Berkeley would face condign punishment. Still protesting his inadequacies all the while, he acceded to the House's proffer and concluded his remarks by asking "leave to return where I began, which is, to give the honorable House most Humble Thanks for their intended munificence to me, which I shall the more Cheerfully doe; because those are engredients to put an acceptable Tincture upon this Apologie; For considering my present Condition (if I had not irrefragable reasons on the Easiness it is proposed to dissuade me from it,) I should be worthily thought hospitall mad, if I would not change povertie for wealth—Contempt for honour."[3]

Apart from accepting his election, Berkeley intended two further results from his address. One was to put his views on the record. The other telegraphed his desire to rekindle the friendly arrangements that had ruled his dealings with the House in bygone days. By inclination reviving that harmony came easily to him, but practicalities drove him too. He was in a weaker place politically than he had been in 1642, and he was about to encounter burgesses who were mostly strangers to him.

As in the past, cooperation with the House would also strengthen his hand with the Council of State. Although the council was subservient to the burgesses, it was still a formidable body and a possible source of difficulty for Berkeley. Its membership had changed considerably in the years since he last sat in the center chair at the council table. All but one or two of Berkeley's appointees were either dead or in retirement. Richard Bennett and William Claiborne remained from the old Mathews faction. As for the newer councillors, Francis Moryson, Abraham Wood, and Edward Hill were close to Berkeley, whereas Thomas Dew was a dyed-in-the wool Puritan. The rest were men he knew more by reputation than from personal acquaintance.

Those characteristics explain why he insisted that the councillors concur in his election. Having them vote on him was both a way of gaining their public acceptance of him as governor and a means of corralling likely adversaries. Thereby he hoped to avoid difficulties similar to those he had experienced when he first arrived in Virginia.

On 21 March Berkeley met with the councillors, all fourteen of whom were present.[4] No minute of what passed between them has survived, though he got what he sought. Their approval brought forth a short speech of thanks from him.

3. Address to the House of Burgesses, 19 Mar. 1659/60, Virginia Miscellaneous Papers, 1606–92, 142.

4. The fourteen are listed in order of their seniority in Hening, *Statutes at Large*, 1:527.

Similar in tone to his address to the burgesses, this talk differed in one important respect. He openly courted the councillors' support. After thanking them for their vote of confidence, he exclaimed, "you have made me the general hope of the Colony . . . [and] You have made me to command overall." Such a "great Treasure" would be little more than a "vaine gift" unless "you helpe me to carry it to a place of safetie . . . but you must instruct and prompt me how to satisfye it." In short, if they would but join and work with him, then their "admirable Harmony of Consents" would be an example that would make peace "at last returne to our long afflicted, miserable, distracted Country."[5]

The speech concluded the formalities of returning Berkeley to power, and he took over either on 21 or 22 March. Whichever day it was, the newly ensconced governor promptly threw himself into regular legislative business. Given the flurry of activity, it seemed that his pleas for cooperation had struck responsive chords. His nomination of William Claiborne for secretary of the colony gained easy approval. So did his recommendation of a batch of appointments to various local and militia offices, which sailed through the House without incident. House and council voted favorably on orders that provided him with various stipends, including the take from port charges levied on all arriving ships and a salary of seven hundred pounds.[6]

Sanctioned, too, were negotiations for a commercial treaty with New Netherlands. The endorsement derived from a statute to encourage foreign trade, which itself was one in a bevy of bills that passed during the session. In early April Berkeley initialed the laws, and the assembly adjourned. It would resume a year later, on 20 March 1660/61, "unless the governour find occasion by the importance of affaires to convene it sooner." Most members scattered to their plantations, content that they had a governor who would honor their interests as he led them through the uncertainties of the coming months.[7]

Berkeley and Theoderick Bland stayed behind to frame the trade agreement with the Dutch colonists. Bland proved a beneficial addition to the negotiations.

5. Speech to the Council of State, 21 Mar. 1659/60, Virginia Miscellaneous Papers, 1606–92, fol. 140, DLC.

6. Appointment of William Claiborne, Hening, *Statutes at Large,* 1:547; commission to Anthony Hoskins, 27 Mar. 1660, NoOB, 1657–64, fol. 65, Vi; commission to Daniel Wild, 27 Mar. 1660, YDWI, 1657–64, Vi; commission to Richard Conquest, LNOB, 1656–66, 253, Vi; commission to John Holmwood, 27 Apr. 1660, CCOB, 1655–65, 228, Vi; commission to Mainwaring Hammond, Hening, *Statutes at Large,* 1:545; order for payment of port duties, Hening, *Statutes at Large,* 1:543–44; order for paying the governor's salary, Hening, *Statutes at Large,* 546.

7. Hening, *Statutes at Large;* 1:540, 530–42, 54; Jon Kukla, ed., "Some Acts Not in Hening's Statutes: The Acts of Assembly, October 1660," *Virginia Magazine of History and Biography* (*VMHB*) 83 (1975): 80–85.

His being speaker added the weight of the House of Burgesses to the talks, and he brought the heft of a well-seasoned merchant-planter as well. He and Berkeley dealt with the New Amsterdamers through Governor-General Peter Stuyvesant's representatives, Nicholas Varleth and Brian Newton, who had been cooling their heels in town ever since the end of February. The four came to an understanding within a matter of weeks, and they put it to paper. Berkeley wrote to Stuyvesant, informing him that he was sending the draft agreement to Sir Henry Moody, who would complete the deal on behalf of the Virginia government. And, in another deferential gesture to the General Assembly, he insisted that Bland also sign the letter to Moody.[8]

Moody did as he was bid, and, as of mid-May 1660, "Articles of Amitie & commerce" between New Netherlands and Virginia took effect. The pact contained four provisions. Merchants in the two colonies could trade freely with one another, though the Dutch would pay export duties on Virginia tobacco at the same rate as "others Neighbouringe English & strangers." Colonists in both places would enjoy equal access to each other's courts, and the respective governors had the right of granting retrials in the event of "Injustice done." Runaway servants would be returned to their lawful owners at "the first [Convenient?] passadge," and the costs of their repatriation would be borne "Either by the Master or Else by the tresurer of the Country." The final clause dealt with the manner of processing debt claims in the courts.[9]

Aside from its commercial merits the treaty represented a most emphatic rejection of current English trade legislation, which was designed to exclude the Dutch from the Chesapeake. It was also a first for Berkeley. Despite his affinity for free commerce and his endeavors to promote Holland traffickers, he never dared to push for a similar compact during his first ten years as governor. Any such agreement was unthinkable then, given the opposition arrayed against it in Britain and in Virginia. Things were different in the spring of 1660, and he snatched an opportunity from the political confusion of the moment to advance the material interests of Virginia as well as his own. Seen in this light, the treaty with New Netherlands points to Berkeley's renewed goal of diversifying Virginia's economy. Whether that dream ever became a reality depended partly on his ability to sell the concept to the General Assembly and partly on the play of politics in Britain.

Like every other Virginian, Berkeley awaited news of what was happening on the other side of the Atlantic. His restoration preceded that of his sovereign by

8. Berkeley to Peter Stuyvesant, 18 May 1660, Dutch MSS, 1634–60, N.
9. Articles of amity and commerce with New Netherlands, ca. 18 May, Dutch MSS, 1634–60, N.

two months—too short a time for word of it to reach Charles II before he returned to London in May. Rather speedily thereafter, the king moved to reclaim his authority in Virginia. Reasserting it constitutionally required little because he regarded the commission he gave Berkeley a decade earlier as still in force. Thus, on 17 June 1660 he ordered a warrant for his signature which "Graunt[ed] unto our trusty & welbeloved Sir William Berkeley knt. of the Place of Governor of Virginia." The paperwork took about six weeks to complete before Secretary of State Sir Edward Nicholas posted the sealed warrant, a newly copied commission, and an official notice of the king's restoration to America.[10]

The dispatches arrived at their destination around mid-September. Tearing them open, Berkeley hastily digested their contents, and, just as hurriedly, he drew up two proclamations for the sheriffs to read throughout the colony. One heralded Charles II as the rightful ruler of Virginia and commanded all Virginians "most humbly & Faithfully" to "Submitt" to that "most potent mighty & undoubted King." The second required that "all officers whatsoever within this Country doe remaine & continue within their severall offices untill further order to contrary . . . and that all Writts and warrants from henceforth issue in His Majestyes name."[11]

Reestablishing monarchy as the basis of authority in Virginia implied more than Berkeley's publicly proclaiming Charles II. Restoring royal rule meant framing the colony's existing constitution anew, and that was something that could not be accomplished by proclamations alone, as Berkeley knew only too well. A General Assembly must now undo what its predecessor had done in 1652. Here, then, was an "occasion by the importance of affaires" that demanded a prompt summons to the assembly.

The immediacy of the moment thrust a decision upon Berkeley not unlike the one he had faced before he met his first General Assembly. Should he recall the recessed legislature, or should he dissolve it and issue writs for an election? His commission empowered him to act on his own mere motion, and, if he opted for a dissolution, there was no disputing the legality of his choice. On the other hand, promises made were promises to be kept. He had pledged back in March that he would honor the colony's "auncient lawes," which were still in force. True to his word, he convened the existing assembly on 11 October 1660.

Unfortunately, fire consumed the session journals when Richmond burned in

10. Antonia Fraser, *Royal Charles: Charles II and the Restoration* (New York, 1979), 164–76; letters patent from Charles II, 3 June 1650, CO 5/1354, 243–252, PRO; warrant from Charles II, 17 June 1660, CO 1/14, 10, PRO; letters patent from Charles II, 31 July 1660, C.66/2941, PRO.

11. Proclamation of Charles II, 20 Sept. 1660, SDWI, 1652–72, 157; proclamation continuing all magistrates in office, 20 Sept. 1660, SDWI .

April 1865, but a text of the acts remains, and it affords a window into what happened. Members cheerfully greeted the return of the colony to its old loyalty, a few zestfully. Even so, certain individuals questioned the legality of the session, which had been called, as they noted, "with out a new election," but Berkeley and others quickly perfected a way around such "doubte & Scruples." The preamble to the acts justified Berkeley by saying that "uppon the Immergent occasions of the Countrey which could not well admitt of soo much delay As must uppon necessitie have attended a new ellection, the authoratie of this present Grand assembly, is by president in England warrantable and legall" and that the ensuing enactments were "good and valid . . . to all intents & purposes."[12]

With the issue of legitimacy composed in the manner of the Convention Parliament that restored Charles II, the next order of business was reforming Virginia's constitution. To that purpose the assembly called for Berkeley to "interceede" with Charles II for a general "pardon of the Inhabitants of this Countrey, and the reacceptance of them into his sacred Majesties favour and protection." In the same vein the House designated a committee—Berkeley, Speaker Bland, and burgesses Nathaniel Bacon, Miles Cary, Robert Ellyson Henry Soane, and Robert Wynne —to memorialize the king for confirmation of "several favours," which included validation of land titles, free trade, and recognition of the General Assembly as the colony's legislature. Next, members voided various acts passed throughout the interregnum that were in any way inconsistent with a royal regime. All other laws "not hereby repealed" were to "Continue and bee in force." Thereupon, the assembly declared that the only "authoraty" in the colony was that of "the Kinges most excellent majestie."[13]

These constitutional remedies satisfied the primary concern for reestablishing royal authority, but they were quite modest in comparison to those of the General Assembly of April 1652. That assembly had used the device of a top-to-bottom revision of the laws in force as the means of its accommodation to the parliamentary regime and a new constitution of government. An equally thorough overhaul was as necessary in October 1660 as it had been a decade earlier, but, in an abundance of circumspection, the usually intrepid Berkeley left that task to another day.[14]

He introduced bills that foreshadowed changes in the direction of Virginia's economy. One taxed exports of tobacco to anywhere but England. Several en-

12. Kukla, "Some Acts Not in Hening's *Statutes*," 86–87.

13. Ibid., 86–87.

14. Warren M. Billings, ed., "Some Acts Not in Hening's *Statutes:* The Acts of Assembly, April 1652, November 1652, and July 1653," *VMHB* 81 (1975): 22–72.

couraged the production of silk, leather goods, and yarn, while another declared Jamestown the colony's sole port of entry. This legislation signaled more of Berkeley's intention to foster agricultural diversification. Now, however, he was adjusting his original approach to the problem. No longer did he expect to lead by example alone, because he had come to realize that his successes at Green Spring were an insufficient means of lessening the planters' dependence upon tobacco. Effective curbs on tobacco cultivation required the cooperation of the Maryland authorities as well as incentives that encouraged the planters to switch to other staples. Berkeley understood that the requisite political and monetary inducements could only be found in England. He was therefore reluctant to proceed further until he had a better feel for how the Crown would take to his ideas, and he let the matter rest once the assembly had enacted his proposals.[15]

Budget bills came up for consideration during the final days of the session, and they were adopted, evidently without incident. Their passage left some nonlegislative items to tidy up before the assembly finished its work. Among the latter was an order that gave Sir Henry Moody ten thousand pounds of tobacco for his "paines" in representing Virginia at New Amsterdam, plus two others that levied sums of corn and tobacco to cancel the arrears that the colony still owed Berkeley. At the specific request of the House of Burgesses, he agreed to take "into his care the building of a state-house" to replace the one that fire had destroyed some years before. For that purpose he received full power to spend whatever funds were necessary and leave to "presse tenne men of the ordinarie sort of people" as construction workers. The council confirmed a number of his appointments before it took steps to rectify some land disputes in favor of the Indians.[16]

At last all was done. Berkeley ceremoniously signed the acts. Speaker Bland initialed them too, and they became law. Berkeley dissolved the assembly and rode back to Green Spring House, where he tended to other things.

His return to office improved his financial situation at a fortunate moment, considering that he was expanding his silk operations and adding to the mansion. The infusion of cash from salaries and perquisites moved those projects along at a faster pace than Berkeley had anticipated when he set them afoot. He also resumed the management of the Governor's Land, which involved him in renegotiating leases with the tenants. One of his renters was William Drummond

15. Hening, *Statutes at Large*, 1:86–87, 88, 90–91, 92–93; Warren M. Billings, "Sir William Berkeley and the Diversification of the Virginia Economy," *VMHB* 104 (1996): 445.

16. Hening, *Statutes at Large*, 2:10, 11, 12, 13, 13–14, 15, 16.

(?–1677), whom he would grow to despise intensely and whom he would hang one day with the greatest of glee.[17]

Being governor again meant that Green Spring House became the center of society once more. Always hospitable, Berkeley thrived on opportunities to entertain as he could not during his retirement. He renewed old acquaintances, but he concentrated on attracting newer politicians and planters. None of the latter was more prominent than Thomas Ludwell (1629–78) and his brother Philip (1638?–1717?). The two arrived in Virginia in the fall of 1660. Considering their affiliations, quite possibly it was they who conveyed Berkeley's commission and notification of the king's restoration.

Thomas and Philip Ludwell belonged to a family, rooted in Bruton, Somerset, that had long been entwined with the Berkeleys. Berkeley did not know either of them until they met in 1660 because he had emigrated to the colony when both Ludwells were small boys. Their tie to his generation of Berkeleys was with his brothers, John and Charles. Thomas campaigned with John during the Civil War and served him in other ways as well. In return the baron used his influence with Charles II to secure Thomas's appointment as secretary of the colony. Philip, on the other hand, was still in his twenties. With few prospects in England, he tagged along to see what becoming a colonist might offer him by way of an improvement of fortune.

Berkeley preferred a secretary of his own choosing, but Thomas Ludwell was graced by John's blessings and a royal warrant of office, which took precedence over his wishes. Actually, Ludwell turned into quite an unexpected asset. Beholden to Baron Berkeley, he sought to ingratiate himself to Governor Berkeley. Knowing little or nothing about the office of secretary, he took pains to learn its intricacies and to improve its administration. More important, he never looked upon it as an alternative to gubernatorial power, as William Claiborne had done, and he presented no threat. Quite the contrary, he avoided Berkeley's adversaries and matured into a thoughtful, reliable ally in the Council of State. Above all, Ludwell's temperament and outlook drew the two men naturally into an ardent friendship that lasted until death parted them. Philip was equally as close to Berkeley.

With such intimacy went the rewards of proximity, and Berkeley was quite generous to both brothers. To Thomas he gave collectorships, a colonelcy in the

17. Lindley S. Butler, "The Governors of Albemarle," *North Carolina Historical Review* (*NCHR*) 46 (1969): 281–89; Warren M. Billings, "Sir William Berkeley and the Carolina Proprietary," *NCHR* 76 (1995): 336.

militia, and the remunerative post of escheator-general,[18] which he created especially for him. Philip became deputy surveyor-general. That position allowed Ludwell to appoint all county land surveyors and to receive a substantial portion of every survey filing fee. He gained a councillor's seat too. Ultimately, the relationship numbered the brothers in a tight, small circle of individuals whom Berkeley trusted absolutely and whose advice he almost never ignored.[19]

Thomas's appointment as secretary put William Claiborne out of a job that had been his off and on since the 1620s. Changing from one secretary to another seems not to have occurred immediately because, as late as March 1661, Claiborne had yet to hand over the records to his successor. Indeed, a mandate from the General Assembly ordering him "upon oath" to deliver the archives to Ludwell suggests that Claiborne had dragged his feet. So does the order's rather pointed reference to Ludwell's "comysion from his sacred majestie." Claiborne relented and retired to private life and lived quietly at Romancoke, his plantation in New Kent County, until his death in 1677. Thus ended the political career of a towering early Virginia leader who had been Berkeley's chief competitor for upward of two decades.[20]

Claiborne's departure spared Berkeley the challenges of a determined adversary. He could be glad of that bit of good fortune. If he exulted at his rival's comeuppance, he never voiced his delight, as far as anyone knows, but news from abroad may well have brushed aside his inclination to gloat.

Throughout the winter of 1660–61 those tidings were filled with signals that simultaneously cheered and alarmed Berkeley. From what he could discern, Charles II seemingly favored drawing the British Isles and the colonies into an empire centered on London. Supposedly, too, the king had even appointed an advisory board of knowledgeable colonists and merchants to inform him of American conditions. The latter tip proved accurate, when in early 1661 Berkeley received a commission from Charles naming him to a place on a newly formed Council for Foreign Plantations. That was the reassuring news. As for the bad

18. Berkeley raised the office to claim and dispose of lands belonging to planters who died heirless, whereupon the ownership of such land was said to escheat, that is revert, to the provincial government. After real estate escheated, it could be acquired by third parties through the courts. The purpose of the office, aside from aggrandizing Ludwell, was to provide an institutional mechanism for handling such legal proceedings. As escheator-general, Ludwell kept track of escheated lands and saw to their eventual distribution, and for his troubles he was entitled to fees.

19. Douglas L. Hayward, ed., *The Registers of Bruton, Co. Somerset* (n.p., n.d.), 1:22; Junius Rodes Fishburne, "The Office of Secretary of State in Colonial Virginia" (Ph.D. diss., Tulane University, 1971), chap. 8; Jon Kukla, *Speakers and Clerks of the Virginia House of Burgesses, 1643–1776* (Richmond, 1981), 89–94.

20. Hening, *Statutes at Large,* 2:39.

news, it bore two items that dismayed Berkeley greatly. One hinted at efforts to revive the Virginia Company. The other was the Navigation Act of 1660, whose clear purpose was to eliminate the Dutch from the American trade. Both developments imperiled Virginia's autonomy and institutions, and they jeopardized his visions of the colony's relationship to the Crown.[21]

He pondered ways of combating the threats. At the moment there was no one in Whitehall protecting Virginia interests. The need for an agent was therefore of utmost importance, and who better to fulfill that role than he? He had connections like no one else in the colony, and it was quite appropriate that he should go to court to plead Virginia's cause. The seat on the Council for Foreign Plantations implied his presence in London too. Legally, his commission permitted him "to go out of the Country" in emergencies. The Council of State and he need do no more than agree on which of them would act in his stead. He also wanted the political blessing of leading planters, which would further brace his hand, and he sought the backing of the General Assembly.

Writs for an election went out about a month before the meeting, which he scheduled for 23 March 1660/61. The ensuing poll returned a scattering of holdovers from the previous assembly. Most of the burgesses, however, were Berkeley's allies. They included his neighbor and confidant, Henry Soane, who took the speaker's chair. Although no one realized it at the time, this General Assembly would sit through seventeen consecutive sessions before it dissolved in March 1676, which would make it the longest of any in the history of Virginia.

That the assembly remained so long says something of the political beliefs that guided Berkeley after he returned to office. He took annual sessions as a given, but he put no store in regular elections and rotation of the burgesses. Those practices, so cherished in modern representative democracies, were quite unconventional in the seventeenth century, and they made little impression on him or anyone else in Virginia. By contrast, continuing the assembly was for him a pragmatic way of governing. It not only raised the standing of the House of Burgesses and eased bills into law; it also held the allegiances of politicians loyal to him.

21. Commission and instructions, 1 Dec. 1660, CO 1/14, 112–16; Charles M. Andrews, *British Committees, Commissions, and Councils of Trade and Plantations, 1622–1675*, Johns Hopkins University Studies in Historical and Political Sciences, ser. 26 (Baltimore, 1908), 49–51, 69–74; 12 Car. II, cap. 18, John Cay, comp., *An Abridgment of The Publick Statutes in Force and Use of The Publick Statutes in Force and Use From Magna Carta, in the ninth year of King Henry III. To the eleventh year of his resent Majesty King George II. Inclusive* (London, 1739), under "Plantations"; Charles M. Andrews, *The Colonial Period of American History* (New Haven, Conn., 1934–38), 4:1–108; Lawrence A. Harper, *The English Navigation Laws: A Seventeenth-Century Experiment in Social Engineering* (New York, 1939), 51–58.

And it evinced a modus operandi he tacitly struck with the great planters. He allowed them virtually unrestrained authority in local politics, and in return they gave him great leeway in charting public policy that affected Virginia province-wide or impinged upon its external affairs.

Concern for such things was not uppermost in the thoughts of the burgesses and councillors as they listened to Berkeley's opening speech. The text of his address has vanished, but its substance is implicit in the acts and orders that passed the session. Berkeley brought everyone up-to-date on developments as he knew them and summarized a letter he had just written to the king. (The letter reiterated his gratitude for the king's trust and prayed that Charles would "yett think me worthy of your Royall Commands," though it conveyed no notice of Berkeley's intention of returning to England.) Next, he besought the assembly's designation of him as agent for Virginia. He then urged consideration of ways to finish the job of recasting Virginia's constitution, recommended selection of a committee to revise the laws in force, and called for additional economic legislation.[22]

The assembly did all that Berkeley asked. In a gesture that signified the importance it ascribed to the agency, it put the enabling statute at the head of the session laws. That act levied a special appropriation of two hundred thousand pounds of tobacco to support Berkeley, whom it bid to "present our grievances to his sacred majesty's gracious consideration and endeavour [to] redresse" them. With a series of statutory changes to local government, the church, and the assembly itself, the members adjusted governing structures to accord with royal rule. As for the laws in force, Francis Moryson and House clerk Henry Randolph were chosen to redact them and to present their draft revisal to the next regular session. Finally, the assembly revived a law encouraging cultivation of mulberry orchards, and it banned setting out tobacco plants after 30 June, "Provided that if Maryland joyne not with us in observation of this act . . . then this to be null."[23]

After the assembly rose, Berkeley rode the whirligig as he readied for his journey. There were arrangements for the management of Green Spring to make, a passage to book, papers to compile, trunks to pack. Besides planning for the trip, he still had to preside at the spring meeting of the Quarter Court. Spring brought with it the usual commissioning of county justices and sheriffs. This year, however, picking who would gain reappointment or who would fill vacancies was anything but usual because the assembly had just reduced the size of the benches

---

22. Berkeley to Charles II, 18 Mar. 1660/61, Virginia Miscellaneous Papers, 1606–92, fol. 169, DLC.
23. Billings, *Little Parliament,* chaps. 2 and 11; Hening, *Statutes at Large,* 2:17–32, 34.

to the eight most senior justices, which complicated a routine task. Berkeley needed to settle on a stand-in too.[24]

Amid the preparation he stopped long enough to succor an abused indentured maidservant. The woman, Mary Rawlins, turned up on his doorstep begging protection from a master who treated her "Most unchristianly and Cruelly." Her plight brought forth a swift response. Berkeley dashed off a note to York County justice Joseph Crowshaw telling him to investigate the matter, and Rawlins gained her freedom.[25]

He finally settled upon Francis Moryson as his replacement. The choice was a natural one. Moryson was an intimate friend and confidant. He had been speaker of the House, so the burgesses respected him, and his fellow councillors regarded him highly too. His selection made good political sense for another reason. Being deputy governor would help him ease the revision of the laws in force through the next meeting of the assembly. Berkeley, as his commission required, nominated Moryson to the council, and on 11 May the colonel was confirmed "Governor and Capt. General of Virginia according to the tenor of the said Commission, whose authority is to begin Upon the Governors setting out."[26]

Another month passed before Berkeley "set out." A pile of patents awaited his signature. He named Moryson and Thomas Ludwell the colony's cotreasurers. The Quarter Court adjourned after he acted upon several outstanding petitions and determined a few civil judgments. He awaited the issue of a lawsuit that he had pending in the Northumberland County court against the Dutch merchant Nicholas Boot. A favorable ruling came down on 6 June. About that date he set off on his mission to London.[27]

24. Hening, *Statutes at Large*, 2:21.

25. Berkeley to Crowshaw, 2 Apr. 1661, YDWI, 1652–62, fol. 121; order of court, YDWI, fols. 122–24.

26. Commission naming Francis Moryson governor, 11 May 1661, LNDWI, 1654–1702, 220–21.

27. Patent Book, 4, 1655–1662, 467, Vi; commission naming Francis Moryson and Thomas Ludwell cotreasurers, 15 May 1661, Conway Robinson, comp., "Notes and Excerpts from the Records of Colonial Virginia," Conway Robinson Papers, ViHi, 244; petition of John Hill 5 June 1661, LNDWI, 1656–61, fols. 312–13; judgment in *Berkeley v. Boot*, 6 June 1661, NuOB, 1652–61, fol. 141.

9

MISSION TO LONDON

 fast passage brought Berkeley to his destination a little more than a month after his ship slipped her hawsers at Jamestown dock. Servants off-loaded his luggage and transported it to Mayfair, where his family readily sheltered him. Even as he settled in, he went about renewing acquaintances and taking political soundings.

London seemed a decidedly happier town than it had been on his last visit. His return after a fifteen-year absence roused sour-sweet memories because so many familiar haunts were no longer as he had recalled them countless times in his mind's eye. "Tradeskins Ark" had closed during the interregnum. The once lovely Oatlands was a ruined pile, its gardens and silk works in shambles. Similar fates had befallen other royal residences where Berkeley had attended Charles I or amused Henrietta Maria with his fellow Wits.

Whitehall Palace again stood at the center of court life. Beehive busy as in the old days, it looked even more dilapidated than Berkeley remembered it. All the Van Dyck paintings and every other artistic piece that manifested the majesty of the late king had gone to market after commonwealth officials stripped the palace of its treasures. The building itself had decayed, though a bustle of renewal was just beginning to mitigate the neglect. Builders and other craftsmen labored busily at refurbishing palace fixtures and refitting the accoutrements of royal existence to a semblance of their former splendor. Lack of money not only slowed repairs to the palace; it was symptomatic of a more general shortage of cash that sorely afflicted the Crown. Royal coffers were bare, and Charles II was constrained to beg his upkeep from Parliament.[1]

Droves of the great and the would-be mighty noisily flocked into Whitehall's precincts pressing for royal favor. Most were strangers to Berkeley, but others were not. His brothers Charles and John sat on the Privy Council. So did a cousin, Henry Jermyn, now earl of St. Albans. Sir Edward Nicholas, one of the secretaries of state, was an acquaintance. Henry Bennet, another cousin, was keeper of the privy purse and on a trajectory that would soon propel him to succeed Nicholas, an ancient man who was beyond his prime. And not to be overlooked was a new sister-in-law, Christiana Riccard, baroness Berkeley of Stratton, who had wed John the previous year. She equipped the marriage with an enormous dowry and furnished the Berkeleys with an equally invaluable political connection via her father. Merchant prince, London alderman, former parliamentarian, one-time president of the Turkey Company, and about-to-be governor of the East India Company, Sir Andrew Riccard brought Will Berkeley close to the ears of the most influential members in the city's mercantile establishment.

As for the Wits, nearly all of them had died years earlier. Henrietta Maria thrived, though she left for France some months before Berkeley turned up in London, and the two were not reunited. John Earle had recently been consecrated bishop of Salisbury. Sir John Denham survived and was now a retainer of Baron Berkeley. And then there was cousin Thomas Killigrew. He still wrote plays, but he was more renowned as an occasional diplomat and an impresario whose productions routinely drew the king and other grandees to his Theatre Royal. (It was he who staged *The Lost Lady, A Tragi-Comedy* for its short revival in January 1661.) Sir Edward Hyde, plus one or two others, remained from the Great Tew Circle. Lately graced earl of Clarendon, Hyde was the lord chancellor, which put him in a place of authority just below the throne.[2]

As for Charles II, Berkeley honored him as his rightful ruler. Charles regarded Berkeley as his subject, but neither man had any claim upon the other that arose from close personal proximity. Their affiliation, if it could be called such, was entirely superficial. A mere boy of eleven when Berkeley sailed to Virginia in 1641, Prince Charles rarely, if ever, recognized him. They did not see one another for

1. Prudence Leith-Ross, *The John Tradescants: Gardeners to the Rose and Lily Queen* (London, 1984), 114–34. The Tradescant collection subsequently passed to Elias Ashmole, who transferred it to the University of Cambridge, where it formed the basis of the museum that now bears his name.

2. Robert C. Latham and William Mathews, eds., *The Diary of Samuel Pepys* (Berkeley, Calif., 1970), 2:18–25.

two decades, and in the intervening years their only contact came as the result of infrequent correspondence, not all of which were happy exchanges. Conversely, Charles and John Berkeley shared tight bonds with the king. They had fought for him, protected him, and lived in exile with him. The ever grateful Charles lavished them with preferments that Will Berkeley never received, though he benefited from his brothers' relationship to the extent that it ensured him a channel to the highest levels of government.

Berkeley left no detailed impressions of Charles that we know of. He couched his existing letters and addresses in the ornate, deferential idiom of the courtier, which betrayed little, if anything, of his inner feelings. When he encountered the king in the flesh, he met someone quite unlike his late royal master. Charles I was small and delicately featured, whereas Charles II was not. Charles I was orderly to a fault; Charles II was lazy. Charles I loved only his queen; Charles II bedded mistresses and sired bastards with abandon. Charles I lacked political instinct, whereas Charles II was cunning. And Charles I died violently at the hands of his enemies, whereas Charles II, having outlasted his foes, departed this world from the comfort of his own bed.

Such distinctions of character and circumstance more than partially accounted for what Berkeley immediately recognized as contrasting styles of kingship, but other changes had happened too, and they were differences that he may not have caught onto instantly, if ever. When Berkeley was a courtier, Charles I and the government were synonymous. Who served in the royal household reflected that king's aims as well as his personality. Charles II was a potent monarch, no one would deny that, but his was a circumscribed power. Like Berkeley, he had been restored by legislative invitation. And, again like Berkeley, the statutory terms of his return limited his authority in ways his father would have found unimaginable. Then, too, from the Restoration onward Parliament largely underwrote the cost of public office. The king's ministers answered to it more than to him. Boards, committees, and departments assumed ever greater administrative responsibility, which distanced the business of governance still further from Charles's household. And nascent parties tussled for kingly favor in order to sway the turn of national politics. These changes led to the further unfolding of a modern bureaucratic polity, wherein the entity of the state and the person of the monarch were finally no longer one and the same.[3]

Berkeley may not have fully fathomed the import of another, more highly visible difference. Soldiers were everywhere. George Monck's troops, who paved

3. David Ogg, *England in the Reign of Charles II,* 2d ed. (Oxford, 1961), 152–67; Kevin Sharpe, "The Image of Virtue: The Court and Household of Charles I, 1625–1642," in David Starkey et al., eds., *The English Court: From the Wars of the Roses to the Civil War* (London, 1987), 262.

the way for the Restoration, now threw protective rings around Charles. Their regiments intimidated Londoners and kept the capital grudgingly peaceful, just as other garrisons billeted strategically across the country held the larger populace under guard as well. That standing armies were yet needed to preserve order, much as they had under Cromwell, bespoke fallen hopes.

Charles II picked up crown and scepter intending to repair his kingdoms to their condition in the halcyon days of the mid-1630s, which meant restoring them to their former unarmed state. He began the demobilization of parliamentary forces as he absolved his adversaries, save for the regicides who had executed his father. To some former foes he gave high posts and noble titles. From others he sought counsel and inspiration on virtually every important matter of state. But the things he could forgive and forget his subjects could not. Twenty years of civil war and revolution cut wounds that healed slowly or not at all. Royalists hankered for revenge on their enemies and recompense for their loyalty. Charles's generosity to their old adversaries displeased them mightily. Anglican high churchmen had scores of their own to avenge, and avenge them they would. Not every parliamentarian gladly donned a monarchist's cloak. Steadfast convictions constrained thousands of republicans to cling unwaveringly to their beliefs, and the bellicose among them posed a genuine danger to a still unsettled realm. Such, indeed, was the actual concern for the king's safety that on Coronation Day, 23 April 1661, detachments of Coldstream Guards lined the processional route to deter trouble.[4]

Persistent threats to public order, whether authentic or pretended, soon convinced Charles to consent to a militia act of 1661 that vested absolute control of all military and naval forces in the Crown. The law effectively wrapped standing armies in statutory legitimacy and forsook a safeguard that had been fought over during the Civil War. And, together with other harsh measures that marked the period of Clarendon's ascendancy, the statute pointed Britain in the direction of an armed camp, ever fearful of religious and political dissent rather than toward a peaceable kingdom where sometime Roundheads and Cavaliers tolerated their differences and lived in harmony.[5]

Berkeley also witnessed stirrings that figuratively and literally laid the keels

4. Ogg, *England in the Reign of Charles II*, 252–82; Clifford E. Walton, *History of the British Army, A.D. 1660 to 1700* (London, 1894).

5. 13 Car. II, cap. ii, John Cay, comp., *An Abridgment of The Publick Statutes in Force and Use of The Publick Statutes in Force and Use From Magna Carta, in the ninth year of King Henry III. To the eleventh year of his resent Majesty King George II. Inclusive* (London, 1739), 2, under "Militia"; Ogg, *England in the Reign of Charles II*, 189–217; Antonia Fraser, *Royal Charles: Charles II and the Restoration* (New York, 1979), 215–23.

for a modernized royal navy and a revitalized merchant marine. Charles quickly resurrected the navy board and the post of lord high admiral, both of which he charged with the civil administration of the fleet. His brother James, duke of York, a seasoned soldier-seaman, became lord admiral anew. Former commonwealth naval officers Sir William Penn and Sir William Batten joined with Baron Berkeley, Sir George Carteret, Samuel Pepys, and Sir Robert Slingsby to make up the navy board. Together, the admiral and the board devised a combination of expert understanding of seamen and ships with sound organization that promised a better navy that could challenge Dutch maritime supremacy.[6]

By the 1660s Britain's merchant marine was a shabby collection of vessels that belonged to private men who were mostly independent of the Crown's centralized direction. The industry long suffered from hard times resulting from the Civil War, owner backwardness, and constant, fierce competition from Holland. By contrast, superior knowledge of the nautical arts and maritime technology set the Dutch a world apart from any of their commercial rivals. Better designed, better built, and better kept, their merchant fleet outnumbered those of England, France, and Spain combined. And, in places such as Virginia, Hollanders dominated the carrying trade to the near extinction of the British. English merchants desperately wanted to shorten the odds in their favor, and they pressed Charles II for help.[7]

Charles was sympathetic to their plight. Relief appeared in the shape of an embryonic colonial policy that Parliament initially set forth in the Navigation Act of 1660. The scheme called for a closed economic order that gathered the nation and its colonies into a transatlantic empire, which in concept drew strength and prosperity from military security, political obedience, and social discipline. Much about the design had a familiar face to it. In fact, large portions of the statute itself were intentionally modeled on the commonwealth navigation law of October 1651. Foreigners could no longer trade with the colonies, and the settlers had to ship enumerated commodities, such as tobacco, only to England and only in British bottoms.[8]

---

6. J. C. Sainty, comp., *Office-Holders in Modern Britain: Admiralty Officials, 1660–1870* (London, 1975), 1, 18–20; J. M. Collinge, comp., *Office-Holders in Modern Britain: Navy board Officials, 1660–1832* (London, 1978), 1, 6, 18–22; Ogg, *England in the Reign of Charles II*, 257–58; John Callow, *The Making of King James II: The Formative Years of a Fallen King* (Thrupp Stroud, Gloucestershire, 2000), 33–34, 192–200.

7. Charles M. Andrews, *The Colonial Period of American History* (New Haven, Conn., 1934–38), 4:22–50; Jan de Vries ad van der Woude, *The First Modern Economy: Success, failure, and perseverance of the Dutch economy, 1500–1815* (Cambridge, 1997), 404.

8. Andrews, *Colonial Period*, 4:50–85; Sister Joan de Lourdes Leonard, "Operation Checkmate: The Life and Death of a Virginia Blueprint for Progress, 1660–1676," *William and Mary Quarterly*, 3d ser., 24 (1967): 44–74; Stephen Saunders Webb, *The Governors-General: The English Army and the*

For Berkeley these limitations were obnoxious and highly detrimental to Virginia, and he admired them no better in 1661 than he had liked them a decade earlier. At that time he had noisily spurned the commonwealth act because it came from a government that he abhorred for its illegitimacy. Open defiance was out of the question now. Charles II willed the present law, which meant that Berkeley must adopt a less hostile approach. Tactically, he needed ways of manipulating the Crown's nascent trade schemes to mitigate their restrictive features or, better yet, to exempt Virginia from them altogether. He knew about London tobacco merchants who had opposed the strictures on free trade, and he figured he could recruit willing supporters in that quarter. Other promising possibilities appeared to lie in the contents of a circular letter that he brought with him from Jamestown. Composed by the Council for Foreign Plantations and addressed to all governors-general in America, the message sought specific information about conditions in their jurisdictions that might aid the commissioners in formulating advice to the Crown on forthcoming colonial policies. Among the express demands upon him was a call for an explanation of any advantages Virginia brought at present "not onely to his Majesties Revenue but to his Navigation trade and Manufactures." The letter went on to urge the appointment of knowledgeable persons who could "represent and agitate" to the council "such things as may tend to the advantage of his Majestie and of you his Collonie of Virginia." It also encouraged Berkeley to foster sericulture and all those "commodities soe many wayes beneficiall and considerable" that would "drawe certaine profit and reputation upon your Plantations, [and] stirr up his Majestie to give you his most particuler favour and indulgence as often as your affaires shall have occasion thereof."[9]

The chance to respond afforded Berkeley his opening to bring the commissioners around to his point of view. In requiting the council's quest for information, he could wax lengthily on how Virginia was the right place to produce silk, iron, flax, hemp, rice, pitch, and other long-desired staples. No mere theorist he, he would speak as one who had actually cultivated such products for years and at a profit. He could hold as well that his example should be extended throughout Virginia with the encouragement of the Crown's "particuler favour" to will-

Definition of the Empire, 1569–1681 (Chapel Hill, N.C., 1979), 57–101; J. M. Sosin, *The Restoration Monarchy of Charles II: Transatlantic Politics, Commerce, and Kinship* (Lincoln, Neb., 1980), 5–91; Jack P. Greene, *Peripheries and Center: Constitutional Development in the Extended Politics of the British Empire and the United States, 1607–1788* (Athens, Ga., 1986), 7–19.

9. The Humble Remonstrance of John Bland, 1660, *Virginia Magazine of History and Biography* (*VMHB*) 1 (1894): 142–55; circular letter from the Council for Foreign Plantations, 17 Feb. 1660/61, CO 1/14, 149–52, PRO.

ing colonists. His arguments, he thought, gained additional weight by virtue of his being a member of the Council for Foreign Plantations.

Forty-eight men besides Berkeley had seats on the Council for Foreign Plantations. He knew five of them—Clarendon, Baron Berkeley, Sir John Denham, Edward Digges, and John Jeffreys—quite well. At least four others—Sir John Colleton, Secretary of State Sir Edward Nicholas, Sir Andrew Riccard, and Secretary of State Sir William Morrice—were acquaintances. As for the remaining members, some were Stuart loyalists or former parliamentarians who held prominent government positions. Others were eminent merchants or, like Berkeley and Colleton, noted colonizers. And there were several, such as Thomas Povey and Martin Noell, who were esteemed as indispensable experts in how the Crown might realize its visions of empire.[10]

Berkeley went to his first council meeting on 5 August 1661. He was the center of attention for that entire day because his fellow commissioners used the contents of the circular letter to quiz him about conditions in the colony. His interrogators allayed his suspicions about a revived Virginia Company. No one broached that possibility as an alternative to the present government, which revealed the rumors in Virginia as so much wild speculation that he could dispel from his concerns without further ado. Just before adjourning, the council asked him "to bring in . . . on this day fortnight" an "Accompt" that rehearsed his answers to their interrogatories in writing. He missed his deadline, and 1661 passed into a new year before he finished the assignment.[11]

His delay had more to do with his changing perceptions of the obstacles that lay in his way than with torpor. Virginia's interests crisscrossed and rivaled those of other provinces, the Crown, and London's mercantile establishment, which were complexities that Berkeley understood even before he left Virginia. It took but a single council session to reinforce his grasp of the complications he faced in achieving uniform policy recommendations that protected Virginia and advanced his goal of royally sponsored diversification. The sheer number of commissioners made for balky deliberations and delays in attaining results. Each member brought his own opinion of colonial affairs, which ranged from slight to intense. His was merely one voice in a huge, clamoring chorus, and, for him to be heard above the others, he needed to do more than dash off a hastily drawn "Accompt."

10. J. C. Sainty, comp., *Office-Holders in Modern Britain: The Board of Trade, 1660–1870* (London, 1974), 20; Charles M. Andrews, *British Committees, Commissions, and Councils of Trade and Plantations, 1622–1675,* Johns Hopkins University Studies in Historical and Political Sciences, ser. 26 (Baltimore, 1908), 69–74.

11. Minutes of the Council for Foreign Plantations, 5 Aug. 1661, CO1/14, fol. 152.

Doing more involved his continued effort at influencing the Council for Foreign Plantations while directly lobbying Charles II through the Privy Council. The first sign of that approach revealed itself in late August. Berkeley collected a group of friendly merchants who on 28 August joined him in an appearance before the Privy Council and asked Charles to allow Virginians free trade and to prevent ships from arriving in the Chesapeake "before the First of May next." (The latter plea represented a prescriptive method of stabilizing tobacco prices through the imposition of regularity in the market relationship between planters and dealers.) After a surprisingly short debate, the privy councillors favored the petitioners. More than that, they commanded the drafting of letters to Berkeley and to Maryland authorities that proclaimed their rule. Then a shoe dropped. Opponents, who had not been heard, demanded and got an audience. They trotted out a bevy of puissant Londoners, who protested loudly about the unfairness of the newly announced policy. The objections gave the privy councillors sufficient pause to suspend their decision pending further "Consideration of the whole matter." A hearing convened on 27 September, and after all parties had their say "His Majestie did . . . absolutely revoke his said former Order."[12]

Stymied, but by no means discouraged, Berkeley regrouped. Attending to the request from the Council for Foreign Plantations now took on greater urgency, and he threw himself into preparing his *Accompt.* Instead of responding exactly to the interrogatories in the circular letter, he reached for more. Here was his opportunity to make the case for diversifying Virginia's economy not just to his fellow commissioners but to the king and the Privy Council, who held the actual power of decision. The result turned into something more than the Council for Foreign Plantations expected or he anticipated at first. And, to enhance its visual impact upon the intended readers even more, he hired a printer, who smartly set his handwritten text as a small quarto pamphlet that bore the title *A Discourse and View of Virginia.*[13]

The *Discourse,* which Berkeley distributed in late January 1661/62, ranks with the finest extant examples of his prose. Much as *The Lost Lady, A Tragi-Comedy* exhibited his deftness as a captivating writer of plays, so the *Discourse* displayed his aptitude as a resourceful polemicist. Sprightly crafted elegance fused with crisp diction to create a clean, spare argument that was all the more compelling because of its brevity. Indeed, the pamphlet from beginning to end exuded its

12. PC 2/55, 357, 370, 384–85 PRO.
13. Berkeley, *Discourse,* 1–2. The source text for these and subsequent quotations is my copy of the Thomas R. Stewart facsimile edition of the *Discourse* published at Norwalk, Conn., in 1914; Warren M. Billings, "Sir William Berkeley's *Discourse and View of Virginia:* A Note on Its Authorship," *Documentary Editing* 24 (2002): 33–36.

author's utter confidence in his gifts of language and his capacity to persuade through the written word.[14]

Aware that most of his readers had never seen the colony, Berkeley opened with a sweeping sketch of the place. He depicted Virginia as "a glorious flourishing Country" that surpassed "all his Majesties Plantations" in advantages. Its "six eminent Rivers," which fed Chesapeake Bay, allowed the largest of merchantmen to sail "near two hundred miles" into the interior free of "Pirats" or other hazards to navigation. The climate complemented an "admir'd fertility" of the soil to give forth great quantities of pitch, tar, and timber, which abounded natively and awaited only the harvest. Weather and soil and the colonists' "industry" yielded bumper crops of foodstuffs too.[15]

That same combination of ingredients could just as easily produce iron, silk, flax, hemp, and potash or other desirable staples. But why, asked Berkeley, had Virginians refrained from making these commodities? A bit of history furnished his explanation. For decades, he claimed, the colonists had struggled merely to survive. Their fight for existence kept their numbers small because, as he put it, "there was not one woman to thirty men, and *populus virorum* is of no long duration any where." Strife with the natives retarded propensities for agricultural experimentation as well. Although not defeated, the Indians had been "terrified to a suspension of arms" in recent years, and of late the colony "began to be of more plenty and security."[16]

He observed how hundreds of men, like himself, "of as good Families as any Subjects in *England*," emigrated to Virginia only to be surpassed by thousands upon thousands of servants who had "no Art or Trade." Driven westward by "hunger and fear of prisons," those desperate immigrants tilled nothing but tobacco on an ever larger scale. Therein lay the great reason Virginians had made so little "progression" toward any other means of livelihood. Tobacco had long since become the "Foundation of our wealth and industry," with the result that chronically huge crops annually depressed prices and brought the colonists to the verge of poverty. Thoughtful planters were primed to seek alternatives, but a lack of a public will and investment capital discouraged them. So did what Berkeley termed the "dis-membring" of Virginia into other provinces, which in his mind increased the difficulty of trying to limit tobacco crops or to stimulate other staples. And he viewed the Navigation Act of 1660 as a major impediment too. Here he struck a cautious line. "No good Subject or Englishman" could

14. Billings, "Berkeley's *Discourse*," 33–36.
15. *Discourse*, 2–3.
16. Ibid., 4–7.

rightly oppose such a law if it advanced Crown or country, but he continued, in tones reminiscent of his play-writing days,

> if it shall appear that neither are advantaged by it, then we cannot but resent, that forty thousand people should be impoverish'd to enrich little more then forty Merchants, who being the only buyers of our *Tobacco*, give us what they please for it, and after it is here, sell it how they please; and indeed have forty thousand servants in us at cheaper rates, then any other men have slaves, for they find them Meat, Drink and clothes, we furnish our selves and their Sea-men with Meat and Drink, and all our sweat and labour, as they order us, will hardly procure us course clothes to keep us from the extremities of heat and cold; yet if these pressures of us did advance the Customes, or benefit the nation, we should not repine, but that it does the contrary to both, I shall easily evidence when commanded.[17]

Admitting that one tobacco ship brought more money to the Crown than five laden with Barbadian sugar, Berkeley was quick to contend that a variety of staples would be to England's greater benefit in the long run than the "vicious ruinous plant of Tobacco." Virginians could as easily raise such desirable commodities, as had he, but they needed the inspiration of the Crown's sanction and, more important, its direct financial investment. To attain those ends, he favored proposals that "at my departure from *Virginia* [were] desired by the Assembly." If the king-in-council would add an additional penny to the duty on tobacco and give it to his government, the extra income would pay all the colony's "publick charges" and underwrite all the expenses of diversification besides. Should that method of financing seem unacceptable to the Crown, then he suggested an alternative: the General Assembly should lay a tax of three to four shillings on each exported hogshead of tobacco, which planters, not merchants, would pay. Next, he urged that the owners of colonial-built ships be permitted to "carry their goods to what Port they pleased," which was his way of skirting the restrictions in the navigation law.[18]

Armed with royal guarantees of free trade and a steady source of investment capital, he claimed he could persuade the planters to follow his example. In seven years' time, he reckoned, Virginia would exceed the commercial value of Barbados, the colony that he regarded as the "mistress" of the American plantations. After all, he concluded, flax, hemp, iron, and silk were certainly "Commodities more lasting and necessary then Sugar or Indico." Besides, he said, Barbadians were already compelled "to expend one fifth part of their Merchandise to provide

17. Ibid., 8–9.
18. Ibid.

Victuals for themselves and Servants." Virginians, by contrast, fed themselves, meaning that they had proportionally greater amounts of cash to spend on British goods than their West Indian cousins. Hence, a diversified economy would further enrich Virginians and make them able to buy still more out of England. He closed by invoking the blessing of the God "that has made us so instrumental to the Wealth and Glory" of the nation.[19]

Berkeley timed his presentation of the *Discourse* to coincide with his appearance on 29 January 1661/62 before the Privy Council, where he and others set forth a variety of views about improving Virginia's economic situation. Although he repeatedly expressed his disdain for tobacco throughout the *Discourse*, he did not champion abandoning it as a cash crop. Advocating such a solution would have gotten him nowhere because it was too drastic an antidote both practically and politically. Raised in moderation, tobacco had always fetched decent prices. Consequently, the treatment he sought lay in restraining production, not in banning the weed altogether. Diversification held the promise of the ultimate cure, which was the point of the *Discourse*, but time and capital must be added to the healing salve for it to have any effect. Therefore, more immediate regimens were needed to combat the chronic disease of too much tobacco.[20]

Haunting the lobbies of Whitehall and the Inner Court of Wards, Berkeley tirelessly pressed the Privy Council and the Council for Foreign Plantations to adopt his intermediate remedies. He often appeared before both bodies as well. Just as frequently, he worked out of public view enlisting aid from willing merchants and others interested in the tobacco trade or colonial commercial policy. By such means he welded those individuals into a pressure group that barraged the government again and again with pleas for relief throughout much of 1662. If Berkeley did not always draw up the position papers himself, he at least counseled in their preparation and saw to it that they consistently articulated the five short-term remedies he had in mind. One called for the building of more towns across Virginia. Another recommended a form of debt relief for planters. A third aimed at ending tobacco culture in the British Isles, whereas a fourth proposed halting production in Virginia and Maryland until prices rose. The last, he argued, should require tobacco fleets to convoy before leaving colonial waters and to limit sailing dates to late-spring departures.

There was little new in these propositions. Several had kicked around in one guise or another for years. The novelty lay in Berkeley's combining them with diversification in the manner that he did.

19. Ibid., 12.
20. Minute of council meeting, 29 Jan. 1661/62, PC 2/55, 527–28, PRO.

His inspiration for joining town building and diversification sprang from several directions. An ally, the merchant John Bland, rekindled the old arguments in a remonstrance against the Navigation Act of 1660 that he sent to the Privy Council. Instead of limiting with whom the colonists traded, Bland contended, the Crown should restrict colonial commerce to a few places in Virginia, namely at selected locales on each of the colony's main rivers. Those sites would naturally attract skilled artisans to settle, towns would rise, trade would increase, and there would be no need for the navigation act. Another paper, the probable handiwork of Martin Noell, repeated many of the same justifications, only it went a step beyond Bland's reasoning. The surest, fastest means of encouragement, insisted Noell, was for the king to reward colonists who founded towns and to compel merchants to trade in those places only. Then, and only then, would ports sprout up and settlers cease to live scattered about the countryside. Even the clergy got into the act. The Reverend Roger Green, who served in Virginia, put forward arguments why the church hierarchy should join its voices to those of Noell and Bland. In a memorial to his immediate ecclesiastical superior, Gilbert Sheldon, bishop of London, Green maintained that "the unhappy State of the Church in *Virginia*" stemmed from dispersed settlements that allowed colonists to fall away from religion and out of right relationship with God and civil society. Accordingly, God had visited His just curse upon those wretched sinners. The obvious remedy for their lapse from grace was for the church to throw the weight and majesty of its authority behind the current push for urban development.[21]

Distribution of Green's memorial in print discloses how Berkeley used the parson to advance his cause. The two men were obviously acquainted because Berkeley had licensed him to perform his clerical duties in Virginia. Besides that, Green associated with another highly regarded colonial clergyman of Berkeley's acquaintance, the Reverend Philip Mallory. When the General Assembly of March 1660/61 dispatched Berkeley to London, it also sent Mallory in search of money to fund a college and to recruit additional priests. Green accompanied him. Berkeley, Mallory, and Green were acting on behalf of the assembly, so it is not too much of a stretch to assume that they sailed to England together and kept in constant touch afterward. As Berkeley marshaled his forces in favor of town building, he turned to Green and gave him a copy of the *Discourse*, portions of which Green incorporated into the printed text of his original plea to Bishop

21. John C. Rainbolt, "The Absence of Towns in Seventeenth-Century Virginia," *Journal of Southern History* 35 (1969): 343–60; "The Humble Remonstrance of John Bland," *VMHB*, 1:152; Martin Noell [?], Proposalls concerning building of Towns, ca.1662, Egerton MS 2395, 666, BL; [Roger Green], *Virginia's Cure: Or, An Advisive Narrative Concerning Virginia* (London, 1662), 1.

Sheldon. The amended version became *Virginia's Cure: Or an Advisive Narrative Concerning Virginia* (London, 1662), whose author was identified on the title page only as "R.G." That touch of anonymity fooled none of the intended readers, though it is indicative of Berkeley's flair for dramatic gestures.[22]

In the end Charles and his advisors came down foursquare in favor of encouraging Berkeley to renew his earlier efforts at town building. Their decision was more or less predictable, considering how their predecessors had prodded the colonists on that score for a half-century. This time, however, the chances of success seemed more promising, given the tie between urban development and agricultural diversification.

Berkeley made the pitch for his second goal himself. In a paper he tabled before the Council for Foreign Plantations in July 1662, he asked his fellow commissioners to recommend royal confirmation of six Virginia statutes. All but one of those laws were his creations, and they had been on the books for many years. He admitted that they diverged from English commercial practices in some particulars, but he justified the deviation on grounds that they fostered a business climate that put the planters on a more competitive footing with tobacco traders and shippers. To make the environment more favorable still, he urged the council to sanction enactment of a new Virginia law. This one should require "That for fower yeares to come wee should not make any debts in tobacco as now wee solely doe but assigne the payment in money, corne, cattle, horses silk, flax, hempe." The advantages of the statute were palpable. Such an act "would facilitate that universall desire which the merchants & planters have to lessen the too great quantities of tobacco." It would also "advance those staple commodities . . . for the ballance of our trade" because in "those yeares all debts to the Merchants would be payd what were due under what denomination," and the planters could cut back the size of their crops "without prejudicing the Merchant who cannot be compelled to lessen his debt." Ultimately, the substitution would suffice as a type of temporary debt relief because it would spare planters from having to grow more tobacco just to keep abreast of their financial obligations.[23]

The recommendation passed to the Privy Council. In due course it received

22. William Waller Hening, ed., *The Statutes at Large; Being a Collection of All the Laws of Virginia from the First Session of the Legislature, in the Year 1619,* facsimile ed. (1809–23; rpt., Charlottesville, Va., 1969), 1:424; 2: 30–31, 34; [Green], *Virginia's Cure,* 15. No manuscript of Green's text is known to exist.

23. Petition to the Council for Foreign Plantations, [23 July] 1662, fol. 183–84; PRO; Hening, *Statutes at Large,* 1:287, 301–2, 260, 248–49, 491–92.

the councillors' tacit approval and formed the basis of legislation that Berkeley later proposed to the General Assembly.[24]

As for the third remedy, stopping tobacco culture in the British Isles was a perennial aim of the colonists that reached back in time almost to the days of John Rolfe and the beginning tobacco farming in Virginia. James I and Charles I both prohibited the practice by proclamation before Parliament banned it by statute. Lax enforcement inevitably resulted in ever larger yields, which by the 1650s provoked colonial planters to insist upon further action from the lord protector. Cromwell tried but failed to solve the problem. After the Restoration demands for help rekindled, and Parliament responded with yet another law that the Crown seemed determined to execute. Island growers now found themselves in an extremely exposed position. Their numbers were few, and, being concentrated mainly in the counties of Gloucester, Devon, Somerset, and Oxford, they lacked much in the way of mutual interests with county magnates. They offered no political advantages to Charles, and their crops yielded no direct monetary benefit to the royal Treasury. Hence they were vulnerable.[25]

With the home growers out of the picture, their enemies readily concluded that the value of Virginia's crop would improve in every respect, as would the king's take from the import duties. Berkeley argued those very points in a petition that he laid before the Privy Council on 26 August 1662 on behalf of Sir Henry Chicheley, Edward Digges, Richard Lee, himself, and "other Planters & inhabitants in Virginia & Maryland." Once more he reminded the council of the problem of low prices, only this time he laid the cause specifically at the feet of British producers. The solution was at hand. Charles had only to give his "Royall Injunction" to put existing law into "full & due execution." That would stifle the competition, the problem would soon disappear, and the colonists would "be induced & incouraged to essay some further wayes for the advancement of Trade and increase of your Majesties people Shipping and Revenue."[26]

24. Instructions from Charles II, 12 Sept. 1662, CO 5/1354, 265–76, PRO; Hening, *Statutes at Large*, 2:189–90, 208.

25. Cay, *Abridgement*, 2: under "Tobacco"; W. L. Grant and James Munro, eds., *Acts of the Privy Council of England, Colonial Series* (London, 1908–12), 1:27, 592; C. F. Firth and R.S. Rait, eds., *Acts and Ordinances of the Interregnum, 1642–1660* (London, 1911), 2:870; various petitions from merchants, planters, and traders to Oliver Cromwell demanding the elimination of British grown tobacco, 1653–55, CO 1/12, fols. 13, 14, 18, 20, 47, 48, 63, 95, 96–97, 101–3, PRO; Charles M. MacInnes, *The Early English Tobacco Trade* (London, 1926), 51–105; Andrews, *Colonial Period*, 4:14n–15n.

26. Petition of Sir William Berkeley et al. to the Privy Council, [26 Aug. 1662], CO 1/116, fol. 220, PRO.

The Privy Council pounced on Berkeley's suggestions and seized them with alacrity. In truth, of all his proposals these drew the strongest royal backing. Charles promulgated additional proclamations that called upon local authorities to enforce the statute to the letter, and the Crown sent troops into the tobacco-growing counties with orders to destroy the crops. The effort eventually put British producers out of business.[27]

Berkeley's fourth and fifth remedies were not so happily met. They were vastly more difficult to apply, however, given the combative opposition that immediately coalesced against them. "Stinting," that is imposing limits on colonial production as a means of driving up the price of tobacco, was an idea that first surfaced in Virginia in the 1630s, but it never got far legislatively until Berkeley latched onto it. At his behest the General Assembly of March 1660/61 adopted a law that forbade planting tobacco seedlings after 1 June on the grounds that such a restriction would lead to an "improvement of the price" and an "amendment of the quality of tobacco." The act included a stiff fine that penalized any planter who was tempted to ignore it. Implementation was conditional upon the willingness of the Maryland assembly to pass similar legislation. No such law came down from St. Mary's City, and Berkeley sailed to London knowing that his scheme for a stint needed royal orders for it to succeed.[28]

To that purpose Berkeley rounded up several groups of his mercantile allies, who began talks with the Crown. For openers, on 26 May 1662 they sent the Privy Council petitions outlining the merits of a royally enforced stint. If tobacco production was limited, they claimed, then prices would improve, merchants and planters could pay customs duties without falling into destitution, investment capital would accumulate, and more desirable staples would be forthcoming. But the thing that was needed to ensure those happy results was the king's proclamation prohibiting planting tobacco in Virginia and Maryland after 10 June of every year for the future. "Consideration thereof being had," the council rejected the petition.[29]

The council minutes failed to record the "considerations" that led to the decision, although they are easily guessed. No councillor knew the effect of a stint upon royal income, and, at a time when the Treasury was thin, the king's closest advisors were reluctant to forestall a proven revenue stream. For a stint to yield the benefits claimed for it by its advocates, it must be enforced diligently, and

27. MacInnes, *Early English Tobacco Trade,* 105–30.

28. Hening, *Statutes at Large,* 1:206; 2: 32; Russell R. Menard, "A Note on Chesapeake Tobacco Prices," *VMHB* 84 (1976): 401–11.

29. Privy Council minutes, 26 May 1662, PC 2/55, 641, PRO.

there was little reason to believe that the authorities in Virginia and Maryland could effectively control growers. If anything, the task would be even more arduous for them than it was for their British counterparts because plantations were scattered and because colonial officials had fewer means to impose their will than the Crown could command. All knowledgeable individuals did not accept the rationale for a stint. The size of the opposition is difficult to calculate precisely, but its numbers were plainly plentiful enough to sway the Privy Council. Quantity did not tell all because there were individual opponents whose opinions alone gave the Privy Council pause.

One such critic was Cecilius Calvert, second baron Baltimore. As lord proprietor of Maryland, he had good reason to be dubious of Berkeley's claims. Marylanders and Virginians were not the happiest of neighbors because, from the founding of Maryland, the very existence of his colony was a source of irritation that continually vexed Virginians. Marylanders were no less annoyed by the antics of William Claiborne and other Virginians who interfered in their affairs even to the point of open warfare. Little wonder, then, that Maryland officials disdained Berkeley's proffer of cooperation to achieve legislative limits on tobacco production. Their rebuff fueled his strictures against Maryland in his *Discourse*, which did little to endear Berkeley to Baltimore.[30]

Whatever the reasoning, the Privy Council's rejection of the petition was a serious setback for Berkeley. An even greater blow was the simultaneous declaration "that [the Privy Council] henceforth would not receive any petition of that nature." That pronouncement, if upheld, closed off any further debate on the merits of a stint, and, unless Berkeley could keep alive the possibility of additional discussion, his entire scheme for redirecting Virginia's economy would be seriously flawed. He and his allies wasted little time before pressuring the council to withdraw its order. Details of their lobbying are scanty, but they evidently pushed hard the contention that a blanket refusal to countenance another consideration of a stint was a denial of the subject's right to solicit the king for redress of grievances. The councillors conceded as much when, on 13 June 1662, they reversed themselves and admitted "That it was not their Intention to forbid or discourage [anyone] from making their addresses to them." They also gave "the said Planters, Merchants & Traders for Virginia, & all Persons therein concerned, as also the Lord Baltimore," ten days to prepare for a hearing. Both sides resubmitted their position papers, and the issue received a thorough airing.[31]

30. Petition to the Privy Council, ca. 26 May–13 June 1662, CO, 1/16, fols. 165–66, PRO; Aubrey C. Land, *Colonial Maryland: A History* (Millwood, N.Y., 1981), 57–73.

31. Privy Council minutes, 26 May 1662, PC 2/55, 641; Privy Council minutes, 13 June 1662, PC 2/56, 10, PRO; instructions from Charles II, 12 Sept. 1662, CO 5/1354, 265–76, PRO.

Neither group overwhelmed the other with the strength of its case, which left the Privy Council at an impasse. If the council favored one, then it faced inescapable repercussions from alienating the other, and the councillors had no stomach for that, given the uncertainties of the remedy and the depth of the opposition to it. Someone offered an elegant way around the impasse. There would be no recommendation for a royal edict for a stint. Instead, the council ordered Berkeley to treat with the Marylanders and gave the king's blessing beforehand to any stint that he might negotiate. That solution made good political sense because it ended the debate in a seemingly equitable fashion with little or no risk to the privy councillors or to the Crown's overall colonial policy objectives. Whether Berkeley succeeded or failed, the burden of the eventual outcome was his, not the king's.

Berkeley's reaction is unrecorded. As any astute politician would, he accepted the decision as the best result he could have gotten under the circumstances. After all, he did not go away empty-handed. He could claim Charles's support for the principle of stinting, which was more than he started out with, and that backing conferred a decided advantage in dealing with the Marylanders. Whatever his feelings, he may well have decided to mask them because any outward show of displeasure would jeopardize his final proposal, arguably the most problematic of his short-term remedies.

The suggestion of a royal mandate to convoy tobacco fleets and to embargo departures to late-spring sailing dates aroused such intense controversy that it threatened the coalition Berkeley had built to lobby for diversification. Two of his principal backers, John Jeffreys and John Bland, opposed each other. For Jeffreys, who typified substantial, well-situated London merchants, the proposal foretold an ordered, stable market that operated through established channels. To Bland it held the potential for radically recasting the ways planters and tobacco merchants did business. Such a prospect was singularly unappealing to him and to similar smaller independent traders, who found the existing methods of marketing quite to their liking.

As the current practice stood, individual merchants controlled the ebb and flow of the trade. Every year traders dispatched their ships to Virginia and Maryland in the fall, each according to his own schedule. Vessels reached the Chesapeake intermittently, whereupon the captains worked the streams that fed the great bay in search of cargoes. Never knowing how many ships would show up, or when, planters frequently bargained with the first skipper who tied up at their landings. The hope of a quick sale was for a high return in England, assuming their crops arrived at the market before someone else's, but the race to be first tended to keep prices low because early buyers rarely offered top prices. On the other hand, ships that sailed alone or in small numbers made inviting targets for buccaneers, whose unpredictable raids added to the hazards of the seas.

Safety was in numbers, so convoying lessened the danger considerably, and, if the fleet sailed at a date certain every spring, then the planters would be in a more competitive position when they came to dicker with their buyers. Prices would go up as a matter of course, and the colonists would have additional capital that would flow into diversification projects. Those claims informed two petitions that certain "planters and traders to Virginia" advanced. Drawn up around the end of May 1662, the documents begged Charles to command "that no Shipp or Vessell carrying any Tobacco shall come forth of the Capes of Virginia before the first day on May next." Implicitly, the embargo would continue until such time as prices stabilized in the future.[32]

Scarcely had the petitions landed on the Privy Council desk than they were countered by the vehement pleas of merchants, shippers, and planters, who stiffly protested what they viewed as a completely unwarranted attempt at limiting how they conducted their trade. The counterclaims, in the main, denied any connection between the price of tobacco and the time of year when ships arrived or departed from Virginia. Restricting departures to late-spring sailing dates worked undue hardship on traders, who would be forced to set out for the Chesapeake "in the dead of Winter, which will prove verie dangerous to the shipps & outward lading & alsoe to the passengers & seamen." Such passages meant that planters would not "receive their cloathing and other necessaries which they shall want for the winter season untill Januarie or February," whereas "Hys Majestie will be hindered and debarred if his Early customes from Virginia att least four months." There was also an issue of fairness. "This designe" was a "debarring of his Majesties subjects their birth right" to trade "att such times and seasons as they shall find fit and expedient." Was it not reasonable, moreover, to take the pulse of the Virginia and Maryland legislatures, which "represent the voice of the whole people in both places (there being a very small Number of them resident here) should not be first consulted with and then heard to offer their reasons against this designe before any order or determination be made thereupon Considering what consequences a lymityation or restriction of tobacco may produce where soe many thousands are concerned, liveing at soe great distance and haveing soe bad a neighbor to blow the Coales"?[33]

32. Petition of planters and merchants to the Privy Council, ca. 14 May 1662, CO 1/16, fol. 145, PRO; same to same, ca. 26 May 1662, CO 1/16, fol. 160.

33. Petition of merchants, ship owners, masters, and others to the Privy Council, 13 June 1662, CO 1/16, fols. 165–67; same to same, ca. July 1662, CO 1/16, 207; same to same, ca. July 1662, CO 1/16, 228, PRO.

Once again, the Privy Council confronted a hard choice. And, again, it wriggled off the hook and passed the decision to Berkeley. It charged him to work out a solution with the Marylanders and other interested parties after he returned to Virginia. Intentionally or not, the directive closed the rifts in Berkeley's mercantile coalition, which retained its vigor for the remainder of his stay in London.

Spring slipped into summer, and it became increasingly evident that his work was nearing its end. Charles and his advisors thought as much because in late July 1662 they commanded that Berkeley "do Forthwith repaire to his Government." They went on to direct that new instructions "be written to him from his Majestie to endeavor by Consulting with the Planters there and with the Lord Baltemores Lieutenant in Maryland or Commissioners appointed by him to Agree upon the promoting of the Planting of Hemp, Flax, and Silke &c. in those Plantations and the lessening of the Planting of Tobacco there, and that the restraint for the Planting of Tobacco may be alike in both places."[34]

Those orders took upward of two months to perfect into letters patent. Meanwhile, Berkeley remained on the alert, making sure to protect the gains he had won. He also prodded the Privy Council to get on with drafting his instructions so that he might go home to Virginia. For all of that, he still found time to follow up on other business more than at any other period of his stay in London. It may well have been during this interlude when the artist Sir Peter Lely (1618–79) executed the three-quarter-length likeness of him that hangs now in Berkeley Castle in Gloucestershire (see fig.).

Lely posed his subject boldly and in a way that radiated Berkeley's soaring presence. Berkeley stands sideways to the viewer, with his head glancing over his left shoulder. His right hand purposefully grasps a baton of office. Palm facing outward, his left hand rests on his left hip. He is smartly garbed in the military attire of the early Restoration era. Generous folds of a cravat accentuate the head and complement the blouse with its billowy sleeves, which are cinched at the elbows with broad ties and at the wrists by snugly fit cuffs. A wide, loosely gathered sash winds around half-armor that provided more decoration than protection. The hilt of a finely wrought rapier hangs from its supporting belt. Shoulder-length hair cascades from the crown of the head in tight ringlets that frame a long oval face, and an angular nose separates broad-set eyes. A fashionable, pencil line moustache decorates the upper of the thin, firmly drawn lips. The entire countenance is of a man well into his middle years. Deep lines underscore the eyes and run from the corners of the mouth. The skin along the jaw line is no

34. Draft order, ca. 21 July 1662, CO 1/16, fol. 165, PRO; journal of the Council for Foreign Plantations, 21 July 1662, CO 1/14, PRO.

Sir William Berkeley. Portrait by Sir Peter Lely, c. 1662.
Courtesy of the Berkeley Will Trust, Berkeley Castle, Gloucestershire

longer taut, though the jaw itself has a purposeful jut to it. Ultimately, the eyes are the portrait's most riveting feature. Their haughty gaze conveys the self-assurance, perhaps even the arrogance, of a man at the top of his form.

Lely well and truly captured his subject. Berkeley stood justifiably proud in the summer of 1662. He went to London bent on protecting Virginia interests, and he won the Crown's blessings, if not its outright encouragement, for his ideas about diversifying the colony's economy. Family connections enabled him to navigate the highest court circles effortlessly, and men in government sought his opinions. Skill, determination, and forceful reasoning assured him audiences that not only heard him but listened intently and were swayed by the close logic of his arguments. To move Charles II and his councillors in that way was heady wine for any British subject, but it was especially intoxicating for Will Berkeley. For once in his life he had achieved something at court that conspicuously distinguished him from his brothers. Not only that, his attainment safeguarded his beloved Virginia and kept faith with his followers back home.

Whatever Lely's painting tells about Berkeley's personality, it says little about what brought sitter and artist together. Sir Peter Lely was no ordinary limner. A

Dutchman, he had alighted in England shortly before the Civil War and plied his talents with an increasing success that handsomely enriched him. He ingratiated himself with the Stuarts, who looked upon him as something of their painter-in-residence and treated him accordingly. It is no exaggeration to say that engaging Lely was a bit of a coup for Berkeley. The painting signified royal favor and something besides. Lely's portraiture represented ever so much more than mere still life renderings of vain, high-placed individuals who patronized him. His portraits of mighty men were meant to instruct, and he carefully showed his subjects as distant, awesome beings whose authority was to be revered, even feared. He depicted Berkeley in just that fashion. And who was Berkeley trying to impress? His fellow Virginians may be the obvious answer, but the painting was never theirs to view either at Jamestown or at Green Spring House. It stayed behind after Berkeley left for America, and it was eventually deposited at Bruton Abbey, where it remained until it passed to the Gloucestershire branch of the family.[35]

While Berkeley was sitting for Lely and keeping a weather eye on Crown officials, he looked to improve his financial situation. With a bit of effort he turned a one-time gift from Charles II into an annual grant. Sir Charles Berkeley used his place as treasurer of the king's household to divert unspecified amounts of cash to his brother, and he helped him reclaim various pre–Civil War benefactions. The sum of these additions amounted to a significant, albeit inexact, increase in Berkeley's personal fortune.

A most astonishing opportunity for gain came via his involvement in a speculative venture of enormous proportions. Berkeley and seven other men—Baron Berkeley; Sir George Carteret; Sir Peter Colleton; Anthony Ashley Cooper, baron Ashley of Wimborne St. Giles and later first earl of Shaftsbury; William Craven, first earl of Craven; Edward Hyde, the earl of Clarendon; and George Monck, first duke of Albemarle—joined forces to create themselves lords proprietor of a vast land to the south of Virginia, which was soon known as "Carolina."[36]

The eight were improbable bedfellows. Clarendon and Baron Berkeley roundly abominated each other. Will Berkeley and the lord chancellor got on rather better if only because years and distance had long parted them. Baron Ashley was a former parliamentarian who never quite earned the royalists' trust. A free thinker, he galled the older, more conservative Clarendon, whose timidity

35. C. H. Collins-Baker, *Lely and Kneller* (New York, 1922), 1–61. In his will the last Baron Berkeley of Stratton, who died in 1773, bequeathed the painting to the Berkeleys of Berkeley Castle, who were collateral relations of the governor (David J. H. Smith to WMB, 20 July 2001, Sir William Berkeley Papers Project archives).

36. Petition of Sir Charles Berkeley, Sir William Berkeley, and Thomas Middleton, 12 Nov. 1661, SP 44/13, PRO; warrant from Charles II, Sept. 1661, indexes 6813, PRO.

in foreign affairs and animosity to religious dissenters he challenged persistently. He and Will Berkeley took opposite sides on issues relating to the imposition of the navigation system. Craven and Carteret were Stuart loyalists who had served Charles's court-in-exile. Albemarle was an old parliamentarian, who, as Sir George Monck, helped ease Charles back to his throne. Friendly toward Clarendon, he was more interested in his place as the king's general-in-chief than anything else. Regarding Colleton, he was a royalist kinsman of Albemarle's who had fled to the West Indies, where he became a prominent Barbadian sugar planter.[37]

Drawing Berkeley into the group made good sense from a practical standpoint. His proximity to Carolina guaranteed that one of the proprietors would at all times be near enough to supervise its development on a regular basis. Besides, he had actual knowledge of the terrain that reached as far back as the 1640s, when he sent men to scout its upper parts and explored it for himself too. He witnessed the region's uncontrolled growth as Virginians streamed south in ever larger numbers throughout the period of his enforced retirement. (One of them was the Reverend Roger Green, who hoped to become a real estate developer after acquiring a ten-thousand acre tract south of Nansemond County in 1653.)

For all of that, becoming a proprietor was not part of the agenda that took Berkeley to London in the first place. And he had no previous personal connections to any of the group, apart from his brother and the lord chancellor. His first demonstrable associations with Colleton, Ashley, and Carteret happened when he joined them on the Council for Foreign Plantations in August 1661. About the same time, he grew familiar with Craven and Albemarle, who were privy councillors.

Those contacts sowed the idea for a proprietary colony, and, as the would-be landlords thought on it, they framed a case for easing their way to a royal charter. Arguably, English colonies to the south of Virginia advanced the nation's interest. Not only would settlements afford a buffer for the Old Dominion; they would also deny valuable real estate to the French, the Dutch, and the Spaniards as they consolidated English control of the east coast of North America. Realistically, however, the Crown lacked the means to fund such undertakings. That being so, the eight were willing to assume the risks of colonizing to ensure that the king would attain a worthy objective without draining his Treasury. Altruism aside, members of the group had something else in mind. As proprietors, they could repair broken fortunes and redeem their substantial financial claims against the Crown, which they could use as bargaining chits with Charles II. The king, the thinking went, would jump at a chance to cancel some large debts in exchange for granting away his "rights" to a portion of the American wilderness.

37. William S. Powell, *The Proprietors of Carolina* (Raleigh, N.C., 1963), 12–43, 47–49.

From the outset the proprietors figured their investment in Carolina would require no more than a nominal venture of capital and influence, which were necessary to move their charter through the royal bureaucracy to the king's signature. Patent in hand, they expected to populate their grant with little added cost to themselves. Seasoned colonists would emigrate out of Virginia, New England, or the West Indies, would bear all their expenses, and would pay for the privilege of renting the land. Rents, in turn, would provide the proprietors a steady, rising supply of income.[38]

Maneuvering for the charter, which included ejecting rival claimants, was in hand by late summer 1662. Who among the proprietors actually took charge of the lobbying is unknown, except to say that Berkeley was not one of them. His impending departure for America eliminated him as a potential lobbyist. That consideration aside, there seems to have been an understanding that his particular talents were better applied elsewhere. Specifically, upon his return to Virginia he would actively promote colonization of the proprietary, sanction existing land claims, appoint temporary officials, and, just as soon as the charter was perfected, receive detailed instructions about how the future advancement of Carolina should proceed.[39]

In the midst of these preparations there was another land grab that boded ill for Berkeley and his government. In August the surviving Northern Neck proprietors leased their rights to a consortium of Bristol merchants, who were keen to exploit the property. Evidently, neither the earl of St. Albans, Baron Berkeley, Sir William Morton, nor John Trethewy bothered to inform Berkeley about renewing their claims to the Northern Neck, which they had done the year before. There is no evidence to tell that they let on about their successful negotiations with the Bristolians before or after the fact. Reviving the long dormant land grant threatened Berkeley's plans for diversification and undercut his control over a

38. Andrews, *Colonial Period,* 3:182–91; Craven, *Southern Colonies in the Seventeenth Century,* 310–25; William S. Powell, ed., *Ye Countie of Albemarle in Carolina: A Collection of Documents, 1664–1675* (Raleigh, N.C., 1958), xiii–xxii; Herbert R. Paschal Jr., "Proprietary North Carolina: A Study in Colonial Government" (Ph.D. diss., University of North Carolina, 1961), 66–76; William S. Powell, *The Proprietors of Carolina* (Raleigh, N.C., 1963), 13–49; M. Eugene Sirmans, *Colonial South Carolina: A Political History, 1663–1729* (Chapel Hill, N.C., 1966), 3–6; Wesley Frank Craven, *The Colonies in Transition, 1660–1713* (New York, 1968), 54–57; K. H. D. Haley, *The First Earl of Shaftsbury* (Oxford, 1968), 227–31; Daniel W. Fagg Jr., "Carolina, 1663–1683: The Founding of a Proprietary" (Ph.D. diss., Emory University, 1970), 31–34; Robert M. Weir, *Colonial South Carolina: A History* (Millwood, N.Y., 1983), 49–51; Warren M. Billings, "Sir William Berkeley and the Carolina Proprietary," *North Carolina Historical Review (NCHR)* 72 (1995): 329–34.

39. Paschal, "Proprietary Carolina," 1–6, 83–86; Paul E. Kopperman, "Profile of Failure: The Carolana Project, 1629–1640," *NCHR* 59 (1982): 1–23.

significant portion of Virginia. And there is not the least hint in the extant record of Berkeley's learning about their plans for the Northern Neck until after he was back in Virginia. Charles II wrote him of the grant's renewal when he sent orders early in 1663 to assist the lessees in every way possible. It is curious that no one seemed to have considered the political fallout from a revived proprietary. Because St. Albans had a thirty-year history of advancing his first cousin's career, it is odd that the earl merely forgot to apprise a favored relation. The disregard of Baron Berkeley is stranger still. He and his brother were deeply implicated in the Carolina venture. All of which points to an inescapable conclusion. Money trumped blood, and St. Albans and Baron Berkeley put profit ahead of consanguinity. On a distant day that choice cost their kinsman dearly. Their duplicity and greed fostered Berkeley's hugely expensive campaign to buy the proprietary, the price of which helped fire Bacon's Rebellion.[40]

Other events moved Berkeley ever closer to a fixed departure date. On 3 September 1662, noting that "his Majesties Governor of Virginia is speedily to transport himself to his Charge," the Privy Council commanded that "the Business & Concernes of that Plantation be taken into consideration at the Board on Fryday next at Three in the Afternoone." To that purpose it ordered Berkeley, the secretary of the Council for Foreign Plantations, and the chancellor of the Exchequer to attend. When the council reconvened on "Fryday next," 5 September, it discussed the final content of Berkeley's instructions and incorporated such of his advice as it deemed appropriate. Satisfied that the last details were properly in place, the council turned the amended version over to scribes, who engrossed it. Charles signed and sealed the clear text on the twelfth, and it passed to Berkeley.[41]

Berkeley pocketed instructions that differed markedly from the ones Charles I had given him in 1641. His old orders were retreads of directives that dated from when Virginia first became a Crown colony. They had set forth lengthy, broadly drawn prescriptions for a novice governor, who had no say whatsoever in their preparation. By contrast, his new instructions were more an economic blueprint for progress than a general guide to governing. Narrower in scope and more focused in purpose, they were targeted at specific aims. Most notably, they bore the distinct press of Berkeley's fingerprints. They are thus a yardstick of his success at bagging the things he had gone to London to collect.[42]

Certain articles, which were construed as purely governmental in nature, re-

40. Lease to Humphrey Hook, John Fitzherbert, and Robert Vicaredge, 20 Aug. 1662, Clarendon Papers, 80, fols. 132–35, Bodleian Library, Oxford; Douglas Southall Freeman, *George Washington: A Biography* (New York, 1949), 1: app. I-1, 456–57; Charles II to Berkeley, 5 Dec. 1662, SP 44/10, PRO.

41. Privy Council minutes, 3 Sept. 1662, PC 2/56, fols. 66, 67–69, PRO.

42. The phrase is that of Sister Joan de Lourdes Leonard, "Operation Checkmate," 44.

sponded to the political concerns of colonial leaders. One of them addressed the future state of ecclesiastical affairs. It decreed that Virginians honor God according to the authority and "the Rights [*sic*] of the Church of England," though it left the matter of public support for the clergy wholly to Berkeley's discretion. Another extended Charles's general pardon to all colonials who had supported the parliamentary cause. A third recognized the General Assembly's right to exist. In effect the latter affirmed the constitutional changes the assembly had adopted when Berkeley resumed office, just as it implicitly endorsed the assembly's latest full-scale revision of the statutes in force. Yet another article dictated the more efficient collection of quit rents, and the final one granted Berkeley "a Commission of Oyer & Terminer for the better Administration of Justice and punishment of Offenses within that Our Colony."[43]

Relatively quiet about how he should govern, these articles codified a salient achievement for Berkeley. Their silence denoted a royal willingness to refrain from intruding unduly in Virginia's internal affairs. Such silence would play well in the colony. It allowed political Virginians still to distance themselves from Whitehall much as they had done in the past, and soothing colonial fears of a meddlesome Crown was a principal reason for Berkeley's trip to London. In the same way the king's silence permitted Berkeley to manage as he pleased, which strengthened a hand already bolstered by the economic instructions. Those orders vouchsafed concessions he had negotiated over the course of his lobbying. Fundamentally, he won the Crown's embrace of diversification and his ability to bring the concept to timely fruition. To that purpose he gained detailed backing for the short-term prescriptions that he argued were necessary to the realization of the overall scheme.[44]

These successes notwithstanding, three of his major objectives miscarried. The Crown flatly refused to allow Virginians freedom of trade, it watered down his arguments for the stint and limits on the tobacco trade, and it rejected his pleas for subsidies out of the royal Treasury. Those outcomes were inescapable, given the odds against Berkeley. Despite the many supporters he mustered, their per-

---

43. Instructions from Charles II, 12 Sept. 1662, CO 5/1354, articles 1, 2, 3, 8, 9, and 12, PRO; Hening, *Statutes at Large*, 2:42–148; Warren M. Billings, *A Little Parliament: The Virginia General Assembly in the Seventeenth Century* (Richmond, 2004), 195; Francis Moryson, comp. *The Lawes of Virginia Now in Force. Collected Out of the Assembly Records, and Digested into one Volume* (London, 1662). In all likelihood Berkeley arranged for the printing of Moryson's compilation, which incorporated the General Assembly's revision of Mar. 1661/62.

44. Kukla, "Some Acts Not in Hening's *Statutes:* The Acts of Assembly of October 1660," *VMHB* 83 (1975): 87–88, 92–93; Hening, *Statutes at Large*, 2:17; instructions from Charles II, articles 4, 5, 6, 7, 10, and 11.

sistent advocacy could not override the opposition to free trade within and outside the government. Hence, there was no way that Charles would exempt Virginia from the commercial restrictions in the evolving navigation system. Enemies of stinting and regulating tobacco traffickers were no less potent. Article 6 of his instructions pointedly reminded Berkeley of the debates "*at which . . . you have been present, and in all which Our Privy Councill have foreborn to give any determination by reason of the difference of opinions between the Merchants & Planters & Masters of Ships, no one party of which seem to be of the same mind and opinion,*" even as it empowered him to go forward to reconcile the discord. There was little money in the Treasury, and there was even less disposition to spend any of it on Berkeley's experiments, and he received no subsidy. Yet he did not leave entirely empty-handed. He now had authority to levy a two-shilling export duty on every hogshead of tobacco "or any other Imposition Our Assembly shall Judge fitt and reasonable." After defraying the costs of "Our Government there," including Berkeley's annual salary of a thousand pounds, the remainder would go toward diversification.[45]

Were those miscarriages fatal to Berkeley's dream for Virginia's future? His superiors did not think so, and neither did Berkeley. He left London convinced that he carried an ample license for his great project, and he resolved to bend the king's instructions as he saw fit. That said, everyone ignored the incompatibilities between the predicates of diversification and the bases of Stuart colonialism. Only time would reveal the harvest of their ignorance.

For the moment, however, Berkeley busied himself with final preparations for his return passage. Included with the papers he packed away was the duke of York's warrant to arrest several sailors, who were alleged to have committed murder at sea, to the High Court of Admiralty. York also informed Berkeley that the suspects and witnesses were already in the custody of Virginia authorities, awaiting service of process and transportation back to London. In and of itself, the duke's order was hardly extraordinary, though it is a very rare peek into the exercise of Berkeley's admiralty powers.[46]

A similar peep betrays a devious side to Berkeley. An apothecary, William Gape, treated Berkeley for various illnesses, only to have his remedies go unpaid.

45. Italics added.

46. Warrant from James, duke of York, 9 Sept. 1662, HCA 1/9, pt. 1, PRO; depositions of Jane Alicocke, Francis Awborne, and John Berkenhead, which are in the hands of the Virginia council clerk Francis Kirkman, PRO. The outcome of the case is uncertain, owing to the incompleteness of the files. Coincidentally, Awborne and Berkenhead were to figure in later events that touched Berkeley. Berkeley appointed Awborne to succeed as clerk of the Council of State upon Kirkman's death in 1670. Berkenhead betrayed a servant rebellion in Sept. 1663.

Learning that his patient was about to decamp for America, Gape desperately tried to collect his debt, but his efforts at squaring the account were for naught. An acquaintance of both men told why. "There is," the friend wrote, "a joke against the good apothecary that he has been 'choused [i.e., cheated] by Sir Wm. Berkeley,' who has given him the slip and embarked for Virginia, apparently in Gape's debt." Berkeley's behavior was of a piece with the way men of his station treated entrepreneurs such as Gape. The apothecary might sue, but the costs of litigating his action in Virginia exceeded its value, and hauling someone like Berkeley before a court, or even threatening to, did Gape's business no good at all. Berkeley knew that, and he sailed away, leaving Gape to sputter in frustration.[47]

Fair winds blew him homeward. Now came the real test of his ability. Could he persuade the Virginians that he held the keys to their future? If the charter passed the seals, could he make a go of Carolina too?

47. Margaret Varney, ed., *Memoirs of the Varney Family* (London, 1899), 4:33.

10

CAROLINA

harles II initialed the Carolina patent in March 1663. Strokes of the royal pen thus made Berkeley the greatest landowner in Virginia, for they entitled him to an eighth share in the proprietary. Charter in hand, his fellow proprietors and he were at last free to promote their colony, and to him fell the responsibility for its actual development. Happy as this news surely was, Berkeley knew nothing of it for the better part of a year.[1]

Unexpected legal complications caused the delay. In hurrying the patent through the bureaucracy, Clarendon and the other London-based proprietors did a slipshod job of ferreting out any rival claims to Carolina, and they missed an overlapping grant that Charles I conferred on Sir Robert Heath back in 1629. Heath never succeeded in settling the place he named "Carolana," but there were those yet alive who came forward to assert their interests because of Heath's charter. Their claims clouded the proprietors' title and drove the contending parties to law. An ensuing suit dragged on through the summer of 1663 before it yielded an order-in-council voiding all prior gifts and reaffirming the proprietors' rights.[2]

---

1. Letters patent to Edward Hyde, earl of Clarendon; George Monck, duke of Albemarle; William Craven, earl of Craven; John Berkeley, baron Berkeley of Stratton; Anthony Ashley, baron Ashley of Wimborne St. Giles; Sir George Carteret; Sir William Berkeley; and Sir John Colleton, 24 Mar. 1662/63, NcAr. This chapter derives in part from my essay "Sir William Berkeley and the Carolina Proprietary," *North Carolina Historical Review* (*NCHR*) 72 (1995): 329–42.

2. Herbert R. Paschal Jr., "Proprietary North Carolina: A Study in Colonial Government" (Ph.D. diss., University of North Carolina at Chapel Hill, 1961), 1–6, 83–86; Paul E. Kopperman, "Profile of Failure: The Carolana Project, 1629–1640," *NCHR* 59 (1982): 1–23.

His colleagues sent Berkeley an explanation for their long neglect of him soon after the Privy Council found in their favor. Their letter, dated 8 September 1663, contained advice about confirming existing land titles, prescriptions for future grants, and a set of orders for him to follow. Among the latter was authorization for a government in the region around Albemarle Sound, and to that purpose Berkeley received power to name such governors and councils of "fitting persons" as were needed. The missive went on to counsel that he pick men capable of keeping "well, good & peaceable government" who, with "the advise and consent of the freeholders or freemen or the Major parte of them there deputyes or delligates," would enact "good and wholsome lawes."[3]

The holdup seems not to have troubled Berkeley unduly. When he got back to Virginia, he saw that orderly settlement in the Albemarle country was already well in hand. Months before Berkeley's return, Deputy Governor Francis Moryson began issuing land warrants to eager planters, and he had even gone so far as to establish a rudimentary government in the settlement. Knowing all of this, Berkeley did nothing to reverse Moryson's actions as detrimental to his proprietary rights, and months rolled by before he doled out his first Albemarle patents.[4]

Granted, Berkeley may have hesitated for want of direction from London. That was unlikely. Boldness came easily to him, especially when the interests of Virginia were at issue. Notably, the interval between his return and his signing of the Albemarle patents on 25 September 1663 was a period when he threw himself boundlessly into maneuvering key diversification legislation through the General Assembly, rebuilding Jamestown, and dickering with the Marylanders for the stint. These priorities, to his way of thinking, were of far greater magnitude than exploiting the proprietary. Not even his coproprietors' letter of 8 September prodded him to consider otherwise. His indifference was indicative of the importance he ascribed to proprietorial duties—Carolina came a distant second to Virginia. That attitude forever colored his regard for the venture, and, because of it, Carolina received less of his attention than its people and his own private affairs deserved, and it brought only unhappy consequences for both in the long run.

Berkeley concentrated on two aspects of Carolina's development: crafting management documents and appointing governors. His hand is visible in the "Concessions and Agreements," promulgated on 7 January 1665, which super-

3. From Edward Hyde, earl of Clarendon, and others, 8 Sept. 1663, CO 1/20, fols. 3–6, PRO; Mattie Erma Parker, ed., *North Carolina Charters and Constitutions, 1588–1683* (Raleigh, N.C., 1963), 62–73.

4. Virginia Land Patent Book No. 4, 1655–63, 93–101, Vi; commission to Samuel Stephens, 9 Oct. 1662, Conway Robinson, comp., "Notes and Excerpts from the Records of Colonial Virginia," Conway Robinson Papers, ViHi, 244; Daniel W. Fagg Jr., "Carolina, 1663–1683: The Founding of a Proprietary" (Ph.D. diss., Emory University, 1970), 7–28.

seded the orders that the London proprietors had sent him fifteen months earlier. In addition to an agreement with settlers to colonize near Cape Fear, the concessions presented a more systematic form of government for the entire province. The parts that set forth the duties of governor, council, and assembly contemplated a legislative body with powers decidedly comparable to those of Virginia. That similarity betrays the handiwork of someone who knew the innermost details of Virginia government and how they might be fitted to a Carolina setting, and among the proprietors only Berkeley fit that description.[5]

As for his choices of governors, he first picked William Drummond. A shadow now, Drummond shone among the many colonists whose lives closely entwined with Berkeley's, but the two were never friends. It is no exaggeration to say that they came to detest each other to the very bottoms of their souls. Scots born and bred with commercial upbringing and smatterings of formal education, Drummond wound up in Virginia in 1637 after he indentured himself to a planter named Theodore Moyes. Moyes bartered him away to an abusive master. When Drummond could abide his mistreatment no longer, he did what indentured servants often did in his situation. He plotted with a band of his fellows to run away, but the conspirators were all soon caught and stood trial in the Quarter Court. They expected no leniency, and they got none. Instead, each received extra service and a severe public lashing as his punishment. The experience tamed Drummond to the extent that he behaved himself for the duration of his remaining bondage.

Once Drummond was set free, he leased a tenement on Jamestown Island, which was the first in a series of properties he rented or bought in James City and Henrico counties. Among the rentals was acreage in the Governor's Land that he leased from Berkeley, and there he built his principal residence. Commercial ventures linked him to local planter-merchants and assorted London traders. He benefited as well from land surveying and representing his fellow colonists in the courts. His daughter Sarah's marriage to Samuel Swann, whose father was a councillor of state, connected the Drummonds to the upper gentry. Berkeley appointed him to the James City County bench and gave him a turn as county sheriff. Sheriff Drummond received extra earnings because the shrievalty was a local office that entitled its incumbent to fees. Being sheriff of James City was better still in that it made Drummond bailiff of the Quarter Court and a sergeant-at-arms for the General Assembly, both of which drew him near provincial leaders in the two bodies and yielded him additional income too.[6]

5. Parker, *North Carolina Charters*, 109–27.

6. Virginia Land Patent Book No. 2, 1643–53, 150, Vi; Survey of the Governor's Land, 1683, Staffordshire Record Office, Stafford; William Byrd II Title Book, 1637–1744, 18, ViHi; H. R. McIlwaine, ed., *Minutes of the Council and General Court of Colonial Virginia, 1622–1632, 1670–1676*, 2d ed. (Richmond, 1979), 315, 467; Lindley S. Butler, "The Governors of Albemarle County, 1663–1689," *NCHR*

Carolina beguiled Drummond. Its moneymaking prospects and its choice real estate opened up opportunities he did not have in Virginia. He apparently stole a march on the competition when he teamed with Virginians Thomas Bushrod, Cuthbert Potter, and Sir Gray Skipwith to form a partnership with a London merchant called Gawen Corbin. Using his Carolina plantation as his base of operations, he was the middleman who marketed a huge line of cloth and other consumer goods that his partners regularly sent to Albemarle, and they financed a line of credit so that he might make loans to his neighbors as well. The combination turned him into one of the most important entrepreneurs in the colony.[7]

Drummond's route to the governor's chair was quite circuitous. Sir George Carteret thought to give the seat to a retainer, but, when nothing came of that idea, the proprietors left the choice to Berkeley. Berkeley dawdled for months in 1664 before settling on Drummond. His procrastination was problem enough, but an unanticipated legal entanglement caused still more months to slip away. Although Berkeley could select whomever he wished, his colleagues made no allowance for him to commission his nominee, which meant that his appointment of Drummond lacked the full force of law. The only way around that complication was for the commission to issue from London. Hence, the added delay while word of the nomination crossed the Atlantic and the commission was prepared. The proprietors finally signed and sealed the commission on or about 3 December 1664, but it was January 1665 before they mailed it and a set of instructions to Albemarle. Thus, more than a year passed before Drummond legally qualified for his office.[8]

None of this says anything about why Berkeley picked Drummond, and there is no clue to his thinking in his remaining papers. Circumstantially, his reasoning appears to have been guided by several considerations. He sought in a prospective governor someone with the wit and parts to oversee the Albemarle colony with only minimal guidance from him, and, from what he knew of his choice, Drummond filled the suit. Drummond picked up an awareness of law and court procedures during his time as a member of the James City County bench. Being sergeant-at-arms imparted insight into the workings of the General Assembly.

46 (1969): 281–89; William S. Powell, ed., *Dictionary of North Carolina Biography* (Chapel Hill, N.C., 1986), 2:107–8.

7. Drummond to "Deare Friend," 3 Sept. 1666, Miscellaneous Virginia Papers, 1606–92, 119–20, DLC.

8. Sir Robert Harley to Sir Edward Harley, 3 Nov. 1662, Royal Historical Manuscripts Commission, *14th Report: The Portland Manuscripts*, 3 (1894), app. pt. 2, 268; commission to William Drummond, ca. 4 Dec. 1664, in William S. Powell, ed., *Ye Countie of Albemarle: A Collection of Documents, 1664–1675* (Raleigh, N.C., 1958), 3–4; London proprietors to Drummond, Jan. 1664/65, in William L. Saunders, ed., *The Colonial Records of North Carolina* (Raleigh, N.C., 1887–90), 1:93.

(Actually, Drummond possessed more practical political experience than did Berkeley when Charles I named him governor-general.) Drummond's business partners were Berkeley's intimates. Their wide-flung commercial contacts would undoubtedly lure much needed settlers and trade to Albemarle, which meant that the colony would prosper without Berkeley or his colleagues investing much of themselves or their purses in building it up. No one among the other immigrants who alighted in Albemarle stood above Drummond in qualifications, nor did any of them scurry toward the job as eagerly as he. In the end it was proximity that won Berkeley's nod. The two men rubbed shoulders in the courts, in the General Assembly, and as landlord and tenant. These associations were close enough for Berkeley to take the measure of Drummond and to conclude that he would suffice.

Drummond proved a bad choice. He failed to match Berkeley's hopes for him in every respect, and he turned peevish at answering to Berkeley. The rupture between them was quite probably unavoidable, owing to their differences in mettle and the difficulties of Drummond's task. Streaks of unyielding stubbornness ran through them both, and they were quick to take umbrage at the merest of excuses. Drummond was rapier tongued and brazen. Berkeley was haughty and wholly unforgiving of anyone who crossed him.

Albemarle drew a disparate collection of land-hungry settlers, many of whom left Virginia believing prospects were better in the proprietary than in the Old Dominion. In that they were often disappointed because their desire for cheap land collided with the proprietors' design to realize income off quit rents and to reserve choice parcels for themselves. Rather than permitting Drummond to designate his own provincial secretary and surveyor-general—who mainly dispensed patents and laid out parcels of ground—the proprietors controlled those appointments. Immigrants came to regard these policies as troublesome and costly, and they complained loudly to London and to Berkeley. Then, too, ambitious Carolina colonists tussled to push themselves to the head of Albemarle's arising polity, and these contests contributed their fair share of dissonance in a society in the throes of being and becoming. Climate and geography also conspired against Albemarle. Disease, scorching heat, drought, crop failure, and hurricanes compounded the early toils of settlement. A shoal-ridden coastline afforded no good harbors so vital to ready supplies of goods and laborers. Isolated from easy outlets to the Atlantic and the Caribbean, the colonists depended inextricably on Virginia. They also relied on tobacco as the backbone of their emerging economy, which put them in competition with Virginia planters and complicated Berkeley's scheme for a stint.[9]

9. Peter Carteret's account of settling Albemarle, 1666–1673, in Powell, *Ye Countie of Albemarle*, 62; Craven, *Southern Colonies in the Seventeenth Century*, 322–28.

Somehow Drummond had to keep the lid on while contenting the settlers and following orders from Jamestown and London. It was not an assignment that came easily to him. His frustrations with the job mounted. Heedless of the consequences, he indiscreetly vented his exasperation in a letter to a friend. He bitterly complained that Berkeley and his colleagues "Obstructed the removall of my whole family to Albemarle." More pointedly, he bemoaned the requirement that land grants must be occupied within twelve months or else the property reverted back to the proprietors. Other "unreasonable parts of there [sic] Instructions," he claimed, "have hindered a thousand people already that weare really reminded to remove" to the colony and "make those that are there already leave," and he "hate[d] to see where I can doe [the proprietors] any service nor my selfe noe good." He attacked Berkeley openly, if cryptically, saying, "here are abundance of people that are weary of Sir Williams Government more I could say as to his obstructing all things of Carolina, but I conceive it not safe in regard I live soe neare him."[10]

A mischief maker passed the letter to Berkeley. Drummond's words incensed him and fueled his displeasure even more. His annoyance rose to greater heights after he and Drummond quarreled about the terms of a leasehold. Their spat bloomed into an acrimonious lawsuit that ricocheted from the James City County court to the General Court to the General Assembly to a rehearing by the assembly. Berkeley prevailed, but the case distracted him just as he was amid shepherding a stint bill to law. Drummond angered him yet again by declining to participate in negotiations with Maryland on tobacco controls, which hindered the much-sought agreement. Fed up, Berkeley dismissed Drummond in 1667. His removal effectively ended Drummond's flirtation with Carolina and finished him politically, but it was not the last that Berkeley saw of him.[11]

Drummond continued to rent from Berkeley. He even returned to his house at the Governor's Land and farmed his leasehold. Nearness embittered their sour feelings for each other, but they kept their dislikes mainly to themselves, at least until another incident set them off publicly once more.

In the early 1670s Drummond agreed to refurbish the Jamestown bastion "At

10. Drummond to "Deare Friend."

11. *Drummond v. Berkeley*, 8 June 1666, Virginia Colonial Documents, 1652–1776, fol. 1, Vi; ruling of House of Burgesses, 8 June 1666, Virginia Miscellaneous Papers, Jefferson Papers, DLC; denial of petition for rehearing, 29 Oct. 1666, H. R. McIlwaine, ed., *Journals of the House of Burgesses of Colonial Virginia, 1619–1658/59; 1659/60–1693* (Richmond, 1914–15), 37; William Waller Hening, ed., *The Statutes at Large; Being a Collection of All the Laws of Virginia from the First Session of the Legislature, in the Year 1619*, facsimile ed. (1809–23; rpt., Charlottesville, Va., 1969), 2:224–26; Berkeley to Drummond, 24 Oct. 1666, McIlwaine, *Journals, 1659/60–1693*, 35.

a Certaine Rate" within "A Certain Time." He still had not finished the job when word of the outbreak of the Third Anglo-Dutch War reached Virginia. Making matters still worse, a survey revealed the use of shoddy brick and timbering on the parts he had fixed. His shortcomings as a contractor left the capital with little protection amid the threat of a possible attack. Alarmed and greatly aggravated, Berkeley sought advice from a hastily gathered council of war, which he convened in April 1673. The council severely censured Drummond, but its members realized that they were stuck with him. They threatened further legal action if he did not immediately perform his contract to its exact letter. That warning received an additional reinforcement when the Council of State refused to pay Drummond until "such time as the said Fort be . . . Erected and Built According to the Conditions" of his agreement. Drummond appeared to comply, but in 1674 it came to light that he was still building with inferior materials and was far from done. The council fined him heavily and compelled him to redo his work. He blamed Berkeley for his costly rebuke. The contretemps drove an unbridgeable gap between them, and in 1676 Drummond joined with Nathaniel Bacon. He was among the last of the rebel's commanders to fall into Berkeley's hands after the uprising foundered. Berkeley, who regarded him as the principal instigator of the revolt, condemned him to dance for the hangman, and Drummond swung to his death in January 1677.[12]

Berkeley's second choice of governors, Samuel Stephens (1629?–70), was far happier. A native Virginian, Stephens was the child of parents with means and influence. His father Richard, a London painter-stainer, had established the family in the colony. Sailing for the Chesapeake in 1622 stocked with goods worth three hundred pounds and a share in a land grant from the Virginia Company of London, the elder Stephens fashioned himself into a prosperous tobacco exporter and an ally of Abraham Peirsey, one of the wealthiest colonial merchants of his day. Peirsey helped his protégé to abundant properties in Warwick County and to seats in the General Assembly and the Council of State. The Peirsey affiliation brought Stephens a wife too. He wed Elizabeth Peirsey about a year before Samuel was born.[13]

12. McIlwaine, *Minutes of the Council and General Court,* 334, 342, 367; Berkeley to Robert Beverley, 21 Jan. 1676/77, Hening, *Statutes at Large,* 3:569; court-martial of Drummond, McIlwaine, *Minutes of the Council and General Court,* 454; Thomas Mathew, "The Rise, Progress, and Conclusion of Bacon's Rebellion in the Years 1675–1676" [1705], printed in Charles M. Andrews, ed., *Narratives of the Insurrections, 1675–1690* (New York, 1915), 38; [John Cotton?], "The History of Bacon's and Ingram's Rebellion," Andrews, *Narratives,* 95–97.

13. Susan Myra Kingsbury, *The Records of the Virginia Company of London* (Washington, D.C., 1906–35), 1:625; 4:245, 257, 269.

Stephens died while Samuel was a small lad. His widow married Governor Sir John Harvey. When the Harveys returned to England in 1639, Dame Elizabeth left Samuel behind and conferred the management of him and his substantial legacy on a succession of guardians. Her selection of trustees was indicative of the standing of the boy's late father. She nominated such prominent men as Richard Kemp, George Ludlow, Samuel Mathews, and William Peirce. Although nothing is known of how the guardians educated their charge, they did well by him financially because they increased his real estate holdings by several thousand acres at least. And their own prominence ensured his insertion into the colony's political establishment once he came of age.[14]

About the time young Stephens attained his majority, he married Frances Culpeper (1634–95?), and their union brought advantages of its own. For Frances a deed of trust executed before the wedding conferred all of her soon-to-be husband's holdings upon her in the event he died without heirs. Marriage into the Culpeper family elevated Samuel socially and politically. Frances Culpeper belonged to genteel Kentish parents of royalist leanings who fled to Virginia in 1650. The Culpepers lived on Mulberry Island in Warwick County, not too far from their Filmer relations and Stephens's plantation, Bolthorpe. Frances's father, Thomas, was a member of the Virginia Company, an original proprietor of the Northern Neck, an associate of Sir John Berkeley, and an acquaintance of Governor Berkeley. After the couple took up residence at Bolthorpe, Samuel became a militia captain and likely sat on the bench in Nansemond or Warwick too. In the early 1660s, if not sooner, he was extending his holdings and interests southward into Carolina. He was sufficiently acquainted with Albemarle to catch the eye of Francis Moryson, who in October 1662 appointed him "commander of the southern plantation." Something about the way Stephens fulfilled his duties so impressed Berkeley that he decided to appoint Stephens as he was about to cashier Drummond.[15]

Stephens governed more or less to the satisfaction of everyone. He displayed flashes of political acumen of a sort that Drummond lacked, as when he gave

14. Virginia M. Meyer and John Frederick Dorman, eds., *Adventurers of Purse and Person: Virginia, 1607–1624/5* (Richmond, 1987), 586–88.

15. Terri L. Snyder, "Frances Culpeper Stephens Berkeley," in John T. Kneebone, J. Jefferson Looney, Brent Tarter, and Sandra Gioia Treadway, eds., *Dictionary of Virginia Biography* (Richmond, 1998), 1:450–51; commission to Samuel Stephens, 9 Oct. 1662, Robinson, "Notes," 244; commission and instructions to Samuel Stephens, 8 Oct. 1667, Powell, *Ye Countie of Albemarle*, 10–28; summary of deed of trust between Samuel Stephens and Frances Culpeper Stephens, 1 Jan. 1652/53, Hening, *Statutes at Large*, 2:322. Dame Frances's known papers, a mere twenty-two items, will appear in an appendix to Warren M. Billings, ed., *The Papers of Sir William Berkeley, 1605–1677* (forthcoming).

Peter Carteret, one of his councillors and Sir George Carteret's fourth cousin, overall command of the colony's militia. The London proprietors eased his task somewhat by allowing him to permit settlers to "hold the land upon the same tearmes the people of Virginia hold theirs." On the other hand, they refused to ratify acts of the Albemarle assembly until the laws were put in a "forme" that they prescribed, and they urged him to select "fitt places" for building a capital and other towns. Berkeley praised Stephens as an effective governor, saying that, "though he had not the fullness of understanding which men bred in Europe and early accustomed to manage affaires of great Importance usually have yett to supply this he was a man of approved Courage great integrity and a lover of the Collony & had many other personall vertues which usually make men lov'd and desired by those that know them."[16]

As much as Berkeley admired Stephens's "vertues," he noted in a letter he sent to Albemarle just after Stephens died how a mild temper and a gentle hand had inadvertently fomented "great factions" and offers of violence. He intimated that those troubles may have hastened the late governor's demise. Whatever its cause, Stephens's untimely death vacated his office, and Berkeley allowed the Albemarle assemblymen to elect a replacement.[17]

Frances Stephens bore no children, and in the spring of 1670 she suddenly found herself the owner of large amounts of land and married for a second time. Her new husband was none other than Will Berkeley. The attraction between the newlyweds can only be guessed. Both were in the market for spouses, both had known one another for many years, and the necessity of liquidating Stephens's estate and affairs in Albemarle unexpectedly threw them together. There were practical advantages to the union. Berkeley was sixty-five and in declining health. His first wife was years dead, and he was in search of a companionable consort. Frances Stephens's property, family, and relative youthfulness—she was thirty-six—raised her allure in his eyes. For Frances Stephens wedding the governor represented a step up the social ladder and a generous marriage settlement that included a life interest in Berkeley's English properties and an annual income of six hundred pounds, plus the prospect of inheriting Green Spring House and the rest of Berkeley's great fortune.[18]

16. Commission to Peter Carteret, 28 Oct. 1668, Powell, *Ye Countie of Albemarle,* 32–33; London proprietors to Samuel Stephens, 1 May 1668, Powell, *Ye Countie of Albemarle,* 29; same to same, Jan. 1670[?], Powell, *Ye Countie of Albemarle,* 34–35; Berkeley to the General Assembly of Albemarle, 7 Mar. 1670, 38.

17. Berkeley to the Albemarle assembly, 7 Mar. 1670, 38.

18. Probate of the estate of Samuel Stephens, 21 Apr. 1670, McIlwaine, *Minutes of the Council and General Court,* 211; deed of trust between Sir William Berkeley and Alexander Culpeper and Anthony St. Leger, 19 May 1670, Robinson, "Notes," 257.

At the time of his marriage Berkeley had already lost much of his interest in Carolina. The place never sprouted forth as the bounteous new Eden of his and his fellow investors' dreams. A stout measure of blame lay in his doorway because from the outset he had failed in his part as the nearly resident proprietor. Nourishing the Albemarle colony was only one of his many projects, but he bestowed far less care on it than he lavished on Virginia or Green Spring House.

Fault for Carolina's difficulties lay in London as well. Berkeley's partners devoted far less of themselves, their time, and their money to the colony than even he, and by the late 1660s their inattention put the colony in a desperate condition. Baron Ashley stepped forward and, together with John Locke, reorganized the operation. He began by negotiating a five-point agreement that promised a steady, adequate sum of working capital for the colony's future development. Each of the proprietors—save Colleton, who was dead, and Clarendon, who was exiled—put up five hundred pounds apiece to create a fund that John Portman, a London alderman and member of the Company of Goldsmiths, banked for them. The bulk of that money would go toward "shipping Armes, Ammunition, tooles, & Provisions for the Setlement of Port Royall" in the southern part of the province. A person, nominated by a majority of the proprietors and termed in the agreement as "an husband," would make the actual purchases and present his bills to Portman for payment. As a check against fraud, the husband was "obleidged to render unto any one of the Proprietors an account of his proceedings whenever therunto required." Finally, everyone agreed to contribute up to two thousand pounds on an annual basis for a period of four years. If someone failed to honor that commitment, the other proprietors would buy him out. Having secured the province financially, Ashley looked to Locke, who drew up a new, more elaborate frame of government that took form as the Fundamental Constitutions of Carolina.[19]

Ashley's assumption of control, plus the concentration of effort on Port Royal, left Berkeley with less to do than in the past, and he withheld more of his hand from Carolina affairs. He put it back briefly when he advised the Albemarle assembly about replacing Governor Stephens. His marriage involved him in settling Dame Frances's affairs in the Albemarle courts, but he entrusted those matters to an attorney, his brother-in-law John Culpeper. He also donated some £270 worth of provisions, which he packed off to the Port Royal settlers at his

19. Articles of agreement between the Carolina proprietors, 26 Apr. 1669, Shaftsbury Papers, PRO 30/24/48, pt. 1, PRO; Fundamental Constitutions of Carolina, Shaftsbury Papers, PRO 30/24/48, pt. 1; K. H. D. Haley, *The First Earl of Shaftsbury* (Oxford, 1968), 241–42; Fagg, "Carolina, 1663–1683," 119–21; J. R. Woodhead, *The Rulers of London, 1660–1689: A Biographical Record of the Aldermen and Common Councilmen of the City of London* (London, 1965), 132.

own expense. Apparently remiss in keeping up his other promised contributions, he became a target for Ashley, who wanted to squeeze him out. In 1672 Ashley exercised the buyout clause in the funding agreement and tried to exchange all of Albemarle for Berkeley's share of the proprietary. Henry Norwood, Berkeley's agent in the negotiations, squelched the deal, and the subject never arose again. Four years later Berkeley was peripherally implicated in the first stirring of Culpeper's Rebellion. His last Carolina involvement of record happened in April 1676, when Joshua Lamb, a Boston merchant, bought Roanoke Island from him. Berkeley died within a year of that transaction.[20]

For all of his knowledge of the place, Berkeley ought to have been more engaged with Carolina. That he was not spoke to his judgment of the proprietary as merely a gamble. If the cards broke right, he would add to his wealth. If not, then he would not be greatly out of pocket, and he still owned a great chunk of real estate. Virginia mattered more.

20. Henry Brayne to Ashley, 20 July 1670, Shaftsbury Papers, PRO 30/24/48, pt. 1, fols. 27–28, PRO; Minutes of meeting of the Lords Proprietors, 29 Mar. 1672, MS Locke c. 30, 3–4, Bodleian Library, Oxford; deed of sale to Joshua Lamb, 17 Apr. 1676, Suffolk County Deed Book 13, fol. 180, Boston; quieta est for Frances Culpeper Stephens, 21 Apr. 1670, McIlwaine, *Minutes of the Council and General Court,* 270; order-in-council regarding the will of Samuel Stephens, McIlwaine, *Minutes of the Council and General Court,* 235; Hugh F. Rankin, *Upheaval in Albemarle: The Story of Culpeper's Rebellion, 1675–1689* (Raleigh, N.C., 1962), 26–30; William S. Smith, "Culpeper's Rebellion: New Data and Old Problems" (master's thesis, North Carolina State University, 1990), 31–32, a copy of which Mr. Smith kindly gave me. Berkeley's attorney, John Culpeper, was a brother of Dame Frances and of no discernible relation to the John Culpeper who gave his name to the uprising in Albemarle.

11

VIRGINIA'S CURE

ome from his travels to London in November 1662, Berkeley wasted little time in sending forth "Conveneing Writts" to the General Assembly, where he would introduce his cure for Virginia's economic woes. Two days before Christmas, burgesses and councillors gathered at Jamestown for the rare winter meeting, and, as they greeted him, Berkeley missed seeing some familiar faces in the press of men who crowded around him. Councillors Henry Browne, Henry Perry, and Thomas Pettus and burgesses John Warren and Robert Soane were dead. Berkeley felt Soane's passing the keenest. Death not only claimed a neighbor and an intimate; it also deprived him of a congenial politician who had been his reliable leader in the House of Burgesses. Now Robert Wynne (1622–75) was speaker. Elected in March 1662, Wynne adroitly shepherded passage of the Moryson-Randolph revision of the statutes in force and moved an important batch of diversification bills into law. That display of acumen alerted Berkeley to the likelihood that he and Wynne could work together. Already friendly with each other, the two men allied easily, and they cooperated comfortably as the session wore on. So began a decade-long, close partnership that consistently garnered legislative backing for Berkeley even as it raised the General Assembly to its pinnacle of power as a little parliament.[1]

1. Berkeley to Henry Coventry, 6 Feb. 1676/77, Coventry Papers, 77, fol. 283. General Assembly accounts, Sept. 1663, Clarendon Papers, 82: fol. 275; Jon Kukla, *Speakers and Clerks of the Virginia House of Burgesses, 1643–1776* (Richmond, 1981), 63–64; William Waller Hening, ed., *The Statutes at Large; Being a Collection of All the Laws of Virginia from the First Session of the Legislature, in the Year*

Texts of the opening speech have vanished, but the drift is readily supposed from the session's laws. Berkeley recounted the results of his mission, summarized the king's instructions to him, announced his intention to negotiate a stint with the Marylanders, and said he would send Francis Moryson to succeed him as Virginia's agent at Whitehall. With that, the burgesses and councillors fell to business, and, when they recessed in mid-January, they presented some two dozen bills that he and Wynne signed into law.[2]

Berkeley got two statutes that were key ingredients in his economic remedies, one for imposing a two-shilling export duty on tobacco and another "An act for building a towne." He probably drafted both bills himself. If so, then he introduced them in the council, where they were debated and adopted before they went down to the House for its approval. Shorter of the two, the impost law derived its constitutional warrant directly from Berkeley's instructions. Therefore, it did not enumerate the uses to which the tariff would go. Instead, it merely forbade anyone from lading tobacco before payment of the duty, which was returnable either in sterling or "goods or merchandize." To curb evasion it required that shipmasters file compliance papers with one of an unspecified number of new customs officers whom Berkeley would appoint.[3]

Berkeley's instructions also provided the point of departure for the town bill. Article 4 expressed the king's wish "that there may be at least one Town in every River, and that you begin at James River, which being first seated wee desire to give all Countenance, and to settle the Government there." The article commanded leading colonists to be "good Examples . . . by building some Houses" at Jamestown, and it admonished Berkeley to "give a particular account by a letter to Ourselves of the success of this Our design."[4]

Translated into law, these stipulations set forth a plan for starting cities across Virginia. After Jamestown, additional towns would rise at Accomack on the Eastern Shore and in unnamed locations on the York, Rappahannock, and Potomac rivers. The act spelled out the manner of Jamestown's repair in elaborate detail. Berkeley would be in charge. All wooden structures within city limits would be demolished, to be replaced over time with ones made of brick. Thirty-two new brick houses would rise on a location of Berkeley's choosing, and they would be "regularly placed one by another in a square or such other forme" as he might direct. Each house would have the same floor plan, which consisted of an interior

1619, facsimile ed. (1809–23; rpt., Charlottesville, Va., 1969), 2:41–162, esp. 119, 120–21, 121–22, 122–23, 124, 125–26, 128, 133–34.

2. Hening, *Statutes at Large*, 2:163–79.

3. Ibid., 176–77; instructions from Charles II, 12 Sept. 1662, article 7, CO 5/1354, PRO.

4. Instructions from Charles II.

floor space that measured forty by twenty feet. Walls would be two bricks thick below the water table, a brick and a half above, and they would rise to a height of eighteen feet from ground level. A steeply pitched roof, covered with pan tiles or slates, completed the design. Built to these standards, the new Jamestown would become less susceptible to fire.

Funding would come from a special colony-wide head tax of thirty pounds of tobacco per poll, rather than appropriations out of ordinary provincial revenues. To keep costs down, the act capped worker wages and fixed the price of materials at set rates per item. It authorized every county court to impress enough crafts-men and goods to put up one house, which meant that local governments would bear responsibility for seventeen of the new buildings in toto. Individual colo-nists would erect the remaining fifteen. Court and colonist alike would receive subsidies of ten thousand pounds of tobacco per unit.

Private developers got other incentives. Just as soon as one of them began a house, he became exempt "during the tearme of two yeares" from "arrest, execu-tion or process of lawe, dureing his abode within the limitts of the said towne, or in his comeing to or going from thence." He was also promised free land on which to raise a warehouse that he would own in perpetuity and from which he would collect rental fees. To ensure him a steady flow of income, the act dipped into the pockets of colonists whose highway to trade was the James River. Plant-ers in Charles City, James City, and Surry counties were obliged to deposit their tobacco in the warehouses until it went to market. A similar requirement touched planters who lived along the lower James down to Mulberry Island, the midpoint between the capital and the river's mouth.

"Because the end for which the towne [was] being built would be wholly frus-trated unles expedition [was] used in effecting it," the act mandated that the en-tire project would be completed within two years from March 1663. Participants were given only until 31 March to file signed performance agreements with the secretary of the colony. Thereafter, anyone who failed to meet his pledge stood liable for a fine of fifteen thousand pounds of tobacco.

The statute said little about the other towns. In truth its section that dealt with them seemed no more than an afterthought. Dead silent about the look of the other towns or a precise timetable for their founding, it merely promised that the special tax would underwrite putting them up. And none would start before Jamestown was rebuilt.[5]

Of the remaining laws enacted at the session, one granted justices of the peace sole power to pass ordinances that were as "fully [binding] as any other act."

5. Hening, *Statutes at Large*, 2:172–76.

That warrant magnified the justices' authority in two significant ways. It codified a division of power between province and locality that was afoot since the 1630s, and it gave local magistrates a nearly absolute freedom to run their counties as they saw fit.[6] Another act took aim at a perceived threat to civil order—growing numbers of Quakers who refused to baptize their children. Several perfected court procedures that had been instituted incompletely in the revisal of 1662. There were additions to an already substantial body of labor law, and the most notable of them was one that statutorily defined chattel slavery for the first time. It declared that a child born to an African and a Briton inherited its mother's condition, rather than its father's, as was the English custom. (Very likely, the inspiration for that designation of status was a Roman law doctrine that came straight from Henry Swinburne's *Treatise of Testaments and Last Wills,* a book well known to members of the House, to councillors, and to Berkeley as well.) The remaining acts assessed horses, encouraged colonists to take up shipbuilding, levied payment of fort duties in powder and shot, suspended tax exemptions for tradesmen and "handy craftsmen," and forbade the exportation of animal hides.[7]

Taken as a whole, these laws say something about how Berkeley traded horses with the assembly before he made a bargain for the two-shilling statute and the town act. Bartering was understandable, indeed inevitable, given the nature of legislatures, but, considering what was at stake for Berkeley and the General Assembly, their dickering took on added gravity. Having sold his brief for diversification in London and having won the blessing of Charles II, Berkeley had now to peddle it in the colony. If the assembly failed to deliver what he wanted, his grand purpose for Virginia would fall into a jumble of spoiled dreams and broken hopes, his ability to govern would diminish, and his standing in Whitehall would be tainted too. On the other hand, few among the burgesses or the councillors doubted, even momentarily, the urgency of heeding royal orders. But these men were not of one mind about *how* to obey the king and *how* to turn his commandments and Berkeley's ideas into workable public policy. Some lacked

6. Ibid., 171–72; Warren M. Billings, "The Growth of Political Institutions in Virginia, 1634 to 1676," *William and Mary Quarterly* (*WMQ*), 3d ser., 31 (1974): 230–32.

7. Hening, *Statutes at Large,* 2:163–71, 177–79; Warren M. Billings, "A Quaker in Seventeenth-Century Virginia: Four Remonstrances by George Wilson," *WMQ* 33 (1976): 127–40; Edward L. Bond, *Damned Souls in a Tobacco Colony: Religion in Seventeenth-Century Virginia* (Athens, Ga., 2001), 161–74; Warren M. Billings, "The Law of Servants and Slaves in Colonial Virginia," *Virginia Magazine of History and Biography* (*VMHB*) 99 (1991): 45–63; Henry Swinburne, *A Treatise of Testaments and Last Wills, Fit to be understood by all men, that they may know, Whether, Whereof, and How to make them* (London, 1677), 52.

their governor's vision. Others balked at urban development as no more than a costly frippery never to match the claims of its advocates. Diversification had detractors too. Its existing legal supports already tapped the ratepayers, who would pay still higher taxes if Berkeley's proposed export duty and town bills were enacted.

As he always did whenever he found himself boxed in politically, Berkeley played to the House of Burgesses and gave ground where necessary. His tactic explains why he consented to the county bylaw statute. The law derogated his constitutional powers in local matters, but, in return for less control over the county courts, he coined political capital with the House. Justices of the peace to a man, the burgesses regarded the act not only for its enhancement of their magisterial power; they also cherished it for its aggrandizement of their social status. Then, too, the promise of additional collectorships ensured Berkeley succulent new patronage plums with which to tempt members in both chambers, and that sweetener eased passage of the two-shilling duty bill into law. Subsidies and other incentives in the town act rendered it more palatable as well, and in the end Berkeley got the things he wanted most.[8]

Work on Jamestown started around the time the assembly recessed. First on the agenda was picking where to build the new quarter. Berkeley chose to reorient the town, and he opted for an undeveloped tract of land at some remove from the inhabited areas. He hired a surveyor while he searched for developers, and he engaged to raise several houses himself. Loggers felled trees. (Because the sap was down, wood cut in cold weather had a reduced moisture content, which lessened drying time.) Sawyers and their pitmen prepared sawpits, rigged their gang saws, and laboriously cut logs into lumber. Carpenters fashioned rough-sawn blanks into window frames, door cases, joists, rafters, flooring, and other structural timbering. Brick makers baked bricks and pan tiles in the hundreds of thousands. Lime burners fired their kilns. Masons gathered great quantities of marl and sand for mortar. Construction supervisors rounded up teams of oxen and gangs of laborers, who stockpiled the various building materials and scaffolding strategically about the site.[9]

All was set, and building began in earnest in the spring of 1663. The following

8. Accounts for the years 1664, 1675, and 1676 are the only surviving record of collections for the two-shilling impost. They suggest that Berkeley distributed the collectorships to members of the council and the House in roughly equal numbers (General Assembly accounts, 1664, Clarendon Papers, 82: fol. 277; auditor-general accounts, 1675, CO 1/35, fol. 211; auditor-general accounts, 1676, CO 1/37, fol. 43, PRO).

9. General Assembly accounts, Sept. 1663, Clarendon Papers, 82: fol. 276; YDWI, 1657–62, 475; Berkeley to Edward Hyde, earl of Clarendon, 30 Mar. 1663, Egerton Mss 2395, fol. 362, BL.

September the General Assembly appropriated an additional allotment of thirty thousand pounds of tobacco, plus "what ever more it shall amount to next yeare," so that Berkeley would erect a statehouse "of such dimensions [as he] shall find Convenient for the Reception of Generall Courts and Assemblyes and accommodation of the Committees." Of necessity this purpose-built capitol would suit the space needs of a bicameral legislature. House and council would have places of their own, in which each body could debate out of earshot of the other. The council room would also suffice for a judicial chamber whenever the General Court met. Other spaces quartered the secretary of the colony, the house clerk, and committee hearing rooms.[10]

Any assessment of Berkeley as an urban designer and builder is sketchy at best. For sure, he was no Christopher Wren, who oversaw the rebuilding of London after the Great Fire of 1666. Neither was he a precursor to Pierre Charles L'Enfant, who laid out Washington, D.C., nor did his remodeled Jamestown ever approach the look of Francis Nicholson's Williamsburg. Instead, Berkeley comes across as someone who accomplished less than he envisioned in the town law but rather more than has been supposed by modern investigators.

An oft-examined spot of elevated ground, which holds a cluster of foundations quite unlike any elsewhere at Jamestown, serves as a starting point for rating his achievement. The patch sits in the northwest corner of the island, a short distance below where the isthmus once was and a few hundred yards slightly north of the church tower ruin. Civil engineer and pioneer archaeologist Colonel Samuel H. Yonge first explored the site a century ago. Delving into it, he found remnants of what he took to be four houses lying end to end in a straight line that ran eastward from the river's edge. Each enclosed an interior space of approximately forty by twenty feet, and Yonge thought the four conformed to the statutory specifications of the town act. He uncovered rear additions that doubled the size of every one. A fifth foundation shared its twenty-foot party wall with the easternmost house, though it ran to a length of seventy-four feet. It, too, had been modified at some subsequent point in its existence. Using such documents as he knew, Yonge judged the entire pile to be the remains of a capitol complex that Philip Ludwell projected from the substructures after fire had reduced the block during Bacon's Rebellion. Therefore, he called the ruins the "Ludwell Group."[11]

10. H. R. McIlwaine, ed., *Journals of the House of Burgesses of Colonial Virginia, 1619–1658/59; 1659/60–1693* (Richmond, 1914–15), 26.

11. Samuel H. Yonge, *The Site of Old "James Towne," 1607–1698* (Richmond, 1904), 84–97, esp. 89. Yonge simultaneously published his discoveries in book form and as a series of four articles under the same title in *Virginia Magazine of History and Biography* 11 (1904): 257–76, 393–414; 12 (1904):

His deductions were not unshakable, owing to disparities between clues he quarried from the earth and those he plucked from the documents. Attempts at refining or rejecting his inferences vexed later investigators, who proved no better at reconciling the inconsistencies than he. Their frustrations seem less compelling now. Recent probes of the Ludwell Group foundations yield a clearer understanding of how builders put up various elements on the site. Archaeology at Jamestown now relies on a sophistication of method unknown to Yonge and unimagined by his successors in the 1930s and 1950s, and there have been important documentary recoveries over the past half-century as well.[12]

At the outset house wrights started the two units nearest the waterside, which they finished in an initial period of construction. They joined a second pair to the first and put it up in a single campaign too. Four more houses were added, which shared long walls with the original buildings. The fifth foundation came last, though not necessarily before someone had expanded the smaller buildings. Such findings establish an order of construction, but they do not date when particular segments actually arose. Nonetheless, connecting the sequence to clues from paper records results in a rather precise building chronology.[13]

The provincial budget adopted by the General Assembly in December 1662 contains a disbursement of twenty-five hundred pounds of tobacco to John Underhill. A York County justice of the peace, Underhill received the payment for "his Extraordinary Paines in surveying the Ground for the Towne." Although the entry fails to pinpoint the site, it corroborates Berkeley's decision to build in an uninhabited section of town. It also dates Underhill's survey to sometime between 20 December 1662 and mid-January 1663, when the assembly rose.[14]

A subsequent order of the General Assembly divulges that four county houses neared completion in September 1663, implying that houses 1 through 4 went up in rapid succession. The assembly then went on to direct that "next yeare foure

3–53, 113–33; James M. Lindgren, *Preserving the Old Dominion: Historic Preservation and Virginia Traditionalism* (Charlottesville, 1993), 121–23.

12. Henry Chandlee Forman, *Jamestown and St. Mary's Buried Cities of Romance* (Baltimore, 1938), 165–74; John L. Cotter, *Archaeological Excavations at Jamestown, Virginia* (Washington, D.C., 1958), 25–28. Architectural historian Carl Lounsbury rejected these earlier interpretations. He contended that the Ludwell State House Group was in actuality the row house Berkeley had started in 1643 (Lounsbury, "Statehouses of Jamestown," MS [1995], 13–15, a copy of which Mr. Lounsbury gave me). His argument was gripping, though I was not persuaded by it (WMB to Lounsbury, 29 Feb. 1996, Sir William Berkeley Papers Project Archive).

13. Those results are set forth in William M. Kelso and Jamie May, "Review of the Archaeological and Documentary Evidence: Structure 144, Jamestown," MS (2002), and I am indebted to Dr. Kelso for giving me a copy.

14. General Assembly accounts, Dec. 1662, Clarendon Papers, 82, fol. 275.

houses more [were to] be built, and soe yearly foure houses untill the number of houses undertaken for by the Counties be accomplished." Besides, the assembly empowered Speaker Wynne "to make and Signe agreements with any that will undertake to build, who are to give good Caution for the effecting thereof with good sufficient bricks, Lime and Timber, and that the same be well wrought, and . . . approved of" before succeeding county contractors got paid.[15]

Budgetary records from 1663 disclose the courts of York, Nansemond, Isle of Wight, and an unidentified county as the first local governments to build in the new quarter. These documents also pinpoint Thomas Harris, Thomas Hunt, John Knowles, Thomas Ludwell, Francis Moryson, plus the improbably named Herman Smevin, as the first contractors for a portion of the privately built brick houses. Moryson and Ludwell lived in James City County. The others were Jamestonians. This revelation substantiates the great planters' lack of ardor for urban development, which Berkeley remarked on when he wrote to the earl of Clarendon that few councillors were "forward" in heeding the king's admonition to promote towns. On the other hand, Secretary Ludwell's observation to Henry Bennet, first earl of Arlington, about accommodating "the publique affaires of the country" in April 1665 indicates that Berkeley readied the capitol for occupancy in less than two years' time.[16]

The 1663 budget also records two outlays to Berkeley. One subsidized him because he promised to erect eight houses. The second represented the General Assembly's down payment on the capitol. This latter allocation is important for two reasons. It fixes 1663 as the starting date of the statehouse, and it suggests that Berkeley managed several building projects simultaneously.[17]

But was his statehouse part and parcel of the Ludwell Group in its original configuration? Both the archaeological data and the written record argue in the affirmative. As Colonel Yonge noted a century ago, four foundations in the block correspond to the provisions of the town law. Fiscal records illustrate how justices in four counties arranged to fabricate houses. Legislative decrees demon-

15. McIlwaine, *Journals, 1659/60–1693*, 28.

16. Berkeley to Clarendon, 30 Mar. 1663, Egerton 2395, fol. 362; Philip Alexander Bruce, *Economic History of Virginia in the Seventeenth Century* (New York, 1895), 2:536–45; John C. Rainbolt, "The Absence of Towns in Seventeenth-Century Virginia," *Journal of Southern History (JSH)* 25 (1969): 343–60; John W. Reps, *Tidewater Towns: City Planning in Colonial Virginia and Maryland* (Williamsburg, 1972), 52–55; Ludwell to Arlington, 10 Apr. 1665, CO 1/19, fols. 75–76.

17. General Assembly accounts, Sept. 1663, Clarendon Papers, 82, fols. 275–76. The provincial budgets for Dec. 1662 and Sept. 1663 are the only such fiscal documents of the period that have come down to us. They were not generally known to archaeologists or historians, and so they were not used in earlier attempts at trying to establish the implementation of the town statute.

strate that those four houses were finished by the time the General Assembly convened for its regular session on 10 September 1663. Budget lines and assembly orders document Berkeley's becoming house wright for a capitol. The largest foundation in the Ludwell Group supported a building that could seat separately thirty-nine burgesses,[18] a dozen or more councillors, and committees, with room left for the secretary and the clerk.

Councillors took up much of the ground floor. Berkeley probably kept an office there as well, though that supposition cannot be confirmed with certainty. Burgesses, committeemen, and the House clerk used the upstairs, which they had to themselves until 1673, when Secretary Ludwell was assigned a second-floor garret for his office. That arrangement proved less than congenial. As the burgesses observed long after the fact, "there [was] nothing Spoken or proposed in the house, that was not equaly heard there, as wel as in the Assembly room itselfe, besides the same gave continual opportunity to all sorts of persons to crowd before the Assembly room, under pretence of coming to the office." The secretary's quarters remained upstairs until after Bacon's Rebellion.[19]

Berkeley's eight houses have never been found. Perhaps he did not finish all of them, though nothing in his remaining papers, nor in any collateral record, points to that eventuality. More likely, the houses stood near the capitol complex on an as yet unexplored site. And there is a third possibility. He may have set them on ground that has since eroded into the James.[20]

Well east of the capitol, by several hundred yards, sat a distinctive brick structure, with interior measurements of 20 by 160 feet, which was erected during the 1660s. Laid end to end, its four components related to one another much in the manner of the original elements of the Ludwell Group. Conceivably, unnamed county courts put it up, or it was the handiwork of some private contractor.[21]

There is no telling what number of planters Berkeley corralled as house builders or how many actually followed through on their pledges. Berkeley intimated that Francis Moryson and Thomas Ludwell made good on their promises when

18. By the time the statehouse was ready for occupancy, two new counties, Accomack and Stafford, had been carved from existing ones, which raised the number of burgesses from thirty-five to thirty-nine. The odd number resulted from the fact that voters in Jamestown got to pick a burgess of their own. Presumably, the new courts were each liable for building a brick house. The Stafford County records are all but nonexistent, so there is no way to determine if the justices ever contracted for a house. On the other hand, the Accomack records are silent on the matter.

19. McIlwaine, *Journals, 1659/60–1693*, 60; McIlwaine, ed., *Executive Journals of the Council of Colonial Virginia* (Richmond, 1925), 1:93–94.

20. William M. Kelso, *Jamestown Rediscovery II* (Richmond, 1996), 21–22.

21. Cotter, *Archaeological Excavations at Jamestown*, 121–29.

he told Clarendon that by "their Councills, Encouragements, and Purses" both had "largely contributed to the building of our Town." Other contractors were less forthcoming. Thomas Harris, for instance, ran afoul of the General Assembly when he neglected to finish his houses within two years. He paid his fines, though he negotiated an extension from the assembly by offering cancellation of his subsidies. Thomas Hunt finished three dwellings, but he was forced to repay his allowances for two others. John Knowles returned several of his grants too, and Herman Smevin just disappeared, apparently without doing anything.[22]

With the onset of the Second Anglo-Dutch War (1665–67) Berkeley diverted resources to defend against an attack, and work on Jamestown slowed or stopped entirely. Once peace returned, there were additions to the compound. Of these newer elements perhaps one was the "Countie Brick house" that the James City County justices had in mind when they petitioned the General Assembly for the right to maintain a jail for "fellons and other publique prissoners." The assembly responded positively, and Speaker Wynne signed a seven-year lease with the court on the understanding that it would bear conversion costs and would return the house in "Sufficient repaire."[23]

Truth be told, Jamestown's residents never warmed wholeheartedly to urban redevelopment. They were slow to tear down dilapidated wharves or to pull up pilings of docks that had rotted into disuse. Many ignored the legal requirement to replace wooden buildings with ones of brick. The number of nonconformists grew to such an extent that it forced the assembly to heed agitation for an easing of the restriction. In 1671 the assembly "thought fitt to grant them libertie to repair their old wooden houses," and the next year it permitted the raising of wooden "out houses" that adjoined any dwelling or lacked brick chimneys. Planters up and down the James River complained mightily about storing their tobacco at Jamestown. Their grievance found lusty voice in a sharply framed memorial wherein the burgesses "intreated" Berkeley and the council to consider the impracticality of "build[ing] warehowses." Bringing tobacco to town was "Inconvenient and prejudiciall" because "the greatest parte" of their constituents were "in wante of Boates and not able to procure them." The conclusion that the difficulty would only be prevented "by every man keepinge his owne comodity and deliveringe it from his howse" was hardly a ringing endorsement of urban renewal.[24]

22. Berkeley to Clarendon, 30 Mar. 1663; McIlwaine, *Journals, 1659/60–1693*, 44, 50.

23. McIlwaine, *Journals, 1659/60–1693*, 53.

24. Memorial from the House of Burgesses to Berkeley and the Council of State, ca. 5 June 1666; McIlwaine, *Journals, 1659/60–1693*, 25, 56, 58.

Berkeley responded to the foot dragging in telling fashion. Spurred by a rush of enthusiasm that surged through him whenever he tackled some new project, he at first threw himself into improving Jamestown with great eagerness. Met with resistance and confronted with other demands upon him, he lost interest, and the inner push that prodded him to finish a job waned. So, he did not rebut the House when it begged him to ignore the warehouse provisions in the town act, nor did he resist loosening legal restrictions on wooden construction, and he all but gave up on urban renewal in the 1670s.

If he had not achieved everything that he set out to do, he could at least console himself at having done his duty to the king. A new capitol and standing county houses testified to that. Something else had always figured into his calculations. Town building fit his overall design of diversification, but it never sat atop his list of priorities. Raising cities in the wilderness counted more for him as a means of winning political support in London than as a major goal. His scheme could flourish *only* if he limited tobacco production and substituted diversity for single-crop agriculture. And throughout the 1660s his efforts at negotiating a stint and cajoling planters into growing exotic staples commanded the greatest of his energies.[25]

Naming Francis Moryson Virginia's agent opened the maneuvering for the stint. The appointment seemed ideal. It rewarded Moryson for his past services as deputy governor, and it bespoke Berkeley's unbounded faith in the colonel's political usefulness. Moryson still had good royalist connections, though he had not been in England for more than a decade, and his ties would certainly be assets as he roamed the corridors of Whitehall. For his pains he would be paid an annual stipend of two hundred pounds, plus expenses. His was a threefold charge. Generally, he acted as the main conduit between Jamestown and London, meaning that Berkeley would funnel all manner of important business through him. He was also responsible for lobbying against the king's recent revival of the Northern Neck proprietary. Most important of all, he would join with Sir Henry Chicheley, Edward Digges, and John Jeffreys to ensure that Lord Baltimore did not frustrate the stint. Berkeley used the occasion of his departure to give him a packet of letters for Clarendon and Sir Henry Bennet, one of which flamboyantly attacked Maryland for hindering "the growth, wealth, and Reputation of this Colony, more then both the Massacres, by . . . not complying with us in those designes, which were for the Advancement of both our Interests & Trade." Mory-

25. The eighteenth-century historian Robert Beverley drew notice to this tendency of Berkeley's (Beverley, *History and Present State of Virginia*, 135). It is also noteworthy that after 1663 Berkeley never mentioned town building in any of his extant letters.

son sailed to his new assignment at the end of March 1663, not knowing that fourteen years would pass before he would see Virginia once more.[26]

Having bid Moryson farewell, Berkeley sought out the Marylanders. His overture was barely off the ground before difficulties on the Eastern Shore threatened the very possibility of talks between the two governments, let alone negotiations as sensitive as those to limit tobacco. The Eastern Shore troubles traced to the presence of Quakers who lived in a contested area along the borders of Virginia and Maryland. Sorely persecuted, the Quakers flourished from the moment of their arrival in Virginia in the mid-1650s, and some of their largest concentrations were in Northampton County. Their presence there particularly annoyed Edmund Scarburgh. Scarburgh—Northampton justice of the peace, surveyor-general, deputy treasurer, burgess, one-time speaker of the House, and staunch Berkeley ally—held all Marylanders in contempt. He not only badgered Quakers who lived in Northampton, but he harried those who fled into the disputed territory and who looked for succor to Lieutenant Governor Charles Calvert. Calvert and the Maryland council objected against Scarburgh in a letter to Berkeley that also declared their intention of drawing the boundary as they saw fit and at a time they would "appoynt."[27]

With a bit of fancy diplomatic footwork Berkeley sidestepped the potential deadfall. He isolated Scarburgh, first by promising support for more anti-Quaker legislation at the next session of the assembly and then by going along with Scarburgh's wish to make the upper part of Northampton into a new county, to be called Accomack. To calm Calvert, Berkeley telegraphed his willingness to appoint a board of surveyors to draw an equitable boundary between the two colonies, though he cautioned that creating such a board required legislative action, which could come no earlier than the fall. Pretending the border dispute was but a trifle, he sent Calvert a letter that expressed his interest in perfecting a stint. He named a commission to represent Virginia and asked Calvert to nominate a comparable team. Next, he proffered the Northumberland County courthouse as the meeting place, which lay just over the Potomac River from Maryland at the home of Isaac Allerton. To add weight to his propositions, he informed Cal-

26. License to Francis Moryson, 26 Mar. 1663, CO 1/17, fol. 42; Berkeley to Sir Henry Bennet, 30 Mar. 1663, CO 1/17, fols. 43–44; Berkeley to Clarendon, 28 and 30 Mar. 1663, Egerton MS 2395, fols. 360, 362, BL.

27. Susie M. Ames, *Studies of the Virginia Eastern Shore in the Seventeenth Century* (Richmond, 1940), 230–37; Clayton Torrence, *Old Somerset on the Eastern Shore of Maryland* (Richmond, 1935), 3–81; Spotswood Hunnicut, "Quakerism in Virginia" (master's thesis, College of William and Mary, 1957), chap. 1; Calvert and the Council of State to Berkeley, *ca.* 8 Apr. 1663, Proceedings of the Council of Maryland, 1661–76, Liber H.H., 172–73, MdAA.

vert that he was acting on royal instructions that expressly directed him to initiate negotiations and to report the outcome to King Charles. He ended by saying, "Both I & Mr. Secretary unlesse hindered by the interposall of some unexpected and pressing occasion would come to wayte upon you att the time & place appoynted." Ever sensitive to the niceties of diplomacy, he entrusted delivery of the message to Councillor Richard Bennett, who had warm family relationships with Maryland through his son and namesake.[28]

Calvert replied affirmatively on 28 April. He promised that he and Secretary Henry Seawell would appear at Northumberland, providing "other Business" did not "disapoynt" them. Days later, he named Philip Calvert, Henry Causey, and Edward Lloyd as his commissioners. Predictably, the three were close to the proprietor. Besides being a Calvert, Philip was a councillor of state and chancellor of the province. Causey sat on the council too. Lloyd had Virginia connections. He emigrated in the 1620s to the area that became Lower Norfolk County. An early member of that county's court, he also went to the House of Burgesses soon after the General Assembly became bicameral. His Puritan beliefs led him to Maryland in 1650 and to a new political career that eventually exalted him to the council.[29]

John Carter, Richard Corbin, Richard Lee, and Robert Smith treated for the Old Dominion. Founder of the Virginia Carters, Carter (?–1669) settled in Nansemond County in 1641 and now lived in Lancaster County at Corotoman, along the banks of the Rappahannock River. He filled various local and provincial offices before he joined the Council of State in 1658. Corbin (1629–76) emigrated to Lancaster County in 1654. He, too, passed up the political ranks and arrived at the council soon after Berkeley's return to power. A former royalist soldier and one of three major generals in the colony's militia, Smith (?–1683?) was a recently appointed councillor. Lee was Berkeley's friend of twenty-years' standing, the incumbent attorney general, and a councillor. The four were experienced traders who favored reducing colonial dependence on tobacco. That stance lined them up behind Berkeley's diversification plan, but they also belonged to a group of newer council members who were his intimates.

28. NoOB, 1657–64, fol. 166; ADWI, 1663–66, fol. 1; Susie M. Ames, "The Reunion of Two Virginia Counties," *JSH* 8 (1942): 536–48; Berkeley to Calvert, ca. 28 Apr. 1663, Proceedings of the Council of Maryland, Liber H.H., 173–75; J. Frederick Fausz, "Richard Bennett," in John T. Kneebone, J. Jefferson Looney, Brent Tarter, and Sandra Gioia Treadway, eds., *Dictionary of Virginia Biography* (Richmond, 1998), 1:446.

29. Calvert to Berkeley, 28 Apr. 1663, Proceedings of the Council of Maryland; Virginia M. Meyer and John Frederick Dorman, eds., *Adventurers of Purse and Person: Virginia, 1607–1624/5*, 3d ed. (Richmond, 1987), 390–91.

Mutuality of interest and friendship aside, there was an added reason why Berkeley picked only councillors, and it had to do with political considerations. From past experiences he knew only too well that Maryland planters were lukewarm toward stinting. Their assembly voted down a stint proposal in 1661. It was likely to do so again, so he needed a way over that barrier. His solution was to leverage the Maryland assembly. That could be done, he thought, if he appointed councilmen as emissaries and if he attended the conference along with Secretary Ludwell. Such moves would compel Governor Calvert to respond in kind, lest his team be outshone by commissioners of more eminent stature. The stint could then be negotiated council to council, as it were, and the ensuing treaty could be promulgated by executive fiat. Calvert responded just the way Berkeley had predicted, and Sir William rode off from Green Spring House encouraged that his objective lay within reach.

The two entourages reached Northumberland about mid-May. Nothing like them had ever descended upon the courthouse before, and, as titular host of the conference, Berkeley left nothing to chance. He meant to put everyone in a right frame of mind, so he arranged for one of the local justices, Peter Ashton, to lay on an elaborate welcoming "Enterteynment."[30]

Afterward he and Calvert withdrew, but the secretaries stayed behind as their personal spokesmen. There are no minutes of conference deliberations, though it is clear that conviviality and the makeup of the delegations got the talks off to a pleasant start. The dickering happened so speedily that commissioners and secretaries initialed an agreement within a day or two. Quite short, the compact contained three articles. The first "proposed to the Respective Assemblyes of each Government that noe Tobacco shall bee planted, or sowed in Either Colony in the succeeding yeare of 1664 after the Twentieth day of June upon such Forfeiture, and punishments as shall bee thought fitt by the said Assembly & effectuall for such a restraint, and that such a Restraint bee continued for one yeare onely unless the said Assemblyes shall thinke fitt to continue it Longer." Next, the Marylanders promised to convene their legislature in September for a vote on the terms and to send the result "with all possible speed" down to Jamestown. Finally, both governors pledged "their utmost Endeavours" to enforce the agreement.[31]

The treaty was not what Berkeley had gambled for, but, like it or not, the compact brought him closer to a stint than at any time in the past. Always the pragmatist, he took what the conference gave him and sought more. Reaching

---

30. General Assembly accounts, 1663, Clarendon Papers, 82, fol. 276.
31. Articles of agreement, 12 May 1663, CO 1/17, fol. 230.

into his political trick bag, he found something he thought might have a favorable influence on the vote in Maryland. He reconvened the General Assembly a month ahead of schedule and introduced two bills to heighten the pressure on Governor Calvert. One ratified the May agreement. The other set up the commission to reconcile the boundary differences on the Eastern Shore. His ploy utterly failed to impress Maryland House members, who overwhelmingly vetoed the stint.[32]

As much as anything, Berkeley's ignorance and more than a touch of presumptuousness accounted for the treaty's failure. Berkeley had misunderstood the dynamics of politics in Lord Baltimore's province. Planters there suffered the ill effects of too much tobacco the same as Virginians, but they were always leery of any arrangement that smacked of an advantage to Virginia, which is how many of their representatives read the stint treaty. Alternatively, some took the view that there could be no effective controls unless restrictions were imposed uniformly throughout English North America and the British Isles as well. Then, too, the Maryland assemblymen were a fractious lot who resented the proprietary family and its dominance on the council. They vented their exasperation to Governor Calvert and hedged his leadership in ways Berkeley had never experienced. Predictably, they were unimpressed when they heard that the Virginia assembly had ratified the treaty and enacted the boundary commission. The dissenters in their ranks likewise recoiled at the harsh new Virginia law against Quakers that made good Berkeley's pledge to Edmund Scarburgh.[33]

Berkeley did not read his defeat as his doing. He attributed the setback to obstinacy and shortsightedness. Frustrated, but not to be denied, he tried to turn the Marylanders' mulishness against them. To that purpose he prepared an appeal to Charles II, which he and Speaker Wynne signed on behalf of themselves and the General Assembly. The petition opened with a rehearsal of "your Majesties Royall Commands" for both colonial governments "to treat of the most convenient way of lessening the quantities of Tobacco, thereby to improve the Commoditie." Berkeley then related that the negotiations had led to a treaty.

32. Hening, *Statutes at Large*, 2:179, 183–85, 190–91; William Hand Browne et al., comps., *Archives of Maryland* (Baltimore, 1883), 1:484–85; 5:16.

33. Hening, *Statutes at Large*, 2:180–83; Michael Dalton, comp., *The Countrey Justice: Containing the Practice of Justices of the Peace Out of their Sessions* (London, 1677), 180–81; Melvin G. Herndon, *Tobacco in Colonial Virginia: "The Sovereign Remedy"* (Williamsburg, 1957); Michael G. Kammen, "The Causes of the Maryland Revolution of 1689," *Maryland Historical Magazine* 55 (1960): 292–313; John C. Rainbolt, *From Prescription to Persuasion: Manipulation of Eighteenth Century [i.e., Seventeenth] Economy* (Port Washington, N.Y., 1974), 57–59; David W. Jordan, *Foundations of Representative Government in Maryland, 1632–1715* (Cambridge, 1987), 97–112.

Unfortunately, it was only an agreement in principle because, as he noted, the Maryland commissioners "[pretended] that they had not a power to impose any such Law upon those Inhabitants without the Consent of theire Assemblie." By the stubborn "refusall of theire Conformitie" to the treaty, the Marylanders not only nullified the king's "Princely Care and favor"; they also left planters in both colonies without relief and still burdened with the "inconveniencies" of too much tobacco. Berkeley closed with a prayer for Charles's direct intervention, which he asserted would be the only sure means of realizing the stint.[34]

Dispatched in June 1664, the petition made its way to London and into the hands of Francis Moryson. It scarcely came as a surprise to him. Contacts in mercantile quarters and regular correspondence with Berkeley kept him abreast of the turn of events in the Chesapeake.[35] Once he learned the fate of the treaty, he knew Berkeley well enough to anticipate the petition. When it reached him, he quickly put the paper in play. Protocol dictated that he present it to the Privy Council, rather than directly to the king. He handed the document over to one of the council recording clerks on 3 August and requested an immediate hearing on its contents. He was told to return in a week's time. On the appointed day Moryson appeared together with Sir Henry Chicheley, Edward Digges, and John Jeffreys, Berkeley's great ally among the London merchants. A reading clerk intoned the petition for the benefit of the king and the attending privy councillors. They considered what they heard but took no action. Instead, they ordered a copy made for delivery to Lord Baltimore, and they summoned all parties, plus the farmers of customs, to a second meeting that they set for "the first Councell day after Michaelmas day next."[36]

The Privy Council convened on the matter again on the appointed day, 5 October. Baltimore and the Virginians were called in and asked for a recapitulation of views. Listening to both sides at length, the council ordered that the parties "do speedily meete" and reconcile their differences. If an accord was impossible, then each side must draw up "distinct proposalls" that were to go to the Council for Foreign Plantations for its consideration and recommendation. Negotiations dragged through to mid-November, but there was no union of minds. The Virginians stuck to the provisions of the 1663 agreement. Baltimore was not at all keen for stints, but, if one was to be, then it should only occur every third year,

34. Petition to Charles II, ca. June 1664, CO 1/18, fol. 202.

35. Nearly all of the exchanges between Moryson and Berkeley are gone. The few that remain, in addition to references to lost letters in other correspondence, clearly indicate that the two were in frequent communication about the stint and other matters.

36. Privy Council minute, 10 Aug. 1664, PC 2/57, 94–96. Michaelmas Day fell on 29 Sept., and it was a holy day in honor of St. Michael the Archangel.

and he also stiffly held out for his colonists gaining a longer time to plant to offset Maryland's shorter growing season. Deadlock put the dispute before the Committee for Foreign Plantations. The committee took the issue under advisement on 19 November, and within a week it utterly repudiated the stint. As a sop, it urged the king to promote cultivation of other staples by allowing them into England duty free for a period of five years. To appease Berkeley it counseled that he be permitted to export duty free three hundred tons of tobacco for every three hundred tons of silk or other exotic staples that he shipped to England. The Privy Council called the parties together on 25 November to announce that it had taken the committee's advice, which it promulgated immediately. The stint was dead.[37]

Rebuffed, Moryson and his colleagues retired, shocked by a result they had not foreseen. Berkeley's immediate reaction is unknown. He can only have marveled at so sudden a reversal of fortunes, but he should not have been surprised by it. Inherently, his faith in curing Virginia's economic ills with a stint carried the risk of just such a turnaround. The remedy always inspired as many doubters as believers. He had overborne the dubious when he convinced Charles II to let him give stinting a chance. The skeptics remained steadfast in their unbelief, and, after he sailed back to America, they steadily chipped at his support in Whitehall and in the London mercantile community. His foes gained more advantage as changes in the Crown's political fortunes swayed the balance toward their judgment of England's best interests with respect to tobacco regulation. Seizure of New Netherlands and Dutch ports on the African coast intensified a drift toward war with Holland. Anticipating just such a conflict, the lord high admiral, James, duke of York, launched a major buildup of the royal navy. The king's own finances were in tatters too. All of which made the want of Crown income much more desperate in the fall of 1664 than it had been in the summer of 1662. Depleted coffers brought the Privy Council to a conclusion it deemed as apparent as it was undeniable. Any policy that limited tobacco production inevitably cut down the duties on tobacco, which were a steady source of much needed cash. Relieving the distress of far-off colonists came a pale second at the very time when demands for royal revenues were as great as they were now. And, so, the Privy Council repudiated the concessions that it had authorized in Berkeley's instructions a mere two years earlier.

Defeat failed to daunt Berkeley. He would find his way around this latest impediment, only he needed time to regroup and invent another approach to win-

37. Privy Council minute, 5 Oct. 1664, PC 2/57, 151–52, 156–57; memorial from Francis Moryson et al. Nov. 1664, CO 1/18, for 254.

ning over the Marylanders. If he could do that, then he could secure the Crown's blessing. Staving off Indians and Dutchmen sidetracked him for much of 1665. A short tobacco crop that year dampened his feelings of urgency, but in November he indirectly broached the possibility of stinting with another appeal to the king.[38]

He avoided blaming Lord Baltimore or the Privy Council for the defeat both had dealt him the year before. Instead, he pointed out flaws he perceived in the council's fear that stinting diminished royal revenues. Merchants, he wrote, never imported more tobacco into England than could be sold for high "prizes." Invariably, they bought only the top grades; the rest they left behind. That rule applied whether the annual crops were small, average, or excessive, and it bore no relation to a stint. More damaging to the intake of royal revenues were the "Frauds" perpetrated by the farmers of the customs. As proof of his point, Berkeley reckoned the combined crop from Virginia and Maryland for 1665 came to forty thousand hogsheads of vendible product. At a rate of 50 shillings per hogshead, the Crown should realize £100,000 in duties, "yet on search" he claimed that the farmers turned in only a quarter of that amount to the Treasury. His conclusion was obvious. Honest collection methods yielded greater revenues. The most remarkable part of the letter was its admission that he had mistakenly favored altering "the usuall way of trade & commers." He argued for that highly controversial proposition while he was in England, and he was instructed to try it, but he never did after his return to the colony. Lately, he told the king, unnamed individuals had advocated requiring shippers to sail for colonial waters only once yearly on the theory that such a timetable would minimize tobacco exports and drive up prices. He expressed his opposition, which he justified with the same reasoning his adversaries had used against him back in 1662. The letter ended with an entreaty that Charles not load his most "conspicuously Loyall Country" with a burden not asked of other colonies.[39]

Charles's answer was not recorded, and Berkeley did not explain his change of heart. His about-face may have had a connection to feelers he had received from Maryland authorities before and after he wrote to the king. Governor Calvert approached him with a view to ending the Eastern Shore border dispute. He sent his brother to Jamestown, where Philip Calvert and Berkeley worked out an equitable settlement. Their encounter led to others that reestablished cordial relations between the two governors and their top advisors, which encouraged

38. Berkeley to Richard Nicolls, 7 July 1665, Blathwayt Papers, CsmH.
39. Berkeley to Charles II, ca. Nov. 1665, CO 1/20, 11.

letters and off-the-record discussions about ways to handle too much tobacco. Berkeley discerned an opening that he capitalized on in an unexpected way.[40]

In the deep winter of 1665–66 and at some hazard to his health, he left Green Spring House for a cold journey to St. Mary's City. He sat down with "the Leift. Governor . . . & others of the most understanding persons of that Government," who listened as he outlined a new approach to the problem of too much tobacco. Instead of promoting a "stint," he pushed something he styled a total "cessation" of tobacco growing. His choice of words was deliberate. Calling a duck by another name avoided unpleasant memories, while it circumvented the royal prohibition against stinting. The experiment could begin in 1667. If it worked, then trials could be extended in succeeding years until surpluses disappeared and prices improved. He conceded the honor of initiating the cessation act to the Maryland assembly, and he guaranteed that, if a law passed in St. Mary's City, the Virginians would promptly follow suit. His last suggestion was the creation of commissions to tuck in ultimate arrangements. After his hosts had heard him out, they promised to introduce his proposals at their next assembly. Berkeley left for home, hopeful that the two governments might actually succeed.[41]

True to his word, Calvert submitted a cessation bill, which quickly picked up majority support in the council. The House of Delegates objected strenuously, and it refused to budge unless Calvert conceded certain conditions. Mainly, the assemblymen wanted the Albemarle colonists to be included in the agreement, they insisted on easing debt payments during cessation years, and they pressed for representation on the colony's negotiating team. Calvert had little choice but to acquiesce. No statute would materialize without those compromises, and, unless he wanted defeat, he must yield to the delegates' demands. They were written into the bill that passed into law on 10 April 1666. The ink had scarcely dried on the engrossed text before messengers hotfooted off to Jamestown with a copy for Berkeley.[42]

Berkeley "joyfully received" the document and immediately set a meeting of the General Assembly for 5 June, though the burgesses lacked their governor's cheer. Much like the Maryland delegates, they doubted the efficacy of this latest

40. Berkeley to Philip Calvert, 22 Mar. 1663/64, Conway Robinson, comp., "Notes and Excerpts from the Records of Colonial Virginia," Conway Robinson Papers, ViHi, 245; commission from Charles Calvert, 3 June 1664, Robinson, "Notes," 244; articles of agreement with Philip Calvert, 7 June 1664, Robinson, "Notes," 244, Hening, *Statutes at Large*, 2:221–22.

41. Berkeley to Charles II, 24 June 1667, CO 1/21, fols. 118–21.

42. Brown et al., eds., *Archives of Maryland*, 2:35–43, 43–49, 143–44; 5:18; Jordan, *Representative Government in Maryland*, 103–4; Berkeley and the Council of State to Charles II, 21 June 1667, CO 1/20, fols. 118–21.

attempt to manipulate the tobacco economy. Of equal concern was the financial impact of reduced crops on their constituents, who faced the burdens of paying for diversification, urban renewal, and defense against the Dutch. They voiced their frets to Berkeley in a pointed memorial that imperiled passage of the reciprocal enabling statute. His reply is lost. The law passed, so he obviously had his way with the burgesses. One of the provisos in the cessation statute reveals what he gave up to calm the House in order to get what he wanted. That section designated the commissioners by name. Councillor Richard Bennett, Secretary Ludwell, and Major General Smith were on the list, but so were Speaker Wynne and five other senior House members. In other words, Berkeley had not browbeaten the House into submission. He had struck a deal. In return for a favorable vote on the bill, he traded a majority of the nominees and the right of their appointment to the House. Furthermore, he was willing to incorporate the roster in statutory language. That concession not only codified the deal; it also safeguarded the bargain from executive tampering. The compromise was vintage Berkeley. More to the point, it worked, which was what counted most.[43]

Both commissions met at Jamestown. Joining them were representatives from the Albemarle settlements, Governor William Drummond and Surveyor-General Thomas Woodward. Berkeley, always hospitable and always eager for company, may well have hosted a reception for the delegations at Green Spring House. Whatever the case, the discussions went expeditiously, and, within a day or two of arriving in town, the commissioners agreed on how to implement the enabling laws. No tobacco would be planted for the twelve-month period after 1 February 1666/67. Officials from governors to county clerks would swear an oath to uphold the statutes and the agreement. Each colonial government could appoint inspectors who could travel freely in the other colonies to check on enforcement of the cessation. Failure on the part of the Albemarle assembly to enact a cessation statute and to transmit copies to Jamestown and to St. Mary's City before the end of September would annul the treaty.[44]

That fail-safe nearly destroyed everything. Even as the talks proceeded, Drummond was suing Berkeley in a dispute about land he leased from Sir William. The litigation turned nasty. Drummond lost and went away angry. Berkeley had

43. Berkeley to Charles II, 21 June 1667, CO 1/21, fols. 118–21; memorial from the House of Burgesses to Berkeley and the Council of State, ca. 5 June 1666; McIlwaine, *Journals, 1659/60–1693,* 53–54; Hening, *Statutes at Large,* 2:225. The five burgesses were Thomas Ballard, Joseph Bridger, Peter Jennings, Daniel Parke, and Nicholas Spencer.

44. Commission to Philip Calvert and others, 26 June 1666, CO 1/20, fol. 178; articles of agreement for the reduction of tobacco planting, 10 July 1666, CO1/20, 193–94; Berkeley to Arlington, 13 July 1666, CO 1/20, fols. 199–200.

second thoughts about the wisdom of his having appointed Drummond. His irritation multiplied after that nameless mischief maker handed him a copy of the highly critical letter that Drummond had sent to his anonymous friend. Reported Indian tumults in Albemarle had prevented the assembly there from passing the cessation law until the start of October. The Marylanders interpreted the delay as having voided the treaty, even though Calvert verged on proclaiming the cessation, and they insisted on renegotiating terms. Virginia's General Assembly was already in session when Berkeley learned that disaster loomed. On 24 October he shot off letters to Calvert and Drummond informing them that the assembly would ratify the agreement. He urged that the cessation go forward, and, to ensure that it did, he got a section in the ratification statute authorizing him to send envoys to St. Mary's City "upon the seaventh day of December next, or as soone as wind and weather will permitt."[45]

Squandering no time debating the appointment of new commissioners, Berkeley and the House agreed that the men who had spoken for Virginia in July would do so again. Wind and weather permitted the emissaries to sail the icy waters of the James River and Chesapeake Bay up to St. Mary's City in the first days of December. Their task went smoothly and quickly. On 11 December everyone signed off on additional articles that confirmed all previous accords. Bidding their hosts farewell, the Virginians sped the happy news back to Berkeley as fast as their shallop could sail to Jamestown. An elated Berkeley proclaimed the cessation three days before New Year's. The long-contested prize was his. With the cessation in place, planters could concentrate on raising other staples.[46]

Sixteen sixty seven would be a good year, thought Berkeley. It was anything but.

In England, about the time the Virginia commissioners were preparing to leave for St. Mary's City, Lord Baltimore was finishing a directive for his son in Maryland. He informed Governor Calvert that he had disallowed the province's cessation law. The order reached Calvert in January and left him dumbstruck. Months passed before Berkeley learned about the blow his old adversary had struck him. He did not refer to it in any of his correspondence during the first half of 1667. Quite the contrary, his letters convey the impression that he took for granted that all was progressing according to plan. He was not alone in that

45. Berkeley and the Council of State to Charles II, CO 1/20, fols. 118–21; Berkeley to Charles Calvert, 24 Oct. 1666, Bland MS, 234–35, DLC; Berkeley to Drummond, 24 Oct. 1666, ibid.; Brown et al., eds., *Archives of Maryland,* 2:547–48, 550–52, 558–60; Hening, *Statutes at Large,* 2:229–32.

46. Commission to Thomas Ludwell and others, 8 Nov. 1666, CO 1/20, fols. 337–38.; further articles of agreement for the reduction of tobacco planting, 11 Dec. 1666, CO 1/20, fol. 295; proclamation of a cessation of tobacco planting, 28 Dec. 1666, LNOB, 1666–75, Vi.

assumption. Secretary Ludwell wrote exactly that when he told Lord Arlington in February that the cessation was afoot. When at last Berkeley saw the "Signature & Seale at Armes of the Lord Baltemore," he described his feelings this way. Baltimore's veto caught him and other Virginians "like a storme and enforced us like distressed marriners after wcc had long strived against all oppositions here & beene at three hundred thousand pounds of tobacco charge to provide their & our happiness to throw our deare bought Commodities into the sea, when wee were in sight of our harbour, & with them to drown'd not only our present releifes but all future hopes of beeing able to doe our selves good."[47]

Still, he persisted. Once more he indited a lengthy letter to Charles II in which he detailed all his efforts and how he had been stymied at every turn. Once more he reminded the king how the colonists suffered because of low tobacco prices. Once more he excoriated his adversaries as short-sighted, obstinate, self-interested opportunists. Once more he extolled the advantages of a diversified Virginia economy. And once more he begged that "your Majestie & the Lords of your most honorable Privy Councell will bee pleas'd upon consideration of our whole complaint herein represented to your Majestie to put such a determination to it as shall seem most just, & that you will bee pleas'd to apply such a remeady as may be proportionable to our distresse." But he also pressed Charles for permission to return to London, apparently believing that, with a personal appearance in the precincts of Whitehall, he could influence colonial policy like no other Virginian. Charles ignored him, and, though he gave permission, Berkeley's return visit to London failed to happen.[48]

Nature temporarily solved the problem of too much tobacco. A monstrous April hailstorm stripped trees bare and beat half-grown fields of grain and young tobacco shoots to pieces. What hail did not destroy, forty days of rain in June and July inundated. A towering "Hurry cane" struck in late August. Its desolating winds raged unabated for twenty-four hours and drove mountainous swells that surged over lowlands and piled killing floodwaters far up Chesapeake Bay and its estuaries. The storm destroyed upwards of four-fifths of the year's crops; it knocked down homes, saltworks, silk houses, tanneries, looms, and boatyards; it uprooted score upon score of orchards, vineyards, and mulberry trees; and the

---

47. Baltimore to Charles Calvert, 24 Nov. 1666, CO 1/20, fol. 319; Jordan, *Representative Government in Maryland*, 104–5; Berkeley to Richard Nicolls, 22 Jan. 1666/67, Blathwayt Papers, CSmH; same to same, 4 May 1667, Add. MS 28218, BL; Berkeley to Arlington, 5 June 1667, CO 1/21, 100–101; Ludwell to Arlington 12 Feb. 1666/67, CO 1/21, fols. 37–38; Berkeley to Charles II, 24 June 1667, CO 1/20, fols. 118–21.

48. Berkeley to Charles II, 24 June 1667, CO 1/20, fol. 118–21; Berkeley to Nicolls, 4 May 1667, Blathwayt Papers, CSmH.

effects of saltwater intrusion lingered long after the storm blew itself out. Sadly for Berkeley, so much devastation seriously crippled diversification.[49]

Berkeley had easily sold diversification to the General Assembly before he went away to London in 1661. The body voted up necessary legislation while he was gone, and it added more after he came back. Laying the legal foundations was the easy part. Persuading planters to build as the law laid out was more difficult, but Berkeley hit upon ways to lower that obstacle. He learned from trials he ran at Green Spring throughout the 1640s and 1650s which exotic staples worked and which did not. As he had argued in *A Discourse and View of Virginia,* silk, flax, potash, and hemp could profitably substitute for tobacco. Hence, diversification statutes encouraged their cultivation, but that was not all. Other acts promoted tanning leather hides, boiling salt, weaving woolen cloth, and building ships—things that Virginians already manufactured in small quantities, which convinced Berkeley of the colonists' ability to make such products on a larger scale.

Silk making required a high initial investment, and for that reason Berkeley expected larger, more well-off planters to follow his example. But it was also possible for small planters to participate in the industry without actually taking up the craft. Anyone who lived near a silk works could tend mulberry orchards and become a supplier of leaves. Potash had many industrial uses, though imports of the stuff supplied English needs because of shortages of wood, the basic ingredient, in Britain. Neither great skill nor large capital outlays were necessary to produce the stuff. With modest direction indentured servants might prepare it as readily as anyone else. All they had to do was burn wood into ashes, leach the ashes with water, and boil the residue in vats or pots (hence the name *potash*). Flax and hemp were field crops, and anyone interested in raising them need only get seed. There was even the possibility of flax men marketing the waste product, oakum, to shipwrights as caulking material. Processing flaxseed into linseed oil or rough dressing flax fibers for export to England demanded crafts not found in the colony. Craftsmen were also needed to turn hemp plants into fiber for rope, cordage, sailcloth, and coarse sheeting and to render its seed into oil. (Whether anyone marketed the leaves for smoking is an open question.) Berkeley relied upon the planters to recruit skilled workers who would ply their craft and teach others as well.[50]

49. Ludwell to John Berkeley, baron Berkeley of Stratton, 4 Nov. 1667, CO 1/21, fols. 282–83; Sir William Berkeley to Arlington, 11 Nov. 1667, CO 1/21, fol. 286.

50. Jon Kukla, ed., "Some Acts Not in Hening's *Statutes:* The Acts of Assembly, October 1660," *VMHB* 87 (1975): 88–89; Hening, *Statutes at Large,* 1:520, 536–37; 2:32, 120–24, 128, 185, 186.

He himself continued to set an example. His silk operation brought in greater yields as a result of an expansion that he undertook in the early 1660s. Investing some five hundred pounds in workmen's wages, he expanded potash production. He exported a ton of the stuff in 1663, and he told Clarendon, "if it yeilds but a reasonable price I shall by gods Blessing send home 200 Tunns more made by. my own family besides what the Country will do when they hear my Labours are successfull." Success with flax got off to a slower start. The London merchant John Bland shipped four hundred bushels of seed to Virginia, which were parceled out to "the severall counties" with disappointing results at first. What happened to Berkeley exemplified the problems of others. He capitalized his trial with a thousand pounds, only to watch his investment drop down an empty hole. The reason, he explained to Arlington, was "want of experienced men that would impart their knowledge and skill. For frenchmen I had procurd at great charges but wilfully and disastrously they spoyld almost al the flax I had."[51]

That theme of "want of experienced men" was one Berkeley invariably sounded throughout the 1660s. On several occasions he volunteered to travel into Italy and France to search out trained men, but his offers came to nothing. His faith hardly seemed to flag. Adversity only made him more relentless. Again and again, he implored his superiors for assistance, but they heard not a word of what he said. He persisted tirelessly. Careful not to blame anyone at Whitehall, he railed against "London merchants," censuring them for their bad advice, lack of vision, and unwillingness to help.[52]

Silence, whatever else might be said of it, implies that those most frequently on the receiving end of his incessant importunities—Charles II, Clarendon, Arlington, his brothers—came to regard him as a tiresome bore besotted with pipe dreams. Nonetheless, the question remains: Did planters take his cure? His letters cheerily touted his successes, despite their rants against obstacles thrown in his way. Such assertions are suspect, given his stake in the remedy and his knack of theater, though bits of this and that offer independent, modest support for Berkeley's claims.

There is the testimony of Secretary Ludwell to the effect that "wee have built severall small vessells to trade with our neighbours & are building others bigg enough to trade to England [and] Wee have gotten the skill of making silke flax [and] Potashes." On three separate occasions the General Assembly sent Charles

51. General Assembly order, 23 Dec. 1663, CO 5/1376; Berkeley to Clarendon, 30 Mar. 1663 and 18 Apr. 1663, Egerton MS 2395, fols. 360, 365, BL; Berkeley to Arlington, 1 Aug. 1665, CO 1/19, fols 202–3.

52. E.g., Berkeley to Clarendon, 20 July 1666, Clarendon Papers, 84, fols. 230–31; Berkeley to Charles II, 22 July 1668, CO 1/23, fols. 42–43; Berkeley to Charles II, ca. 12 June 1669, CO 1/24, fols. 121–22; Berkeley to Arlington, 1 June 1669, CO 1/24, fols. 121–22.

ll gifts of silk cloth that totaled upwards of nine hundred pounds in weight. Thomas Walker, a Gloucester County justice of the peace, kept over seventy thousand mulberry trees. An orchard of that size supported a major silk works that put him in the same league as Edward Digges, Sir Henry Chicheley, the Reverend Alexander Moray, and Berkeley himself. Then there were planters who took bounties on their produce. Individually, they made silk in amounts of six to ten pounds, woolen cloth that ran to quantities of less than ten yards, or they built vessels that ranged to fifty tons in size. Intriguingly, an extant list of these planters recorded few prominent names. Another tantalizing bit comes from a statute of 1666, which set aside the staple subsidies and the requirement that colonists plant mulberry trees. The assembly justified itself by saying that colonists were "now convinced of the profitts accrewing" from diversification and would of "their owne accord vigerously prosecute those now apparently profitable designes," and repeal therefore eased the "public taxes." Tellingly, the law originated at a legislative session for which the journals survive in the main, but these records have nothing to say about the politics of the repeal.[53]

Conclusions that emerge from these snippets are in no way definitive, although they are suggestive. Colony-wide, diversification had passed beyond the experimental stage by the middle of the 1660s. Planters across the economic spectrum were as willing gamblers as their governor, and, like him, some made quite a go of diversification. Salt boiling failed. As for flax, hemp, and potash, the jury was still out, but no one abandoned any of them yet. The silk industry seemed sufficiently established as to do without government support. Unhappily, those trends petered out in the late 1660s.[54]

Destructive though it was, the great hurricane of 1667 proved more a coup de grâce than a *cause de mort*. The loss of legal ways to limit tobacco weakened diversification before the storm swept across Virginia, but more fatal was the precipitate decline in Berkeley's interest. His exertions wore him down, and it began to dawn on him that his grand design was failing. Once the realization settled into his thoughts, his attention waned. The Reverend John Clayton explained the volte-face this way: "Sr Wm Berkeley [was] a man . . . that . . . tried experiments that others might reap the Advantage Leaveing them when he was satisfied they might be made beneficial, thus he did when he had expended many

53. Ludwell to Arlington, 1 Aug. 1665, CO 1/18, fol. 213; Charles II to Berkeley and the General Assembly, 20 Feb. 1662/63, Egerton MS 2543, BL; order from the House of Burgesses, 5 June 1666, CO 5/1376, fols. 87–103; Berkeley to Charles II, 22 July 1668, CO 1/23, fols. 42–43; McIlwaine, *Journals, 1659/60–1693*, 39; General Assembly accounts, 1663, Clarendon Papers, 82: fols. 275–76; Hening, *Statutes at Large*, 2:241–42.

54. Hening, *Statutes at Large*, 2:236–37.

hundreds of pounds about Sope, & Potashes, whereby he might have got a greater Estate than he spent in all his Contrivances."[55]

Amid attempts to convert the economy the other business of governing pressed upon Berkeley because there was no surcease from the innumerable routine chores that went with his office. He had a colony to defend as well, and countering Indian threats, servant unrest, or attacks by the Dutch persistently demanded his attention all the while he concentrated on revitalizing the economy.

An uneasy peace reigned nominally ever since the end of the Anglo-Powhatan War of 1644–46, and the tensions between Indians and Englishmen scarcely relaxed. Throughout the 1650s expanding settlements gobbled up ever more of the native homelands and sorely pressed tribes who were not signatories to the Treaty of 1646. Repeated skirmishes with those natives were the order of the day. To keep them from boiling over into serious conflicts, Governors Bennett, Digges, and Mathews relied on Berkeley's defense policies, which remained in effect after 1660.

Berkeley had no sooner resumed office than the Lancaster County militia mustered to quell a disturbance there. About that time, too, a detachment of men from York also crossed Chesapeake Bay to help still a ruckus on the Eastern Shore. More trouble erupted in Charles City and Henrico a few months after Berkeley left for England. To combat that menace, military leaders in both counties overhauled their force structure and chain of command. Their reform was so successful in meeting the emergency that it became the prototype for the entire colony's militia. The makeover was largely in place by the time Berkeley returned from London. As in the past, every able-bodied free male above the age of sixteen was liable for militia duty, and he was expected to provide himself with the necessary arms and ammunition. Enlisted men from each county formed regiments of foot and dragoons and drilled at least twice yearly. Officers below the rank of colonel came from the county courts, whereas the colonels who led the regiments were councillors. The regiments were parceled into four "associations," three of which were commanded by Major Generals Abraham Wood, Robert Smith, and Richard Bennett, respectively. (The fourth was under Berkeley.) Superior to those three was Lieutenant General Sir Henry Chicheley, who answered to the captain-general.[56]

55. Edmund Berkeley and Dorothy S. Berkeley, eds., "Another 'Account of Virginia' by the Reverend John Clayton," *VMHB* 76 (1968): 427.

56. Hening, *Statutes at Large*, 2:13–15, 34, 35, 36, 39; LOB, 1655–66, 113, YOB, 1657–62, 241; CCOB, 1655–65, 279, 284–88; Thomas Ludwell to Arlington, 17 Sept. 1667, CO 1/20, fols. 220–21; William L. Shea, *The Virginia Militia in the Seventeenth Century* (Baton Rouge, 1983), 73–83.

This arrangement nominally allowed for better coordination, flexibility, and swift reaction than had formerly been true, but it still left much of the responsibility for defense where it had always been, in local hands. Even so, colonists continued to look to Berkeley for leadership in troubled times, though his responses to crises did not always satisfy the settlers. In 1663, for instance, natives in Rappahannock County killed "2 or 3 but wounded more of such English as were nearest adjoining to [them]." The attack aroused such fear among area planters that they approached Berkeley in "a petitionarie way for speedy redress." Berkeley ordered a call-up of area units and promised to sustain them with supplies from elsewhere about the colony, should the need arise. The troops caught nine Indian "kings," suspected ringleaders, who were sent to Jamestown for trial as murderers. Berkeley and the General Court acquitted them. Their exoneration angered many a Rappahannock resident, including Justice John Catlett, who vented his outrage to a cousin in no uncertain terms. "Now I dare not tell you," he said, "why these Indians were cleared, I blame not the Governor, for I believe he is a very just Judge, yet being a man, may have things presented to him through false glasses. I say no more, but onely, that private interests doth too often pervert justice it self. Wee are now at peace blessed bee God." He concluded darkly that, should a similar incident occur again, "I believe wee of the northern parts fronters to the Indians shall not be so forward as wee have been for publique redress of our wrongs."[57]

Three years later another series of depredations in Rappahannock proved Catlett wrong. Instead of taking matters into their own hands, Catlett and his fellow justices informed Berkeley in June 1666 of certain "vale [i.e., vile] Execrable murders" done by "a Combination of our Northern Indians particularly the Doagge" and begged his assistance. Catlett's intelligence panicked Secretary Ludwell into believing a full-scale war verged on breaking out. Ludwell wrote rather excitedly to Clarendon that the natives killed settlers at will and made "dayly shew[s]" of themselves along the frontiers in great numbers. His letter voiced not only his own anxieties but also those of other colonists, who feared fighting the Indians even as they guarded against the depredations of their servants and the Dutch.[58]

For his part Berkeley reacted cautiously. He pressed Catlett for more details, and he asked Major General Smith for his assessment of the situation. Evidently, Smith confirmed Catlett's claims because Berkeley ordered him to destroy the

57. John Catlett to Thomas Catlett, 1 Apr. 1664, ViWC; Hening, *Statutes at Large,* 2:193–94. The record of the Indians' trial no longer exists.

58. John Catlett et al. to Berkeley, ca. 22 June 1666, RDWI, 1663–68, 57; Ludwell to Clarendon, 16 Sept. 1666, Clarendon Papers, 84, fol. 228.

Indians, though he counseled that local officials and "the Councell nere you" must concur in any ensuing action. He warned that the costs of an operation could not be charged to the provincial treasury. Instead, they might be defrayed by the sale of captive women and children. Finally, he coldly advised, "If your young men will not undertake it alone there will be Some from hence will undertake it for their share of the booty."[59]

Details of what happened next are sketchy. In July the Council of State confirmed all of Berkeley's orders to Smith. It took the further step of specifically commanding the utter annihilation of Indian villages and the "whole nation of the *Doegs* and *Potomacks*." Beyond that it left prosecution of the campaign to the discretion of Berkeley, who seems to have kept to his original intention of letting Smith and the Rappahannock militia mount the colonists' response. It is unclear whether the Indians suffered as he and the council intended, but the campaign seems to have been a short one. There was no mention of it in the records of the October meeting of the General Assembly. The house journals, which are quite extensive, dealt mainly with the stint and Berkeley's effort to prod the burgesses to continue funding Francis Moryson's agency at Whitehall. Then, too, Ludwell had recovered from his initial alarm and played down the incident. He wrote to Arlington in February 1667, saying that Virginia was "very peaceable and undisturbed by any enimy except some few Indians from whom we cannot feare any great misfortune."[60]

Another near brush with open warfare came about as a consequence of Edmund Scarburgh's harassment of the Accomacks. "The Conjurer," as the Accomacks knew Scarburgh, had a long history of sharp dealings with them and other Eastern Shore natives. Scarburgh, who was close to bankruptcy, tried to grab Accomack lands for a speculative venture that he hoped would clear his debts. The Accomacks made noises about taking up arms, but they also sought help directly from Berkeley, who arrested Scarburgh to the General Court. Charged with threatening "the Peace long since established between us & the Indians," the Conjurer was summarily dismissed from all offices, and his removal prevented further trouble.[61]

These outbursts were only the more extreme manifestations of constant tense

59. Berkeley to Smith, 22 June 1666, RDWI, 1663–68, 57.
60. Order-in-council, 10 July 1666, Robinson, "Notes," 116–17; McIlwaine, *Journals, 1659/60–1693*, 32–45; Ludwell to Arlington, 12 Feb. 1666/67, CO 1/21, fols. 37–38.
61. Warrant for the arrest of Edmund Scarburgh, 12 Sept. 1670, ADWI, 1664–71, fol. 3; order suspending Edmund Scarburgh from all offices, 25 Oct. 1670, McIlwaine, *Minutes of the Council and General Court*, 238; Billings, *Little Parliament*, 167–69; Ames, "Reunion of Two Virginia Counties," 539–43.

relations between the Indians and the English after 1660. Given the cultural dissimilarities, such edginess was unavoidable. The stolen land or the provocations of men such as Scarburgh and pilfering or revenge killings by the Indians stood out as perpetual, irritating reminders of the differences between two peoples who contested for control of Virginia's bounty. Although Berkeley's policy was peace, colonists who daily confronted the natives took a less tolerant view whenever they were set upon. An isolated attack upon a remote community suddenly became a raid of unparalleled proportions. To be sure, the colonists' itch for land was at the root of the simmering troubles, but few were the settlers who looked upon the Indians as anything other than a peril always to be guarded against.

Compounding that siege mentality were the endless annoyances caused by the meanness of indentured servitude. Servants constituted over half of the colonial population. Young, restless, and mostly male, they were difficult to control in a society that had few efficient means of calling any of its people to account. Servants stole, malingered, ran off, set upon their masters, and, most fearful of all, sometimes plotted to rebel. The great concern, as Secretary Ludwell once expressed it, was the provincial government's being pressed simultaneously "att our backs with the Indians [and] in our bowells with our servants." Berkeley faced just such a frightening combination in the fall of 1663, when a group of servants to various prominent planters in Gloucester and York counties nearly pulled off a mutiny.[62]

The plot leaders were former Cromwellian soldiers who secretly conspired at a small house in a wood in Gloucester County. They agreed to recruit additional men and to purloin as many weapons as they could. Then they would march in force to Councillor Francis Willis's plantation to seize a large supply of muskets and gunpowder that was cached there. Armed thus, the conspirators would range about the countryside enlisting more followers and arms. With this mighty army they would slay anyone who opposed them on their trek toward Jamestown. Once they were in the capital, they would negotiate with Berkeley to set them at liberty. If he refused them, then they would leave Virginia to settle elsewhere as free men.[63]

John Berkenhead, a tepid conspirator who had only been in the colony a few months, betrayed the would-be rebels. He alerted his master, former Speaker

62. Warren M. Billings, "The Law of Servants and Slaves in Colonial Virginia," *VMHB* 99 (1991): 45–63; Ludwell to Clarendon, 24 June 1667, Clarendon Papers, 85, fol. 341; Berkeley to the Northampton County Court, 30 Dec. 1669, NoDWI, 1668–80, fol. 11.

63. Affidavits of Thomas Collins and others, 8 Sept. 1663, Miscellaneous Virginia Papers, 1606–1692, 3–5, DLC.

John Smith, who with his fellow magistrates quickly frustrated the plot, and nothing came of it. The ringleaders were rounded up, examined, and bound over for trial before the General Court. Their fate was swiftly sealed. On the day their case was called from the docket, a grand jury indicted them, whereupon they immediately went to trial, and they were just as swiftly convicted of treason. Berkeley sentenced them to die, and straightaway they hanged on the gallows. Berkenhead gained his freedom and a reward of five thousand pounds of tobacco. A shaken Berkeley and the General Assembly enacted a pass system for servants and proclaimed 13 September, the day the plot would have happened, a perpetual holy day of commemoration.[64]

The conspiracy not only kept Berkeley ever mindful of the eventuality of like intrigues in the future; it also compelled him to try to put a stop to one of their causes, the routine importation of convicts as servant laborers. He and Secretary Ludwell embarked on an intermittent crusade to prohibit the use of prisoners in Virginia. Their drive stretched on to 1670 before the Council of State and the Crown finally banned the shipment of felons to the colony.[65]

Within a year and a half of the suppression of the servant plot, Berkeley faced the problem of mounting a defense against a Dutch attack. Relations between Virginia and New Netherlands regressed after the imposition of the navigation laws, which effectively killed Berkeley's commercial treaty with the Dutch colony. Settlers still traded with one another, albeit surreptitiously, but the once cordial connections between Berkeley and Peter Stuyvesant spoiled. The souring was symptomatic of the deteriorating relations between England and Holland that produced the Second Anglo-Dutch War. James, duke of York, contributed to the breakdown when he dispatched Richard Nicolls with a force of ships and men to seize New Amsterdam. Apparently, Nicolls and Berkeley were acquaintances, because the two men opened a regular correspondence quite soon after Nicolls became governor of New York. It is evident that their exchanges alerted Berkeley

64. Robinson, "Notes, 251; indictment of John Gunter and others, ca. 16 Sept. 1663, Virginia Miscellaneous Papers, 1–2; McIlwaine, *Journals, 1659/60–1693*, 28; Hening, *Statutes at Large*, 2:197, 191; John Catlett to Thomas Catlett, 1 Apr. 1664, ViWC; General Assembly accounts, Sept. 1663, Clarendon Papers, 82, fol. 276; Billings, *Little Parliament*, 266 n. 45. Berkenhead arrived on the merchant ship *Mary & Elizabeth* in the fall of 1662. So far as can be determined, he was a run-of-the-mill indentured servant rather than an old Cromwellian warrior (warrant from James, duke of York, to Sir William Berkeley, 9 Sept. 1662, HCA 1/9, pt. 1, 53, PRO).

65. Order-in-council, 20 Apr. 1670, McIlwaine, *Minutes of the Council and General Court*, 209–10; Ludwell to Arlington, 29 Apr. 1670, C.O. 1/25, fol. 62; order banning transportation of felons to Virginia, 2 Oct. 1670, PC 2/62, 302; Robinson, "Notes," 257.

to the possibility of an impending war, but he would not act without orders from Whitehall.[66]

Sixteen sixty-four yielded to a new year without any tidings of a formal proclamation of hostilities. January became February, February slipped into March, March passed to April, April turned into May, and still Berkeley had no news of the war's progress or what the king expected of him. At last, on 3 June, a ship brought him a packet of mail from London. A letter from Charles II told of the Crown's declaration of war, and it ordered Berkeley to prepare Virginia against an almost certain Dutch strike. Others were directives from George Villiers, second duke of Buckingham, commissioner of prizes, which authorized Berkeley to dispose of any captured Dutch shipping.[67]

Berkeley instantly summoned his councillors to a meeting, which he set for 21 June. It was apparent that, although the reorganization of the militia worked well, the armed forces faced a critical deficit in armaments. There were but fourteen pieces of heavy ordnance in the colony, and they were in disrepair. The council authorized Berkeley to petition Charles II either to send over more cannon or to allow him to sequester two guns from every merchantman or to use money from the two-shilling duty to buy additional great guns. Powder and shot were dangerously low too, and, to offset that shortage, the order went out for the purchase of two hundred pounds' worth of ammunition. To combat the immediate threat of invasion, tobacco ships were required to anchor at havens in the James, the York, the Rappahannock, and on the Eastern Shore that would be protected by emplacements "for battery and small shott." Berkeley and the council recognized they could not deny Dutch men-of-war entry into the Chesapeake Bay, but they reasoned that the militia might thwart the invaders. Some would man the emplacements that guarded the anchorages. Others could suffice as marines to repulse boarders. The rest would rebuff landing parties. And, so, the council called up four thousand men who "shall stand and remain ready to march and obey any other order from the Governour at two days warning." A more durable defense depended upon heavily fortifying Jamestown, thereby

---

66. Kenneth Scott, ed., "The Arms of Amsterdam: An Extract from the Records of the General Court of Virginia, 1664," *VMHB* 77 (1969): 407–40; Jaap Jacobs, *Een zegenrijk gewest: Nieuw-Nederland in de zeventiende eeuw* (Amsterdam, 1999), 164–66; C. R. Boxer, *The Anglo-Dutch Wars of the Seventeenth Century* (London, 1974), 20–42; Berkeley to Nicolls, 4 and 22 Oct. 1664, Blathwayt Papers, CsmH.

67. Berkeley to Nicolls, 4 Mar, 1664/65, Blathwayt Papers, CsmH; Berkeley to Arlington, 10 April 1665, CO 1/19, fols. 71–72; orders for the defense of Virginia, 21 June 1665, Robinson, "Notes," 107; circular letter from Charles II, 27 Jan. 1664/65, Jefferson Papers, DLC; commissions and instructions from George Villiers, second duke of Buckingham, 25 and 28 Feb., 1664/65, ibid.

making it the safest harbor in Virginia. To that end the council made two decisions. It agreed to push enabling legislation through the upcoming session of the General Assembly, and it ordered the removal of the colony's heavy ordnance from a derelict bastion at Old Point Comfort to the capital.[68]

Berkeley introduced the legislation for the fort to the October assembly session, and it passed into law. To pay for the fort, the assembly levied an appropriation of £100,000 of tobacco, £80,000 of which were to come from increased taxes and the remainder from the "sale of the king of Potomacks land." Berkeley received discretionary power to locate the fort on a site of his choosing, and the assembly empowered the militias of James City and Surry to help him raise the battery, which it garrisoned with the governor's guard.[69]

The decision to build a single fort at Jamestown rested on several quite practical considerations. Placing the limited number of heavy weapons in one location massed all the available firepower that could be brought to bear against an attacker. Anchoring tobacco fleets under the fort's guns provided them with greater protection than they might find anywhere else. With the fort situated so far inland, the Dutch would not go unnoticed, and they would have great difficulty mounting an assault within range of its guns. Jamestown was also the focal point of political and commercial activity. Having the fort there would prove psychologically uplifting to the colonists, and it would ease Berkeley's responsibilities as commander in chief. Besides, because it would be manned by his guard, its garrisoning could be maintained at minimal additional expense to the colony's ratepayers.[70]

These preparations were under way by the time another instruction reached Berkeley. This one told him that he should return to Whitehall because Charles "thought it expedient for Our Service that you should repaire to Our Royall presence to informe & give us an accompt of the state of that Our plantation & to consult with us upon the good & welfare thereof & what is fit to bee done for the security of Our subjects & for the increase & prosperity of the Trade there." Charles's reasons for the recall are not clear, though they may have had to do with war planning or Berkeley's push for the stint. Whatever the explanation, the summons was most untimely, and Berkeley ignored it.[71]

As the fort neared completion in the spring of 1666, Berkeley received direct

68. Order-in-council, 21 June 1665, Robinson, "Notes," 107–9; Berkeley to Arlington, 1 Aug. 1665, CO 1/19, fols. 202–3; Berkeley to Charles II, CO 1/19, fol. 200.

69. Hening, *Statutes at Large*, 2:220–21.

70. Ludwell to Arlington, 18 July 1666, CO 1/20, fol. 218; Ludwell to Clarendon, 17 Sept. 1666, Clarendon Papers, 84, fol. 228; Berkeley to Clarendon 20 July 1666, Clarendon Papers, 84, fol. 230.

71. Order to return to England, 13 May 1665, SP 44/20, PRO.

orders to abandon it in favor of another at Old Point Comfort. The commandment came about as a result of some effective lobbying on the part of Bristol merchants, whose factors based their operations in the lower James River basin and were resistant to convoying their vessels upriver. Berkeley and Ludwell protested vigorously. Sir William remarked acidly to Arlington that "all the Forts that wee can build [at Old Point Comfort] though never soe strong will not absoulutely answere what they are designed for the Entrance into the Province is soe large that any Enemy Shipp may ride out of all possible dainger of the greatest Cannon in the world and shipps may be taken goeing out or Comeing in without all possible assistance from us." Ludwell made much the same argument, though he added that, since the Virginians were better acquainted with the country, it should be left to them to decide the best sites, rather than rely upon persons "to often byased by their owne Interests."[72]

Whatever his disappointment, Berkeley acceded to the king's wishes. Back down the James went the heavy artillery. A call went out for men to start on a new bastion at Old Point Comfort. Construction went slowly. Bad weather slowed the project, but so did Berkeley's lack of enthusiasm, especially after a lone Dutch raider stole into the James and out of gunshot easily made prizes of two merchant vessels. A disgusted Berkeley sent word to the workmen to bury the cannon as a safety precaution, and, though he urged them to continue their building, he did not push them very hard. When the assembly met in October 1666, the House implored him to plead with Charles II "to Excuse us from further prosecuting the said Work." Berkeley responded "most willingly," though he was quick to point out that any effort to lobby the king was severely hampered by the burgesses' reluctance to pay Francis Moryson a timely salary. The builders left the fort unfinished, and Virginia remained ill defended against the Dutch.[73]

One bright spot, if it could be called that, was the Crown's response to the pleas of Berkeley and others for war matériel and a frigate to patrol Virginia waters. The royal navy dispatched the HMS *Elizabeth*. She got caught in a storm that so damaged her that she arrived barely able to "keep the sea for want of masts and some reparations in her hull." Sir Thomas Chicheley, the royal master of the ordnance, shipped ten artillery pieces of varying sizes, five hundred round shot, and ten barrels of powder. These supplies were but a drop in the bucket of Berkeley's wants, but they were all the Crown could muster, given its own needs

72. Ludwell to Arlington, 18 July 1666, CO 1/20, fol. 218; Ludwell to Clarendon, 17 Sept. 1666, Clarendon Papers, 84, fol. 228; Berkeley to Clarendon 20 July 1666, Clarendon Papers, 84, fol. 230; Berkeley to Arlington, 13 July 1666, CO 1/20, fols. 199–200.

73. Robinson, "Notes," 112–16; Berkeley to Arlington, 13 July 1666, CO 1/20, fol. 199; McIlwaine, *Journals, 1659/60–1693*, 42.

and its decision to invest more of its limited military stock in protecting the West Indian colonies than in guarding Virginia.[74]

None of the added ordnance did any good when the Dutch at last attacked in force in June 1667. Fresh from a stunning sea campaign in the West Indies, Admiral Abraham Crijnssen stood his squadron of five men-of-war and a smaller "dogger boat" northward for the Chesapeake in search of prey. Off the Virginia capes he caught two merchantmen. Learning from his captives that *Elizabeth* and nearly two dozen tobacco ships lay anchored at Newport News, he decided to feast on opportunity. On 5 June, guided by one of his hostage vessels, he worked his fleet up the James toward the anchorage. The colonists gave no thought to the approaching flotilla because it flew English flags and its crews bawled out soundings in English. Nothing seemed amiss until Crijnssen hove into range and loosed withering broadsides that quickly drove *Elizabeth*'s skeleton crew to surrender. The tobacco ships, though armed, offered little resistance or tried to escape, and the Dutch easily made prizes of them. By dusk Crijnssen not only controlled the lower reaches of the river; he had also trapped all the ships above Newport News, and, if he chose, he could attack Jamestown itself.[75]

When messengers brought Berkeley word of the disaster and the impending threat to his capital, he hastily devised his counter moves. He reckoned that his best defense lay in trying to snare Crijnssen between Newport News and Jamestown. That could be done by marshaling the ships in the York River and at Jamestown. The former would sail around the Peninsula and attack head on, while the latter would close from the rear. Additionally, Major General Bennett's militia regiments would repel any Dutch landing parties. Riding over to the York, Berkeley commandeered nine of the largest ships he could find. To their guns he added cannon he had stripped from all of the small vessels, and he put some

74. Moryson to the Privy Council, 4 Jan. 1666/67, Coventry Papers, 74, fol. 136; order-in-council for the dispatch of a frigate to Virginia, 11 Jan. 1666/67, Coventry Papers, 74, fol. 137; Ludwell to Clarendon, 24 June 1667, Clarendon Papers, 85, fol. 34; An account of Ordnances and other Stores of War Sent to the Plantations 1660–1688, CO 323/24; order-in-council regarding ammunition for Virginia, 10 Mar. 1667/68, PC 2/60, 221, PRO. An account drawn up in 1677 listed the guns and powder that were dispatched in Feb. 1666 and valued them at twenty-four pounds. That list, by contrast, showed that between 1660 and 1676 the master of the ordnance shipped nearly nineteen thousand pounds worth of munitions to Jamaica (CO 1/40, fols. 138–39, PRO).

75. Ludwell to Clarendon, 24 June 1667, Clarendon Papers, 85, fol. 34; Berkeley and the Council of State to Charles II and the Privy Council, ca. 24 June 1667, CO 1/21, fols. 109–10, PRO; J. C. M. Warnsinck, *Abraham Crijnssen de Verovering van Suriname en zijn Aanslag op Virginië* (Amsterdam, 1936), 3–91; De instructie voor Abraham Crijnssen van den 23sten December 1666, ibid., 105–29, esp. 116–18; E. B. O'Callaghan, ed., *Documentary History of the State of New York* (Albany, 1849–51), 2:518–19; Thomas Waltham to [?], 2 June 1667, Rawlinson Mss A195a, Bodleian Library, Oxford.

three regiments of militia on board as well. The merchant mariners seemed eager to follow Berkeley into battle, but, once he was ready to weigh anchor, their ardor for a fight cooled, and they played for time. Their timidity cost Berkeley the element of surprise. Whatever chance he had of victory slipped from his grasp when Crijnssen sailed off unscathed.[76]

His effort to oppose Crijnssen and his failure to exact any price for the Dutchman's raid wore Berkeley down, and for a time he contemplated retirement. As Secretary Ludwell wrote to Baron Berkeley worriedly, Sir William planned on soliciting "the king by your Lordship and my Lord Arlington to displace him, and (by sending in another governor) for the future better government of this place." Ludwell went on to say that he and his fellow councillors hoped the baron would use his influence with his brother and the king to keep Berkeley "amongst & over us." His pleading succeeded because Berkeley remained at his post.[77]

The August hurricane swept the Old Point Comfort rampart away. Berkeley tabled a new scheme of fortifications that the General Assembly enacted when it met in September. By law the Jamestown fort would be completed, and there would be four others raised at strategic choke points on each of the colony's major rivers. They were to be situated where all ships "trading to those respective places may conveniently, and in all probability securely ride and load." Freeholders in the surrounding counties would form associations that commissioners drawn from the county courts would lead. The associations would build and man the forts, and the costs would be borne by local ratepayers. Once the forts were up, all vessels would unload and take on cargo under protection of their guns. The work did not proceed very far before Berkeley learned that the Peace of Breda, which was agreed in July 1667, had ended the war. Construction halted, and, "since God hath restored unto us the blessing of an universall peace," tobacco transports no longer had to anchor under the guns of the batteries that were already complete.[78]

The return to peace aroused little enthusiasm for diversification in Berkeley and even less among the planters. Indeed, to all intents and purposes, Berkeley's remedy had failed to cure Virginia's economic woes. His own overconfidence was partly to blame, but so were the predicates for diversification. They put his economic ideas at odds with Stuart goals of empire, and the inconsistencies be-

76. Ludwell to Clarendon, 24 June 1667, Clarendon Papers, 85, fol. 34; Berkeley and the Council of State to Charles II and the Privy Council, ca. 24 June 1667, CO 1/21, fols. 109–10, PRO.

77. Ludwell to John Berkeley, baron Berkeley of Stratton, 24 June 1667, CO 1/21, fol. 117, PRO.

78. Hening, *Statutes at Large*, 2:255–59, 265; Boxer, *The Anglo-Dutch Wars*, 42.

tween the two visions loomed ever more apparent as the 1660s rolled by. Bad luck dogged Berkeley too. He had never bargained for the loss of the Dutch trade, war with the Hollanders, domestic discord, the failure of the stint, or natural disasters, let alone the way the Crown consistently undercut him after 1662. And yet, being governor, he bore the onus of meeting unexpected contingencies even as he tried so relentlessly to achieve his cherished dream of a diverse Virginia economy.

His failures distanced him from constituents who had long relied upon his judgments of what was best for them. Planters, great and small, who feared for their safety and chafed by high taxes, grumbled at the prices they paid for urban development, crop experimentation, and defense. Their growls found voice in the General Assembly, where Berkeley usually quieted them. And, as the 1660s closed, he began to exhibit a tone deafness to the reasons for the complaints.[79]

79. Henry Norwood to Joseph Williamson, 17 July 1667, CO 1/21, fols. 156–57, PRO; Ludwell to Clarendon, 12 Feb. 1667, Clarendon Papers 85, fol. 348.

12

Age and Misfortune Have Withered My Desires

urden of years and weight of office lay heavily on Berkeley. He sought to lighten his load when he asked permission to retire in 1667. "What I shall say my Lord," he wrote to the earl of Arlington that spring, "age and misfortune has withered my desires as wel as hopes and the truth is I cannot in this time of my very old age so wish my selfe happy but that I possibly repent of my desires to be so, the way I proposed when the time was that I could have taken any gust in the favour of princes I wanted the help of a frendly Angel to put me into the Poole when the waters were made seasonable for hopes and powerful to treate dispayre." Arlington, reacting to the exigencies of the Dutch war and the pleas of Secretary Ludwell, ignored the request. Berkeley persisted to no avail, and in a while his "dispayre" became melancholic acceptance.[1]

Thus, it was a languid Berkeley who marked his sixty-fifth birthday in 1670. Weariness dulled his mental acuity. Poor health altered his personality. Death deprived him of dependable patrons and dear friends. But he soldiered on.

Observers first noticed a change in Berkeley during the mid-1660s, but, except for deafness, none of them ever specified the exact nature of what they saw. Ludwell, who worked with the governor almost daily, called attention to an impair-

1. Berkeley to Henry Bennet, earl of Arlington, 5 June 1667, CO 1/21, fol. 100, PRO; Berkeley to Richard Nicolls, 14 Nov. 1667, Blathwayt Papers, BL 79, CsmH; Berkeley to Charles II, 22 July 1668, CO 1/23, fol. 25; Berkeley to Arlington, 12 June 1669, CO 1/24, fol. 121.

ment when he remarked to the earl of Clarendon and Baron Berkeley that his friend was in the "saddest condition he ever saw." The ailment, whatever it was, worsened by 1674 to the point that even Berkeley seemed to fear his end might be close. That February he designated Sir Henry Chicheley his successor in the event that he became incapacitated. The appointment was uncharacteristic because for three decades Berkeley had always managed without a deputy, save for his two absences in London. Moreover, he took steps to put his real estate holdings in order. Among others he had the Council of State renew his rights to Green Spring, plus a large tract in New Kent County in April 1674. Four months later he got the General Assembly to confirm his freehold of Green Spring by statute and to codify his recent sale of Bolthorpe plantation to William Cole.[2]

Deafness was the clearest extant indicator of a pronounced personality transformation that overcame Berkeley in the 1670s. Whoever greeted him—friend, casual visitor, suitor, antagonist—had to shout at him just to be understood, if at all. Engaging Berkeley in such a manner heightened his natural tendency to irascibility, and the need of loud talking made him seem in a perpetual state of irritability. The Quaker evangelist William Edmundson captured a telling insight into the impact of the hearing loss on Berkeley's temperament. While on a visit to Virginia, Edmundson called at Green Spring House. He found his host "very peevish and brittle" and not in the least inclined to his vaunted hospitality. Afterward Edmundson spoke of his encounter with Councillor Richard Bennett, who had known Berkeley for thirty years. Asked about his reception, Edmundson responded that the governor had seemed in a foul mood. Said Bennett, "Did he call you 'a dog, rogue, etc.?'" "No," answered Edmundson. "Then," came the retort, "you took him in his best humor, those being his usual terms, when he is angry."[3]

2. Ludwell to Edward Hyde, earl of Clarendon, 12 Feb. 1667, Clarendon MS 85, fol. 348, Bodleian Library, Oxford; Ludwell to John Berkeley, baron Berkeley of Stratton, 24 June 1667, CO 1/21, fol. 116, PRO; Nicholas Spencer to [?] Spencer, 13 June 1672, Sloane MS 3511, BL; the General Assembly to Charles II and the Privy Council, 3 Oct. 1673, CO 1/30, fol. 177; the Council of State to Charles II, ca. Oct. 1673, CO 1/30, fol. 179; Giles Bland to the commissioners of customs, 1675, Egerton MS 2395, fols. 515–16, BL; commission to Sir Henry Chicheley, 28 Feb. 1673/74, Jefferson Papers, DLC; William Waller Hening, ed., *The Statutes at Large; Being a Collection of All the Laws of Virginia from the First Session of the Legislature, in the Year 1619*, facsimile ed. (1809–23; rpt., Charlottesville, Va., 1969), 2:318–25; renewal of patent rights to land in New Kent County, 4 Apr. 1674, in H. R. McIlwaine, ed., *Minutes of the Council and General Court of Colonial Virginia, 1622–1632, 1670–1676*, 2d ed. (Richmond, 1979), 367.

3. William Edmundson, *A Journal of the Life, Travels, Sufferings, and Labour of Love in the Work of the Ministry, of That Worthy Elder, and Faithful Servant of Jesus Christ, William Edmundson, Who Departed This Life, the 31st of the 6th Month, 1712* (Dublin, 1715), 61–63; Edward D. Neill, comp., *Virginia Carolorum: The Colony under the Rule of Charles the First and Second* (Albany, 1886), 339–41.

Admittedly, these are slender bits on which to found judgments about the state of Berkeley's health or its effect upon how he ruled after 1670. Nevertheless, from the mid-1660s onward it was common knowledge among outspoken colonists that Berkeley was unwell and continually out of sorts. For them the possibility that "hee [could] not be expected long to continue" was unsettling. He had governed so many years that Virginia without him was unthinkable. And that was why his being "antient" and sickly troubled observers sufficiently to remark upon his condition among themselves and in their correspondence.[4]

A powerful web of patrons supported Berkeley at court throughout the first years of the Restoration, but the netting tattered as one by one most of his champions left their places. Clarendon fell into disfavor during the Second Anglo-Dutch War and scurried into exile. Death took Sir Charles Berkeley. Baron Berkeley traded London for Dublin and the lord lieutenancy of Ireland. Lord Arlington gave up his place as secretary of state. The Carolina proprietors were either dead or inactive, save the earl of Shaftsbury, who disagreed with Berkeley over the management of Carolina and tried to buy him out. Other committees supplanted the Council for Foreign Plantations, and that change of policy denied Berkeley another of his fulcrums of influence. As for the king, he owed Berkeley nothing. He had favored him only because of his debts to Berkeley's brothers, but, once they were gone from the royal presence, Charles II had little cause to be generous toward their sibling, and he was not. The successors to Berkeley's cronies on the Privy Council or in the colonial bureaucracy were mainly strangers who had more of the king's ear than he could gain from afar. Not invested in him, they came to regard him as something of a nuisance who promised more than he delivered and cast blame on others for his shortcomings. All of which left Berkeley increasingly isolated from Whitehall.[5]

A like loss of stalwart intimates and close colleagues on the Council of State or in the House of Burgesses compounded his detachment. Richard Lee, John Carter, Theoderick Bland, Thomas Stegge Jr., Edward Digges, Richard Bennett, Augustine Warner Sr., Richard Corbin, Edmund Scarburgh, and Robert Wynne all passed away in the decade after 1664. A feeble Abraham Wood rarely attended the council. Moryson remained in England, where Secretary Ludwell and Robert Smith went to work against the Northern Neck Proprietary in 1674. Berkeley replenished his losses with younger politicians or newer immigrants, but they stood at a distance from him, and few earned his trust. He depended, instead,

4. Nicholas Spencer to [?] Spencer, 13 June 1673, Sloane MS 3511, BL.
5. See chap. 10.

Dame Frances Culpeper Stephens Berkeley.
Courtesy of the Museum of Early Southern Decorative Arts,
Winston-Salem, North Carolina

upon an ever narrowing circle of advisors that came to include only the Ludwell brothers, Robert Smith, Robert Beverley, and Dame Frances Berkeley.[6]

Dame Frances was her husband's "frendly Angel" after their marriage in April 1670. Lack of detail frustratingly cloaks the nature of their union, but the occasional tidbits hint at a compatible, beneficial relationship. The new mistress of Green Spring House was a lively, durable, and intelligent woman. Perspicacious, articulate, and skillful, she was not in the least minded to play her role as Virginia's first lady in a minor key. She soon advised Berkeley in all things great and

6. Berkeley to the Committee for Trade and Plantations, 21 June 1671, CO 1/26, fol. 196, PRO; circular letter from the Lords of Trade, 11 Aug. 1675, CO 323/4, PRO; Charles M. Andrews, *British Committees, Commissions and Councils of Trade and Plantations, 1622–1675, Johns Hopkins University Studies in Historical and Political Science,* 26th ser. (1908): 96–106; R. P. Beiber, "The British Plantation Councils of 1670–4," *English Historical Review* 40 (1925): 93–106; Winfred T. Root, "The Lords of Trade and Plantations," *American Historical Review* 23 (1917): 20–41; Berkeley to Thomas Osborne, earl of Danby, 1 Feb. 1675/75, Tracy W. McGregor MSS, Alderman Library, ViU; Berkeley to Thomas Ludwell, 1 Apr. 1676, CO 1/36, fols. 67–68, PRO.

small. He cheerfully accepted her judgments, and, as his faith in the soundness of her counsel deepened, he trusted her more than anyone else. The tightness of their bond made her a formidable political presence who was for Berkeley not unlike what Edith Bolling Wilson would be for President Woodrow Wilson— chief executive in everything but name alone. And, like Mrs. Wilson, Dame Frances's closeness to her husband had partisan repercussions. It fed rumblings that "old Governor Barkly [had been] altered by marrying a young wyff from his wonted public good." Supposedly, she and other "interested persons" seduced her husband "continually with strange stories which being antient [he] is apt to believe." The nature of the "strange stories" is unclear now, though the content is less significant than the welling up of the tales themselves. That they surfaced at all portended a hitherto unseen level of disaffection with Berkeley.[7]

By the very nature of the office being governor-general always threatened to undermine popular confidence in him. In the past skill, determination, and boldness, laced with a keen sense of timing, had fended off harm to his leadership. The challenges of the 1670s were as serious as any that ever confronted him. In each instance, however, he failed to stanch the damage to his government because little by little he fell out of touch with the lessons of statecraft that had long sustained him.

One such was the fraying of his bargain with the great men. In return for a free hand to devise policies that benefited the colony as a whole, Berkeley conceded ample measures of self-government and control of local affairs to the great men. That quid pro quo had been essential to his political survival throughout the 1640s and 1650s and had been vital to his grand design for Virginia after his restoration. Once diversification fell to pieces, the bargain needed repairs, but Berkeley still clung to his faith in the vision. He never conceded his failure publicly. Instead, he lost interest, made no attempt to advance alternatives in its stead, and seemed insensible to the damage to his reputation.

He also missed the imperative of constraining the great men. Left to their own devices and desires, the great men had cemented their access to power for themselves and their progeny. More ruthless than tender toward colonists they presumed to rule, they readily corrupted their vast, often poorly drawn authority. As of the 1670s, their insecurities and elbowing for place invested local politics with a reckless, mean-spirited quality that irritated middling and lesser planters as well as prosperous settlers who had lost out in the contest for place and preferment. The cumulative ill effects of such behavior stirred passions as it corroded popular support for Berkeley, though, here again, he displayed few signs that he grasped the injury to him. His reliance upon the General Assembly became an

7. Giles Bland to the commissioners of customs, Egerton MS 2395, fols. 133–34.

annoyance too. To his constituents annual sessions increasingly seemed only to result in ever higher taxes and legislative expenses, and once more Berkeley missed the ramifications of such a sentiment.[8]

Berkeley's unsuccessful effort to extinguish the Northern Neck Proprietary added to popular frustrations with the assembly and ultimately with him. The proprietary originated in 1649, when King Charles II conferred land between the Rappahannock and Potomac rivers on a group of favorites that included Sir Henry Jermyn; Dame Frances Berkeley's father, Thomas; John Culpeper, first baron Culpeper of Thoresway; and Sir John Berkeley. Sir John Berkeley subsequently named Governor Berkeley as his agent, though neither he nor any of the other proprietors could exploit their gift because they were in exile. Charles II renewed the grant in 1661. In turn the surviving patentees leased their interests to several Bristol merchants about the time Berkeley ended his mission to London, though they hid their transaction from him. The first glimmer he had of the deal was when the king wrote in 1663, ordering him to assist the Bristolians in developing their claims.[9]

To Berkeley the proprietary posed threats on a number of fronts. Some of the land within its supposed limits was already occupied by settlers who held their tracts by virtue of patents that he had issued. Helping the proprietors would throw those titles into turmoil and run the risk of alienating the planters, some of whom were important allies. A proprietary in his midst reduced the size of Virginia and imperiled the significance of his government. Worst of all, a proprietary jeopardized diversification. As a first line of defense against the hazards, Berkeley refused to cooperate with the Bristolians. Next, he dispatched a stern protest to Lord Chancellor Clarendon. His appointment of Francis Moryson as Virginia agent was meant as the mainstay in his desired solution—repeal of the proprietary.

Moryson left Jamestown in the spring of 1663 with instructions to negotiate a royal charter that voided the grant and vouchsafed Virginia from any such land grab in the future. Frequently diverted by other agency business, Moryson lobbied quietly without much noticeable success until he struck an arrangement whereby the proprietors would solicit another patent that removed provisions in

8. Warren M. Billings, *A Little Parliament: The Virginia General Assembly in the Seventeenth Century* (Richmond, 2004), chaps. 2, 5.

9. Douglas Southall Freeman, *George Washington: A Biography* (New York, 1949), 1: app. I-1, 447–82; Fairfax Harrison, *Virginia Land Grants: A Study of Conveyancing in Relation to Colonial Politics* (Richmond, 1925); Harrison, *Landmarks of Old Prince William: A Study of Origins in Northern Virginia* (Richmond, 1925); power of attorney from Sir John Berkeley to Sir William Berkeley, 8 Nov. 1649, Add. MS 15857, BL.

the original grant that were unacceptable to Virginians. Sealed in 1669, the new patent limited the size of the territory to whatever land the proprietors actually "possessed, inhabited or planted" within twenty-one years. It also removed another of Berkeley's objections by compelling Northern Neck residents to obey Virginia laws and to pay colonial taxes. Nevertheless, existing land titles remained cloudy, and that uncertainty was a running irritant. To speed things along, Berkeley sent Councillor Robert Smith to help Moryson. Time seemed to favor the agents as one by one the proprietors died or transferred their interests until only the earl of Arlington, Lord Culpeper's son Thomas, and Thomas's cousin Alexander were left. Moryson and Smith, at Berkeley's insistence, concentrated on persuading them to sell out. The three were thought to be amenable to a quick sale. All had noses for fast money. A cash settlement might seem more appealing than the chore of trying to develop a far-off property, and to that purpose Sir William ventured twelve hundred pounds from his own pocket to cover some of the sale price. Besides, because the Culpepers and Arlington were related to Berkeley, he seemed to think that family ties counted for something in the negotiations. (Arlington was a Berkeley cousin. Alexander Culpeper was Berkeley's brother-in-law and cousin to Thomas, Lord Culpeper.)[10]

The proprietors had other ideas. In 1673 they inveigled the king to confirm their rights and then some. They not only received a renewed title to the Northern Neck; they also got their hands on all the unpatented land in Virginia and the rights to all colonial quit rents for a period of thirty years.[11]

Word of this latest twist reached Jamestown in the summer of 1674. As Berkeley digested the news, he grasped its implications. The new patent effectively ended the head right system because it took control of the unseated land from the provincial government and gave it to the proprietors. Who could say what terms of possession those strangers intended to lay down, but, as a result of his Carolina experience, Berkeley knew they would regard patenting procedures as a source of income. He realized, too, that Arlington and the Culpepers expected to enrich themselves with quit rents, which meant they would aggressively try to collect a levy that Virginians had long avoided rendering up to the king.

When the General Assembly sat for its annual meeting in September 1674,

---

10. Billings, "Thomas Culpeper, 2d baron Culpeper of Thoresway," in Colin Mathew et al., eds., *The Oxford Dictionary of National Biography* (Oxford, 2004); Charles II to Berkeley, ca. Feb. 1669/70, CO 1/25, fols. 8–9, PRO; H. R. McIlwaine, ed., *Journals of the House of Burgesses of Colonial Virginia, 1619–1658/59; 1659/60–1693* (Richmond, 1914–15), 57, 61, 237–40; McIlwaine, *Minutes of the Council and General Court,* 250; Ind 6815, 603, PRO; Hening, *Statutes at Large,* 2:569–78.

11. Quit rents were fees collected from landholders that went to the king as the presumptive owner of all Virginia real estate. Freeman, *George Washington,* 1: app. I-1, 461–65.

Berkeley informed the members of the latest developments, and he presented a solution that he believed would put an end to the proprietary. Secretary Ludwell, who already had royal permission to go to London, would join Moryson and Smith. The three agents would not only redouble the efforts to purchase the Northern Neck; they would simultaneously seek a royal charter under the Great Seal of England that overturned the Arlington-Culpeper grant. Next, to support the agency and to buy the proprietary, Berkeley called for a special tax of £120 of tobacco per tithable and an increase in court fees. Finally, he promised to indite a memorial to the king that made the brief for why Charles II had erred in his generosity toward the proprietors, and he offered to make a direct appeal to Arlington on behalf of himself and the assembly. Hearing him out, the members readily voted his proposals into law, thereby committing themselves and their constituents to another of Berkeley's costly gambles.[12]

Berkeley grounded the memorial to Charles II upon a single theory of law. The king had been badly advised, and, in making the Arlington-Culpeper grant, Charles inadvertently set aside an old royal promise to the colonists. That pledge, maintained Berkeley, was to be found in long-settled law. For proof of his argument he cited a dozen documents that ran from the original Virginia Company charter to his own commission and instructions, copies of which he provided for Charles's edification. The bulk of the brief rested on how these good precedents absolutely guaranteed Virginia's integrity as a Crown possession. "Therefore," he begged,

> wee doe on our bended knees most humbly pray your majestie to grant soe much to the peace and happiness of this Collony & the security of us your officers here and your revenue comeing from hence (which is more then the yearely valew of all our labours) as seriouslie and with your wonted Princely Prudence and care to weigh our present hazardous condition & at once by recalling those grants, calme and quiett the harts of all your good and loyall subjects here, and by granting them such a Charter as may forever prevent the designes of those who may seeke (by separating us from our imediate dependence on the Crowne) againe to disturbe our peace and wellfare which would secure us from all future feares of beeing divested of our priviledges.

Berkeley's letter to Arlington was neither legalistic nor argumentative. It expressed a profound hope that the earl would "consider our present condition,

12. Hening, *Statutes at Large*, 2:311–14; Charles II to Berkeley, 10 Apr. 1672, CO 324/2, PRO; license to Thomas Ludwell, 19 Nov. 1674, in Conway Robinson, comp., "Notes and Excerpts from the Records of Colonial Virginia," Conway Robinson Papers, ViHi, 262.

and hear those reasons, which we have ordered our agents . . . to present to your lordship, why we are unwilling, and conceive ought not to submit, to those, to whom his majesty (upon misinformation) hath granted the dominion over us."[13]

Just as soon as Ludwell found passage and all of the papers were done up, he bid Berkeley farewell and sailed to London. None of his succeeding correspondence with Berkeley is extant, so how much or how little Berkeley knew of the negotiations or the nature of his advice to the agents is purely speculative. Berkeley's exchanges with the proprietors are gone too. (Truth be known, Berkeley may not have kept in close touch with either the agents or the proprietors because of the disruptions of the Third Anglo-Dutch War [1672–74].) On the other hand, the record of the agents at work is quite complete. It reveals the three men working diligently and deftly for nearly two years before they pulled together all of the pieces of a deal. The proprietors agreed upon an asking price in early 1676. Around that time Ludwell, Moryson, and Smith also procured the draft for a royal annulment of all proprietary grants present and future. A Virginia free of proprietors seemed within reach, but the proposed charter never passed the seals. News of Bacon's Rebellion stayed it.[14]

13. Berkeley to Arlington, 21 Sept. 1674, in John Daly Burk, *History of Virginia from First Settlement to the Commencement of the Revolution* (Petersburg, 1805), 2: app. 33; Berkeley and the General Assembly to Charles II, 22 Sept. 1674, Coventry Papers, 76, fols. 305–10, Longleat House; certificate to Charles II, and the Privy Council, 21 Nov. 1674, Coventry Papers, 76, fol. 330. The certificate authenticated the following documents as "true Coppys" from Virginia's provincial records:

A Patent to Sir Thomas Gates &c. dated Aprill xth in the fourth yeere of King James.

A patent to Robert Earle of Salisbury &c. May 23 in the 17th yeere of King James.

A Perpetuity to the first Collony of Virginia March 12th in the 9th yeere of King James.

Orders of Councell of the 8th, 17, and 24th of October 1623.

A letter of King Charles the first Dated July 5, 1642.

A letter of the Lords of the Councill July 22, 1634.

Sir Francis Wyatt's Commission, whose instructions are the same word for word as Sir William Berkeleys.

Sir William Berkeleys Commission from his Majesty that now is dated July 3 in the second yeere of his reigne.

Sir Georg Yardleys commission and Instructions.

Sir William Berkeleys instructions September 12 in the 14 yeere of the king.

The certified documents wound up in the hands of Secretary of State Henry Coventry, who succeeded Arlington, and they are filed at the beginning of volume 76 of the Coventry Papers at Longleat House.

14. Authorization for Robert Smith to purchase the Northern Neck Proprietary, 2 July 1673, Robinson, "Notes," 263; Thomas Jefferson Wertenbaker, "The Virginia Charter of 1676," *Virginia Magazine of History and Biography* (*VMHB*) 66 (1948): 263–66; David S. Lovejoy, "Virginia's Charter and Bacon's Rebellion, 1675–1676," in Alison G. Olson and Richard Maxwell Brown, eds., *Anglo-American Political Relations, 1675–1775* (New Brunswick, N.J., 1970), 31–51.

Berkeley's determination to kill the Northern Neck Proprietary did not meet with universal fervor. It drew enthusiastic support from planters who speculated heavily in land or those who lived on the Northern Neck. Planters outside the proprietary saw no immediate benefit to themselves if the proprietary died, and they resented having to pay the added taxes and higher court costs that allowed Berkeley to lobby against it. Most merely grumbled or privately cursed their governor and opened their wallets. Others resorted to direct action and refused to pay their taxes, which compelled Berkeley to intercede. His intervention squandered political capital that he lessened further as the result of an ugly altercation with Giles Bland, the Crown customs collector for Virginia.[15]

Giles Bland (1647–77), son of Berkeley's mercantile ally John Bland, was also nephew to Councillor Theoderick Bland. His father-in-law was the consequential royal bureaucrat Thomas Povey, which probably accounted for Bland's appointment as a customs officer. Around the time Bland received that rank, his uncle passed away. Councillor Bland's death saddled his widow and executrix with a tangle of debts and claims against the family's Virginia ventures. A desperate Anna Bennett Bland wrote to her brother-in-law, pleading with him to come to Virginia and help her settle the accounts. John opted to send his son, instead, and in 1673 Giles Bland traveled to Virginia, armed with his father's power of attorney and the king's commission.[16]

Caustic and free-spirited, Bland immediately squabbled with his aunt over the best way of resolving the family's financial difficulties. He tried to shove her aside, but, not one who budged easily, she shoved back, and their disagreements wound up in litigation before the General Court, where the odds favored her. Anna Bennett Bland could count on support from Berkeley, Sir Henry Chicheley, Secretary Ludwell, and her father, Richard Bennett, all of whom cared a great deal more for her than for her saucy, spiteful nephew.[17]

The incident that opened the breach between Bland and Berkeley happened in September 1674. Berkeley was presiding at the General Court when it ruled on a suit in favor of Mrs. Bland, despite Bland's tart objections. After the court had recessed for the day, an indignant Giles Bland called at Thomas Ludwell's house to harangue the secretary for siding against him. Ludwell, thinking to calm Bland, invited him in for drinks. The wine, instead of pacifying his guest, magni-

15. Proclamation against mutineers in New Kent County, 18 Nov. 1674, Robinson, "Notes," 445.

16. Warren M. Billings, "Giles Bland," in Sara B. Bearss, John T. Kneebone, J. Jefferson Looney, Brent Tarter, and Sandra Gioia Treadway, eds., *Dictionary of Virginia Biography* (Richmond, 2001), 2:7–8.

17. Joan R. Gunderson, "Anna Bennett Bland," in Bearss et al., *Dictionary of Virginia Biography*, 3–4.

fied Bland's ire, and the two men soon were loudly swapping harsh words. Not content to let their dispute slide, as Bland left Ludwell's, he filched one of his host's gloves, which he nailed to the door of the statehouse. Under it he hung a snippy note that proclaimed the glove's owner "a Sonn of a Whore mechanick Fellow puppy and a Coward." No one in the General Assembly was amused, least of all the burgesses. The note, they protested, "Publique[ly] Affronted" not only them; it also sullied Ludwell, and they demanded that Berkeley arrest Bland to answer for his misbehavior. Without considering all of the political consequences of the burgesses' request, Berkeley rose to the defense of his friend and promptly issued the warrant. Brought to the bar of the General Court, Bland excused himself with a "Slight and Scornefull" air. The court also fined him five hundred pounds for his contempt, but it abated that penalty for two years, after Bland announced his intention to appeal to the king-in-council.[18]

Rather than await the outcome of the appeal, Bland decided to tweak Berkeley. He leveled an accusation that he knew would upset the old man and make its way to the eyes of his superiors. Berkeley, he whispered, had for years been derelict in enforcing the navigation laws, and, now that the governor was aged, his enforcement was looser than ever. (Owing to the destruction of the pertinent records, Bland's allegation can neither be proved nor disproved.) Bland hectored Berkeley in other ways too, and they argued repeatedly over the bounds of Bland's authority as customs collector. Finally, Berkeley lost all patience with Bland. The thing that set him off was a contemptuous, accusatory letter from Bland that charged Berkeley with intentionally countenancing countless infractions of the trade statutes and promised to expose him to the Crown. In an uncontrolled rage Berkeley summoned Bland to the Council of State. He demanded proof under oath of Bland's accusations. There was none. Bland "would not or could not otherwaies Justifie himselfe," though he confessed to having sent a copy of his charges to the customs board. On hearing that admission, Berkeley suddenly moved to suspend Bland from office and to jail him until he posted a peace bond. His motion passed without dissent. Out of a job "untill his Majesties Pleasure shall be further Knowne," Bland made his bond and looked for other ways to stir up trouble.[19]

The handling of Bland was not the way Berkeley had attended to foes in earlier times. Rather than lashing out, he tempted opponents with preferments, pa-

18. McIlwaine, *Minutes of the Council and General Court*, 399.

19. Berkeley to Thomas Ludwell, Francis Moryson, and Robert Smith, Dec. 1674, Jefferson Papers, DLC; Giles Bland to Berkeley, 16 Sept. 1675, Egerton MS 2395, fol. 511; Bland to the commissioners of customs, 1675, Egerton MS 2395, fol. 515, BL; McIlwaine, *Minutes of the Council and General Court*, 423, 448–49; Robinson, "Notes," 259.

tiently charmed them with his courtly demeanor, or frightened them with an intuitively timed fit of temper, and, if those ploys were unsuccessful, then he adroitly isolated the offender. Even William Drummond, who vexed Berkeley far more than the impertinent young Bland and over a much longer period of time, was treated with greater finesse. Annoying as Bland was, he posed no imminent threat. A more considerate Berkeley would have tried to win him over before aloofly brushing him off as casually as he would have flicked away a gnat. Instead, Berkeley reacted to Bland's bullyragging with an unstudied vehemence that hinted at how the stresses upon him fogged his instincts.

Not least among those strains was the Third Anglo-Dutch War. Renewed hostilities raised the issue of defense once more, and Berkeley was no better prepared to stave off the Dutch than he had been a half-decade earlier. Charles II declared war on Holland on 14 March 1672. He sent Berkeley a copy of his declaration along with orders to prepare Virginia for the likelihood of invasion, both of which did not arrive at Jamestown until July. Berkeley promptly issued a proclamation "in his Majesties Name streightly charging & commanding all Millitary Officers and all other his Majestyes subjects within this his Majestyes Colony to . . . doe and execute all Acts of Hostillity in the prosecution of this Warr." The prospect of fighting the Dutch seems not to have troubled him greatly because he neither summoned a council of war nor called the General Assembly into special session. He waited until the assembly reconvened for its regular meeting in September to advocate a course of action.[20]

Berkeley knew full well that Virginia was in far worse shape militarily in the summer of 1672 than it had been five years earlier. After the Peace of Breda there was less pressure on him and his militia officers to worry about external threats from hostile powers, and they dropped their guard. Militia units were not kept at full strength. The forts envisioned by the act of 1667 fell to wreckage. Fort James was only partially completed before construction was halted, the emplacement at Old Point Comfort was abandoned, and other batteries were never started. The associations created to erect, maintain, and man the forts ceased to operate regularly. Local fort taxes continued to be collected, but they were put to other uses. Depleted provincial stockpiles of munitions went unreplenished. The perennial need for heavy artillery pieces continued unmet. Whether from weariness or frustration, Berkeley ceased begging the Crown for war matériel, though, in response to a query from London in 1670, he again decried not only the shortages of armaments but the lack of military "ingeniers." And it was no secret to trained eyewitnesses that Berkeley was ill prepared to protect the colony

20. Proclamation of war with the Netherlands, 4 July 1672, AOB, 1671–73, fol. 142, Vi.

in the event of another attack from the sea. Sir Thomas Grantham, a naval officer with ties to James, duke of York, stated the case most emphatically when he informed the Committee for Trade and Plantations in February 1672 that "there was not powder enough at Tindall's Point upon York River to charge a piece."[21]

Given these circumstances, Berkeley's recommendation to the assembly in September 1672 was neither imaginative nor bold, but it became law nonetheless. The ensuing statute mainly reiterated the provisions of the fort act of 1667. Dilapidated forts should be quickly rebuilt at taxpayers' expense, and those that were never started were now to be erected. This time, however, the bulwarks should be fabricated in brick rather than in timber or earth. The act also admonished militiamen to refurbish their weapons and to keep them "fitt for service" at a moment's notice. Its only new wrinkle was a clause that promised fines for colonists who boarded "newly arrived vessels" not knowing "whether they be Friends or enemies."[22]

"Newly arrived vessels" were few and far between, which disrupted commerce and constricted the normal flow of supplies. An unusually harsh winter had killed off more than half the colony's livestock, and cold weather and the shortages of draft animals slowed the reconstruction of the forts. By March 1673 Berkeley was at last scrambling to round up stores of ammunition through direct appeals to the Crown. "The Merchants Will not venture Soe precious A Commodity to us," he told the Committee for Trade and Plantations, and "by your Intercession" he supplicated "his Majestie to give us Some Small Quantity of Ammunition." A more specific appeal went to master of the ordnance Sir Thomas Chicheley. Berkeley asked Chicheley to furnish fifty great guns, a thousand muskets, a like number of horse pistols and sabers, shot, and forty barrels of powder. A third letter went to the king. It explained how Berkeley had put the colony in a state of preparedness, but it also noted that the province had no money to pay for the armaments he sought from the royal arsenal. That being the case, Berkeley begged "That your Majestie wilbee graciously pleased to graunt us such a supply as may bee sufficient for our defense against any Enemy."[23]

To reinforce just how desperate he was, Berkeley prevailed upon Sir Henry

21. Berkeley to the Committee for Foreign Plantations, 21 June 1671, C.O. 1/26, fol. 197, PRO; Sir Thomas Grantham, *An Historical Account of Some Memorable Actions, Particularly in Virginia . . .* (London, 1716), 59; Grantham to the Committee for Foreign Plantations, Feb. 1672, *VMHB* 20 (1913): 23–24.

22. Hening, *Statutes at Large,* 2:292–94.

23. Berkeley to the Committee for Foreign Plantations, 25 Mar. 1673, CO 1/30, fol. 14, PRO; Berkeley to Sir Thomas Chicheley, ca. 25 Mar. 1673, fols. 115–16, CO 1/30; Berkeley to Charles II , ca. 25 Mar. 1673, fols. 175–76, CO 1/30.

Chicheley to send his personal military appraisal to London. Chicheley was lieutenant general of forces. That position gave him a singular knowledge, which meant that royal officials might listen to him more than Berkeley. He was also the ordnance master's brother, and Berkeley aimed to pull the tie of blood. When Chicheley framed his assessment, he observed that in an emergency the Virginians could call up twenty regiments of foot and twenty more of cavalry. Impressive as that might sound, not a tenth of them had any arms whatsoever. With the militia in such a state of unreadiness, he shuddered at the possibility of the colonists "fly[ing] to the mountains for our security, and leav[ing] this Country and our estates a prey to the invaders."[24]

The letters arrived at their destination in October 1673. At a meeting of the Privy Council, King Charles stole time from his preoccupation with an unpopular war long enough to listen to the requests. A short discussion followed the reading before an order went out to dispatch up to fifty great guns and whatever shot might be spared, but there is no record of the weapons being shipped before the war ended.[25]

Meanwhile, the Virginians readied themselves as best they could. In April 1673 intelligence drifted into Jamestown that warned of a looming offensive by a Dutch fleet thought to be on the prowl in the Caribbean. For safety's sake Berkeley immediately compelled all tobacco ships that were about to leave for England to sail in convoy, and he named Sir Thomas Grantham admiral-in-charge of the hastily gathered fleet. He called a council of war, at which he and his advisors hatched their defensive tactics. To offset the shortage of small arms, the council directed senior militia officers to muster their men and calculate how many weapons they would need to make their units combat ready. The officers were authorized to "take Care that what Armes shall bee in any Howse more then the people Listed Can use" be appropriated for those of their men who lacked muskets and gunpowder. At the first sight of the Dutch, squads of fifty troopers would board any merchantmen that rode at anchor to protect them "till further Order can be taken for their Better Defense." Concurrently, regiments of foot and cavalry would take up positions along the shoreline or man the forts. Regarding the latter, the fort associations were admonished to hurry the strengthening of the bastions, and it was on the basis of this precept that William Drummond's shoddy workmanship at Fort James came to light. That startling

24. Sir Henry Chicheley to Sir Thomas Chicheley, 16 July 1673, CO 1/30, fols. 114–16.

25. Minute of Privy Council meeting, 3 Oct. 1673, PC 2/64, fols. 107–8, PRO; C. R. Boxer, *The Anglo-Dutch Wars of the 17th Century* (London, 1974), 42–62; Antonia Fraser, *Royal Charles: Charles II and the Restoration* (New York, 1979), 307–33.

discovery raised the level of anxiety and distracted Berkeley as he searched for a means of remedy.[26]

Two frigates provided some welcome, if unexpected, help. In May HMS *Barnaby* escorted some tobacco ships into Virginia waters. Her skipper, Thomas Gardner, offered to help Berkeley for as long as it took the merchants to find cargoes. A grateful Berkeley used *Barnaby* as a sentry. He stationed her at the mouth of the James and told Gardner to cruise Chesapeake Bay and, weather permitting, offshore waters in search of the expected Dutch raiders. An additional warship, HMS *Augustine* under the command of Edward Cotterell, appeared in June, and she shared picket duty as well.[27]

The naval presence paid off. On 10 July, just before the tobacco fleet was scheduled to weigh anchor, coastal sentries spotted masts peeking above the horizon to the southeast. As the hours passed, the forms of nine Dutch men-o'-war loomed nearer, and the alarm went forth. Berkeley called out the militia. Squads took their places aboard the merchantmen, while the regiments trooped into the forts or stood guard along the beaches and the river banks. The Dutch pressed their way past the headlands of the Chesapeake Bay and worked cautiously into the James, not realizing they had lost the element of strategic and tactical surprise. They anchored in Lynhaven Bay as daylight waned, but just west of them they could see an inviting fleet of tobacco ships silhouetted against the setting sun.

Hoping to shorten the odds against them, Gardner and Cotterell commandeered six of the best armed merchantmen they could find, and on the morning of 12 July their hastily cobbled armada made for the Hollanders. In the furious firefight that followed, four of the merchant vessels ran aground and were lost. The rest of the English flotilla held its own, despite being outgunned. As darkness closed in, Gardner and Cotterell broke off the engagement and retreated to the safety of the Elizabeth River anchorage. They had saved the greater part of the tobacco fleet, much of which scattered upriver toward the Nansemond fort and Fort James. The Dutch were afraid to force their way past the ramparts at Nansemond, which actually mounted no artillery, so they "looked on them five Dayes" before they burned six stray tobacco ships and sailed out of the bay.[28]

26. From Charles Calvert, 1 Apr. 1673, Jefferson Papers, DLC; commission to Sir Thomas Grantham, 2 Apr. 1673, in Grantham, *Historical Account*, 8–9; orders-in-council for the defense of Virginia, 22 Apr., 1673, McIlwaine, *Minutes*, 334; Robinson, "Notes," 262.

27. Orders to Captain Thomas Gardner, 23 May 1673, Jefferson Papers, DLC.

28. Berkeley and the Council of State to Charles II, July, 1673, CO 1/30, fols. 114–15, PRO; Ludwell to Arlington, 2 Aug. 1673, CO 1/30, fol. 120; William Sherwood to Sir Joseph Williamson, 4 Aug. 1673, CO 1/30, fols. 121–22; Richard Wharton to [?], 24 Sept. 1673, CO 1/30, fols. 169–70; Donald G. Sho-

Despite minimal losses, there was criticism of Berkeley's defense. "Severall masters of shipps and other persons who (how ignorant soever they ar of the Place)" complained that there would have been no mishaps at all if only Berkeley had fortified Old Point Comfort. Berkeley would have none of that. Acting on his motion, the Council of State appointed Secretary Ludwell, Gardner, Cotterell, the chief river pilot, and several ship captains to "Sound the whole Channell in out and Athwart the said Poynt and Give us a Report of the same under their hands how they find it." Their findings confirmed what everyone in Virginia always knew. Shallow water ran outward from the shore for more than a mile, and ships that anchored beyond the shoals lay outside cannon range. Hence, the Virginia government was not to be faulted for the shippers' misfortunes.[29]

Captains who lost their ships pressed Berkeley for salvage rights or relief from the export duties. The applications for salvage were quickly granted, but reimbursing the excises was not so easily done. As Berkeley pointed out, "the bills which were passed for the said Duty being paid away upon the Country's Credit and the General Accounts Stated and transmitted for England it is impossible to returne them in Kind." Therefore, he and the council ruled, any captain who certified that he had paid the duty would be absolved from paying a like amount on their next cargo. The solution did not satisfy everyone, but it was all that Berkeley was prepared to do for them, and the disgruntled were left to sputter in frustration.[30]

Those discontents paled in comparison to the growls of the colonists. Demoralization crept over officers and soldiers alike. Some grew fidgety after being called up and then not seeing any action. Others fretted about possible dangers, which Berkeley described this way. "Wee leave at our backs," he explained to the king,

as Many Servants (besides Negroes as their are freemen to defend the Shoars and all our Frontiers [against?] the Indians). Both which gives men fearfull apprehentions of the dainger they Leave their Estates and Families in, Whilest they are drawne from their houses to defend the Borders, Of which number alsoe at least one third are Single freemen (whose labour Will hardly maintaine them) or men much in debt, both which Wee may reasonably expect upon any Small advantage

mette and Robert D. Haslach, *Raid on America: The Dutch Naval Campaign of 1672–1674* (Columbia, S.C., 1988), 138–48.

29. Order to sound the James River channel at Old Point Comfort, 1 Aug. 1673, Council Records, 1663–76, 198; reports in response to the order, 8 Aug. 1673, 199; order-in-council to John Powell, 1 Aug. 1673; salvage order to John Letchington, 1 Aug. 1673—all in Jefferson Papers, DLC.

30. Reply to petition for relief from export duty, 1 Aug. 1673, Jefferson Papers, DLC, 200.

the Enemy may gaine upon us, would revolt to them in hopes of bettering their Condition by Shareing the Plunder of the Countrey With them.

Berkeley sent the troops home quite soon after the Dutch sailed away, and he made a progress throughout the colony in a bid to dampen the discontent.[31]

Playing for the planters' affections got Berkeley less than a ringing endorsement. His popularity still held, but more than a few signs indicated an erosion of confidence, much of which stemmed from his failure to stave off the Dutch and his inability to provide adequate defenses. In a memorial to Charles II, the Council of State found it necessary to defend him against the aspersions "of Some ill affected Persons who [were] vexed with their losse." His conduct was "beyond what could be expected from a man of his years." And, argued the councillors, Berkeley still retained "the love and reverence" of all Virginians.[32]

Commotions in the fall of 1673 betokened a lack of universal "love and reverence" for Berkeley or for his policies. Berkeley presided at the court-martial of a York County militiaman, who was convicted of striking his superior officer and disobeying orders. Ordinarily, such behavior merited execution, but in a show of mercy the trooper got off with an apology and a fine. A more direct confrontation came from Benjamin Egglestone of James City County, who "most presumptuously and impudently intrenched upon the prerogative and abused the Authority of the Right Honorable the Governor." The exact nature of Egglestone's insult is unrecorded, though it was deemed heinous enough for the General Court to sentence him to "have Thirty Nine Lashes unless he forthwith Give Good Security . . . for payment of Three Thousand pounds of tobacco and Caske to be Disposed of for buying of Armes for this Country" and court costs. In contrast to the ruling of the court-martial, this was not a sentence that Berkeley mitigated.[33]

Far more serious than incidents such as these was popular resistance to increased defense expenditures. The Crown could not, or would not, furnish the militia with muskets; there was no money in the provincial treasury to buy weapons, but the militia still needed to be brought up to strength. Berkeley embodied his remedy in a bill he pushed through the General Assembly as the militia act of October 1673. The statute passed the primary responsibility for a well-armed

31. Berkeley to Charles II, ca. July 1673, CO 1/30, fols. 114–15; PRO.
32. The Council of State to the Privy Council, Oct. 1673, CO 1/30, fols. 179–80.
33. Court-martial of Richard Clarke, [20?] Oct. 1673, Jefferson Papers, DLC; *Berkeley v. Egglestone*, 21 Oct. 1673, McIlwaine, *Minutes of the Council and General Court*, 348.

militia to the local magistrates. Officers were required to calculate shortages, and on the basis of their reports the courts were compelled in turn to purchase the necessary weapons. The costs, which represented public outlays on a scale not seen in decades, would be borne by the local taxpayers. When the courts met in November and December to impose their annual levies, they raised their taxes sharply. And so it was that fourteen planters in Lawne's Creek Parish, Surry County, refused to pay their assessments.[34]

Strength lay in numbers, the ringleaders thought, and they contrived to round up as many of their neighbors as they could who felt as they did. Their plan was simple enough. They would reason with the court in the hope of persuading the justices not to increase their taxes. If persuasion failed, then they would stop the sheriff from collecting the levies within Lawne's Creek Parish. The boycott started on 12 December, the day the sheriff, accompanied by several justices, arrived at the parish church to publish what individual parishioners owed the county. As the magistrates announced the assessments, the protesters attempted to express their feelings. The sheriff commanded silence and ordered them to disperse. They refused, whereupon they were arrested on charges of unlawful assembly, contempt of authority, and hindering the sheriff. At trial in the Surry County court, nine of the dissidents escaped with no more punishment than signing peace bonds. Three others were fined a thousand pounds of tobacco for seditious utterances, and they too posted bonds for good behavior. The reputed architect of the affair was bound over for trial at the General Court, where he was judged guilty of all charges and fined heavily. Then in a show of goodwill Berkeley pardoned all the convicts and remitted their fines on their promise to admit their crimes in open court.[35]

Berkeley's conciliatory gesture quieted Surry taxpayers. His show of gentleness would not still complaints against higher taxes elsewhere, especially after they went up again in September 1674 to defray the lobby against the Northern Neck Proprietary. Nor did it lay the defense question to rest. Some county courts swiftly restocked their forces. Others moved more cautiously or not at all, which left the colony no better prepared for an emergency than it had been before the Dutch war. The magnitude of Berkeley's failure to enforce quick, uniform com-

---

34. Hening, *Statutes at Large,* 2:304–5.

35. Warrants for the arrest of Matthew Swan and others, 3 Jan. 1673/74, SDWI, 1671–84, 41, 42; depositions of Francis Taylor, Jan. 1673/74, SDWI, fol. 43; order remanding Matthew Swan and others for trial at the General Court, 6 Jan. 1673/74, SOB, 1671–91, 41–42; judgment against Matthew Swan and others, 6 Apr. 1674, McIlwaine, *Minutes,* 367; pardon for Matthew Swan and others, 23 Sept. 1674, SDWI, 1671–84, fol. 69.

pliance with the militia act of 1673 became horribly plain within a year of his pardoning the Surry dissidents.[36]

On "a Sabbath day Morning in [July] Anno 1675" a party of Doeg Indians struck an outlying farm situated in the remote northwest frontier county of Stafford. The natives looted the house, stole a few hogs, killed two men, and then slipped away as suddenly as they had appeared. Word of the attack came to Colonel George Mason and Major George Brent of the Stafford militia, who called out their men and went off in search of the marauders. Picking up the track, the troopers followed it across the Potomac River into Maryland, where they surprised the raiders and killed a dozen. Mistakenly, they also dispatched an equal number of friendly Susquehannocks before returning to Virginia. The incident seemed akin to flare-ups that were commonplace, but this one boded more serious repercussions. Indignant at the Virginians' incursion into their colony, Maryland authorities sternly reprehended Berkeley for allowing the violation of their territory. More threatening were the outraged Susquehannocks, who struck murderously at undefended settlements everywhere along the frontiers of Maryland and Virginia.[37]

At first Berkeley seemed content to let the regional militia officers deal with the trouble as best they could, and he did no more than instruct Mason and Brent to "expell the Enimy if they made further attempts." He heard more rumors of trouble as the weeks went by, and the tales led him to conclude that the situation verged on getting out of hand. Not certain what to do, he summoned all of the councillors who lived nearest to him for a meeting at Green Spring House on 31 August 1675. The councillors advised against a show of force that involved a colony-wide call-up of the militia. They recommended the appointment of John Washington and Isaac Allerton to make a "full And thorough inquisittion" of the "true causes of the Murthers and spoyles by which Nation or Nations of Indians donne" and to "transmitt the whole business to the next Generall Court." Washington and Allerton were also charged to punish the natives, and, if that meant crossing into Maryland, they should inform the "Honorable Governor of that province Who is pleased . . . To promise if occasion be all necessary assistance."[38]

36. County grievances, 1677, CO 1/39, fols. 195–255; AOB, 1673–76, 94–95; LOB, 1660–80, 292; MOB, 1673–80, fols. 7, 58; YOB, 1672–94, 139.

37. Thomas Mathew, "The Rise, Progress, and Conclusion of Bacon's Rebellion in the Years 1675–1676" (1705), printed in Charles M. Andrews, ed., Narratives of the Insurrections, 1675–1690 (New York, 1915), 17; Sir John Berry and Francis Moryson, "A True Narrative of the Late Rebellion in Virginia, by the Royal Commissioners, 1677," Andrews, Narratives, 105–6; proceedings of the Council of Maryland, 1671–75, Liber R. R., 37–38, MdAA.

38. Minute of council meeting, 31 Aug. 1675, WDWI, 1665–77, fol. 232.

Bent on retaliation, Washington and Allerton never held the "inquisittion." Instead, they gathered a detachment of men and contacted the Marylanders for help in trailing the enemy. The Marylanders provided troops, and the joint force set forth in search of the Susquehannocks. In late September the colonists approached the Susquehannocks' fortified encampment and negotiated a parley. The Virginians accused the Indians of killing settlers, an allegation that the natives denied vehemently. Washington and Allerton refused to accept the protestations and perfidiously executed five of the chiefs before investing the stronghold. Their seven-week siege failed when, under cover of darkness, the defenders quietly abandoned their fort and slipped into the interior. The expedition had been a costly, disheartening failure.[39]

Worse was to come. The Susquehannocks, intent on exacting a toll for their murdered leaders, hit border outposts all along the frontier. Their most deadly stroke fell in January 1676, when they killed some three dozen persons in a single attack. Satisfied that they had taken their full measure of revenge, they sent messengers, who conveyed their desire for peace to Berkeley. Berkeley refused to deal, and they withdrew deep into the interior, well out of reach of the English.[40]

Welcome though the Susquehannocks' retreat was, it did not end the bloodletting. Other natives saw opportunity in the colonists' distress, and they set about avenging wrongs done them for decades. Who these "others" were quickly turned into a hot feud between Berkeley and the frontiersmen that remains controversial to this day, but the effects of their handiwork was indisputable. The Susquehannocks had been satisfied with killing Englishmen and capturing provisions. These Indians not only slaughtered colonists; they also killed livestock, burned fields, torched houses, and razed every settlement they attacked. Their scourge stampeded the English into a mass panic.[41]

Convinced that a long-feared league of all Indians from Canada to Virginia had come to pass, the frontier settlers urgently appealed for Berkeley's help. Berkeley responded by ordering Sir Henry Chicheley to march a detachment of

---

39. [John Cotton?], "The History of Bacon's and Ingram's Rebellion, 1676," in Andrews, *Narratives*, 47–48; John Gerard, "A narrative of the transactions of the Susquehannock Fort," 1677, WDWI, 1665–77, fol. 288; Alice L. Ferguson, "The Susquehannock Fort on Piscataway Creek," *Maryland Historical Magazine* 337 (1941): 1–9.

40. [Cotton?], "History of Bacon's and Ingram's Rebellion," 48.

41. Berkeley to Ludwell, 16 Feb. 1675/76, Coventry Papers, 77: fol. 56; same to same, 1 Apr. 1676, CO 1/36, fol. 66; Berkeley to Charles II, 24 Mar. 1675/75, Coventry Papers, 77, fol. 67; Beverley, *History and Present State of Virginia*, 77; Wilcomb E. Washburn, "Governor Berkeley and King Philip's War," *New England Quarterly* 30 (1957): 363–77; Francis Jennings, *The Invasion of America: Indians, Colonialism, and the Cant of Conquest* (Chapel Hill, N.C., 1975); Jill Lepore, *King Philip's War and the Origins of American Identity* (New York, 1998).

three hundred foot and cavalry up the Rappahannock and to destroy whatever pillagers he encountered. Chicheley had barely assembled his men when, without warning, Berkeley disbanded them, saying that he had decided to put the whole matter of the Indian troubles before the General Assembly. His reversal flabbergasted everyone. So did his refusal to offer so much as a hint for why he rescinded Chicheley's order, and not even his closest friends could explain it. Strangest of all, Berkeley was wholly oblivious to the effect of his change of mind. In a moment of crisis, when daring was needed, he was irresolute and seemingly fainthearted. Perchance there was truth in the murmurs that the old man had lost his edge, after all.[42]

Berkeley set the meeting of the General Assembly for 7 March 1675/76. Members streamed into town amid frenzied alarms and tales of imminent new attacks. The burgesses were all the more unsettled because Speaker Wynne had died a few weeks earlier, and they would miss his steadying hand, as would Berkeley. No one in the assembly had an inkling of Berkeley's plans. As much as the Indians terrorized them all, Berkeley scared them too, but his critics, among the burgesses and councillors, were reluctant to face him off. He might yet regain his balance, and then they would look foolhardy for having doubted him. Foe and friend alike held their tongues, content for the moment to follow his lead.

Just as soon as the burgesses picked Augustine Warner Jr. to replace Speaker Wynne, Berkeley laid a three-point plan before the assembly, and it was adopted. One act committed a defensive war that left the major military decisions to him. It called for a special task force of five hundred rangers, some of whom would raise and garrison nine forts located at the heads of the main rivers and other prominent places. As for the remaining troops, they would march between the forts in search of hostile Indians, but they could not attack "untill order shall come from the governour." And to no one's surprise the costs of this defense would be paid with new taxes. A second law prohibited, under penalty of death, arms trafficking with the natives, though it permitted the sale of other "necessaries" with "such Indians who are amongst us in peace," and it restricted trade in those items only to colonists who held licenses from Berkeley. The third act forbade the exportation of corn so as to ensure adequate provender for men and livestock.[43]

Here was nothing that comforted hysterical colonists nor erased any doubts about Berkeley. Planters universally derided the plan as useless in the face of a

42. Berry and Moryson, "True Narrative," 107; grievances of Rappahannock County, 13 Mar. 1676/77, CO 1/39, fol. 107, PRO.
43. Hening, Statutes at Large, 2:326–39.

mobile enemy who attacked suddenly and disappeared just as swiftly. Settlers in the outlying areas volunteered to fight Indian fashion and beseeched "that your gratious Honor would be pleased to grant us a Committion and to make choice of Committioned Officers to name someone as their commander." Berkeley coldly refused to receive all such plaints, and he even banned additional petitions on the subject.[44]

In April a tale flew about Charles City County that rumored the massing of sizable bands of marauding natives within fifty miles of the county's borders south of the James. Although the news later turned out to be erroneous, it was credited long enough to arouse the local planters. Some "beat up the drum for volunteers to go against the Indians," while others hustled to Jamestown seeking the appointment of a commander. Once more, Berkeley hotly turned them aside. Not to be denied, the Charles Cityites armed themselves and began to look for someone who would lead them anyway. They found their man in Nathaniel Bacon.[45]

44. Petition to Berkeley, spring 1676, CO 1/36, fol. 139.
45. Berry and Moryson, "True Narrative," 109.

13

A Bacon! A Bacon! A Bacon!

athaniel Bacon's open defiance of Berkeley caused the rebellion that bears his name and made him a central actor in colonial Virginia. His followers cherished him as their deliverer. His enemies branded him a traitor. Reverberations of that partisanship still resound in the opinions of modern scholars, who rarely agree about Bacon's character or his impulses to rebellion, let alone his proper place in Anglo-Virginia history. The difficulty arises chiefly because no one can say who Nathaniel Bacon was. There are no portraits or diaries or volumes of letters to depict him. Only snippets remain, scraps that are plastic enough to fashion Bacon into an Indian hater who demolished the fame of the ever-popular Berkeley, a patriot who struck the first blow for American independence, or someone else.

The bare facts of his origin and his appearance on the Virginia stage made Bacon an improbable choice for the fate destiny dealt him. Born in 1647, he came of well-to-do East Anglian gentry stock. His parents, Sir Thomas and Elizabeth Brooke Bacon, named their son after a kinsman who had served Oliver Cromwell as master of requests and who was honored by parliamentarians for his polemics against Charles I. Bacon rose to adulthood in the cozy surroundings of the family seat, Friston Hall, in Suffolk. When he turned thirteen, he enrolled at St. Catherine's College, Cambridge. The pleasures of being away from home and extravagant living distracted him and caused his recall to Friston Hall. Squire Bacon hired the highly regarded linguist John Ray for his son's tutor, but the boy showed no more inclination for study under Ray's instruction than he had at university. Ray decided to take his pupil on a tour of the Continent. They set off in 1663 on a journey that tracked Berkeley's thirty years before, though Bacon fell victim to a lengthy bout of smallpox. Returning to England, he resumed his studies at St. Catherine's and gained his master's degree. Diploma in hand, Master Bacon matriculated at Gray's Inn, in London, where all the Bacon men had learned the law.

Again like Berkeley, Bacon balked at walking the path his father intended for him. He returned to Suffolk and courted Elizabeth Duke. The couple married, despite their parents' adamant opposition. Sir Edward Duke so disliked his new son-in-law that he disowned his naughty daughter and never spoke to her again. Bacon was without means before he married, he had none after he wed, only now he had to support a family, and his scramble for income entangled him in unsavory business deals that earned him a swindler's reputation. Greatly annoyed, Sir Thomas Bacon shielded his roguish son once more. He handed Nathaniel eighteen hundred pounds and packed him, Elizabeth, and their two daughters off to Virginia. The money staked the couple to a fresh start. There was the hope, too, that their colonial kinfolk would establish the twenty-seven-year-old Bacon in a respectable living. (One of Bacon's relations was Dame Frances Berkeley. Another was Councillor Nathaniel Bacon, who was both childless and well-heeled.)[1]

So began Bacon's Virginia adventure. Landing at York County in August 1674, the couple stayed briefly with Councillor Bacon, who introduced them to the Berkeleys. Dame Frances invited them to Green Spring House, where they remained until Bacon sealed the purchase of Curles Neck plantation, which was situated in Henrico County some forty miles upriver from Jamestown. A working farm, replete with house and outbuildings, Curles Neck afforded Bacon instant stature as a great planter, which he rapidly enlarged after he acquired additional property near the falls of the James and Berkeley licensed him as an Indian trader.[2]

Well established, accomplished, inquisitive, but of a morose, sometimes haughty, makeup, and given to impulsiveness, Bacon swiftly found favor with his

---

1. "Strange News from Virginia" (London, 1677), in Harry Finestone, ed., *Bacon's Rebellion: The Contemporary News Sheets* (Charlottesville, Va., 1956), 8–9; Thomas Jefferson Wertenbaker, *Torchbearer of the Revolution: The Story of Bacon's Rebellion and Its Leader* (Princeton, 1940), 39–59; Brent Tarter, "Nathaniel Bacon," in John T. Kneebone, J. Jefferson Looney, Brent Tarter, and Sandra Gioia Treadway, eds., *Dictionary of Virginia Biography* (Richmond, 1998) 1:271–74; Warren M. Billings, "Nathaniel Bacon," in Colin Matthew et al., eds., *The Oxford Dictionary of National Biography* (Oxford, 2004).

2. Bacon to Berkeley, 18 Sept. 1675, Coventry Papers, 77, fol. 6.

fellow upcountry planters. Nearness to the governor bore him higher still. In March 1675 Berkeley did something most extraordinary and wholly uncharacteristic for him. He named Bacon—a man of no political seasoning whatever—to a vacancy on the Council of State. The seat at the council table made Bacon a "man of great Honour and Esteem among the people," but he was not captivated by his conciliar duties and rarely attended meetings.[3]

Such newfound prominence surrounded Bacon with a coterie of conspicuous men. Thomas Blayton, William Byrd, James Crews, Henry Isham, Francis Poythress, John Poythress, and John Sturdivant were neighbors. Byrd and Crews held junior militia commissions and seats on the Henrico County court, but they were estranged from the justices who ran the county. Blayton, Isham, the Poythress brothers, and Sturdivant were prosperous planters who associated with a faction that contested Edward Hill, a Berkeley ally and one of the leading politicians in Charles City County. All seven men disdained Indians but profited from commerce with the natives. Giles Bland and William Drummond befriended Bacon too. So did Richard Lawrence and William Carver. The elusive Lawrence, an Oxford don of formidable intellect, kept a tavern at Jamestown and occasionally represented Lower Norfolk County in the House of Burgesses. A Bristol seafarer turned planter, Carver was an unpredictable man who had once held seats on the Lower Norfolk bench and in the House. He was dismissed from both after he stabbed a man to death in a frenzy. Others included two York County militia officers, Thomas Hansford and Thomas Cheesman, and the recently arrived traders Joseph Ingram and Gregory Walklate, who lived on the New Kent County frontier.[4]

These were men who questioned their governor's abilities but who trembled at leading the frightened planters against the Indians or publicly opposing Berkeley. They were drawn to Bacon because his comet-burst rise marked him as someone with special influence over Berkeley. Sudden notoriety seduced Bacon too. Amid the Susquehannock attacks in September 1675, he presumed to counsel Berkeley on the proper way to deal with the crisis and to press for a greater share

3. Sir John Berry and Francis Moryson, "A True Narrative of the Late Rebellion in Virginia, by the Royal Commissioners, 1677," in Charles M. Andrews, ed., *Narratives of the Insurrections, 1675–1690* (New York, 1915), 109–10; Robert Beverley, *History and Present State of Virginia,* ed. Louis B. Wright (Chapel Hill, N.C., 1947), 78; H. R. McIlwaine, ed., *Minutes of the Council and General Court of Colonial Virginia, 1622–1632, 1670–1676,* 2d ed. (Richmond, 1979), 401.

4. Thomas Mathew, "The Rise, Progress, and Conclusion of Bacon's Rebellion in the Years 1675–1676" (1705), in Andrews, *Narratives,* 24n; Thomas Jefferson Wertenbaker, "Richard Lawrence: A Sketch," *William and Mary Quarterly,* 3d ser. 16 (1959): 244–48; LNDWI, 1666–75, fol. 41; LNOB, 1666–75, fols. 17, 18, 22, 34, 41, 55, 84, 127.

in the fur trade. Not one to accept advice from his juniors, Berkeley sharply rebuked his kinsman to mind his own affairs and candidly told Bacon to leave the Indians to him. (Berkeley's pique was the more intense because Bacon owed him money, and Elizabeth Bacon quarreled with Dame Frances.) Bacon ignored the admonition.[5]

Months later, in April 1676, he, Isham, Crews, and Byrd sat down for drinks. Their talk was not about planting or fur trading. It turned on "the Sadness of the times" and "the Fear they all lived in." Bacon and Byrd had lost servants during a recent Indian attack, and they were perplexed by Berkeley, who seemed inept in the face of the onset of a much-feared combination of Indians from New England to the Chesapeake. The static defensive scheme he had pushed through the last General Assembly was no shield against the crafty foe. His refusal to allow the backcountry settlers to safeguard the frontiers and his insistence on protecting tributary natives reeked of preferential treatment toward Berkeley's favorites, who controlled the Indian trade. The conversation continued in that vein until someone remarked that planters were arming themselves. Supposedly, hundreds were already massed in an encampment on the south side of the James. The four companions decided to see for themselves, and, as they drew near the campground, shouts of "A Bacon! A Bacon! A Bacon!" roared out as the would-be soldiers cried for him to command them. Bacon answered their call.[6]

He led the men across the river and into New Kent County looking for action. Finding none there, they marched to the falls of the James, forded the river once more, and tracked deep into the southwestern wilderness. Along the way Bacon dashed off a hurried note to Berkeley. "The whole Country," he wrote, "is much alarmed with the feare of Generall Combination and I thinke not without reason." Despite his avowal ever to be "esteemed by your Honor as a loyall subject and your Honors most humble servant," his justification that he took command in "his owne defense and the Countrys safety" conveyed a none-too-subtle criticism that angered Berkeley. Berkeley scribbled a stern message in reply that warned that commanding unauthorized volunteers was mutiny. Bacon, perhaps believing that his office and his kinship sufficed to excuse him no matter what, retorted that he was "just now goeing out to seeke a more agreeable destiny then you are pleased to designe mee."[7]

Bacon's blithe disregard threw Berkeley into an even greater fury. The last

5. Berkeley to Bacon, 14 Sept. 1675, Coventry Papers, 77, fol. 3; Bacon to Berkeley, 15 Sept., Coventry Papers, 77, fol. 6.

6. Berry and Moryson, "True Narrative," 109, 110.

7. Bacon to Berkeley, 28 April 1676, Coventry Papers, 77, fol. 73.

thing he wanted was reproach from an insubordinate upstart. He rashly called up three hundred militiamen and set off after Bacon, on 3 May, intent upon heading off his obstreperous young relative. Bacon beat him to the falls and got away. Saddle sore and marrow tired, Berkeley sickened. He was not just ill and irate; he looked asinine and incompetent. Bacon stood vigorous and bold, and out of reach, which outraged Berkeley all the more.

His failure to catch Bacon finally awoke Berkeley to the precariousness of his political situation. Never before had a rival endangered him so. He was in peril of losing control, and he must swiftly regain his authority or Virginia would spin into chaos and worse for him. Shaken from the torpor that had gripped him for months, he bid to right himself. To that end he published two proclamations from the field on 10 May. One declared Bacon a rebel and suspended him from all public offices. Berkeley meant that decree to wipe away any legitimacy that attached to Bacon because of his being a councillor of state, and it likewise was intended as a caution to those planters who contemplated joining Bacon. The second proclamation dissolved the General Assembly and ordered the election of an entirely new House of Burgesses. Customarily, election writs were brief documents that merely announced the dissolution and set the polling date. This one was different. It broadened the franchise to include all free adult white males, and it contained a stratagem that had served Berkeley well in the past. It dared the voters to fault Berkeley, promising that, were he the chief source of complaint, he would promptly ask Charles II to recall him.[8]

To isolate Bacon further, Berkeley told militia commanders across Virginia "to spare none that has the name of an Indian for they are now all our enemies." He followed his order with specific commissions to the officers and informed them that the Council of State would "publiquely" declare war against all Indians just as soon as he returned to Green Spring House. Managing a flash of his old courtliness in a postscript to one of those commissions, he apologized to William Claiborne Jr., saying: "I write many letters howerly and dayly and have noe Clerke to assist mee. Therefore I desire you to send a Coppy of this Commission to Col. Goodrich which is as instructive and significant to him as to you." None of these moves deterred Bacon, who was bent on running the natives to ground, though they gave him pause sufficient to exculpate himself once more in a letter he posted to Berkeley on 25 May.[9]

8. Proclamation suspending Nathaniel Bacon Jr. from all offices, 10 May 1676, CO1/37, fol. 3; election writ, 10 May 1676, Tracy W. McGregor, MS, ViU; Declaration and Remonstrance of Sir William Berkeley, 29 May 1676, Coventry Papers, 77, fols. 157–58.

9. To Thomas Goodrich, 15 May 1676, Coventry Papers, 77, fol. 85; commission to William Claiborne Jr., ca. 15 May 1676, ibid.

Bacon expressed his resentment that "for the expence of our Estates and hazard of our lives in the Countrys service," he and his men should be "so falsely represented to your Honor." Far from being rebels, the volunteers were devoutly loyal subjects of the king and always obedient "to your Honor as his servant and our chiefe Commander here under him." Indeed, it was Bacon's "generall preface to all my proceedings to all men declaring that I abhored rebellion or the opposeing of Laws or Government and that if your Honor in person were to lead a Command I would follow and obey and that if noe body were present and I had noe orders I would still goe in the defense of the Country against all Indians in generall for that they were all enemies."

Bacon dismissed accounts of Berkeley's "threatenings against my life which are dayly brought to my eares" as ridiculous and not to be credited to such a wise, just governor as Berkeley. Those tales he put off to the work of evildoers. "Consider," he continued, "what manner of men have aspersed mee whoe never in any thing aimed further then the Countrys quiet and prosperity and the destructions of all Indians of all trade concerned with them which being by them perceaved together with the violence and freedome of my temper and expressions I believe they did combine first to engage with mee in this Indian Warr and then desert mee but I assure you Sir my conscience is cleare to feare and my resolutions to well grounded to stop."

Although he wished to clear himself with Berkeley, Bacon plainly said that he was continuing his "just proceedings" against the Indians. As proof of his intent, he appended a report of his recent slaughter of the friendly Occaneechees and the seizing of an Indian who was "yett protected and defended by Major General Wood against whome wee have by sufficient Witnes severall high and great Complaints and doe expect due Justice According to the Laws of England."

In a postscript Bacon attempted to square himself with Dame Frances too. "I heare," he wrote, that "my Lady has raised severall scandalous and false reports of mee that I was not worth a Groate as a Parliament Captain that my bills were protested." He had "too high an estimation" of her to credit such stories, and he begged "her to bee as generous to mee whoe can heare enough if I would Attend [her]."[10]

Bacon entrusted delivery of the letter to James Crews, who brought it to Green Spring House on 26 May. Crews walked into the dining room, where he found

10. Bacon to Berkeley, 25 May 1676, Coventry Papers, 77, fol. 89; Abraham Wood to Berkeley, 24 May 1676, ibid., fol. 88; "A description of the fight between the English and the Indians in May 1676, Nathaniel Bacon being their General and the number of men 211," CO 1/36, fol. 77, PRO; Wilcomb E. Washburn, *The Governor and the Rebel: A History of Bacon's Rebellion in Virginia* (Chapel Hill, N.C., 1957), 40–49.

Berkeley at the table with Dame Frances, their parish priest, the Reverend John Clough,[11] and Sir Henry Chicheley. When Berkeley finished the letter, he showed it to the others. Crews obviously knew its contents in advance because he said that Bacon "did desire to Answer what he hath donne before his Majestie in England." Berkeley allowed that "Mr. Bacon should have his owne wish," providing he gave himself up.[12]

Dame Frances seized the moment to declare for Crews's benefit that "Being not borne of a Family that hath taught me to lye, and being in the Just defense of my Husbands Honor forst upon the Sladge, I doe Assert that meeting with an universall prepossession in the minds of People that Esquire Bacon would not onely be their Captain, but bear all their charges, releeve and maintaine the wives and children of all those that should goe out with him." She went on to speak in no uncertain terms her opinion of Bacon as little more than a dishonest man who borrowed freely from others with no mind to repay his debts. Bad as that was, he was an ingrate, who abused her husband's hospitality and "rent the Heart off [sic] a woman and his Kinswoman whom by all Laws of Honor and Humanity Hee was bound to protect." She flatly denied that "ever I said Hee was a Parliament Captain."[13]

Crews spent the night at Green Spring House. He left the following morning in the company of Councillor Bacon and Major John White, a New Kent County justice of the peace, both of whom were evidently trying to compose the differences between two stubborn antagonists. The three men caught up with Bacon later that day and told him what had transpired. Hearing the Berkeleys' reaction, Bacon gave White and his cousin another letter. Quite brief, the letter deserves to be quoted in full because it bears the earmarks of Bacon's petulant personality and his willful determination to have his way with Berkeley.

> My submissions are unacceptable my intentions misunderstood. Whoe are my Enemies and misinformers I know not. If I did I would manifest my innocence by their shame whoe have by severall false and paltry inventions bin busie to injure my reputation by oblique and false representations of every sorte. I am sorry that your Honors resentments are of such violence and groweth as to command my appearance with all contempt and disgrace and my disowning and belying soe Glo-

11. Clough (d. 1684) was rector of James City Parish. For a time after Bacon's Rebellion, he held the cure of Southwark Parish in Surry, but he returned to his former place, where he served until his death.

12. Affidavit of Sir William Berkeley, Sir Henry Chicheley, the Reverend John Clough, and James Crews, 28 May 1676, Coventry Papers, 77, fol. 90.

13. Affidavit of Dame Frances Berkeley, ca. 26 May 1676, Coventry Papers, 77, fol. 91.

rious a cause as the Countrys defense. I know my person [is] safe in your Honors word but only begg what pledge or warranty I shall have for my reputation. Sir I as I told your Honor upon severall scores your Honors most obliged servant one that respects your Honors authority and holds your person sacred and that wilbee ever soe although I bee never soe contemned slighted and persecuted and if I may be so happy as to have your Honors Commission I shall most thankfully embrace it. I cannot tell what more to say but only to begg your Honor not to attend to all storyes of my Enemies but to believe mee in my heart Your Honors most humble and most faithfull servant.[14]

No less mulish, Berkeley turned to his councillors for their support of his view that Bacon must yield to him. He outlined his case before a hastily gathered meeting of the council at Green Spring House. They backed him, even Councillor Bacon, who decided that his kinsman was a dangerous fool. In a statement for the record they all pronounced Bacon's activities "rash, illegal, unwarrantable, and most rebellious, and consequently most destructive to all Government and Lawes."[15]

Thus armed, Berkeley shot yet another salvo at his rival. His "Declaration and Remonstrance" stated the question between him as governor and Bacon this way. "If any Ennimies should envade England," he wrote, "any Councelor justice of the peace or other superior Officer might rayse what forces they could to protect his majesties subjects. But I say againe if after the kings knowledge of this invasion any the greatest Prince of England should rayse forces against the kings prohibition this would be now and was ever in al Ages and nations accounted Treason." Such was the case with Bacon, and, because Bacon had acted contrary to his express orders, "I doe therefore againe declare that Bacon proceeding against al lawes of al nations moderne and ancient is a rebel to his sacred majestie and this country." Nonetheless, he promised, "if Mr. Bacon can shew me president or example where such actings in any nation what soever was approved of I wil mediate with the king and you for a pardon and excuse for him." Berkeley was dubious that such "presidents" existed, though he could give Bacon "an hundred examples where brave and greate men have been put to death for gaining victories against the command of their superiors."

Next, Berkeley compared his character to Bacon's. He had lived in Virginia "fower and thirty yeares as uncorrupt and diligent as ever governor was." Bacon

14. Bacon to Berkeley, 28 May 1676, Coventry Papers, 77, fol. 93.

15. Opinion of the Council of State, 29 May 1676, Coventry Papers, 77, fol. 157. Besides Bacon Sr., Chicheley, Philip Ludwell, Thomas Swann, James Bray, Thomas Ballard, and William Cole endorsed the opinion.

was but a "man of two yeares amongst you his person and qualities unknowne to most of you and to al men els by any Vertuos action that ever I heard of." As for Bacon's "boastes" about his military prowess, Berkeley dismissed them with the claim that he had expended fewer men during the entire Anglo-Indian War of 1644–46 than Bacon lost during his brief attack on the Occaneechees.

Berkeley then stood by his decision to distinguish between hostile and amicable Indians. The distinction was militarily sound because the English relied upon the tributaries as spies who could ferret out the "more bloody ennimies." Just as soon as he discovered the treachery of the friendly natives, he gave out instructions to destroy them too, "as the commissions themselves wil speake it." He himself would take the field but only after he brought Bacon "to acknowledge the lawes are above him." Calling himself the voters' "incessant servant," Berkeley asserted he had done all that was possible for friend and foe to "have granted Mr. Bacon those Pardons which he has scornefully rejected supposing himselfe stronger to subvert then I and you to maintaine the lawes by which only and goode and assisting grace and mercy al men must hope for Peace and safety."[16]

To achieve maximum effect upon the voters, Berkeley circulated the declaration a week before the convening of the new General Assembly. He ordered it read out in the churches and at the county courts, but it changed few minds. Amid an overheated political climate the first colony-wide poll in fifteen years produced a General Assembly that was unruly, combative, and decidedly unlike any that Berkeley had ever presided over. He may have sensed that trouble lay ahead of him. On 3 June, two days before the assembly opened, he wrote to Secretary of State Henry Coventry, craving to be relieved by "a *more vigorous Governor.*" He entrusted the request to Dame Frances, whom he sent to England to answer for him at court.[17]

The composition of the new House of Burgesses and who controlled the assembly's legislative agenda determined the outcome of the session. In June 1676 a full House consisted of forty-one members, who represented Virginia's twenty counties and Jamestown. Electors in Middlesex and Westmoreland counties chose a single burgess apiece, in direct contravention of a 1669 statute,[18] which mandated the election of two per county. Therefore, the House had but thirty-nine burgesses. Of that number twenty-two members can be identified by name and constituency. Only two of them, Richard Lawrence and James Crews, allied

---

16. Declaration and Remonstrance, 29 May 1676, Coventry Papers, 77, fol. 157.

17. Berkeley to Coventry, 3 June 1676, Coventry Papers, 77, fol. 103.

18. William Waller Hening, ed., *The Statutes at Large; Being a Collection of All the Laws of Virginia from the First Session of the Legislature, in the Year 1619*, facsimile ed. (1809–23; rpt., Charlottesville, Va., 1969), 2:272–73.

openly with Bacon. Himself an outlaw, Bacon was elected from Henrico County anyway. Of the remainder four lacked political experience, five or six were hold-overs, and the rest were incumbent justices of the peace who had been in and out of the House throughout the 1660s. Unquestionably, many members loathed "Indians." Undeniably, they were out of sorts with Berkeley too, but collectively nothing about them suggests that they were hot to radicalize Virginia. Neither were they necessarily inimical to Berkeley, nor was he antagonistic toward them. After all, the House of Burgesses actually adopted a resolution begging him to remain in office, whereas he showed his customary deference to the burgesses by allowing them to pick Thomas Godwin for their speaker.[19]

Godwin's selection was a tale within a tale. Augustine Warner, who succeeded the deceased Speaker Wynne in March, won reelection as a member for Glouces-ter in the May polling. He stood for speaker again, but his too-close identification with Berkeley kept him out of the chair. Godwin, who represented Nansemond County, had been away from the House since 1659. He was neither near to Berke-ley, the fiery Indian haters, nor Bacon's partisans, and it was this moderation that gained him the speakership. Once Godwin was chosen, he and Berkeley worked together well enough to enact some wide-ranging reform legislation that an-swered voter demands.[20]

The twenty acts of the June assembly came to be known as "Bacon's Laws." Three responded to the Indian crisis and provided for a more aggressive way of carrying the fight to the enemy than Berkeley had proposed three months earlier. Among the others one addressed unauthorized gatherings by codifying English laws against such assemblies and authorizing Berkeley to expend whatever public money he needed to punish offenders. A second statute took dead aim at settlers such as Bacon. One of its clauses prevented Berkeley from appointing newcomers who had lived in Virginia for less than three years. (That proviso, it should be noted, diminished Berkeley's appointing powers under his commission.) A sec-tion of the act also tried to eliminate abuses of local magisterial authority that had gone uncorrected for years. Then there was a law that denied councillors direct participation in local matters and another that removed their tax exemp-tions, which lessened county taxes. A fifth act made it easier for borrowers to

19. Warren M. Billings, "'Virginias Deploured Condition': The Coming of Bacon's Rebellion, 1666–1676" (Ph.D. diss., Northern Illinois University, 1968), app. 2; Cynthia Miller Leonard, comp., *The General Assembly of Virginia, July 30, 1619–January 11, 1978: A Bicentennial Register of Members* (Richmond, 1978), 32 ; H. R. McIlwaine, ed., *Journals of the House of Burgesses of Colonial Virginia, 1619–1658/59; 1659/60–1693* (Richmond, 1914–15), 66.

20. Jon Kukla, *Speakers and Clerks of the Virginia House of Burgesses, 1643–1776* (Richmond, 1981), 65–69.

pay off their debts, while a sixth permitted senior justices of the peace to certify testamentary papers, which spared Berkeley an onerous chore and the affected colonists a trip to Jamestown. The rest of the statutes opened up vestry elections, limited powers of the sheriffs, and closed most alehouses or other tippling places that sold liquor over the counter.[21]

Were these statutes truly Bacon's Laws? At the time Berkeley's allies intimated darkly that the burgesses, drugged by an emanation of "Ill-Humours," were overwhelmingly Bacon's men. They praised their cool-headed governor, who with the assistance of some few loyal followers maintained control until Bacon seized the government. Berkeley explained himself similarly when he wrote to Secretary Coventry in February 1677. With typical hyperbole he claimed that "their was but eight of the Burgesses that were not of [Bacon's] faction and at his direction," and with equal embellishment he commented how "this very factious Assembly . . . absolv'd me from all crimes relating to the Country and desired me not to sollicite his majestie to remove me."[22]

Dramatic though these explanations were, they tell only part of the story. Bacon was absent for most of the session, which ran from 5 to 25 June. Clearly, he had designs on taking his seat, but he was wary of appearing at Jamestown because he was still an outlaw, and he feared arrest. Even so, he sent his friend Crews to inquire about Berkeley's intentions. Berkeley refused to speak with Crews, though several councillors passed the word that they might succeed in reconciling the governor and Bacon. That intimation explains why Bacon left Curles Neck for the capital on or about 5 June. Caution dictated that he not go by himself, so he took a contingent of armed men, sailed down the James, and anchored within gunshot of Fort James on 6 June. His emissary sought out Berkeley, asking if Bacon might take his seat. Berkeley answered by ordering the gunners at the fort to sink the sloop. Shots rang out, but she quickly hoisted anchor and sailed out of range. When night fell, Bacon crept into town and met secretly with Richard Lawrence and William Drummond to consider his next moves. He left Lawrence's house at first light and almost got away undetected. Just as he stepped into his long boat, someone recognized him and sounded the alarm. The alert set off a chase. Rowing with all of their might, his boatmen gained his sloop ahead of their pursuers. The sailors pulled up anchor and tried to escape upriver, but, before they had made much headway, the armed mer-chantman, *Adam & Eve,* bore within cannon's reach, and surrender was their

21. Hening, *Statutes at Large,* 2:340–65.

22. George Jordan to Francis Moryson, June 1676, Coventry Papers, 77, fol. 138; Isaac Allerton to Thomas Ludwell, ibid., fols. 160–61; Berkeley to Henry Coventry, 2 Feb. 1676/77, ibid., fols. 350–55.

only choice. On orders from Berkeley, *Adam & Eve*'s captain Thomas Gardner arrested Bacon and handed him over to James City County sheriff Theophilus Hone. Major Hone deposited his prisoner in the town jail to await Berkeley's further pleasure.[23]

Now that Berkeley had Bacon in custody, what would he do? Of greater concern, perhaps, was what would Bacon's followers do? Those questions buzzed through Jamestown as days passed and nothing happened. Indecision on Berkeley's part accounted for some of the delay. Then, too, certain councillors played for time in order to defuse an explosive situation gracefully. Their effort paid off, at least temporarily. On 9 June Bacon appeared before the Council of State. Confessing himself a rebel on bended knee, he "most humbly begg[ed] of Almighty god and of his Majesties . . . Governor that upon this my most Harty and unfeigned Acknowledgement of my said Miscarriages and unwarrantable practices he will please to grant me his Gracious Pardon and Indempnity." Berkeley not only forgave Bacon; he returned him to his place as a councillor and tentatively offered him a commission to war on the Indians. A few days later, pleading a sick wife, Bacon won Berkeley's leave to go upriver to his plantation.[24]

Berkeley came to regret these decisions. They were choices he could never fully explain to himself, to his superiors, or to anyone else, for that matter. His greatest mistake was to let Bacon get away. It gave the young hot spur a chance to regroup his followers, and together they threw Virginia into civil war. For the moment, however, the General Assembly returned to its legislative business, and it neared the point of readying the bills for final passage by 23 June.

Anxiety still hung heavy in the moist air of early summer that enveloped Jamestown that day. Residents went about their usual daily habits. Some broke from routine and stole a while to quaff a draft of ale or two while trading gossip with willing visitors who always swelled the public houses whenever the General Assembly gathered in session. Troubled times, all agreed, made this particular meeting as tumultuous as any within living memory. The rattle of men under arms broke in without warning as Bacon and five hundred volunteers clanked into town. Some fanned out to seize key positions, while the main force marched with their leader to the statehouse and surrounded it. A messenger from Berkeley

23. William Sherwood to Sir Joseph Williamson, 12 June 1676, CO 1/37, fol. 1, PRO; Berkeley to Thomas Ludwell, 1 July 1676, Coventry Papers, 77, fol. 144; Philip Ludwell to Dame Frances Berkeley, 16 June 1676, Coventry Papers, 77, fol. 117; Philip Ludwell to Sir Joseph Williamson, 28 June 1676, CO 1/37, fols. 37–38, PRO.

24. Warrant for the arrest of Nathaniel Bacon Jr., 7 June 1676, CO 5/1308, fol. 67, PRO; Submission of Nathaniel Bacon Jr., 9 June 1676, Coventry Papers, 77, fol. 116; Conway Robinson, "Notes and Excerpts from the Records of Colonial Virginia," Conway Robinson Papers, ViHi, 260.

asked to know Bacon's intentions. Back came the reply: authorization to lead these and other volunteers against the natives, blank commissions for subordinate officers, justification and pardon for Bacon's earlier acts, a law to debar several Charles City County politicians from office, and compensation for the seizure of Bacon's sloop two weeks earlier. Nothing in these demands hinted that Bacon aimed to oust Berkeley or throw over the government.

Berkeley thought otherwise. No colonist had ever asked, let alone *demanded*, anything like that before, and he was not about to brook such insolence from a presumptuous relative. In a towering rage he strode from his office and confronted Bacon. "Here," he challenged the soldiers, as he ripped open his shirt, "Shoot me, fore god, fair Mark Shoot." When no one stirred, he turned on Bacon, calling him "Rebell and Traytor," as he pulled his rapier from its scabbard and dared the younger man to settle their dispute with swordplay. Bacon turned the bait aside, saying he had no wish "to hurt a haire of your honor's head." But, swore he, "God damne my Blood, I came for a commission, and a commission I shall have before I goe," whereupon he ordered his troops to train their muskets on the statehouse and fire on command. Their menace terrified the burgesses and the councillors, who pressed their elderly leader to give in. Cornered thus, Berkeley yielded to the entreaties, and in two days what Bacon wanted was law.[25]

By capturing Jamestown and forcing a commission from the General Assembly under duress, Bacon altered the political calculus in a dangerous, irrevocable way. No longer was the issue between Berkeley and him a matter of how best to defend against the Indians or who should lead the fight. Now it was a question of whose authority would prevail and who would control Virginia, the king's governor-general or an impetuous upstart? As of 25 June 1676, Virginians stood perilously close to the edge of civil war. Bacon's next moves and Berkeley's counters pushed them over the brink.

Reports of new skirmishes with the Indians drifted into Jamestown while the assembly cobbled Bacon's demands into statutory language. On 26 June General Bacon detached scouts to find the enemy before rejoining him at the falls of the James, where he and his army were headed. Worn-out and dispirited, Berkeley left town some while later and sought respite from his troubles in the comforting environment of Green Spring House. There he remained, seemingly too beaten to care about Bacon. The quiet interlude restored him, so much so that when he received a petition from certain freeholders in Gloucester County, which questioned the legality of Bacon's seizing supplies and pressing men, he responded

25. See n. 23; Mathew, "Rise, Progress, and Conclusion of Bacon's Rebellion," 28–29; Berry and Moryson, "True Narrative," 116–17; Hening, *Statutes at Large,* 2:349, 363–65.

by proclaiming the general a rebel anew and revoking his commission. Then he rode over to Gloucester, seeking men for an army of his own. No one volunteered. Humiliated, Berkeley gathered up a handful of loyalists, packed them on several vessels, and sailed across Chesapeake Bay to the Eastern Shore, where he found refuge in Accomack County at John Custis's Arlington House.[26]

Bacon, in the meantime, got wind of these developments and headed back to Middle Plantation. Camping there on 29 July, he devoted the ensuing weeks to consolidating his hold on the colony. He employed his own considerable gift of words to attack Berkeley in a stirring condemnation that he entitled a "Declaration of the People," just as he vindicated himself with his "Manifesto." Words, in and of themselves, he knew, meant little unless deeds supported them. He kept Sir Henry Chicheley a prisoner in close confinement while he coerced councillors Thomas Ballard, Thomas Beale, James Bray, Thomas Swann, and sixty-five other leading colonists to swear fidelity to him. Their oath bound them to stand steadfast until he could make his case with Charles II and to oppose Berkeley, whom Bacon accused of having abandoned his government, which left the colonists defenseless against their savage enemy. To meet the latter threat, he and the four captive councillors issued orders for the election of burgesses for a General Assembly that would meet on 4 September. And, hoping to take the fight to his enemy, Bacon sent Giles Bland and William Carver across Chesapeake Bay to attack Berkeley.[27]

Believing himself secure in his authority, General Bacon departed Middle Plantation to hunt for Indians once more. This time he and his men fanned out westerly toward the falls of the James. They had not marched far before their rangers discovered the trail of the Pamunkeys, a nation of tributary natives. Bacon opted to pursue them, largely because he suspected them of having colonists' blood on their hands. The track led in the direction of murky wetlands between Middlesex and Gloucester counties, which the English knew as Dragon Swamp. Bacon's men quickly discovered that finding their putative enemy in such a landscape proved a near impossibility. Weeks of trooping through the swamp yielded no result other than mounting frustration. A near mutiny forced Bacon to send dissident troopers home before he finally stumbled across his terror-struck quarry. Most were women and children and old men. No matter. The

26. Petition from the freeholders of Gloucester County, ca. 28 July 1676, Coventry Papers, 77:181.

27. Declaration of the People, ca. 29 July 1676, CO 1/37, fols. 128–29, PRO; Bacon's Manifesto, ca. 29 July 1676, CO 1/37, fols. 178–79; Nathaniel Bacon, Thomas Ballard, Thomas Beale, James Bray, and Thomas Swann to John Washington, 11 Aug. 1676, ibid., fol. 133; [John Cotton?], "The History of Bacon's and Ingram's Rebellion," in Andrews, Narratives, 60–63.

English easily slaughtered those they chose not to keep for prisoners or those who could not retreat deeper into the watery terrain.[28]

Bland and Carver proved unequal to their mission. Good seaman Captain Carver may have been, but he possessed an erratic personality, and he was easily duped. The sportive Bland had no military experience whatever. Consequently Berkeley's chief lieutenant, Robert Beverley, and the merchant mariner Captain Thomas Larramore tricked them into surrendering. Their defeat heartened Berkeley to retake control of the Western Shore. He assembled his troops aboard a flotilla of ships and smaller vessels and set sail for Jamestown. Arriving off the town on 7 September, he learned that about eight hundred of Bacon's men occupied it. A promise of pardon soon gained their capitulation without loss of life or shots fired, and within a day Berkeley was master of Jamestown once more. Mistakenly, he chose to hold fast to await Bacon's next move.[29]

An elated Bacon emerged from Dragon Swamp, believing that reports of his "victory" over the hapless Pamunkeys bolstered his hand. He hoped, too, that Bland and Carver had succeeded in taking Berkeley. One can only imagine how he reacted to the devastating news of his lieutenants' failure and Berkeley's capture of Jamestown. Whatever his thoughts, he wasted little time in rounding up all the reinforcements he could impress in Gloucester. A hurried march brought the army to Glass House Point, located at the northern end of the isthmus that joined Jamestown Island to the mainland. As the men dug in on the evening of 13 September, Bacon and a few of his officers used the safety of nightfall to reconnoiter Berkeley's defenses. Their inspection revealed fortifications too stout to attack headlong, especially without artillery, which Bacon lacked. Bottling up the defenders and playing on their fears seemed the likeliest and least costly means of dislodging them. Bacon held captive the wives of some of Berkeley's men, and he paraded the women across his earthworks. The gambit weakened the defenders' resolve, so much so that their attempted breakout ended in abject failure. Disgusted by what Berkeley saw as cowardice, he had no choice other than to seek the safety of his stronghold in Accomack once more, even though retreat left Green Spring House open to further plundering. Bacon entered the deserted capital on 19 September. After consultations with his officers about the fate of his prize, he put it to the torch and moved his forces to a campsite in Gloucester County.

Setting fire to Jamestown proved to be a mistake. So did a promise to free

28. Washburn, *Governor and the Rebel*, 68–76.

29. Ibid., 77–89; Stephen Saunders Webb, *1676: The End of American Independence* (New York, 1984), 44–103.

bondservants in return for their joining the rebels. Both decisions cost Bacon followers as a result, and, more important, neither brought him any closer to defeating Berkeley. His men grew restless from inaction and fell to pillaging nearby plantations, a behavior that hardly advanced the cause. There was no taking the fight to Accomack because Bacon lacked naval support. He tried to incite the Eastern Shore planters, but the ploy enticed no one to his standard. Indeed, as September lengthened toward October, Bacon faced the dilemma of someone who had not thought through the consequences of his acts. What to do next? Fight Indians? Attack Berkeley? Strike for an independent Virginia? Hold out until he could make his case before Charles II? Death relieved him of his predicament on 26 October, when a "Bloody Flux" and the "Lousey Disease" suddenly killed him at his headquarters in Thomas Pate's plantation, Gloucester Hall. Dumbfounded by their loss, his men hastily interred their leader's corpse in a secret place.[30]

Bacon's demise undid the revolt. Drummond, Lawrence, and his other close subordinates tried to keep it going, but they lacked their general's capabilities and his appeal. The army scattered. Some, sensing their cause was lost or sated by their plunder, drifted away. Others broke into smaller units, hoping to carry the fight to the death or to negotiate terms that would spare their necks and their properties.

News of Bacon's end, which probably came to Berkeley within a day or two of its occurrence, stirred him to action. Luckily for him, a half-dozen armed merchantmen had recently arrived in Virginia waters, and they were pressed into service. Making their way up the York and the James rivers, they were especially useful in eradicating the organized remnants of the rebel army. That work, together with the energetically ruthless suppressions of Robert Beverley on land, soon snuffed out the last flickers of rebellion.

30. Berry and Moryson, "True Narrative," 139.

14

Disgrace

y January 1677 Berkeley had regained the whip hand. He did not use it sparingly. No one who knew him thought he should, but the unremitting fury of his application astonished even the most hardhearted of his adherents. Save Richard Lawrence, who fled the country, and Gregory Walklate and Joseph Ingram, who turned coat, the rebel leaders were his prisoners. Their treasons were capital offenses. They could hope for no mercy from him, and he showed them none. Court-martialed, sentenced, and hanged, they all died within hours of their trials. Not one was spared, least of all William Drummond and Giles Bland, whom Berkeley condemned with unbecoming glee. Even lesser rebels, who might have expected reprieve, were punished with an equal ferocity. They paid heavily in fines or lost estates, which Berkeley confiscated as compensation for their misdeeds, and the seizures quickly surpassed the pillaging the Baconians had done.[1]

Because the uprising was so bitter a cup for Berkeley to taste, there seemed to be no end to his thirst for vengeance. His hatred of rebels knew no bounds. Rebels were to him the most despicable of creatures. Wicked men, they threatened established order like no other. Once they had murdered his king. They had

1. Thomas Grantham to Henry Coventry, Coventry Papers, 77, fol. 301; Sir Thomas Grantham, *An Historical Account of Some Memorable Actions, Particularly in Virginia . . .* (London, 1716), 17–24; Berkeley to Walklate, 1 Jan. 1676/77, Coventry Papers, 77, fol. 177; pardon and commission to Walklate, 1 Jan. 1676/77, Coventry Papers, 77, fol. 178; list of executed rebels, ca. Feb. 1677, CO 1/40, fols. 241–42.

driven him from office, and they had nearly done so again. He, who had given so much of himself to Virginia, could not grasp why his favored young kinsman revolted. How it galled him that this upstart dared extort a general's commission from *him*, the king's governor and captain-general. Nor could he comprehend why, after so many years of mild administration, *his* people had turned away from him so suddenly and so completely. Begging Secretary Coventry for a replacement was a humiliating testament to his incapacity to rule in the midst of trouble. He was angered to walk through the smoldering ashes of Jamestown, the capital he had labored long to build up. The sight of his beloved Green Spring House, which looters had laid waste, pained him exquisitely and reminded him of his other losses, which totaled more than ten thousand pounds. And he was greatly embarrassed at having to answer to King Charles for his conduct.[2]

Such injuries to a proud, sick, bone-tired old man clouded his judgment and dulled that sense of proportion that had always sustained him through past crises. He could not heal without reprisal, come what may. That voracity for revenge set him at odds with the Crown and brought him down to disgrace.

Tales of Berkeley's troubles reached Whitehall throughout the first half of 1676. They were sufficiently alarming to halt the sealing of the charter that ended the Northern Neck Proprietary, which the Virginia agents had negotiated, and the stories drained the residue of Berkeley's influence with royal officials already suspicious of how he governed in Virginia. His request for a successor reinforced a mounting determination to be rid of him. The king's advisors linked Berkeley's replacement not only to smashing Bacon but to a larger task of intervening forcefully in the colony as the Crown had not done since the downfall of the Virginia Company. With a celerity that was extraordinary for Stuart bureaucrats, they mobilized for the reconquest of the Old Dominion. Colonel Herbert Jeffreys received command of a regiment of a thousand redcoats and orders to crush the rebellion. Sir John Berry led a squadron of warships and transports to ferry the troops to America and to provide naval support. He, Jeffreys, and Francis Moryson also constituted a commission of investigation charged with collecting popular grievances and determining the reasons for the rebellion. They carried a royal command for Berkeley to return to England and a commission for Jeffreys to succeed as lieutenant governor as well as a proclamation overturning the acts of the June assembly and pardon for all but Bacon and his chief lieutenants.[3]

2. Instructions to Berkeley, 12 Sept. 1676, CO 5/1355, fols. 99–107; further instructions to Berkeley, 13 Oct. 1676, CO 5/1355, 111–14; pardon for Sir William Berkeley and others, 25 Sept. 1676, CO 5/1355, fols. 97–98; Berkeley to Henry Coventry, 9 Feb. 1676/77, Coventry Papers, 77, 382; petition to Charles II, ca. 16 June 1677, CO 1/40, fol. 245.

3. Minutes of Privy Council meeting, 20 Sept. 1676, PC 1/58, pt. 1, PRO; estimates and orders for provisioning armed forces for Virginia, Oct. 1676, CO 5/1355, fols. 69–77; commission to Sir John

The choice of Berry, Jeffreys, and Moryson bespoke a loyalty, outlook, and experience that neatly fitted the three for their mission. Berry and Jeffreys ranked in a cadre of career military officers, steeled by long service at sea or in the army, that the Stuarts always depended upon to enforce their will in Britain and the colonies. A seafaring man, Berry (1635–90) had joined the royal navy in 1663, just as James, duke of York, was rebuilding the fleet. Duty took him to the West Indies, the Mediterranean, and other places as he steadily rose through the officer corps. He was knighted during the Third Anglo-Dutch War for his part in the battle of Sole Bay, by which time he was closely aligned with the duke of York. Jeffreys (?–1678) first picked up a sword for Charles I in the early days of the Civil War. His bent for war eventually gained him a captaincy in the king's army, though the defeat of the royalists drove him into exile in France, where he, too, found a spot in the entourage of the duke of York. After the Restoration he was posted to Dunkirk, Portsmouth, York, and France before the duke tapped him to dispose of Bacon and his rebels.[4]

As for Moryson, no one in London knew the ins and outs of Virginia better than he. Before he was the colony's agent, he had been a speaker of the House of Burgesses, councillor of state, deputy governor, and a redactor of the revised Virginia statutes of 1662. Given his friendship with Berkeley, which stretched back to the days of the Great Tew Circle, he might more easily impress upon his mentor the king's resolve to impose stricter rule from Whitehall. Besides, Secretary Coventry authorized him to communicate the duke of York's promise to compel Lords Arlington and Culpeper to surrender their claims on the Northern Neck after the charter was quashed. There was yet another reason why Coventry and other royal bureaucrats picked Moryson. They knew that his many years in London had worked a change in his outlook on the Anglo-Virginia connection.

Once the Old Dominion had lured Moryson as a place of new beginnings, but he now regarded England as the source of his future successes. The precise reasons for his about-face are not entirely evident, but the colony never gripped him

Berry, Herbert Jeffreys, and Francis Moryson as commissioners of investigation, 3 Oct. 1676, CO 5/1355, fols. 83–85; commission to Herbert Jeffreys, 7 Nov. 1676, CO 5/1355, 86–90; instructions to Berry, Jeffreys, and Moryson, 14 Nov. 1676, CO 5/1355, fols. 117–20; commission to Berry as commander-in-chief at sea, 3 Oct. 1676, CO 5/1355, fol. 121; commission to Jeffreys as lieutenant governor, 11 Nov. 1676, CO 5/1355, fols. 122–24; instructions to Jeffreys as lieutenant governor, 11 Nov. 1676, CO 5/1355, fols. 125–26; proclamation for suppressing the rebellion in Virginia, 27 Oct. 1676, CO 5/1355, fols. 129–32, PRO.

4. Stephen Saunders Webb, "'Brave Men and Servants to His Royal Highness': The Household of James Stuart in the Evolution of English Imperialism," in Donald Fleming and Bernard Bailyn, eds., *Perspectives in American History* 8 (1974): 55–83; Webb, *The Governors-General: The English Army and the Definition of the Empire, 1569–1681* (Chapel Hill, 1979), 3–57, 122–37; *DNB*, 2:398–99.

as it did Berkeley and other immigrants who fashioned themselves into Virginians. Perhaps, too, he resented the General Assembly's perennial tardiness in compensating him. Money was always a concern for him. Possibly he grew weary of Berkeley's habit of sending colonists such as Secretary Ludwell and General Smith to assist him, which seemed to imply that he was incapable of handling Virginia's most important London business on his own. Whatever his inner impulses, the thirteen years he had spent in the company of royal functionaries had had a palpable effect on him. He absorbed the tenets of Stuart imperialism into his own thinking, and that exposure undermined his commitments to Berkeley's vision of Virginia's welfare. Bacon's Rebellion horrified him and solidified his change of mind. It confirmed the bankruptcy of Berkeley's administration, and it reinforced Moryson's realization of a need to weigh the balance between colony and mother country heavily on the side of Whitehall. Such a calibration would offer the security and economic gain that Berkeley had long promised but never delivered, and those who backed such an adjustment stood to glean much in royal preferments. Sympathy for the Stuart worldview and new realities convinced Moryson to look to King Charles, not Berkeley, as his principal patron.[5]

Those convictions added an unexpected poison to his and the commission's subsequent dealings with Berkeley. So did ignorance and a hurried carelessness on the part of Henry Coventry and the others who drafted the commissioners' directives. None of them knew who controlled Virginia in the fall of 1676. They proceeded on the assumption that Berkeley was either dead or Bacon's prisoner or on the run, and they authorized Jeffreys to succeed Berkeley as governor-general pro tempore. In their haste to smash Bacon and control the colony, they forgot to specify precisely how governor and commissioners should relate to each other legally or practically in the event that Berkeley was alive and in charge of the situation. By failing to take that contingency into account, they inadvertently snarled the lines of authority, which left Berkeley and the commissioners ample leeway to read their instructions as broadly as they saw fit. Such was a recipe for trouble, given the circumstances and the personalities involved. Another potential toxin lay imbedded in how Charles II answered Berkeley's plea to retire. Granting the entreaty, the king assumed that Berkeley would promptly depart, and thus he did not set a date for the retirement to take effect. Instead, he merely

---

5. Henry Norwood, *A Voyage to Virginia. By Col. Norwood* (n.p., n.d.) in Peter Force, comp., *Tracts, Relating Principally to the Origins, Settlement, and Progress of the Colonies in North America, from the Discovery of the Country to the Year 1776* (Washington, D.C., 1836–44), 3: no. 10; Moryson to Coventry, 28 Sept. 1676, Coventry Papers, 77: fol. 54; Longleat House; George Morley, bishop of Winchester to James Scott, duke of Monmouth, 10 Oct. 1676, SP 29/386, PRO; Moryson to Mr. Cooke, 27 Mar. 1677, Wiseman Papers, n.p., Pepysian Library, Cambridge; Webb, *Governors-General*, 336–37.

wrote that "wee are pleased to condescend unto that your request, And doe accordingly hereby order you to repair into this Our Kingdome of England to give us an account of the present commotions in Our said Colony, that Wee may take such farther measures thereupon as we shall judge fit and expedient." The conditional nature of the command allowed Berkeley the liberty of deciding when to return to London, and that discretion set him at odds with Colonel Jeffreys.[6]

Insensible to such lurking malignancies, the commissioners approached their assignment with an abounding eagerness to honor the king's trust. They would smite the rebels to destruction, ease Berkeley into retirement, discover the reasons for the uprising, and recommend ways to strengthen the Crown's dominion over the colony. Duty done, they would return to the plaudits of a grateful King Charles, who would reward them not only with his thanks but with showers of largess greater than the fifteen hundred–pound salary each received for accepting his assignment.

All was in readiness by November 1676, and the three commissioners journeyed from London down to Deal harbor. On the nineteenth Berry and Moryson boarded the ketch HMS *Bristol* and raised sail for the James River. Accompanying them was an advance party of seventy redcoats who shipped on another ketch, HMS *Deptford*. Jeffreys left Deal two weeks later in the merchantman *Henry & Ann*. His vessel and seven additional transports bore the bulk of the troops. Two frigates, HMS *Rose* and HMS *Dartmouth*, rounded out the convoy. Eager to be with her husband as soon as possible, Dame Frances Berkeley booked a cabin on *Rose* too. Her choice of passage proved most unfortunate because her proximity to Jeffreys sparked an intense dislike between the two of them.

Favorable winds blew *Bristol* to the Western Hemisphere within ten weeks of her departure, and she dropped anchor in the James off Kicoughtan (near Newport News) on 29 January 1676/77. Berry sent men ashore in search of information about the dangers ahead. Back came a report that was little short of astonishing. Bacon was dead, Berkeley was alive, the rebellion was over, and most of its leaders were either executed or awaiting trial. That news spared the redcoats from having to fight, though it in no way deterred the commissioners from carrying out the rest of their mission. To that purpose Moryson and Berry decided to confer with Berkeley at once. Berry ordered a barge upriver to Jamestown. His messenger picked up a horse and rode the rest of the way to Green Spring House with a letter that told of *Bristol*'s landing and the impending arrival of the expedi-

6. "Instructions to Berkeley," 13 Oct. 1676, CO 5/1355, fols. 111–14, PRO; Charles II to Berkeley, 5 Nov. 1676, CO 5/1355, fol. 127; Henry Coventry to Berkeley, 15 Nov. 1676, CO 5/1355.

tionary force. Berry also thought "fitt to acquaint [Berkeley], that the King hath given mee full Power of Commanding all Merchants Shipps and Seamen within the Rivers of Virginia, to bee ayding and assisting in His Majesties Service, to the suppressing and Quieting the Disorders of the Country," and he proffered "what shott, Powder, Greate Guns &c. you shall stand in neede of." More pointedly, he noted there were "severall other matters to impart to you, which cannot bee soe well imparted, but upon a personall conference with you," so he demanded that Berkeley meet with him and with Moryson aboard *Bristol* just as soon "as may seeme agreeable to the Kings Honor, and your owne Conveniency." He closed saying that "Col. Moryson writes not now, because hee knowes and suddainly expects wee are to meete face to face."[7]

Peremptory in its tone, the letter annoyed Berkeley, who was as perplexed at receiving such a message from a total stranger as he was by Moryson's failure to send written respects of his own. More troubling was the coming of troops and a commission of inquiry, both of which signaled profound royal displeasure with his handling of the revolt. There was no choice but to do as Berry bid. Feverish, Berkeley left his sickbed and took to the barge for the chilly, damp trip down the James to Kicoughtan.

The barge came alongside *Bristol* about midday on 31 January. Boatmen hooked her fore and aft to tackles that dangled from *Bristol*'s main yard. In a matter of moments they manhandled her aloft to the squeal of creaking sheaves and the cry of a boatswain, who bawled, "Haul away! Haul away!" in a rhythmic voice that fixed the pace of the ascent. As she came abreast of the bulwark, one last tug on the downhauls hove her up and over the railing before she was gently eased down on the main deck. Hands steadied a shaky Berkeley as he disembarked to greet the awaiting Moryson and Berry.[8]

The three men exchanged pleasantries and ambled astern to Berry's cabin below the quarterdeck. Seating themselves around a table, Moryson and Berry read their commission to Berkeley. They told him that Jeffreys would replace him and that the colonial government was expected to maintain Jeffreys's redcoats. Then they gave him a thick packet of documents that he signed for in writing. Berkeley broke the seals, undid the outer wrappings, and saw a royal pardon for all colonists but Bacon, another for himself and the General Assembly, a commission allowing him to absolve offenders, a set of supplemental instructions, a form for use in indicting suspected rebels, and a batch of five

---

7. Log of HMS *Bristol*, n.p., Adm 51/34, PRO.

8. Log of HMS *Bristol*, 29–31 Jan. 1676–77, n.p., Adm 51/134, PRO; Berry to Berkeley, 29 Jan. 1676/ 77, n.p., Wiseman Papers, Pepysian Library, Cambridge.

hundred printed copies of the king's proclamation of pardon. As he scanned the contents, the instructions caught his eye. One enjoined him to lodge the commissioners and to help them conclude peace with the natives. A second rebuked him for enfranchising freemen, and it expressly limited the vote in future burgess elections to freeholders. Several set forth explicit directions for putting Bacon down. Others related to the General Assembly. An order to call the assembly into immediate session was the most innocuous of the instructions. The rest struck down privileges that the assembly had enjoyed for a half-century. Lost was its right to annual meetings. Assemblies to come would sit every other year, and then only for fourteen days, instead of the customary twenty days. Gone was the absolute control of burgesses' salaries, which the king commanded to be lessened so as to ease the burden on taxpayers. Subverted, too, was the liberty to enact laws without royal interference—a limitation that arose from Charles's veto of the acts of the June assembly.[9]

Berkeley masked his thoughts and steered the conversation toward an account of the present condition of the colony. He confirmed what Moryson and Berry already knew and more. Jamestown lay in ashes. The rebel army was scattered and no longer a threat to anyone. Most of the ringleaders were in his hands. He had tried about twenty offenders at martial law, and they had gone to the gallows. The rest awaited their inevitable fate. Negotiations were in hand for a peace treaty with the Pamunkeys. He had already sent out writs for a General Assembly, which would convene at Green Spring House on 20 February. Finding quarters for the commissioner and the troops would be problematic, he continued, because of the desolation at Jamestown and the great damage to nearby plantations, including his own, which had suffered from extensive pillaging. Pride nearly got the better of him when he confessed to his puzzlement at the Crown sending so many soldiers and naval vessels when a frigate or two would have sufficed. More likely than not, in his opinion so huge a display of might would frighten the colonists into abandoning their plantations, and, should his prediction come true, then he would have greater difficulty sheltering the commissioners and the soldiers.[10]

As the talk continued, Berry and Moryson made known their intention of summoning planters from the various counties to say to them why they had

9. Inventory of papers delivered to Berkeley, Wiseman Papers, n.p., Pepysian Library, Cambridge; minute of conference between Berry, Moryson, and Berkeley, 2 Feb. 1676/77, Pepysian Library; "Instructions from Charles II," clause 3, clauses 4, 6, 7–8, clauses 1, 2, 5, 6, 9, fols. 111–14, PRO.

10. Interlocutory heads of matters for the king's service, 2 Feb. 1676/77, Wiseman Papers, Pepysian Library, Cambridge; Berry and Moryson to Coventry and Sir Joseph Williamson, 2 Feb. 1676/77; same to Sir John Werden, 2 Feb. 1676/77, Pepysian Library.

come and to gather the popular grievances, which they would set down in writing for the king's edification and action. They were careful to insist that none of this was a sign of misdeeds on Berkeley's part. The one complaint they had heard about before leaving England was that the burgesses got exorbitant salaries, and they were prepared to redress that complaint. Even though their stated intention consisted with their instructions, it raised the hairs on Berkeley's neck, but he offered no objection.

Instead, he expressed a disinclination to circulate the king's proclamation. His logic was plain enough, at least to him. Publishing that document was useless because much of it was aimed directly at men who were now dead or in captivity, and so its original purposes were diminished by conditions not foreseen when it was drafted. In its place he proposed to issue a proclamation of his own that offered the royal pardon to all but those in custody and eight others that he planned to exempt. Such a compromise, he pointed out, fell within his constitutional prerogatives as governor-general and the king's most recent orders. He also insisted on continuing his expropriation of rebel properties, which he meant to distribute to his adherents as rewards for their loyalties. Moryson and Berry protested mildly. Such a policy, in their view, would only prolong the animosities that they had been sent to quiet, but for the moment they refrained from interfering because the issue of confiscations was beyond the scope of their instructions. They also questioned the legitimacy of trying rebels at martial law now that military operations had ceased, though they did not press that point. With that the conference ended, and Berkeley was invited to remain aboard until his health improved.[11]

In spite of the prickles, the meeting had gone about as well as anyone had reason to expect. Berry and Moryson observed as much in their first dispatches to London, which they showed to Berkeley. They summarized the encounter with little embroidery. Disagreements they noted, but not in a way that cast Berkeley in an unfavorable light. If anything, they were at pains to note that they had discovered no complaint against him, and such was their optimism that they predicted a short stay in Virginia.[12]

Berkeley wrote to London too, but his comments to Coventry conveyed quite a different message. "This will not be a letter," he scribbled, "but a History of our miseries," wherein he recounted his version of the rebellion. Before "I enter into it," he began, "I must cleere one just accusation which you have against me til you heare my justification and that is this that I wrote not to you the state and

11. Berry and Moryson to Coventry and Williamson, Pepysian Library.
12. Ibid.; log of HMS *Bristol*, 2 Feb. 1676/77, n.p., Adm 51/34, n.p., PRO.

Condition of this afflicted country." He excused himself by saying that he had "your letters stil by me at my house," but it had been impossible to send them eastward for want of reliable shipping. Those letters would be on "the next shipp that goes for England . . . and then I hope your goodnesse and mercy wil absolve me from my supposed Crime and neglect of my Duty." With that he set forth his explanation of the revolt. He blamed fear of Indians as the spark, but he attributed root causes to his own pride and to the readiness of the "rabble" to follow Bacon into rebellion. Therefore, God had visited his righteous fury upon him and the colony. The God of wrath was also the God of mercy, and, after humbling Berkeley, God had brought victory to him and death to the "Atheistical" Bacon. Even so, Berkeley had suffered greatly at Bacon's hands, and quite crassly he begged recompense for his losses.[13]

The "History" had none of the snappy cadences, the flashes of wit, the pungent turns of phrase, that characterized the best, most convincing Berkeleian prose. It lacked any acknowledgment of the king's recent instructions, took no notice of the commissioners or the reasons for their being sent to Virginia, and completely ignored the fact that Berkeley's superiors wanted him gone. The tone was surly and presumptuous throughout. A single example makes the point. Berkeley's concluding plea to be put "into a condition of living happyly the remainder of his old age and leaving something to his poore virtuous and now distressed wife" left the impression that his own needs stood higher than his duty to his master, which he did little to allay in subsequent letters to Coventry. Rambling and ill considered, the letter graphically testified to how much age and poor health had diminished his acumen.[14]

Berkeley stayed with the commissioners until 4 February, when Berry's barge took him back to Green Spring House. Before he departed, he drew up a writ for all sheriffs that compelled them "to call a County Court and their to take a report of the Inhabitants . . . [of] what abuses and aggreivances have beene done to them, by whome & for what reason, without regard to the quality of any man in the said Collony at such tyme as you shall receive orders from the said Commissioners & to take care to obey such Commands, and Instructions, as you shall . . . receive from them."[15]

13. Berkeley to Coventry, 2 Feb. 1676/77, Coventry Papers, 77, fols., 350–55, Longleat House; Wilcomb E. Washburn, ed., "Sir William Berkeley's 'History of Our Miseries,'" *William and Mary Quarterly* 14 (1957): 403–13.

14. Berkeley to Coventry, 2 Feb. 1676/77, Coventry Papers, fol. 355; same to same, 8, 9, and 10 Feb. 1676/77, Coventry Papers, fols. 382, 383, 386, 394.

15. Log of HMS *Bristol*, 3 and 4 Feb. 1676/77, Adm 51/134, n.p., PRO; writ from Berkeley to John Mottrom, 3 Feb. 1676/77, Wiseman Papers, n.p., Pepysian Library, Cambridge.

Once Berkeley had initialed the writs, he gave them to Berry and Moryson, who distributed them across the colony. They included their own solicitation for grievants to come forward, and in at least three instances they also sent personal letters to men of Moryson's acquaintance. Each cover letter professed the commissioners' regard for the recipient, and it pointedly sought evidence that the expenses of frequent, lengthy assemblies caused popular discontent even as it urged that it pass from sheriff to sheriff for their perusal.[16]

With little subtlety Moryson used one of the letters to play for the loyalties of a Berkeley confidant, Councillor John Custis. How pleased he was to discover that his friend "Honest Jack" remained a loyal and prudent person. Moryson and Berry were thus depending upon Custis to tell the inhabitants of Accomack and Northampton counties that they eagerly sought complaints. The commission also wished to spare residents the inconvenience of journeying over Chesapeake Bay, and so they could relay concerns through their burgesses. If Custis did as he was bid, then Moryson would personally make known his "just merits" to the king. Custis did no more than convey Berkeley's writ and the commissioners' declaration to Eastern Shore authorities. He may have shown the letter to Berkeley as well. If so, then Berkeley found written confirmation for his suspicion that Moryson was no longer trustworthy.[17]

More overt signs of that distrust surfaced in the days that followed Berkeley's return to Green Spring House. After Berry's barge dropped Berkeley at Jamestown, he tarried long enough to arrange the commission's accommodations at a nearby plantation. His ride home was painfully discomforting, and he arrived weak from a "Terrible Ague and Feavor." Before going to bed, he managed to dash off a quick note to Berry and Moryson saying that Councillor Thomas Swann had agreed to put them up. At Swann's, he told them, you "shall not want any thing hee can supply which I beleeve wilbe in a plentifull manner, for his House and Groundes have not been disturbed all this Warr." (Although Berkeley did not say it, Swann's plantation had the added convenience of sitting just over the river from Jamestown and within easy reach of Green Spring House.)[18]

The reply set him off. Instead of expressing thanks for his effort in their behalf, Berry and Moryson disclosed the arrival of additional redcoats and the "howerly" expectation of more. There was a need for "fitt Magazines and Store Howses for the Kings Ammunition, Provisions &c and good shelter for the

16. Declaration of the commissioners to the people of Virginia, 6 Feb. 1676/77, Pepysian Library, Cambridge; Berry and Moryson to John Armistead and to John Tiplady, ca. 3 Feb. 1676/77, Wiseman Papers, n.p.; same to Custis, Wiseman Papers, n.p.

17. Postscript to Berry and Moryson, ca. 3 Feb. 1676/77, Wiseman Papers.

18. Berkeley to Berry and Moryson, 6 Feb. 1676/77, Wiseman Papers, n.p.

Men," and they insisted on knowing how Berkeley would provide these necessities. The sooner the better, they said, lest "demurrage will be little lesse than a hundred Pounds per diem Charge to His Majestie . . . which wee pray you will consider." As if that were not insult enough, the commissioners next called upon Berkeley to publish the king's pardon at once. "The Generality of the People," they claimed, "looke very amaz'dly one upon another at Our, and the Forces coming." Circulating the printed proclamations would certainly dispel popular "Ignorance of a right understanding of the end and occasion of it." Consequently, they continued, "Wee take leave to impart to Your Honor as our serious Opinion, as also Our earnest desire, that the Trembling People bee putt out of paine in this particular." The crowning insult was their renewed criticism of his sequestration of rebel properties. "For His Majesties service" they sharply advised against Berkeley's proceeding "soe as to give occasion to Merchants and Traders to complaine you obstruct or Retarde their Trading, by causing Hogsheads to bee marked with the Broad-Arrow-Head, as goods forfeited to the King, which (in our opinion) cannot bee justified by any colour of Law."[19]

Signing themselves "Your Honors very true Friends, and Most Faithfull servants," Berry and Moryson appended a postscript that demanded Berkeley's written answer. They insisted that all future communication "bee in writing also which wee apprehend a much Better way than by word of mouth; perceiving it is a greater trouble to you and us, by reason of your defect of hearing, which not onely hinders privacy, but Lookes Angerly, through Lowd talking."[20]

Moryson attached an addendum of his own that revealed how easily he distanced himself from Berkeley. In it he declined a verbal invitation to call at Green Spring House. He was, he claimed, "under some indisposition" and in immediate need of "Phisick" before much "Businesse" prevented him from taking the cure. Thereafter, two sometime friends never met privately or out of earshot of Moryson's commissioner colleagues.[21]

To borrow the commissioners' word, "Angerly" best describes Berkeley's reaction to their insults. Accepting their admonition to carry on all further communication in writing, Berkeley added a stinger when he announced that he would forward copies of all correspondence to Coventry. He denied ever having "Marked one hogshead of Tobacco." Nor would he until such time as he received the king's permission, which he sought via Secretary Coventry. He bluntly told Berry and Moryson that the proclamation would go forth "to morrow," and he

19. Berry and Moryson to Berkeley, 8 Feb. 1676/77, Coventry Papers, 77, fol. 376, Longleat House.
20. Ibid.
21. Ibid.

would incorporate "exceptions which I have Authority from his Sacred Majesty to make." His exclusions were necessary for "Majesties Honor and the futur peace of the country" because too much leniency would only "encline the Rabble to a new Rebellion." As to the business of furnishing "Magasines for the Soldiers Victuals and Ammunition," he sarcastically retorted, "I hope you doe not thinke I am able to doe impossibilities." The rebels, he reminded Berry and Moryson, stripped Green Spring of all its cattle and grain. Left with but a single ox of his own, he borrowed six more. Those beasts could scarcely haul wood and provender enough for some two hundred men who were presently billeted about the grounds and who looked to him for succor. Besides, as "Col. Morrison knowes," Berkeley had already arranged to buy additional oxen and lumber on his own credit, which was too stretched for him to hire the workmen to put up the soldiers' huts. Then, as if to ensnare the commissioners, he said that, if they told him it was lawful to impress extra oxen, he would do it.[22]

Impressing oxen for the king's service did not equate legally with confiscating the goods of rebels for Berkeley or other loyalists, though the two actions bore an outward similarity to each other. If Berry and Moryson admitted the legitimacy of the one, then logically they could not deny the legality of the other, and Berkeley would have undercut their insistence that his expropriations must cease. Moryson did not take the bait. He temporized, saying that he could not comment without first having consulted Berry, who was presently out of touch. When pressed further, he protested that Berkeley acted as though he were impotent "because wee are here." That was a mistaken impression. They had come to "vindicate" his power. "Therefore," he chided, "I shall desire you will not suffer your Better Reason to draw wrong Inferences from our right meaning towards you." With that he skirted the trap and intensified Berkeley's hostility toward the commission.[23]

Release of the king's proclamation, Jeffreys's arrival, and Dame Frances's return widened the distance beyond any chance of repair. On 10 February Berkeley issued the printed proclamation. He accompanied it with an amplifying proclamation of his own. That document reiterated that Berkeley had already granted what the king's proclamation offered—forgiveness to all rebels who surrendered within a designated period—and those pardons were now confirmed. Clemency extended to anyone else who turned himself in to a justice of the peace by 2 March, swore an oath of obedience, and abided by the conditions of the printed

22. Berkeley to Berry and Moryson, 9 Feb. 1676/77, Coventry Papers, 77, fol. 386, Longleat House.
23. Ibid.; Moryson to Berkeley, 11 Feb. 1676/77, Coventry Papers, 77, fol. 395; Berkeley to Moryson, same day, Coventry Papers, 77.

proclamation. Mercy did not reach Richard Lawrence or nearly a dozen insurgents, who were still at large. Nor was it granted to Giles Bland and fellow rebel prisoners, who would stand trial for their lives. Lesser actors, including various councillors and local magistrates "who administred & solicitously advised the takeing of Bacons unlawfull pernitious, & Rebellious oathes," were excluded too. Apart from these exclusions Berkeley excepted the property of Bacon and others who had died during the revolt as well as the goods of those who went to the gallows for their treasons. Furthermore, pardon did not absolve former rebels of their duty to repay those colonists whose estates they had plundered, and victims were encouraged to seek restitution in the courts.[24]

Berkeley's proclamation enraged Berry and Moryson. They rebuked it because of the exclusions Berkeley had written into it. In effect they took the position that, irrespective of his warrant, Berkeley was bound by the king's proclamation to the letter, which meant only Bacon was beyond the pale. They based their opinion on their claim that the printed proclamation trumped Berkeley's commission and instructions because it bore the later date. Such an assertion was of dubious legality, as a man of Moryson's background surely knew, but constitutional niceties were not uppermost in his mind. Restoring peace and order to Virginia were, and, as Moryson judged the situation, Berkeley's proclamation stood in the way of that goal.[25]

All along, Berkeley considered anyone who took or administered Bacon's oath of fidelity guilty of insurrection, no matter his actual degree of participation in the insurgency. Consequently, he believed the defections were massive, which was why he told the commissioners that "there are not above five hundred persons untainted in this rebellion." On the other hand, it suited Moryson and Berry to credit Berkeley's exaggeration. Neither they nor he could say for certain who among the colonists were truly rebellious persons, but from the day of their arrival the commissioners concluded that the overwhelming majority had been enticed or forced to support Bacon. Their judgment inclined them to blanket forgiveness, which set them at odds with the unyielding Berkeley. Berkeley's ruthless lack of charity and his stubborn determination to continue his sequestrations were stumbling blocks to the success of their mission. His proclamation threw up an even greater obstacle because in their minds it breached the king's

24. Proclamation of pardon and indemnity, 10 Feb. 1676/77, CO 1/39, fols. 64–65, PRO. Berkeley had been encouraging loyalists to file claims on rebel estates well before he issued his pardon. Lemuel Mason, a Lower Norfolk justice, entreated him to permit the sale of William Carver's goods to repay the county militia and others for opposing Bacon, and Berkeley complied with the request (petition of Lemuel Mason, 15 Jan. 1676/77, LNDWI, 1674–86, fol. 17, Vi).

25. Berry and Moryson to Thomas Watkins, 10 Feb. 1676/77, Coventry Papers, 77, fol. 389.

mercy. As a result, after 10 February they considered Berkeley the guilty party, and they began to defend the rebels against him. Because neither they nor he would bend, there was little likelihood that the appearance of Colonel Jeffreys would break the impasse amicably.[26]

HMS *Rose* beat *Henry & Ann* to Virginia, which put Dame Frances ahead of Jeffreys by two days, and that was time enough for her to size up her husband's situation and to rally his supporters. When she got to Green Spring House, she beheld its ruin for the first time. The extent of the damage came as a shock because she had no inkling from Berkeley, who had not written since she left back in June. She was greeted by Philip Ludwell and various other councillors who lodged at the mansion in advance of the General Assembly. Berkeley she found weakened by another fever and much agitated by his sparring with Berry and Moryson. They shared their bed for the first time in months, though "nothing but Vocal kindnesse past betweene" them. Whatever "past" that night had the effect of revitalizing Berkeley, who would welcome Jeffreys with courtly courtesy but concede as little as possible.[27]

Jeffreys came ashore on 11 February. The next day he, Berry, and Moryson called at Green Spring House. Berkeley collected the councillors for the reading of Jeffreys's commission. He then asked if he should resign at once. Jeffreys said yes. Berkeley said no. He cited the king's letter of recall and the colonel's commission, which he construed as permitting him to retire when it was convenient to do so. That opinion did not satisfy Jeffreys, or his colleagues, who continued to insist that Berkeley must go post haste. Berkeley sought the council's ruling and promised to abide by it. Jeffreys, Berry, and Moryson hotly insisted that the councillors must decide to what *convenient* applied, the governor's ease or the king's service. Not surprisingly, the council sided with Berkeley. Ludwell and the others grounded their answer in the commission of oyer and terminer that King Charles had sent over. That document authorized Berkeley and the council to try suspects who stood accused of capital offenses. Bearing both the Great Seal and a later date than Jeffreys's commission, it took precedence, and, thus, the councillors held, Berkeley could continue in office until he decided when to give the government up.[28]

26. Ibid.; Moryson to Berkeley, Coventry Papers, 77, 11 Feb. 1676/77, fol. 395; Berkeley to Moryson, same date, Coventry Papers, 77.

27. Log of HMS *Bristol*, 9–11 Feb. 1676/77, n.p., Adm 51/134; Berkeley to Moryson, 11 Feb. 1676/77, Coventry Papers, 77, fol. 395.

28. Commission to Jeffreys, 7 Nov. 1676, *Virginia Magazine of History and Biography* (*VMHB*) 14 (1907): 356–59; Jeffreys to Coventry, 14 Feb. 1676/77, Coventry Papers Papers 77, fol. 403; précis of commission of oyer and terminer to Sir William Berkeley and others, 16 Nov. 1676, CO 389/6, 183–85.

The ruling incensed the commissioners, but they were powerless to reverse it, and they retired in a huff. They sputtered irritably to Coventry, and henceforth they began forwarding excerpts of their correspondence with Berkeley that cast him in the most unfavorable light. Buoyed by the council's judgment, Berkeley prolonged their exasperation. He bedeviled Jeffreys with a taunting note he posted within hours of the commissioners' leave-taking. "Right Honorable," he said, "Since his Majesty has given me leave to throw my selfe at his feet, to give him an account of the Condition of this Colony is in here, I shall doe it with all the hast the miserable Condition of my affaires will permit me, and shall gladly obey his sacred Majesties gratious direction of leaving the Government in my absence in a Person of so worthy a Character, and am Sir Your most humble Servant."[29]

Back came an equally sarcastic retort. "Since yourself and the Councill have beene Plesed to passe your conjunct opinion, that his Majestyes Commission granted mee does not take Place, untill after you shall have left and gone out of this Country," Jeffreys "applied" to Berkeley "(as a matter that highly imports His Majestyes present service) that speedily as the urgency of the occasion requires, I may know your expresse determination of what Provision is to bee made ready for the necessary Reception of his Majestyes Forces under my Command." He and his colleagues also repeatedly berated Berkeley about his refusal to stop taking rebel properties. In the days that followed Jeffreys's coming, there were other feuds over precedents and whether or not the commissioners would participate in court-martialing rebel leaders. Berkeley continued to resent the intrusion of strangers, who questioned his every decision and who treated him as though he were merely an underling rather than the king's vice-regent. He particularly chafed at answering to Moryson, whom he once regarded as a friend and whom he had done much to advance.[30]

Nevertheless, the commissioners went about the business of collecting complaints from anyone who cared to voice them, and they soon compiled a large file of grievances. Jeffreys and Berry also managed the unloading of the troops, some of whom encamped at Swann's Point, whereas the majority settled into barracks near Middle Plantation. There was nothing for them to do, but at least settling them on land transferred the expenses of their upkeep from the king to the Virginia government. How those costs and the colonists' grievances would

29. Berry, Jeffreys, and Moryson to Coventry, 14 Feb. 1676/77, CO 389/6, fol. 401; Berkeley to Jeffreys 12 Feb. 1676/77, Coventry Papers, 77.

30. The exchanges are in Coventry Papers, 77, fols. 378ff.

be met depended upon the upcoming General Assembly, which was scheduled to start on 20 February.[31]

Snowy weather detained most of the burgesses, and their absence delayed the opening of the session for nearly a week. One by one they trickled into Green Spring House, and, as they did, it was obvious that the local magistrates were in full control of the election machinery. Here were no malcontents. Instead, here were loyalists and stout Berkeleyites to a man. They elected Augustine Warner as their speaker, and they picked Robert Beverley as their clerk. Many, including Speaker Warner, had lost heavily at the hands of the rebels, and they were every bit as eager as Berkeley to recover what they could from their former enemies. Small wonder, given those attributes, that the General Assembly of February 1676/77 was in an unforgiving mood.[32]

Despite King Charles's direct command, the session was one of the longest on record, running as it did from late February into early April, but, considering the unusual times and the amount of business, its duration was easily justified. The assembly did little of what the king ordered legislatively. It repealed the laws of the June assembly and then reenacted all the ones that had nothing to do with Bacon or the prosecution of the Indian campaign. Members' salaries were reduced but only by thirty pounds of tobacco per diem. An act of pardon and indemnity codified Berkeley's proclamation and all of its exceptions. Another statute attainted Bacon and everyone else who had been executed for treason. A third appropriated "severall [statutes] of parliament in the 13th year of his majesties raigne" as precedents for inflicting "paines and penalties upon" certain "great offenders," which the act named. And a fourth law prescribed how loyal sufferers such as Speaker Warner might find remedy for their losses in the courts.[33]

Orders of the assembly addressed issues that did not rise to the level of statutory enactment. Principal among them were mandates for liquidating the costs of fighting Bacon, the means of accommodating the redcoats at provincial expense, and the restoration of three Eastern Shore magistrates to office. Additionally, the House and council honored Berkeley in two very public ways. They

31. Log of HMS *Bristol*, 14–27 Feb., n.p., Adm 51/134.

32. Berkeley to Moryson, 24 Feb. 1676/77, Wiseman Papers, n.p.; commissioners to Williamson, 14 Apr. 1677, CO 1/40, fol., 53; Cynthia Miller Leonard, comp., *The General Assembly of Virginia, July 30, 1619–January 11, 1978: A Bicentennial Register of Members* (Richmond, 1978), 42; Jon Kukla, *Speakers and Clerks of the Virginia House of Burgesses, 1643–1776* (Richmond, 1981), 70–73.

33. William Waller Hening, ed., *The Statutes at Large; Being a Collection of All the Laws of Virginia from the First Session of the Legislature, in the Year 1619*, facsimile ed. (1809–23; rpt., Charlottesville, Va., 1969), 2:366–401.

ordered that "he Bee presented with five hundred pounds *Sterll,* out of the Countryes money," as "a token of theire Acknowledgment, and thankfullness for his unwearied Endeavours of the Countreys good and welfare." Then they adopted a showy testimonial to Berkeley's leadership, which ended by saying that "this his majesties people and Country doe most humbly desire, and would accompt it an act of high favor, that his sacred majesty will graciously please, to Continue him in the Government."[34]

Members accepted the commissioners' demand to be heard. They were challenged to become "the HEALING ASSEMBLY." That exhortation, plus advice about what legislation should pass into law, went unheeded. The commissioners also presented texts of the grievances that they had collected. Their suggestions for redress got short shrift too.[35]

A final bit of business took form in a series of addresses that the assembly directed to King Charles, the duke of York, the earl of Arlington, and Secretary Williamson. The one to Charles II conveyed gratitude for his "favours," but, more especially, it thanked him for his recent pardon of the assemblymen and "all the miserable seduced Commonaltie of *Virg'a.*" It climaxed with a spirited justification of Berkeley's conduct. The address to the duke thanked him for his "great and gratious Assistance" in dispatching the expeditionary force. It emphasized that the mere but "certaine knowledge of this Approaching Royall Assistance" terrified the rebels into submission, and it intimated, albeit disingenuously, that the redcoats were a welcomed sign of royal regard for the colony. The memorials to Arlington and Williamson spoke to matters that touched the Northern Neck and attacked proprietary rule in Maryland.[36]

Results of the session strengthened the commissioners' prejudgments. Here was proof positive of an overly independent assembly whose frequent meetings and excessive costs had driven the lesser planters to rebellion. Here, too, was manifest confirmation of Berkeley's mismanagement. Added to the grist that became the commissioners' final report, this evidence led to the recommendation

34. H. R. McIlwaine, ed., *Journals of the House of Burgesses of Colonial Virginia, 1619–1658/59; 1659/60–1693* (Richmond, 1914–15), 68–85. In the eyes of some observers the testimonial seemed a way of easing Berkeley toward England (William Sherwood to Williamson, 13 Apr. 1677, CO 1/40, fols. 51–52).

35. Berry, Jeffreys, and Moryson to the General Assembly, 27 Feb. 1676/77, Wiseman Papers, n.p.; McIlwaine, *Journals, 1659/60–1693,* 87–90. Some of these grievances are printed in McIlwaine, *Journals of the House of Burgesses of Virginia, 1659/60–1693,* 99–113. Contemporary file copies of the entire collection reside in CO 1/ 39, fols. 194–255; and CO 5/1371, fols. 149–69.

36. These letters were all dated 2 Apr. 1677. Printed texts appear in McIlwaine, *Journals, 1659/60–1693,* 95–99.

that the General Assembly stood in prompt need of subordination to Whitehall. As for the remainder of the report, it assessed Berkeley for the lion's share of blame for the Virginians' rebelliousness.[37]

Holding Berkeley responsible was a determination that Berry, Jeffreys, and Moryson had come to well before they drafted their report for King Charles. If one were to pinpoint the likeliest moment when they reached that decision, it was 12 February. From that day onward their dealings with Berkeley grew ever more venomous, and the actions of the assembly merely added more poison. By the time Berkeley dissolved the assembly, he and the commissioners were no longer on speaking terms. Indeed, they rarely even wrote to one another.

With the assembly gone, Berkeley had little excuse for remaining in charge, but he procrastinated in naming a day to retire. There were hints of his intentions. He updated his will in mid-March, which was a common practice for a traveler who was soon to embark upon an ocean passage. Quite short for someone as wealthy as he, the will settled one hundred pounds on his sister Jane Davies, "providing My Dear Wife has three thousand pounds sterling to maintain her in the quallity of my wife." It allotted another ten pounds to Sarah Kirkman, a "virtuous good woman," a family friend and widow of former council clerk Francis Kirkman. Baron John's children had "noe want of that little I can dispose of," and they got nothing. Seeing as how Berkeley was "farr from haveing any obligation" to his other English relations, the will cut them out too. And so Dame Frances became both his chief beneficiary and his executrix.[38]

Berkeley contracted with Captain Thomas Larramore, skipper of the *Loyal Rebecca*, for passage to London, and he began to pack for the trip. It was no secret that he was about to leave, but still he said nothing to Jeffreys. Word got around that he would depart soon after the General Assembly left Green Spring House. A week after the dissolution, Moryson sent a note saying that the commission would pay him a final courtesy call on 22 April. The visit ended disastrously. As the commissioners mounted the coach that Berkeley had furnished, one of them recognized the postilion as the provincial hangman. Highly insulted by the lowliness of their escort, they stormed off on foot in high dudgeon. They wrote Berkeley a threatening letter the next day, accusing him of deliberately contriving so obvious an affront to their dignity as gentlemen and the Crown's representatives and promising to tell the king. Berkeley professed his innocence, as did Dame

---

37. A printed version is in Charles M. Andrews, ed., *Narratives of the Insurrections, 1675–1690* (New York, 1915), 105–41, while a contemporary text may be found in CO 5/1371, fols. 188–205.

38. Updated will of Sir William Berkeley, 20 Mar. 1676/77, Hening, *Statutes at Large*, 2:359–60. Berkeley originally drew up the will on 2 May 1676. Councillors Nathaniel Bacon Sr., Thomas Ballard, William Cole, Philip Ludwell, and Joseph Bridger witnessed the update, as did Robert Beverley.

Frances, who endorsed her protest as the "wiffe of the persecuted Sir William Berkelay."[39]

Jeffreys had had his fill of Berkeley. On 27 April he peremptorily proclaimed himself governor. Berkeley got the message. He realized that the highly exasperated colonel might grab him and ship him off to London in chains. Still, the temptation to have the last word proved irresistible. He shot off a tart letter to Jeffreys in which he taxed his adversary with an "irresistible desire to rule this Country" and forecast that "the inhabitants of this Colony will quickly find a difference between your management and mine." As if to dig the needle deeper, he signed himself "Governor of Virginia til his most Sacred Majestie shall please to determine otherwise of me." Finally, he bade Dame Frances good-bye, boarded *Loyal Rebecca,* and on 5 May he sailed away.[40]

39. Moryson to Berkeley, 21 Apr. 1677, Wiseman Papers, n.p.; Berkeley to Berry, Jeffreys, and Moryson, 23 Apr. 1677, CO 1/40, fol. 62; Dame Berkeley to same, same date, CO 1/40, fol. 63; Berry, Jeffreys, and Moryson to Thomas Watkins, 4 May 1677, CO 1/40, fols. 130–31.

40. A printed text of Jeffreys's proclamation is in *VMHB* 22 (1914): 44–45; Berkeley to Jeffreys, 28 Apr. 1677, CO 1/40, fols. 68–69. Jeffreys did not receive the letter until 7 June (Jeffreys to Williamson, 11 June 1677, CO 1/40, fols. 225–26).

15

THAT HIS DAYS SHOULD BE ACCOMPLISHED

ind and tide worked the *Loyal Rebecca* down the James toward the open sea. Landmarks Berkeley knew well slipped by one by one; Hog Island, which lay off his Chippokes farm; Denbigh, seat of his long-dead rival Samuel Mathews; Mulberry Island, home to Frances's Filmer relations; Bolthorpe, the plantation that Frances and he had lately sold to Councillor William Cole; the ruined fort at Old Point Comfort, that much reviled bulwark that had afforded no defense against attack from seaborne raiders but had cost him so dearly in political capital. At last the mouth of the great river neared. A tiny pilot boat darted from the shore and maneuvered delicately along *Loyal Rebecca*'s windward side. Quickly, the river pilot bade Captain Larramore bon voyage. Just as quickly, he hopped over the railing, scurried the precarious span down the swaying Jacob's ladder, and jumped the short distance to the heaving deck below. His passenger safely aboard, the helmsman of the pilot boat smartly veered her off, while Larramore pointed *Loyal Rebecca* easterly toward England.

In a while Virginia dipped behind the horizon, seemingly swallowed up by the ocean deep as the last vistas of dry land fell into its darkly blue-hued waters. Whatever emotions and thoughts crowded in upon Berkeley at that moment are lost now, as is any mention of how he passed the duration of his journey. The only certainty was his intent vigorously to answer the allegations the royal commission of investigation had laid against him. That done, and by the king's leave, he would return to America and repair his beloved Green Spring House, there to live out his remaining days in quiet, much as he had done during his forced retirement.

Loyal Rebecca caught fair winds. Berkeley reached England within six weeks of her casting off from Jamestown dock. How different London seemed compared to when he had last visited, in 1661. Then he was at the peak of his abilities, and he moved effortlessly around the highest court circles. Men in government, King Charles among them, highly valued his opinions on Virginia. Now he was sick and spirit withered. No one welcomed him. No one sought him. His allies were all gone, even his brother Baron John, who was off in the Netherlands.

For a time he lodged at John's mansion in Berkeley Square. Only one thing mattered, and that was a compulsion "to clear his innocency" with his master. He petitioned for a royal audience. A response came through Henry Coventry, whose note said, "his Majesty would speak with you as soon as you can."[1]

They never did. On 9 July 1677, bereft of friends or loved ones and half a world away from the place he acknowledged as home, Berkeley died suddenly.

Embalmers prepared the corpse. Funeral arrangements were made. The body, encased tightly in lead foil, was transported to its rest at a place not far from Baron John's country estate in Middlesex. On the thirteenth a small burial party strode solemnly down the aisle of the Church of St. Mary the Virgin, just off the high street in the village of Twickenham, barely three miles from Berkeley's birthplace at Hanworth Manor.

Echoes of steel against stone reverberated across the nearly empty building as workmen pried open the entry to the crypt. The way cleared, bearers descended into the undercroft and deposited their burden, whereupon a priest intoned the closing prayers of the Anglican burial rite. When he spoke the dismissal, the mourners quietly retired, leaving the mortal body of Sir William Berkeley, late governor and captain-general of His Majesty's colony and dominion of Virginia, to corrupt to the dust from whence it had come.[2]

1. Petition to Charles II, ca. 16 June 1677, CO 1/40, 244, PRO; Coventry to Berkeley, 16 June 1677, CO 389/6, 207, PRO.

2. Parish register, Church of St. Mary the Virgin, Twickenham, Middlesex; Edward Ironside, comp., *The History and Antiquities of Twickenham* . . . (London, 1797), 42. Berkeley had no connection to St. Mary's, though his friend Sir John Suckling had been baptized in the church. Edward Hyde, earl of Clarendon, once kept a house and pew in the parish, as did Baron John Berkeley, which explains why the governor was buried there. Baron Berkeley, who died in 1678, was also interred near his brother (anon., *The Parish Church of Twickenham: St. Mary the Virgin* [Gloucester, n.d.], 21–22). After the antiquary Edmund Ironside inspected the crypt ca. 1797, he reported that "on opening this vault about a year ago, . . . the body of Sir William Berkeley was found lying on the ground without a coffin cased in lead exactly fitted to the shape of the body, shewing the form of the features, hands, feet, and even nails; and appears to be beat firmly to it, and looks like a figure in armour." Presumably, the remains rest as Ironside found them. When I visited St. Mary's Church in 1989, parish

Few in England mourned Berkeley. Not King Charles, though legend wrongly has it that he hastened Berkeley's end by remarking, "that old fool has hanged more men in that naked country, than I did for the murder of my father." Charles's advisors cared not a whit. With Berkeley gone, they busied themselves figuring out how to reweave the web of the Anglo-Virginia connection more to the advantage of the Crown. The royal commissioners of investigation took no notice. Their work done, they went their separate ways. Lieutenant Governor Jeffreys breathed his last in 1678, very much tormented by Virginians he spurned but could not cower. Colonel Moryson never returned to the Old Dominion. He passed away in obscurity about the year 1680. Sir John Berry died in 1690, though not before poor seamanship doused him in ignominy. He had captained the ill-fated HMS *Gloucester* when she foundered off Lowestoft in 1682 and nearly drowned James, duke of York. Only Baron Berkeley and Alexander Culpeper cared. They tried to restore Berkeley's reputation, but their defense of their kinsman before the Privy Council was puny, and it failed to undo the damage.[3]

Canny colonial leaders grieved not at all for their departed governor. They had little occasion because his going immediately altered their relationship with royal authorities. Bent on minimizing the change, they resisted Berkeley's successors at every turn, and the antics of confrontation stirred Anglo-Virginia political passions for a generation. At the turn of the century they were all dead too—all, that is, save Philip Ludwell, who made his peace with Stuart imperialism and lasted until 1716.[4]

Whatever tears Frances Berkeley cried, she wept them in private. Putting off her widow's weeds, she fixed the damage to Green Spring House, repaired her fortune as best she could, and played a meaningful hand in post-rebellion politics.

She inherited all of Berkeley's earthly goods. And yet, apart from vast real estate holdings, her legacy was mostly a shambles. Thousands of pounds in debt, she appealed to the General Assembly and to the Crown for her dead husband's

archivist Donald H. Simpson pointed out a window that memorializes the Berkeley brothers and told me that the entry to the vault had been built over when repairs were made after World War II.

3. John Callow, *The Making of King James II: The Formative Years of a Fallen King* (Thrupp Stroud, Gloucestershire, 2000), 234–36.

4. Thomas Mathew, "The Rise, Progress, and Conclusion of Bacon's Rebellion in the Years 1675–1676" (1705), in Charles M. Andrews, ed., *Narratives of the Insurrections, 1675–1690* (New York, 1915), 40; Wilcomb E. Washburn, *The Governor and the Rebel: A History of Bacon's Rebellion* (Chapel Hill, N.C., 1957), 139–53; Warren M. Billings, *A Little Parliament: The Virginia General Assembly in the Seventeenth Century* (Richmond, 2004), 49–63.

back dues, only to be denied much of what was owed. Shortages of ready cash forced her to sell her interest in Carolina for a mere three hundred pounds, and she struggled to fend off damage suits lodged against the estate. The hurt Bacon's rebels did to Green Spring House left it destitute of furnishings and in need of massive, costly refurbishment. Despite her straitened finances, she again made the mansion "the finest seat in America & the only tollerable place for a Governour" and invited Jeffreys's successor, Thomas Culpeper, second baron Culpeper of Thoresway, her cousin, to live with her. Implacably hostile to Lieutenant Governor Jeffreys, she rallied the Ludwells, Robert Beverley, and other key Berkeley followers into a faction that unremittingly harassed her hapless enemy quite literally to his death. Green Spring House remained the center of such opposition until a dalliance with Lord Culpeper and marriage to Philip Ludwell pushed her to the political margins. Nonetheless, visits to England invigorated her standing in court circles, so much so that she radiated an aura of importance until death reunited her with Berkeley in the realm of faded memories.[5]

Robert Beverley II (d. 1722) burnished those memories and more when he wrote *The History and Present State of Virginia*, which he first published in 1705 while on a visit to London. His mastery of the documentary record invested the *History* with an immediate credibility with eighteenth-century readers and cloaked it with a reliability that abides with those who turn to it still. Beverley rated Berkeley a "good and just" man but provided little by way of background or personal detail about his hero. He made a brief for Berkeley as the ablest of administrators and a governor nonpareil. Lavish in his praise, he was neither blind to Berkeley's limitations nor unmindful of the difficulties of ruling Virginia.[6]

In Beverley's estimation Bacon's Rebellion was the most troublesome incident Berkeley ever faced, and he had more to say about it than any other episode of

5. Last will and testament of Sir William Berkeley, in William Waller Hening, ed., *The Statutes at Large; Being a Collection of All the Laws of Virginia from the First Session of the Legislature, in the Year 1619*, facsimile ed. (1809–23; rpt., Charlottesville, 1969), 2:559–61; Frances Berkeley to Ann Danby, 27 June 1678, Cunliffe-Lister Muniments, bundle 69, County Hall, Northallerton, Yorkshire; order of the General Assembly, Oct. 1677, Coventry Papers, 78; Wilcomb E. Washburn, "The Humble Petition of Sarah Drummond," *William and Mary Quarterly (WMQ)*, 3d ser. 13 (1956): 354–75; William S. Powell, *The Proprietors of Carolina* (Raleigh, 1963), 53; Warren M. Billings, *Virginia's Viceroy, Their Majesties' Governor General: Francis Howard, Baron Howard of Effingham* (Fairfax, Va., 1991), 24–28; William Byrd to Warham Horsmanden, 21 June 1684, in Marion Tingling, ed., *The Papers of the Three William Byrds of Westover, Virginia, 1684–1776* (Charlottesville, 1977), 1:25; Warren M. Billings, ed., *The Papers of Francis Howard, Baron Howard of Effingham, 1643–1695* (Richmond, 1989), 115.

6. Robert Beverley, *History and Present State of Virginia*, ed. Louis B. Wright (Chapel Hill, N.C., 1947), 61–86.

Berkeley's tenure. Beverley's judgment inadvertently framed metes and bounds for later historians and fiction writers because it fixed the revolt as their starting point for appraising Berkeley. They seldom agreed about how Berkeley handled the upheaval, let alone who he was or what his presence meant for Virginia. Their disagreements sounded and resounded, angrily at times, in their depictions of him as Berkeley the staunch Stuart loyalist, Berkeley the merciless tyrant, Berkeley the friend of native Virginians, Berkeley the architect of Creole culture, and Berkeley the avatar of patriarchy, and he continues a figure of controversy to this day.[7]

To be sure, Berkeley exhibited tendencies ascribed to him both by his partisans and his detractors. Such traits personify his nature and impulses, and they gauge the character of the man rather than his significance as a figure in history. The measure of Berkeley's historical importance exists in the juxtaposition of colonists with colonization, which is a linkage that raises plain but profound ruminations about English settlement in Virginia. What did it matter that Britons, Africans, and Native Americans converged in that place? How did colonization change the Virginia environment? Why did colonists settle? How did acts of settling amend immigrants' views of themselves or alter their outlook on their world? In what ways could the presence of a single settler give shape or purpose or quality of existence to Virginia? These and like queries are singularly pertinent to Berkeley because his life and the events that fashioned it are as useful for composing answers to such questions as they are to discerning him as an individual.

Berkeley stood center stage in Anglo-Virginia politics while the colony passed from an outpost toward a roughhewn imitation of its English origins. Tirelessly, he promoted his adopted homeland for more than a third of a century, during which he pressed deep marks on its people, its society, its politics, and its relationship to the British monarchy, and he had much to do with the settling of the Carolinas, westward exploration, and economic development.

7. The contrariety of these opinions is summarized in Wilcomb E. Washburn, *The Governor and the Rebel: A History of Bacon's Rebellion in Virginia* (Chapel Hill, N.C., 1957), 1–17; and Jane D. Carson, *Bacon's Rebellion, 1676–1976* (Jamestown, 1976), 34–84. See also Stephen Saunders Webb, *1676: The End of American Independence* (New York, 1984); Warren M. Billings, John E. Selby, and Thad W. Tate, *Colonial Virginia: A History* (White Plains, N.Y., 1986); John M. Murrin, review of Webb, *1676, WMQ*, 3d ser., 43 (1986): 119–24; Wilcomb E. Washburn, "Stephen Saunders Webb's Interpretation of Bacon's Rebellion," *Virginia Magazine of History and Biography* 95 (1987), 275–301; Jon Kukla, *Political Institutions in Virginia, 1619–1660* (New York, 1989); David Hackett Fischer, *Albion's Seed: Four British Folkways in America* (New York, 1989); Kathleen M. Brown, *Good Wives, Nasty Wenches, and Anxious Patriarchs: Gender, Race, and Power in Colonial Virginia* (Chapel Hill, N.C., 1996); Michael Leroy Oberg, *Dominion and Civility: English Imperialism and Native America, 1585–1685* (Ithaca, N.Y., 1999).

Hoping to make Virginia a land of close-knit communities with a varied economy and a deferential social order, he befriended leading colonists, fostered the rise of the General Assembly from a unicameral body into a little Parliament, and sanctioned a decentralization of power between provincial and county governments that ensured the planter elite untrammeled control of local politics. In return he won support for his handling of Virginia's external affairs and his schemes for diversifying its economy. By these means he attracted men who saw in his leadership the means to satisfy their own appetites for power. While only a few shared his vision of diversification, others saw in his beloved Green Spring House a model symbolic of their social standing, which they and their descendants copied.

His cultivation of the great planters contributed to a political atmosphere in which the mighty were at liberty to fathom the intricacies of authority in ways that singularly benefited themselves. Such freedom led to habits of self-rule that are the essence of American politics to this day, though liberty for them deprived others less fortunate than they. Berkeley's Virginia was a country where a select few could flee the constraints of Britain and aggrandize themselves at the expense of the overwhelming number of settlers who were slaves, indentured servants, and lesser planters. After his return to power in 1660, he made the Old Dominion a place increasingly out of tune with English colonial policy, and, so long as Virginians walked his way, Stuart dreams of empire remained unfulfilled. Then he bumbled into Bacon's Rebellion, which compelled the later Stuarts to intervene in Virginia affairs as never before. Royal interference took the form of direct assaults on practices that Crown bureaucrats deemed inconsistent with contemporary English policy, law, and custom. Consequently, the Anglo-Virginia relationship passed through a time of redefinition that ushered in an era of tighter control from London. That permutation shifted the focus of colonial politics away from local issues toward provincial and imperial concerns, and Berkeley's like as governor was never seen again.

Will Berkeley lived a succession of inventions of himself. Possessed of a temperament at once winning and wrathful, he was a gifted, clever man with a quicksilver turn of mind and a vaulting ambition. Descended from prominent English West Country stock, he rose to manhood expecting to prosper as a servant to the Crown in the manner of his forebears. He won notice at the court of King Charles I for his literary and diplomatic abilities, but, disgruntled by his lack of achievement, he gambled his disappointments on a chance at new beginnings in Virginia. His subsequent passage mirrored that subtle transformation that happened to women and men who traded the uncertainties of their lives in Britain for the vicissitudes of an American existence. Like all of his fellow immigrants, he arrived in his new world big with expectations. Like them, he became a Virginian, which is to say his colonial experiences slowly gave greater definition to his being than did his English origins. Unlike them, he uniquely marked Virginia. That imprint was both his accomplishment and his failure.

Essay on Sources

overnor Berkeley grouped his papers into two distinct, though often overlapping, collections. He retained documents that he broadly regarded as personal—deeds to his properties in England, Virginia, and Carolina; plantation records; business accounts; personal writings—at Green Spring House. His official records—file texts of speeches, exchanges with his superiors at Whitehall, messages to the House of Burgesses and the Council of State, communications with county officers, proclamations, draft legislation, General Court opinions, commissions, and similar items—stayed either in the custody of the secretary of the colony or with county clerks of court, all of whom maintained Virginia's various institutional records.

Nathaniel Bacon's rebels' damage to the private papers is beyond reckoning. Remnants passed to Dame Frances and then, at her death, to her third husband, Philip Ludwell. Thereafter, extant Berkeley papers commingled with those of the Ludwell and the Lee families. They were scattered intermittently during the eighteenth and nineteenth centuries until the few survivors finally came to rest among the Lee Family Papers at the Virginia Historical Society in Richmond.

As for Berkeley's official records, their route to all but complete destruction was somewhat longer and more circuitous. Successive secretaries of the colony and clerks of the House of Burgesses and the Council of State stored provincial archives in their residences and brought them to Jamestown as needed. Those documents escaped Bacon's burning of the town in September 1676 largely unscathed because they were out of harm's way. They were also spared additional damage from the fire of 1698, which resulted in the transfer of the capital to Williamsburg and in the raising of a purpose-built public record office that stood adjacent to the capitol building at the eastern end of Duke of Gloucester Street. The record office closed after the General Assembly moved the seat of government to Richmond in 1782. Major ruin at last befell Berkeley's state papers on the night of 2–3 April 1865, when fire consumed all but mere fragments. The conflagration also destroyed county court files that had been sent to Richmond for safekeeping, and with them burned an untold number of Berkeley items as well.

This chronology of loss aided in the reassembly of Sir William's extant papers because it circumscribed the limits of the search and dictated the use of known items as the primary source of leads to others. Systematic investigation revealed that a majority of items sat among numerous colonial, state, and private record groups housed at the Public Record Office and the British Library, London; the Bodleian Library, Oxford; the Longleat House Library, Wiltshire; the Magdalene College Library, Cambridge; the Library of Congress, Washington, D.C.; the Library of Virginia, Richmond; the Maryland Hall of Records, Annapolis; the North Carolina Department of Archives and History, Raleigh; and the Henry E. Huntington Library, San Marino, California. Smaller groupings turned up in the Library of the Middle Temple and the College of Arms, London; the Centre for Kentish Studies, Maidstone; Trinity College Library, Dublin; the National Library of Scotland, Edinburgh; the North Yorkshire Record Office, Northallerton; the Royal Swedish Archives, Stockholm; the Folger Shakespeare Library, Washington, D.C.; the Massachusetts State Archives and the Massachusetts Historical Society, Boston; the New-York Historical Society, New York City; the New York State Library, Albany; the University of Sheffield, Sheffield; the Alderman Library at the University of Virginia, Charlottesville; and the Virginia Historical Society, Richmond.

The reconstituted corpus contains at least one item from almost every year of Berkeley's life between 1624 and 1677, and it amounts to approximately eleven hundred documents, about a third of which were previously unknown. A more complete description and a calendar are available at the Papers of Sir William Berkeley Project Web site. That site is accessible at www. uno.edu/history/berkeley.htm, which will remain mounted on the World Wide Web until *The Papers of Sir William Berkeley, 1605–1677* comes into print.

Additionally, two of Berkeley's identified printed writings are available in both original and modern editions. They can be consulted in the Early English Books in Microfilm series, which is keyed to A. W. Pollard and G. R. Redgrave, comps., *Short-Title Catalogue of Books Printed in England, Scotland, and Ireland, and of*

English Books Printed Abroad, 1475–1640 (London, 1926); and Donald W. Wing, comp., *Short-Title Catalogue of Books Printed in England, Scotland, Ireland, Wales, and British North America and English Books Printed in Other Countries, 1641–1700* (New York, 1945–51).

The Lost Lady, A Tragi-Comedy went through three printings before 1640. Witnesses to each of them can be found in the British Library, the Folger Shakespeare Library, the Library of Congress, and other institutions with extensive holdings in early English imprints. The literary scholar D. F. Rowan published the definitive critical edition of the play for the Malone Society under the title *The Lost Lady by Sir William Berkeley* (Oxford, 1987).

As noted in chapter 9, Berkeley intended *A Discourse and View of Virginia* as a brief for Crown support of his plan to diversify the Virginia economy. He wrote the text sometime between August 1661 and January 1662, when a London printer ran enough copies for Berkeley to give to members of the Committee for Foreign Plantations, the Privy Council, and certain other influential individuals. There remain but seven known witnesses to that single printing. Two are in English libraries, one is in Ireland, and four are in the United States. Thomas R. Stewart, an early-twentieth-century book dealer cum antiquary, prepared an edition in facsimile. Naming it *A Discourse and View of Virginia by Sir William Berkeley*, which he published at Norwalk, Connecticut, in 1914, Stewart drew this rendition from the Huntington Library witness, though he wrongly attributed its year of publication. His edition became a rarity in its own right, owing to its having been issued in a press run of only 250 copies. A more detailed description of the origin and subsequent distribution of the booklet may be found in Warren M. Billings, "Sir William Berkeley's *A Discourse and View of Virginia:* A Note on Its Authorship," *Documentary Editing* 24 (2002): 33–36.

Record groups that put the Berkeley papers in their historical context are also to be found in the repositories enumerated here. Printed collections of collateral manuscripts are identified throughout the notes that accompany the text of this volume and need not be rehearsed here.

Index